Ed West is deputy editor of U  publications, including the *Spectat* *The Week* and many more. He is t lad's mag and the *Catholic Herald*, a time. He lives with his wife and three children in nor...

Tory Boy

Memoirs of the Last Conservative

Ed West

CONSTABLE

CONSTABLE

First published as *Small Men on the Wrong Side of History*
in Great Britain in 2020 by Constable
This paperback edition published in Great Britain in 2021

A CIP catalogue record for this book
is available from the British Library.

ISBN: 978-1-47213-081-5

Typeset in Spectrum by SX Composing DTP, Rayleigh, Essex
Printed and bound in Great Britain by Clays Ltd, Elcograf S.p.A.

Papers used by Constable are from well-managed forests
and other responsible sources.

Constable
an imprint of
Little, Brown Book Group
Carmelite House
50 Victoria Embankment
London EC4Y 0DZ

An Hachette UK Company
www.hachette.co.uk

www.littlebrown.co.uk

CONTENTS

INTRODUCTION

One morning, a few months short of my fortieth birthday, I awoke with a monstrous hangover, a vague memory of embarrassing myself the previous night, and the dawning realisation that my worldview is dying. The previous day the Tory government, despite taking on an almost comically inept opposition with a leader wildly to the Left of anyone in British electoral history, had managed to lose their majority in Parliament. More disturbing, though, they had been massacred among the under-forties and professional classes.

The result itself was not the really alarming thing, and would be corrected two and a half years later when the Conservatives won a majority under Boris Johnson. Far more worrying was that, as I headed deep into the happiness U-bend of middle age, no one I knew was becoming more conservative. It had been said before, in the 1960s and 1920s and probably before, that the young were Left-wing and so the future was socialist or liberal; then those cohorts had matured, or perhaps just become more bitter and cynical as they aged, and so had adopted conservative world-views; but this was no longer happening, and my personal observations were matched by growing amounts of data. The Tories could still win elections, but they now depended on the elderly; the generation entering middle age were something different, and would not, as Father Ted put it, become more Right-wing as they got older. They were cut off from the old faith.

Conservative parties could still win elections but conservatism was an endangered creed, as much in demographic decline as the Christianity from which it once emerged, and the degree to which it had become hated by anyone born after 1970 was intense and perhaps irreversible. It was not the young who had turned out to wreck the Tories in 2017, despite the term 'youthquake' being bandied around, but the middle-aged; this wasn't the natural rebelliousness of adolescence but a more permanent shift of social mores, changes that made conservatism socially abnormal and anything associated with it electoral excrement. This was repeated again at the 2019 election when the Tories lost heavily among all age groups under 44.

When I was in my mid-twenties and quite conservative for my peer group I assumed that I was just an anomaly, someone who develops these traits earlier than normal, and conservatism was like baldness or impotence or the other bad things that people get in middle age. One day you just wake up and realise you'd rather go to a country pub than a nightclub, can't be bothered getting into new bands because music was perfected in 1995, and agree with what you read in the *Telegraph*. Most of my friends and acquaintances would catch up at some point, because these things just develop at different speeds.

By my late thirties I realised it's worse than that and almost none of my contemporaries was going to become more conservative; if anything, they had turned more Left-wing than they were ten or twenty years earlier, as the barometer of what is progressive and therefore socially acceptable had shifted. Indeed, despite long-held Conservative assumptions that people will always grow into Toryhood, surveys showed that those from Generation X (born between 1965 and 1980) were actually moving to the Left as they got older, and in the US the proportion identifying as liberal had increased from 29 per cent in the mid-1990s to almost half today.[1] The same thing was happening with the cohort after us, the Millennials (born 1981–96), who were not showing any signs of becoming more Right-wing as they aged.

By any conceivable measure, what is regarded as mainstream, normal opinion had shifted rapidly in the preceding decades, but the rate of change now also seemed to be speeding up, almost as if we were heading for some sort of progressive singularity. The most influential publications and broadcasters among people who matter, the BBC, *Times*, *Guardian*, *Financial Times*, *Economist* and even the *Daily Telegraph*, had all become considerably more socially liberal in that period, a shift that was accompanied by a shrinking bracket of what was permissible to think without social sanction. On almost any non-economic issue most of my friends hitting forty were more progressive than in their early twenties; they might resent paying more tax or even dislike trade unions, but that didn't make them conservative.

Among my contemporaries in the 35–44 age group, some 50 per cent voted for Corbyn in 2017 and even if many did not entirely support his particular interpretation of the Left they were nevertheless totally repulsed by conservatism. Indeed the Brexit referendum had helped to expose how much the Tory party's brand was entirely built around its reputation for economic competence, a reputation now largely pissed against the wall; it exposed just how unpopular conservative philosophy actually was once financial considerations were removed. This sense of revulsion was felt not just by a large proportion of young and middle-aged Britons, but by the overwhelming majority of the most educated and influential.

The daunting realisation was that this cultural shift was permanent and even more pronounced among the cohorts growing up. Faiths abandoned by grandparents and forgotten by parents will not be retained by the children. At my kids' school a mock election that same week featuring made-up parties was won overwhelmingly by 'Change' (this was before Change UK was launched as a party, rather less successfully as it turned out), whose rhetoric was obviously progressive and inclusive, and illustrated how attractive the Left's language and philosophy were to the young – and how difficult was the uphill struggle now faced by con-servatives. Our philosophy is now so counterintuitive, so hampered by the negative undertones of the words associated with it, and so reflexively badly viewed in the surrounding culture, that its long-term prospects seem distinctly gloomy, barring either an unprecedented religious revival or the sort of apocalyptic event that pushes us back to the Dark Ages. And even I would find civilisational collapse a somewhat worse prospect than having to listen to Radio 4 talk about gender equality every morning.

Among the parents at my children's school I'd be one of only a tiny handful who identified as conservative, and the only issue for most would be which Left they identified with, the centrist or more radical wing. And so despite all the liberal lamentation about Brexit and Trump – and the live-action nervous breakdowns of so many members of the commentariat – these events are most likely mere blips in the onward march of progressivism; the former supported by the old and the latter by the prematurely dying in America's depressed, opiate-riddled heartlands.

There are today very few important areas of British or American society in which progressives do not have complete dominance. The influential film industry of southern California is overwhelmingly liberal, as is the even more powerful and vaguely sinister tech industry of northern California. The annual Oscar ceremonies are now heavily political in a way that would have been strange even two decades back, when it would have been considered weird and inappropriate to revel in the industry's liberal sympathies. Technology giants such as Google or Facebook overtly side with progressive causes in funding and policy, the daily Google doodle and its prog bias being a good example of something-which-seems-important-to-conservatives-but-really-petty-to-everyone-else. Within these companies Left-wing identity politics is so embedded that according to one employee at Google 'the presence of Caucasians and males was mocked with "boos" during company-wide weekly meetings', one of many reported examples where 'white males' were subject to abuse.[2] That these progressive outfits are all pretty much led by white males is beside the point; it's a creed with inherent inconsistencies and contradictions, just as Christian leaders throughout history have been absurdly wealthy or warmongers, and yet still genuine believers.

Outside of tech, increasing numbers of corporations, including Nike, Starbucks and Heineken, openly promote progressive causes, either in advertising or in donations, in a way no mainstream company would once have done for fear of alienating a large section of customers. Likewise most prestigious American newspapers and news outlets are not only pro-Democrat but since 2008 have become far more openly partisan, while conservatism has retreated to the shouty, tabloid ghetto comprised of Fox News and smaller non-mainstream sites of varying degrees of sanity.

This cultural trend is reflected in the shifting axis of the two-party system. In the US the Democrats have become the party of graduates with a huge education divide in voting,[3] but in Britain a similar trend is now developing. The Conservatives, once the party of the more educated middle classes, are now haemorrhaging support among all professionals – seen as a 'rejection of the party's values'[4] – while making advances in once improbable ex-industrial towns in the Midlands and north. The Tory party has in the late 2010s enjoyed consistently stronger support among social class C2DE – broadly speaking the lower-middle and working class – something that would have been wildly unlikely once upon a time. This came to fruition at the 2019 election when they won a number of seats Labour had held since time immemorial.

In contrast, in middle-class areas of London it is not just that there are more Labour posters in people's windows, as has always been the case for reasons of conspicuous compassion (and because Tories fear getting their windows smashed). It almost resembles Northern Ireland, where entire streets are covered with the flag of the tribe. Big urban areas are emptying of conservatives, who have been able to cling to only a handful of metropolitan seats due largely to a divided Left.[5] In this we are following the US pattern, where in the 2018 midterms the Democrats won all ten of the wealthiest districts.[6]

It's all very well complaining about the 'liberal elite' while citing semi-exotic vegetarian foodstuffs eaten in upmarket postcodes, but it doesn't really matter if this much-caricatured group are 'out of touch', as we're always reminded. History shows that elite opinions tend to become adopted by society as a whole because people imitate the belief systems of those higher up the social ladder. If Left-liberalism has become dominant among the elite, then like many historical faiths its popularity among a high-status minority will lead to universal adoption in just a couple of generations.

Historically the religions and belief systems that flourish and predomin-ate are those that carry the most prestige, and which bring with them more social benefits than costs to followers. What matters is how much ideologies are associated with high-ranking and successful people, and how much social proof their believers have. Look to the protest movements with the most beautiful people and those are the dominant political causes of the future. If conservatism is becoming a brand certain to cause social leprosy to young, educated people, it will not be long before it goes the way of paganism.

A crucial indication of the way things are developing is the extent to which younger women have become far more Left-wing than men, with a pro-conservative bias among females born before 1955 turning into a heavily Left-liberal one among younger cohorts.[7] In 1974 the Conservatives had an 11-point advantage among women, in an election they lost, reduced to zero in 2017 in one they won.[8] Historically, religions that attract large numbers of women tend to predominate, the most obvious being Christianity, where females heavily outnumbered males in the early centuries, in some areas by six to one. Indeed, the influence of women in spreading successful ideas, because non-elite men tend to follow them, has been noted down the centuries. So the fact that young women backed Labour over the Tories by 65 points to 15 at the 2019 election should be a cause for alarm.

Before she became prime minister, Tory politician Theresa May once commented that they were viewed as the 'nasty' party, which was true, especially after she gave everyone the catchy phrase. The image problem of conservatism more generally, however, is even worse than that – it's seen as low-status, and the number of people in professions receptive to conserva-tive ideas is rapidly shrinking.

Whole fields, among them teaching, academia, journalism and science, have gone from being politically mixed a generation ago to overwhelmingly

Left-liberal today. Indeed there is growing evidence in many areas that dissenting thinkers increasingly keep their opinions to themselves. Among UK journalists, part of an industry that shapes public discourse and to some extent acts as gatekeeper of acceptable thought, only 23 per cent identity as 'Right-of-centre', compared to 53 per cent who see themselves on the Left.[9] And this is nothing compared to education, where in 2017 some 65 per cent of primary-school and 72 per cent of secondary-school teachers voted for the most Left-wing major leader in British history, compared to just 7 and 8 per cent respectively for the Tories.[10]

This domination is just as pronounced in academia, where the leaders of tomorrow are taught how to think and what to think. Universities have seen Leftist activism since the 1960s and in recent years the endlessly tedious no-platforming and 'safe spaces' saga has revealed how extreme some have become. And yet, as with the rise of political correctness a generation earlier, it is the repetitively boring complaints of conservative opponents, droning on about 'snowflakes', that comes to dominate the debate. Even I roll my eyes when I hear a Right-wing pundit mention the subject, because it cannot help but seem inconsequential, and yet universities are the nerve centre of ideological power and a training ground for future leaders. And they have been rapidly moving Leftwards in recent years.

American academia has gone from a political ratio of 2 liberals to every 1 conservative in the early 1990s to 5 to 1 now, and that figure is only that low because less-ideological STEM subjects (science, technology, engineering and mathematics) tend to be quite evenly balanced; in contrast the ratio in the social sciences varies from between 10 to 1 and 40 to 1.[11] In 1990 the proportion of Democrats to Republicans in psychology departments was 4 to 1; by the year 2000 it was 10 to 1; and by 2015 it was 14 to 1.[12] The academic ratio is 18 to 1 at Brown, 26 to 1 at Cornell and 16 to 1 at UCLA.[13] At Williams College in Massachusetts it is 132 to 1.[14] Between 7 and 11 per cent of all faculty members in the US are conservatives, and even a third of liberals agree that conservative academics face a 'hostile atmosphere' on campus.[15]

In some humanities subjects such as anthropology, there are now zero Republican-supporting professors at any elite US college.

The same trend has been happening in Britain. In 1964, some 35 per cent of British academics voted Tory, compared to 47 per cent for Labour and 17 for the Liberals; by 2015 just 11 per cent supported the Conservatives, only half that of the radically Left-wing Green Party (who received 3.6 per cent of the national vote).[16] The changing politics of education correlates with a huge shift in the youth vote. Back in 1979 the Conservatives beat Labour among 18–24-year-olds, and once again came close in 2010 during the party's brief experiment with social liberalism, although both got fewer young voters than the Liberal Democrats. By 2017 the Conservatives were 35 points behind Labour among this demographic, but even in the 30–39 age group the gap was a disastrous 26 per cent.

Elsewhere, among doctors, scientists, in the civil service and even the leadership of mainstream churches, conservativism is becoming marginalised. There are a number of reasons for this, among them the expansion of higher education, as well as changing family patterns and the decline of religion, and Leftist 'capture' of many institutions, including charities, broadcast media, government, social services and education, which have all become culturally progressive.

People's political identity tends to be heavily influenced and shaped by the individuals in their social circles, so the disappearance of conservatives in the professional middle class has a domino effect; people grow older in an ideologically homogenous environment, and so continue to identify as liberal even as their tastes change. Indeed, one of the most popular political insults of the 2010s, 'centrist dad', applies to a growing demographic of men who see themselves as liberal but whose lifestyle is recognisably quite conservative – marriage with children, weekend visits to the Cotswolds in their hatchbacks and rock-based musical tastes frozen in the 1990s.

Pretty much the last refuge of conservatism is the military, and even Sandhurst has equality and diversity classes while the armed forces' social media accounts tweet out prog mantras just as their seventeenth-century forebears would have quoted scripture, as if the raison d'être of the Army was to promote inclusivity and LGBT rights rather than literally killing foreigners.

With domination over broadcasting, film, the universities and schools, so we have come to view the past through a particular progressive lens, a vision in which Victorian and '1950s' are pejorative terms and the era before 1963 seen as one of oppression. Traditional families are hotbeds of hypocrisy and sexual frustration, the churches bigoted and backward, industry invariably linked to poverty, and secular socialism the only saviour of the poor.

Most importantly, the Left has also developed a moral monopoly, so that those outside of the faith are under an unspoken obligation to prove their moral worth before their views can be considered, just as non-believers in highly religious societies have an air of suspicion hanging over their every word. Because of this, one of the de facto expectations for conservatives in public life is that they must denounce those to the Right of them, and so the boundary of what is acceptable shifts Leftward, bit by bit, and ideas that would have been mundane and mainstream one decade become shocking the next (or 'controversial', as the media use as shorthand for 'beyond the pale'). In contrast, there are no social sanctions against proposing even extreme Left-wing ideas because those advocating them are not seen as ethically questionable for doing so – at worst misguided. In fact, there is active competition to come up with ever wilder radical ideas, a trend that has sped up with the 'Great Awokening' of the 2010s, the acceleration of identity politics brought about by competing victimhood narratives on social media.

People still talk of conservatives as 'the establishment', the defenders of the rich and big business, and the Left as being in favour of the poor, socialism and equality, but that's an outdated idea of the industrial age, when a large politicised working class was countered by a bourgeoisie defending its own class interests. That old political polarity, of a pro-free market party representing the middle class and gentry opposed to a socialist or social democrat movement whose core support is the workers, is now gone for ever.

The establishment in the twenty-first century is centre-Left, if by 'establishment' you mean people who hold most power and make the important decisions, rather than those who have archaic titles or take part in Ruritanian traditions. Except for a shrinking number of toffs who follow the old faith, progressive views are the norm among the future leaders of tomorrow, even at Britain's top public schools. Indeed, the most expensive schools and colleges, both in Britain and the US, are now leading the way in liberal causes, whether it's gender-neutral uniforms or no-platforming conservatives, and in America there is a clear correlation between how much a college charges its elite students and how intolerant it is of Right-wing speakers, a phenomenon nicknamed 'radical privilege' by one blogger.[17] What better way to signal high status in the current year than banning conservatives from being able to speak?

The year 2014 saw one of Britain's top actors, the Old Harrovian Benedict Cumberbatch, star in a film about a gay scientist persecuted for his sexuality in the repressive 1950s austerity era. So the following year our other top actor, the Old Etonian Eddie Redmayne, made a film about a transsexual woman. I'm not sure what Cumberbatch will do next to top that, but most recently he has taken to lecturing London theatre patrons on the importance of taking in more refugees, a quintessential moralised high-status cause for a high-status, elite audience. (That the most sanctimoniously right-on actors are often also the finest talents doesn't make it easier for us.)

As Left-liberalism has become the prestige faith with a moral monopoly, dominant in academia and the most elite professions, so conservatism has retreated into comforting stupidity. It has become characterised by shock jocks and outrage merchants, as well as an aversion to commonly accepted science, the most prominent examples being scepticism over climate change and denial of evolution (or 'primate change denial', as someone once quipped). In America it has become the preserve of 'the Stupid Party', as then-governor of Louisiana Bobby Jindal referred to the Republicans in 2013, echoing John Stuart Mill's jibe about the Tories.

Some Right-wing commentators, in an appeal to their increasingly male audience, have tried to make the philosophy seem more macho than it actually is, when in reality many conservatives by nature are quite fearful. Likewise in Britain, where tabloids take on the conservative banner against a socially liberal broadsheet and broadcasting media, the Right has become associated with deliberate anti-intellectualism and even yobbery. Most people in Britain, when the phrase 'Right-wing journalist' comes to mind, would probably think of a tabloid columnist, someone such as former reality-TV star Katie Hopkins, who is a sort of *Guardian* reader's idea of what a conservative is – a deliberately unkind Cruella de Vil figure, a pantomime villain.

Yet by aiming low, to paraphrase Michelle Obama's expression, conservatives are only further helping to make their brand irredeemably vomit-inducing to almost anyone under the age of forty. It is a view summed up by the thirty-something Bridget Jones when she said: 'Labour stands for sharing, kindness, gays, single mothers and Nelson Mandela as opposed to braying bossy men having affairs with everyone shag shag shag left right and centre and going to the Ritz in Paris then telling all the presenters off on the *Today* programme.'[18] Bridget Jones is a fictional character, obviously, but the words reflect widespread middle-class thinking, and apply even more so today than when they were written in the 1990s, at a time when the Tory party seemed to disgrace itself with sexual peccadilloes while they were lecturing the rest of us on morality. Indeed, a Bridget Jones twenty-five years ago would have known many conservatives in her upper-middle-class social circle; today there would be very few indeed, at least openly.

Right-wingers in heavily liberal networks sometimes talk about being in 'the closet' and even liken their situation to that of gay men before liberation, which is a silly comparison, not least because we're not going to be shunned by parents or face prosecution. A better analogy might be that we're followers of the old religion that has lost its place in society, like Catholics after Henry VIII broke with Rome. Of course, conservatives aren't hanged, drawn and quartered for refusing to sign company diversity statements, but then liberals in the 1950s weren't burned to death for heresy either. We don't use violence to enforce moral codes today, but carrying deviant beliefs even in a modern, developed country is certainly a social stigma, and most definitely carries a penalty. There is strong evidence of job discrimination against conservatives in certain professions, most especially academia, where one-third of social psychologists admit that they overlook qualified Right-wingers when hiring.[19]

This is not to claim victim status – at the very least the sacralisation of victimhood is one of the most tedious aspects of political debate right now. It's also true that conservative appeals to be treated with leniency, especially over things such as gay rights, seem pretty hollow since we clearly didn't treat the other side with such tolerance in the past. I'm sure if we could marginalise and stigmatise Left-wing views in the way ours are, we probably would. As that great conservative philosopher Conan the Barbarian reflected on what is good in life: 'To crush your enemies, see them driven before you, and to hear the lamentations of their women!'[20]

Unfortunately, however, it is the Left that is now dominant among the intelligentsia and upper-middle class, while conservatism has been crushed and what few women we have left are lamenting. Since the 1960s the West has gone through the biggest cultural shift in half a millennium, an epochal change similar in some ways to the Christian takeover of pagan Rome and the sixteenth-century Protestant Reformation. Both of these events led to revolutions in public ideas about morality and eventually to cultural conflicts – and conservatives, like the polytheists and Catholics before them, are today on the losing side.

The bad news is that this second reformation is going to be long, painful and boring, and both sides are going to get more tedious and hysterical, just as divisions the last time around drove Catholics and Protestants into prolonged periods of insanity. Conservatism will see revivals but it will become increasingly dominated by the sort of identity politics the centre-Right once hated, a phenomenon already developing in continental Europe and Trump's America.

Conservatism has become increasingly concentrated in more provincial areas, a shrinking and often poorly educated community led by a small, reactionary aristocracy who still support the old faith. This has happened before, when England's declining Catholic population hung on for over a century after the Reformation before dwindling almost altogether, a mixture of the rural, tradition-minded in the more remote west and north, and a conservative sub-section of the aristocracy. At that time Anglicanism was the prestige faith; today Left-liberalism is the creed of the new ruling class. That is why there is no contradiction in public schoolboy Lefties or Labour signs outside £2 million London houses, any more than there was in sixteenth-century aristocrats being radical Protestants. Despite the electoral setbacks of the late 2010s, the Left is winning and we're losing. As the dashing, gentlemanly and high-status liberal Barack Obama said of al-Qaida, another group of guys not entirely comfortable with the modern world, we're Small Men on the Wrong Side of History.[21]

1

1989

Back in the early 1980s my father suddenly found himself in a very dangerous situation. Along with an old journalist friend called Peter Kemp, he had travelled to Nicaragua to cover the civil war between the communist Sandinistas and the American-backed Contras. It was a violent country even in peacetime but had exploded into ideological warfare and the mood was intensely anti-Yankee. At one point the two Englishmen found themselves surrounded by an angry mob of Sandinista-supporting men, increasingly looking like they might turn violent against the *gringos* in their midst. At this point Dad, who spoke fluent Spanish, loudly remonstrated with them, telling the crowd as he pointed to his friend: 'and to think here you are threatening a veteran of the Spanish Civil War'. They backed down, shamefaced and respectful towards the old English gentleman they had only a minute earlier threatened to pull to pieces.

Strictly speaking Dad was telling the truth, of course, although he didn't mention which side of the war his friend had fought on; he was, in fact, one of only twelve people from Britain who had run away to Spain to fight *for* Franco. Sure, that doesn't have quite the same romantic cachet, and no one sang any punk classics about volunteering for the Nationalists; neither did they have Orwell, Hemingway or Laurie Lee in their army. On the other hand, they didn't massacre any nuns, an aspect of the war that horrified a lot of people at the time; as with Syria, which saw a brutal dictator fight an unstable coalition of moderates and fanatics, including foreign volunteers, many weren't entirely sure which side was more awful.

It's fair to say that by this stage Dad's friendship circle had become rather more Right-wing than it was in his youth when he had flirted with communism, which at that time seemed like the future. Indeed, by now he was happy to see the Sandinistas beaten by the thuggish killers who invariably comprised Latin American Right-wing militias, although his real venom was directed at an enemy closer to home, the *Sandalistas* – London's Left-leaning intelligentsia.

The small but unpleasant Nicaraguan conflict was part of a greater ideological struggle, the Cold War, which pitted Western democracy against a radical, world-changing ideology that once boasted it would bury us. Instead we buried them, in 1989, a dramatic time I remember well; I was eleven and had just entered secondary school when the protests in East Germany began to swell and led to the subsequent, rapid collapse of communist rule in Czechoslovakia and Romania. I found it very exciting, having grown up in a politicised household where the imprisonment of eastern Europe was a talking point at home. As you can probably guess, I was hugely charismatic at school, and had no trouble finding girlfriends at all.

My parents were both bohemian conservatives, if that's not too much of a contradiction. Much later in life I rather felt sorry for Ed Miliband and the way his parents' highly political, middle-European household was regarded with suspicion in England; it was considered weird that they sat around discussing Marxist dialectics rather than normal things such as football or TV. I grew up in a similar ideology-obsessed Cold War atmosphere, although on the Right, my father having crossed the entire spectrum from hard Left to reactionary over forty years as a journalist covering the struggle between capitalism and communism.

Like many public schoolboys of his generation, Dad embraced socialism as a young man and when he was stationed in Trieste for national service fell in love with Tito's Yugoslavia. Any youthful ideals, however, were soon knocked out of him by his experience of decolonialisation in Africa. By the time I was around he was deeply pessimistic and cynical, and seriously out of step with the prevailing mood over South Africa. Although he respected and admired Nelson Mandela, he thought the ANC a venal and extreme organisation that would eventually make the country even worse off than it was under apartheid (which he nonetheless thought morally indefensible).

This was, to put it mildly, an unpopular opinion during the 1980s, which despite the popular image of yuppies in pinstripes shouting down brick-sized mobile phones was a time of Left-wing cultural dominance in Britain. The anti-apartheid movement was ultra-fashionable, topping the charts and filling stadiums, and progressive control of areas such as theatre and local government had been hugely extended over the decade. That this was done in opposition to a Right-wing government suited Leftists quite well, since it allowed a cultural narrative of liberation and resistance without anyone actually hitting them over the head with truncheons. Indeed the Thatcher government was not especially into social conservatism, and mostly focused on winning the economic arguments; pretty much the only anti-progressive measure they enacted, the now notorious Section 28 banning the promotion of homosexuality in schools, is stamped into the popular consciousness because it was so unusual. (It's surely only a matter of time before one of our many old Etonian actors appears in a film about Section 28 with, I don't know, a striking miner's son growing up gay or something.)

Academic dominance by the Left, and the inevitable intolerance that accelerated in the twenty-first century, was already a reality. Britain's great conservative philosopher Roger Scruton recalled going to speak at Glasgow University in the mid-1980s where he discovered on his arrival that the philosophy department had staged an official boycott on the charges of 'scientific racism'. Forced to wander aimlessly around campus until the organisers could find a room for him to use, he watched a 'desultory procession of apparatchiks' conferring an honorary degree on Zimbabwean leader Robert Mugabe, already at this stage responsible for mass murder, although he hadn't quite become the wild-eyed geriatric madman of later years.[1]

Scruton's crime was to have founded the *Salisbury Review*, a tiny conservative magazine that caused huge controversy in 1984 by publishing a Bradford headmaster called Ray Honeyford, who argued that multicultural policies were causing segregation to worsen. Forced to walk through a gauntlet of anti-racism campaigners, Honeyford was effectively driven out of his job, although later his arguments became more accepted. The following year Scruton's *Thinkers of the New Left* was published, chronicling the influential intellectuals of the post-war era whose ideas dominated our age. I remember when my brother was sick in his late teens with something like glandular fever, Mum brought him a copy to read in bed – classic light reading material for a nineteen-year-old, obviously. At some age, I can't remember when, it dawned on me that most families wouldn't consider that normal.

By the time I was a teenager Dad was such a reactionary that he had settled on the fourteenth century as the ideal time for human development before everything went downhill (sure, the Black Death and everything, but . . .). He disliked most democratic politicians almost as much as he did the communists, and the only contemporary figure he admired was the King of Cambodia, Norodom Sihanouk, a maverick who was also leader of the Royal Buddhist Socialist Party. Dad spoiled his ballot paper each election because he didn't approve of democracy and shrugged when Mum joined the Reform Club because in his view the Great Reform Act of 1832 was a historic mistake. He believed that we were far better off with rotten boroughs such as Old Sarum, the hillside on which just seven voters elected two MPs until the 1830s, while whole cities had no MPs at all (he'd have been amused to see, post-Brexit and Trump, *Guardian* articles arguing that the franchise should be limited because the people are too thick to understand politics).[2] A non-smoker, he deliberately smoked on National No Smoking Day and hated 'the nanny state' more than anything.

Not that Dad was a Conservative, exactly. He mainly loathed the governing party for being anti-train and pro-car, which struck him as a betrayal of traditionalism, and he also disliked what he saw as their obsession with money. He especially hated what multinationals were doing to the environment and to indigenous groups, and was sued by one mining company over a book he wrote about Papua New Guinea. As a result of this I think he had a small cult status in one part of that country – not quite Prince Philip god tier but somewhere among the minor deities.

Politics and history were always discussed at Sunday lunch, often leading to slanging matches, especially if drink was involved, which it invariably was. My parents' social circle was pretty mixed politically, the most regular visitor being the former *New Statesman* journalist Corinna Adam, a friend of both my parents who lived nearby. She was incredibly bright and witty, but unlike my parents she had not moved to the Right in middle age and they all argued intensely. This was even more so with my godmother Finn, one of Mum's childhood friends from Dublin, and an ardent Irish Republican who had pictures of the Birmingham Six in her window on the Portobello Road. I have strong childhood memories of her storming out on more than one occasion after Dad had said something especially offensive about the Irish. I remember her arguing with Kemp too – they obviously didn't quite see eye to eye over politics.

Our first home was in Bloomsbury, once the intellectual heart of darkness of early twentieth-century Britain but by then somewhat run-down and, as part of the London Borough of Camden, at the centre of crazed Trotskyite local politics. The 1970s were weird; at the time some members of the Camden Labour Party actually supported paedophile liberation, the idea being that kiddie-fiddlers are just another marginalised group kept down by bourgeois repression and their relationship with children was no more exploitative than various other capitalist power structures that commodified people. This particular idea didn't go down very well with working-class Labour voters in places such as Gospel Oak and Kentish Town, you'll be amazed to hear.

After that we moved to fashionably bohemian W11, and so my brother and I went to the local primary school, which was then in the control of the hard-Left ILEA. The Inner London Education Authority was run by former Fabian Society and National Union of Students leader Frances Morrell, a follower of celebrity local resident, Left-wing Labour MP Tony Benn. While the ILEA were themselves on the Left of the Labour Party they were, however, in conflict throughout with the even more radical Inner London Teachers' Association (ILTA). One of my abiding memories of the school was my brother repeatedly getting days off because his form teacher was on constant strike, while mine did not join the boycott, presumably because she was not in the union – much to my annoyance.

Schools at the time were not so competitive and catchment areas were huge compared to today, so many of my friends lived further up Ladbroke Grove beyond the Westway, while we were in the wealthy bit by Holland Park (which was always expensive, although at this point you didn't have to own a Russian energy monopoly to live there). My best friend Ben was just beyond the flyover; his dad was a carpenter and he and his sister Joanna called their parents by their first names and were passionate Labour supporters. I remember even at eight years old being conscious of our families supporting different teams and talking about it competitively, which seems slightly shameful in retrospect. The implication is that I was merely indoctrinated into being conservative rather than having brilliant flashes of insight, or rationally coming to these political conclusions, as we'd all like to believe. It's of course certainly true that I was indoctrinated, but then around four in five people do follow the politics of their parents and the cause is not entirely environmental either – indeed, there is a fair amount of genetic influence.

Even when people go against their parents' politics it's often towards competing creeds that share similarities – many young people grow up to become Marxists in rebellion against Christian mums and dads, but their new faith will share many of the characteristics of the old, including the millennial utopianism, a revulsion against unearned wealth and the wild-eyed certainty that opponents are deviants. Indeed, much of Leftist thinking is basically Christianity with all the magic drained out (which again I'll get back to later).

Ben and I lost contact after primary school but years later I looked him up on Facebook; he was a DJ or something and looked effortlessly cool and laid-back in that way people from Ladbroke Grove always seem to be. In contrast my profile showed a man with a shirt and side parting, the same haircut I'd had for about fifteen years, my face filled with worry and fear, looking every bit like Mark Corrigan from *Peep Show*. I didn't look up Ben's politics – I find Facebook too depressing to actually stalk people in case they're wildly more successful and happier than me – but it's safe to bet he's probably not an active member of the Traditional Britain Group or UKIP.

The first political memory I can definitely recall was in 1986 while on holiday in Berlin. I was eight, we were in a restaurant and Dad was reading the British papers when he suddenly chuckled heartily; I asked what he was laughing at, and Dad replied that the 'GLC has been abolished', with a big grin on his face. I didn't understand what that meant, but he certainly had a spring in his step afterwards. The Greater London Council had ruled the city for decades but by this stage had been taken over by Ken Livingstone and the 'loony Left' (a phrase Dad claimed to have invented, although I'm sceptical). Later Livingstone would become the first mayor of London before being suspended by Labour and then going on to become a sort of professional media Hitler-obsessive, his political career ending with him hiding in the disabled toilets at Millbank television studios while being harangued by a scrum of reporters asking him to explain his most recent bizarre comments about Zionism and the Nazi leader.

Being eccentric conservative intellectuals, my parents had taken us to see East Berlin as well as West; I don't know why exactly, since no one at the time had any inkling the German communist state wouldn't last the decade. My overriding sensual memory of the DDR was tasting the local version of Coca-Cola, which quickly answered any debate in my young, impressionable, sugar-addled 1980s mind over whether capitalism or socialism was superior. East Berlin was a grey, cold place where no one smiled or looked at you, while in contrast I remember the West as basically one big toyshop, with endless treats and sweets, and Dad even took us to Burger King every day because they served beer there. Junk food, permissiveness, toys – it was capitalist heaven for children. (I also remember that billboards featured topless women in that strange not-hung-up-about-sex German way.)

The strongest memory, however, was of the Wall, covered in graffiti on the West side and lined with the crosses of those shot down by snipers while attempting to flee from this socialist paradise. Crossing the death zone was genuinely scary, and in my mind I recalled that some people had been killed just before we visited; in fact, when I looked it up on Wikipedia the most recent had been eighteen months previously, but I had a neurotic fear at the time that one of the snipers might shoot at us. The Wall seemed terrifying and permanent, the Soviet Union unbeatable, and yet just three years later the Cold War was effectively over, so ending a conflict that had defined the modern world. Socialism looked defeated and outmoded, and the Labour Party, almost taken over by Tony Benn a few years earlier, was already making moves towards the centre that would culminate with the election of Tony Blair as leader.

Yet perhaps in retrospect the period of Soviet domination was a glorious time from the point of view of Western conservatism. We were at least sure that our socialist enemies didn't have the moral high ground, since no amount of cognitive dissonance or intellectual obfuscation could compete with the visual metaphor of a wall to keep their citizens imprisoned. Besides which communism was hardly very sexy by this point, represented not by Che but the hard-faced Politburo geriatrics who would turn out for their annual May Day events looking like living corpses, old, tired men addicted to vodka and surviving on dialysis machines. How could anyone say these mirthless half-dead bureaucrats with their failed ideas were the future?

In contrast the United States that decade seemed as magical as those West Berlin toyshops, filled with colour and sound, hairspray and shoulder pads, dynamic films and music. Even its urban decay and squalor was sort of glamorous and exciting. The country seemed to have regained its confidence in this age of cheesy action films with Rocky, Rambo and John McClane beating up various Ruskis, Germans and Arab pantomime villains, not to mention Frank Drebin in *The Naked Gun* fighting the Ayatollah and Gaddafi. Conservative anti-communist writers such as P. J. O'Rourke could even be cool when writing about socialism and how fun-sucking the creed was. Being Right-wing might have almost seemed attractive.

So while only hardline Leftists regret the Berlin Wall falling, it was something of a tactical setback for our side, too. It moved our opponents away from economic arguments, which they're not very good at winning, towards social ones, which they are. The end of 1989 might have looked like the darkest moment for the Left, but it actually heralded the start of their greatest triumph. Now we're the old, grey men, clinging to a dying creed while our opponents appear young, fresh and colourful. Unaware of how to fight back, the Right replies with polemics that are shouty and self-satisfied, and too little explore where our arguments have failed to find an audience and why people find us so repulsive. Where did we go wrong? Or as Michael Douglas's character says in *Falling Down*, one of the few recent Hollywood films that had a conservative message, 'I'm the bad guy? How'd that happen?'[3] (Admittedly he'd shot quite a few people by this stage and was stalking and threatening to kill his ex-wife, so maybe we'll gloss over that bit.)

2

CASSANDRA WAS RIGHT

'Yes, I'm a liberal and I'm sick of it being a bad word. I don't know at what time in history liberals have stood on the wrong side of social issues.' So spoke the famously handsome, charming, decent and progressive actor George Clooney in an interview with the *Sunday Times* a few years back, in which he added: 'We thought that blacks should sit at the front of the bus, that women should be allowed to vote, that maybe McCarthy was a jerk, that Vietnam was wrong and strip-bombing Cambodia was probably stupid. We've been on the right side of all these issues.'[1]

Few would disagree with him, certainly not many university-educated people under the age of forty-five on either side of the Atlantic. For them Clooney is obviously on the right side of these issues, and since the fall of Berlin and even more so since the fall of the Berlin Wall liberals have won almost every single social argument there is to be won. While the Left has been defeated in many economic arguments since – although socialist policies remain popular in British opinion polls – the biggest losers in the period have been Right-wingers.

Conservatives might whinge that people believe George Clooney's narrative of history, but why wouldn't they? Look at him – he's cool, he's sexy, he's obviously kind and caring, you wouldn't find him standing at a bar ranting about immigrants or writing incoherent comments below MailOnline articles. He's a winner, and a charming winner too.

Look at the line-up of people who represent liberalism in the modern

23

imagination: Martin Luther King, Nelson Mandela, JFK, Martin Sheen in *West Wing*, Pope Francis, Oscar Romero, (younger, popular) Tony Blair and Barack Obama.

Contrast with what people picture when they think of the Right: Richard Nixon looking sweaty and suspicious, racist 1970s comedians, South African security forces gripping their salivating Alsatians, semi-literate rednecks shouting at black people, five-foot South American dictators with their trophy wives, sleazy 'back to basics'-era Tory MPs forcing their families to pose with them after they'd been caught engaged in sexual depravities with a dominatrix. And last but not least Donald Trump, a man who seems to possess the unique gift of having no redeeming human qualities whatsoever. Oh, and Nazis obviously.

They have: Clooney, Matt Damon, Scarlett Johansson, Marlon Brando, Sean Penn, Humphrey Bogart, Tom Hanks, Susan Sarandon, Robert De Niro, Meryl Streep, Leonardo DiCaprio, Alec Baldwin and Whoopi Goldberg, plus pretty much all the most talented character actors including Christopher Ecclestone, Mark Rylance and Pete Postlethwaite.

We have: the elderly, senile Charlton Heston at an NRA rally after a school massacre, Clint Eastwood talking to an empty chair, Mel Gibson when he's had a drink and gets onto the subject of 'You Know Who'.

Look at the musicians of the Left: Dylan, Lennon, Woody Guthrie, Johnny Cash, Bruce Springsteen, Joe Strummer, Public Enemy, young, beautiful Elvis, Beyoncé.

Look at ours: dinosaur rocker and gun enthusiast Ted Nugent. Alice Cooper maybe? Late fat, embittered Elvis.

As for comedians, don't even bother asking.

What cool people does the Right have? Chuck Norris, maybe, because he's a meme. Or, meta-ironically, Jacob Rees-Mogg.

Their fashion: jeans, as worn by sexy twenty-two-year-olds with long hair; leather jackets sported by a young Brando; 1968 Paris students, Vietnam War protesters, beatniks and punks.

Ours: driving gloves, sports casual, Alan Partridge cardigans, novelty socks, middle-aged slippers. Jeans, as worn by men in late middle age presenting car programmes.

Even the Left's murderers are cooler. Compare Che with, say, General Pinochet. Sure, we can talk all we like about how the junta in Chile got inflation under control, but there's no contest in the rugged sex-god category.

Who would give a woman a better night of romance, lovemaking and pillow talk afterwards? Lefties, almost every time.

I like George Clooney. Who doesn't? But he's wrong about one thing – although 'liberal' has indeed become a bogey word in some sections of American and British society, they're almost entirely parts that aren't powerful or influential, filled with disenfranchised, angry people. 'Liberal elites' is a cry of rage and despair against the connected and successful by the impotent, the old and the prematurely dying, a low-status signifier as telling and recognisable as mispronouncing a word might once have been, or putting an England flag on your car. In contrast 'Tory' has for some time been used as a casual insult, even by people from privileged backgrounds, while Right-wing in sophisticated circles is almost always a pejorative, and is certainly never a compliment. It's an irredeemably tarnished identity, which is hardly surprising when two generations of educated people have largely been raised in environments where they have encountered few conservatives, except when hate-sharing deliberately provocative opinion pieces from professional irritants (and I was once one myself, a deeply irritating one).

From before their political awakening most middle-class people are given the message by the education system, the broadcast media and the wider political culture that to be Left-wing is to be generous, tolerant and forward-thinking, and so to be Right-wing is to be selfish, uncaring and bigoted. Just as Bridget Jones said.

Unless they encounter the small and shrinking pool of conservative professors, nothing they are taught in university challenges this; nothing they hear or see in the media casts doubt on it, unless they purposely choose to seek out non-mainstream outlets, in which case they are probably conservo-curious anyway. Even in the office, where centre-Left views are increasingly the accepted norm, this view might go unchallenged – especially in the state and semi-state third sector where so many of the brightest and best choose to enter. Their Facebook feed will reflect their worldview and the site will feed them a diet of stories specifically designed to cater to their prejudices (just as, of course, it will with conservative-minded people).

Nothing they pick up from a library or bookshop will alter this, since the politics section will have about three Right-wing books for every hundred socialist or liberal works. And if you ever visit the homes of Left-leaning twenty- or thirty-something humanities graduates (i.e. 98 per cent of them) you'll see that their bookshelves, while heavy on current affairs, contain almost nothing by any conservative writers. The most reactionary books will be from centre-Left authors attacking the hard Left, but even these are theological questions over which way to lead the true faith, rather than any question that it is indeed correct.

Conservatives will generally have more books from the Left, because those are the big must-read tomes, and we will certainly absorb more progressive television and cinema; not because we're more open-minded (by nature we're not) but because those are the prevailing cultural noises and so we have no choice, just as any minority has more awareness of and interaction with the majority. But it's also because we have to live in society, and appear normal to our contemporaries or neighbours or fellow parents, which is why I have books by Owen Jones and Natasha Walter displayed on my bookshelf as well as works arguing for open borders or attacking internalised misogyny, not to mention a fashionable graphic novel about the occupation of Palestine. (Obviously, you have to pull a special lever on my bookshelf to reveal the shelf where my *real* politics books are stored, along with all the Third Reich memorabilia.)

The only time some people seriously engage with conservatives is with older relatives who they meet once a year and argue with about Brexit or

Trump. The 'how to handle Republican relations at Thanksgiving' genre of article has become a staple of the American commentariat, as if the occasional dinner with people with whom you disagree politically is a profound hardship. That's pretty much *every* social event I go to.

But then, being from an unpopular minority, I tend to keep my views to myself. Soon before the election of Barack Obama I was at a dinner party hosted by my wife's friend, who is socially conscientious and, I suspected, a Level 1 *Guardian* reader (this goes up to Level 5, for those truly lost to God). She's very kind-hearted and wanted to go to Africa at the time to work as a medic. We were all getting on fine, when one of the guests, an American who had left when George W. Bush was elected, started making jokes about Republicans and conservatives generally, and talking to me about 'we' and 'us' and 'them'. We hadn't even discussed politics, but because of the setting, with a cosmopolitan circle of graduates in a gentrifying area of London, he perhaps assumed I was of his tribe too.

He was a nice guy, and we got on. I'm fairly adept at putting on an Oscar-loser fake smile when the casual anti-conservative comments come out, hiding my horns and tail and mimicking a humanoid appearance so they don't know I'm not one of them. I just keep quiet, partly because I've learned that alcohol and politics really don't mix, but I suppose mainly it's just abject cowardice and a longing for an easy life. Inevitably if an argument broke out everyone there would be on his side. That's my strategy when anyone begins bad-mouthing conservatives at social occasions, in that effortlessly comfortable way that suggests everyone at the gathering must be a tribal liberal. People make these comments almost in the same way one would feel confident voicing a negative remark about ISIS without worrying someone will say, 'Actually I support radical Islam and I find your comments deeply offensive. I've never been so insulted in my life. Come on, darling, we're leaving.'

I can recall at least a dozen similar events where I've kept my mouth shut, and yet by doing so I am adding to the problem. After all, how many actual conservative arguments will people have heard down the years, except perhaps in political debate shows that are designed to increase outgroup hostility? Indeed, most shared media, whether it's television, radio, newspapers or blogging, is combative and confrontational, the aim being to score points against opponents and to solidify group feeling in the tribe. It would be easy to get a very misleading view of what the opposition think, so perhaps, I've often wondered, people hate us because they don't understand what we actually believe.

American journalist Harry Stein once asked a publishing editor about what she and her colleagues thought about conservatives and what they hold dear: 'Racist, sexist, homophobic, anti-choice fascists. They hate everyone who's not a rich white guy. The kind of idiots who voted for Bush and McCain.'[2] Of course, most people on the Left will have a far more nuanced view than this, but there is research showing that progressives have a poor or hazy understanding of what their opponents think, compared to vice versa. A study by three academics at the University of Virginia looked into how people stereotype their opponents, with both conservatives and liberals asked how they thought a 'typical' member of the opposing tribe would answer a question. The results were 'clear and consistent', they found: 'Liberals were the least accurate, especially those who described themselves as "very liberal".'[3] In particular they thought that conservatives would disagree with statements such as 'One of the worst things a person could do is hurt a defenseless animal' or 'Justice is the most important requirement for a society', when in fact they did agree. So if conservatives don't believe in hurting defenceless animals just for laughs, what do we believe?

We Are Doomed

Perhaps the very first conservative was Cassandra from Virgil's epic poem the *Aeneid*, a Trojan who expressed scepticism that after a bitter ten-year-long war their deadly enemies the Greeks suddenly now wanted peace and, more suspiciously, had gone to the trouble of building a wooden horse as a gift – a horse strangely just large enough to fit loads of Greek soldiers in it.

The daughter of the Trojan King Priam, Cassandra was given the gift of prophecy but after she turned down the god Apollo's attempted seduction (being a good conservative girl) she was cursed always to be right about the future but never to be believed. And so when Cassandra warned that the Greeks were not really seeking peace she was ignored. 'What are you afraid of, Cassandra?' the *Aeneid* recalled them saying: 'It's the year 1200 BC – I can't believe this sort of Hellenophobia still exists. This prejudice belongs in the middle bronze age (because, you know, this is the late bronze age).' Or something to that effect.

She turned out to be right, Troy was sacked, and poor Cassandra was dragged off into slavery where she was murdered by her new owner's jealous wife. Like many people when they first read the story of the Trojan horse, I thought the plot idea pretty silly, because how could people fall for something so transparent? And yet it tells us something about human nature. The Trojans were fooled because they wanted to be fooled; they were sick of war and they wished to believe the Greeks were too, and nagging objections from relentlessly negative doomsayers were the last thing anyone wanted to hear. In real life Cassandra probably was quite annoying to be around, like many conservative pessimists.

Cassandra is a folk-tale explanation for why people never listen to worrywarts who warn about terrible disasters – people who are right but irritatingly so. Optimism and hope is ingrained in us, as another Greek tale, the story of Pandora's box, explained – a requirement in a world filled with suffering. As Daniel Kahneman observes in *Thinking, Fast and Slow*, entrepreneurs underestimate the odds their businesses face – over 80 per cent rating their chances of success as high, when in reality only a third will survive five years.[4]

As a species we have to be optimistic because otherwise nothing would ever get done and life with all its awfulness would just crush us. We'd never get back into relationships that were bound to fail, and in which the odds of romantic bliss were minuscule. We wouldn't become involved in business ventures that had bankruptcy written all over them. We'd certainly never write another book, with all its disappointment and penury. As those Barack Obama posters famously showed, hope is a powerful idea, and one that usually sells better than reality. Optimists also live longer, and if you have a positive outlook in life then that life will be more enjoyable, too. In contrast Jeremiahs think everything will go wrong, and a lot of the time they're not disappointed.

And yet there is good reason to think the party poopers have a better grasp of what's going on. 'People suffering from depression actually have a more accurate perception of reality than those with healthy minds,' according to the theory of depressive realism developed by Lauren Alloy and Lyn Yvonne Abramson of the University of Wisconsin–Madison. Indeed, in one experiment, which estimated completion times for building schemes, professional project managers were found to be less accurate than a random, unqualified group of people suffering from depression. The miserable have a better grasp of what is real 'than their happier friends and family who often look at life through rose-tinted glasses and hope for the best'.[5]

And our personality traits, including our outlook on how things will turn out, heavily influence the political team we pick, for an essential part of the conservative mindset is pessimism, which runs through reactionary thought like the drone of a whining passenger after you've taken the wrong turn. Pessimists are not great to be around but they are arguably useful, since any group needs people who are able to see flaws in a project. This is especially so in politics, where enthusiastic optimists love schemes that are going to make the world a better place, but inevitably just waste loads of money or leave lots of people dead.

And yet conversely humans also have a tendency to spot threats and notice the negative, one of the reasons why the news tends to be relentlessly miserable when by any measurement most things are getting better every decade. People tend to think the world, or the country they live in, is in a worse state than it objectively is, while thinking *their* lives are getting better. This battle between feeling threatened and complacent, and optimism and pessimism, lies at the core of the culture war between liberal and conservative, as much as the traditional Left/Right economic split on who-gets-what.

Back in ancient Greece politics was divided between different factions of the aristocrats and democrats, *aristos* meaning 'the best' although in reality denoting 'the richest'. Most writers at the time tended to identify with the former, and regarded the people, or *demos*, as easily swayed, emotionally giddy morons. Although many Cold War parallels have been made between the two Greek superpowers Athens and Sparta, the one a democracy and the other an authoritarian hellhole, Sparta was viewed at the time as being more conservative and in tune with ancient values such as militarism and order. There was one definite similarity with the Soviet–American conflict, however, in that many writers lavished praise on the ideals of Sparta while few actually wanted to live in such an awful place, just as some Leftists in the West sympathised with the USSR without being particularly keen to spend their days queuing for stale bread and vodka. (Whether Sparta can be called Left or Right depends; it was a racial, supremacist, militarised state but also one where everything was shared equally – either way it was utterly awful.) Yet the intellectual snobs had a point, as within a short space of time the Athenian people did destroy the state by pushing it into needless wars through bad judgements made by excitable mobs. In a very tenuous way this dispute between *aristos* and *demos*, the former supported by the Spartans, could be seen as a prototype to Left v. Right battles, just as in Rome there were 'patrician' and 'plebeian' factions representing the old aristocracy and the poor. Running through the political divide has always been the issue of class, with one side wanting wealth distributed more evenly and the other rather keener on hanging on to what they have.

All modern ideological debates also have their precursors in theological arguments that asked questions of man's nature, about whether we were damned or saved, destined to act according to our natures or imbued with free will, naturally closer to angels or devils. One such division within the Church came down to a debate between two fifth-century theologians, Augustine of Hippo, who came from what is now Algeria, and Pelagius, a sort of monk/wandering holy man from Britain (or maybe Brittany). Pelagius was the typical optimistic do-gooding type who thinks that people are inherently nice, and can't understand why the laid-back youth club for troubled teenagers he's set up has been vandalised and ransacked. Augustine was in contrast the classic sex-obsessed conservative weirdo who thought that, without strong social repression, everything would go to pot and people would indulge in disgusting-and-yet-strangely-arousing carnal depravity.

Pelagius wrote that there was no point in God giving out commandments if mankind was not capable of following them, and so we cannot surely be 'fallen creatures' as the pessimists would maintain. His view was echoed later in Church debates about whether to give people harsh penances for serious offences admitted to in Confession, since many priests thought this would only deter people from confessing and so put their mortal souls in peril. Better to hand out a mild punishment so that they do at least confess, some churchmen argued, a prototype of that core liberal principle, harm reduction, which is most used in areas such as drug decriminalisation.

Augustine had a much more downbeat view of humanity. He stood in opposition to Plato's great idea that some noble elite could rule a society to perfection, because mankind was so irredeemably dreadful in Augustine's view. He argued that we could never achieve the sort of utopian city-state Plato had in mind, and the best that we could hope for was one in which Christians were free to practise their faith, and in which everything didn't basically turn to total hell. He didn't do the whole hopey-change thing and, even more off-putting to modern sensibilities, Augustine had some very harsh ideas about children being born with deformities as punishment for original sin, and that unbaptised babies would burn in hell. St Augustine's downbeat view of the world may have stemmed from his own childhood, of which he later remarked: 'If anyone were offered the choice of suffering death or becoming a child again, who would not recoil from the second alternative and choose to die?'[6]

He was also, like many conservatives, unhealthily obsessed with sex, fascinated and repulsed all at once, and this formed a core part of his morality. If he were around today his internet search history would probably be a terrifying mixture of depraved filth and censorious finger-wagging puritanism. Augustine was at the mercy of his sexual desires and disgusted himself by taking a mistress, who along with their son he then abandoned when he found religion. His entire philosophy rested on the doctrine of Original Sin, that humans are tainted by nature, thanks to Adam and Eve. Because of that we needed regulation, including strict rules for crime and punishment, since for Augustine 'it was possible to imagine the state acting like a stern father, compelling a reluctant offspring to toe the line'.[7]

Augustine's pessimistic view of human nature was blamed by some for justifying authoritarian regimes of later years. Certainly it heavily influenced Catholicism, and in the thirteenth century Pope Innocent III wrote a bestseller inspired by him, called *On the Contempt of the Worlds*, in which he voiced the view that 'Man has been formed of dust, clay, ashes, and a thing far more vile, of the filthy sperm.'[8] Obviously this fits quite well with the popular liberal idea of conservatives being obsessed with sinful lust, spending their darker moments furiously masturbating while crying and muttering 'Disgusting!' under their breath.

And fanatical opposition to sexual licence has been a running theme with some conservative thinkers throughout history. Among the most important of the Middle Ages was the French writer Jean Gerson, a sex-hating zealot who had bullied his six sisters into joining him in a life of celibacy and wrote outraged tracts against masturbation. He denounced the popular work *Roman de la Rose* as immoral because it contained bawdy *Carry On*-style allusions to rosebuds being fertilised by seeds and suchlike. If he had the only copy in existence, he said, and it was worth the vast fortune of 1000 livres, he would burn it. 'Into the fire, good people, into the fire,' he fantasised.[9] Later, in 1583, an English moralist called Philip Stubbes published his *Anatomie of Abuses*, warning that the country faced 'the pathway to all Bawdy and filthiness'.[10] Looking at the newfound wealth on display in London he warned about ale, lawyers, money-lenders, football – which was a 'bloody and murdering practice' – as well as dancing, which led to 'smouching and slobbering one of another'. Stubbes predicted that 'there are three cankers which in process of time will eat up the whole Commonwealth of England, if speedy reformation be not had: namely dainty fare, gorgeous buildings, and sumptuous apparel'. He disliked changing fashions, and got particularly angry by the 'great and monstrous Ruffs' now sported by Tudor gentleman and argued that soft shirts made men 'weak, tender and infirm', and even children these days looked like 'whores, strumpets, harlots and bawds'. While women who wore doublets were the worst and 'may not improperly be called Hermaphroditi'. God knows what he'd make of London today.

Many conservative men like to view themselves as sort of modern-day cowboys, independent-minded tough guys who value freedom and a rugged independence, and yet we are by nature more scared of the world. Indeed, a key component to conservative thought through the ages is fear, both physical fear and a terror that society is in permanent decline. In the 1970s sociologist Stanley Cohen coined the phrase 'moral panic' to sum up a strand of socially conservative thinking about the way things are always getting worse and young people in particular are more badly behaved than their predecessors. Middle-aged people have always complained about the younger generation, but during the 1950s and 1960s, with the invention of the 'teenager' and more widely reported acts of criminality and juvenile delinquency, as well as changing sexual mores and more promiscuity, this accelerated.

Although the Prophet Jeremiah was the original doomsayer, changing social attitudes have been associated with societal disaster throughout history. In the fourteenth century many moralists blamed the Black Death on increasing sexual debauchery, and a trend that many found troubling and unsettling – the button. Whereas most common people had until then worn a simple smock that loosely covered their bodies like a sack, this new invention allowed men and women to dress in a way that emphasised masculine and feminine physical characteristics. It was a still recent enough change at the time of the plague in 1348 that some observers attributed the disease to these new tight-fitting outfits. One chronicler attacked men's clothes 'cutted on the buttok' which 'inflame women with lecherous desires'; another complained that English women 'dress in clothes that are so tight . . . they [have to wear] a fox tail hanging down inside of their skirts to hide their arses'.[11] All of this had brought the Almighty's wrath crashing down on us, one monkish chronicler in particular describing this divine punishment with ill-disguised glee as a 'marvellous remedy'.[12]

It's easy to laugh at all this, just as perhaps our distant descendants will laugh at conservative columnists of our day. And yet Augustine's essential view of human nature, that we are wicked beings who need to be kept in control, is not entirely wrong. Or at least that was the impression I got after starting secondary school.

3

ANOTHER BRICK IN THE WALL [1]

Conservative pessimism was outlined in the seventeenth century by the philosopher Thomas Hobbes, a fantastically downbeat man who lived through the English Civil War and concluded that people needed a strong state to stop them all from killing each other. Even his birth was marked by terror, baby Thomas arriving into the world during the Spanish Armada of 1588, when Mrs Hobbes had gone into labour prematurely as a result of the invasion scare. 'My mother gave birth to twins: myself and fear,' Hobbes quipped in that light-hearted way of his, describing the day he was born. From the outset he had a gloomy demeanour, and his great book *Leviathan* set out as depressing a picture of human nature as is possible, arguing that left to our natural state man's existence was 'nasty, brutish and short'.[2]

Hobbes's father was a vicar in London, but the family had to flee the city after he was involved in a street fight with one of his parishioners – England at the time was rather more violent than it is now, it's fair to say. Although Thomas was taught by a Puritan at Oxford he fell out of favour with the rather intolerant Puritan-dominated Parliamentarians and in 1640 had to flee to Paris, where four years later he became tutor to the Prince of Wales, the future Charles II. From 1645, with the Parliamentarians winning the English Civil War, Paris was flooded with royalists, but when Hobbes's book *Leviathan* came out in 1650 it provoked such a hostile reaction from them that he had to go back to London again.

Without social order, Hobbes contended in his seminal work, men's lives were filled with murder and misery. Although most of his ideas were formulated in the 1630s, events in the coming years were to rather vindicate his uncheerful view of the world. The book advocated a strong ruler, but it was also critical of traditional religion, which upset the Catholic-leaning Anglican royalists. He described good and evil as nothing more than men's appetites, rather than transcendental things in themselves, and that they were only so defined by how they affected the community in general. There is no *summum bonum*, or greatest good, he argued, but there is however a *summum malum*, the greatest evil – which is fear of death, and we come together to form laws and states out of terror of each other. This essentially non-religious theory of politics would become a core part of conservativism.

For Hobbes the 'natural' state of mankind is unbelievably awful, with 'no account of time, no arts, no letters, no society, and which is worst of all, continual fear and danger of violent death, and the life of man, solitary, poor, nasty, brutish, and short'. He must have been absolutely great fun to be around, and indeed after the Restoration in 1660 the magnanimous Charles II didn't bear a grudge and invited his old teacher to court to be his 'pet'.[3] The author fell out with the Church, however, and there was a move to have him tried for heresy; it was not clear whether the law about burning heretics was still valid 'but Hobbes, who prided himself on his timidity, did not want to test it'.[4] The sort of legal test case no one really wants to volunteer for, in fairness.

Hobbes ends the book *Leviathan* with the hope that his doctrines might be taught in the universities, perhaps including his alma mater Oxford, from where 'Preachers and the Gentry' would 'sprinkle' his ideas on the people.[5] Which seems unduly and uncharacteristically optimistic, and when he died the university had his books ceremonially burned.

Hobbes's view that man's natural state is perpetual warfare and misery was countered, a century later, by French-Swiss philosopher Jean-Jacques Rousseau. His famous phrase, 'man is born free but is everywhere in chains', sums up a particular strand of optimistic thought that people would be nice were it not for society corrupting or oppressing them, or as hippies would say (I imagine), 'the system, man'.[6] To conservatives his idea of 'the noble savage', primitive man living in peaceful abundance, makes Rousseau the godfather of all bad ideas; every idiotic proposal thought up on campus, every cretinous *Vox* or *Guardian* comment piece you roll your eyes at, every ill-judged policy announcement that feels good but is obviously open to abuse, every badly thought-out educational reform of the late twentieth century, can trace its lineage back to this one awful man.

Jean-Jacques Rousseau was perhaps the most influential thinker of his and our time, doing more than any other to popularise the idea that people are inherently good. Christian theology holds that we are all born with original sin, tarnished and imperfect from birth. Rousseau's great idea was to see human behaviour as formed by social conditions, so that our wickedness comes not from within but the society we are raised in. Today liberals are far more likely to believe this, with 76 per cent thinking that 'society works best when people recognize that humans can be changed in positive ways' while just 23 per cent believe it works best when 'people recognize the unavoidable flaws of human nature'. The figure for conservatives is in contrast balanced almost at 50–50.[7]

Despite Rousseau's assertion of human goodness he was himself a terrible human being, although in his defence he was also rather mad, and had some cards stacked against him. Although he had had a lively career, as a servant, tutor, music copier and composer, he was broke most of the time, and also suffered persecution from various authorities. His book *Émile* was burned in Paris and he was forced to escape to Switzerland and then to England at the invitation of the Scottish philosopher David Hume.

Before this Rousseau had endured a tough upbringing, with a brutal, unloving father who no doubt influenced his thinking. The old man had Jean-Jacques's elder brother sent to a reformatory on the grounds that he was 'incorrigibly wicked' and the poor boy ran away, never to be seen again. The philosopher later wrote: 'The ambition, greed, tyranny and misguided foresight of fathers, their negligence and brutal insensitivity, are a hundred times more harmful to children than the unthinking tenderness of mothers.'

Rousseau grew to become something of a lady's man, despite his obvious character flaws, his endless financial problems and an apparently misshapen penis, which he called 'a malformation of an organ'. He was also fantastically selfish and cruel towards women, and sponged off them, most of all his aristocratic lover Mme de Warens, whom he addressed as 'maman' (mummy). But he learned that he could impress upper-class women with his ruffian act, and that being transgressive also made him seem more attractive, especially if he could use political virtue as a justification; or as he put it, 'I have things in my heart which absolve me from being good-mannered.' He was a rebel and a bit of a bastard, and that didn't hurt his chances with the opposite sex.

Rousseau grew his hair long, 'my usual careless style with a rough beard', and he also took to wearing a kaftan, becoming a prototype 1960s selfish sexual adventurer, rather like Malcolm Bradbury's protagonist in *The History Man* – the Leftist lecturer who opposes traditional gender roles and wants to promote radical politics and combat sexual hypocrisy and patriarchy, which involves him shagging loads of hot students while his equally right-on wife ends up doing all the housework and trying to kill herself.

This egotism was mixed with enormous amounts of self-pity, although some of it was justified, I suppose: 'Few men have shed so many tears,' he wrote, talking about himself, while his lover Madame d'Épinay, whom he treated terribly, later said, 'I still feel moved by the simple and original way in which he recounted his misfortunes.' On another occasion he wrote 'Show me a better man than me, a heart more loving, more tender, more sensitive.' And also: 'I feel too superior to hate' and 'I love myself too much to hate anybody.' But Théodore Tronchin of Geneva, a former friend, would later ask: 'How is it possible that the friend of mankind is no longer the friend of men, or scarcely so?' (With the sentimentality often found in the awesomely selfish, Rousseau also loved animals and was affectionate to his cat and dogs.)

When Madame de Warens, his former lover and benefactress, fell on hard times and Rousseau's finances improved he sent her 'little' money as it would have been taken by the 'rascals' around her, and when she died in 1761 she was suffering from malnutrition. He had a 'pseudo-wedding' with his mistress Thérèse Levasseur and at the event made a speech all about himself, saying there would be statues erected of him one day and 'it will then be no empty honour to have been a friend of Jean-Jacques Rousseau'. Unfortunately, he was correct. Levasseur was from a lower social class and when he had people around for dinner she was not allowed to sit down; he praised her as 'a simple girl without flirtatiousness' and 'timorous and easily dominated'.

And after his lover gave birth Rousseau had the children sent off to the orphanage. This happened five times and the institution was a virtual death sentence, with two-thirds of babies sent there dying before their first birthday and only five in a hundred reaching adulthood, usually becoming beggars or something similarly awful. Rousseau made almost no attempt to ever track his kids down and argued that having children was 'an inconvenience'. In his defence he said: 'How could I achieve the tranquillity of mind necessary for my work, my garret filled with domestic cares and the noise of children?' He would have been forced to do degrading work 'to all those infamous acts which fill me with such justified horror'.

With his behaviour it's easy to see Rousseau as a stereotypical liberated feminist man who ditches his girlfriend when she gets pregnant because he respects her choice and, you know, he's got a new, younger girlfriend. Like many egotistical men he also chose the company of women who were no intellectual threat to him, and his mistress was apparently so simple she didn't even know what month it was at any one point. (Whereas we conservatives, of course, won't even go to bed with a woman unless she can recite whole passages of Isaiah Berlin.)

Rousseau's political philosophy was that 'The fruits of the earth belong to us all, the earth itself to none' and that the rich and the privileged should be replaced by the state which reflected the general will, whatever that meant. He also insisted that 'The people making laws for itself cannot be unjust' and 'The general will is always righteous.' Despite the fluffy feelings behind them, his ideas for the perfect state were quite totalitarian, involving government control over every aspect of our actions and even thoughts.[8] He was also sceptical of material progress, arguing that agriculture filled our lives with drudgery and that more resources just created more competition, which made us miserable, as well as damaging the world around us. This became a great strand in progressive thinking by anti-capitalists and environmentalists, but also, conversely, among certain reactionaries (my dad included).

After Rousseau's death in 1778 his burial place soon became a shrine, an illustration of how the decline of religion would only lead to the rise of pseudo-religions. One worshipper recalled how: 'I dropped to my knees . . . pressed my lips to the cold stone of the monument . . . and kissed it repeatedly.' His fame only grew, and eleven years later when France erupted in revolution, it was to be led by a number of his followers. The rather reactionary Thomas Carlyle wrote that the second edition of Rousseau's *The Social Contract* 'had been bound in the skins of those who had laughed at the first edition'. Yet Rousseau's real influence would come much later, in the twentieth century, when religion went into free fall and with it the strength of original sin.

After Karl Marx, Rousseau was perhaps the most influential person of modern times, and he was spectacularly wrong, perhaps the most wrong man who ever lived. His beliefs were still hugely influential when I was growing up two centuries later – most of all in the field of education where his idea of 'child-centred' learning took root after the Second World War. This new educational philosophy placed less emphasis on discipline and structure, and became almost universal in the state system; strangely, however, the private sector completely ignored it and by the time I was at school the education gap between the independent and state sectors had grown enormously, as had the proportion of children attending private schools.

That same year we visited Berlin, 1986, my parents took me out of the local state primary, unhappy with its very Rousseauian educational ethos, and sent me to a private Catholic school, a cultural shock that would be repeated in reverse three years later when I went back into the state sector. There were two secondary schools near us. One was the ultra-trendy Holland Park Comprehensive, which had once been nicknamed the 'socialist Eton' because of its progressive ideas about child-centred education. It had no homework and no uniform, gave its pupils great freedom, and was heavily influenced by the fashionable child-centred ethos of the time. The school drew in the children of Notting Hill's elite, including upper-class Left-wing MP Tony Benn, upper-class Left-wing author Lady Antonia Fraser, upper-class Left-wing peer Baron Kennet and upper-class communist theatre critic Philip Toynbee.

Anyway, that was the school my parents didn't send me to.

While Holland Park Comprehensive was like a 1968-er's egalitarian experiment, its near neighbour, the Cardinal Vaughan Memorial School, more resembled New York City under Mayor Rudy Giuliani. The headmaster ruled with a zero-tolerance policy whereby pupils could get Saturday detentions for being seen eating in uniform, haircut regulations were effectively military-standard and expulsion was employed so ruthlessly that one kid was thrown out for using the word 'bent' about a teacher whose writing was crooked.

But then maybe Hobbes had something of a point. I remember the first day of secondary – bearing in mind I had just come from a private prep school with eighteen floppy-haired choristers per class – and seeing two enormous boys from the White City estate punching the hell out of each other, one of whom seemed to be genuinely mentally unbalanced (he was expelled in the second year, for the rather more justifiable reason of urinating in the art-room sink during class). It was a culture shock.

Cardinal Vaughan had been a grammar school that became a comprehensive in the 1960s but didn't seem aware of it. It maintained school houses, named after four Catholic martyrs, taught Latin and even Greek, gave out lots of homework, even more detentions, and had walls commemorating those who died for their country in Flanders. It's strange that, perhaps thanks to the popularity of Harry Potter, these things sit well with progressive sensibilities today, but back in the 1980s they were considered ludicrously outmoded by the educational establishment. Yet despite this most parents still really wanted this kind of traditional school experience for their children. The Vaughan was therefore absurdly oversubscribed, especially popular with aspirational immigrant parents who weren't so keen on Holland Park Comprehensive – for, incredibly, by this stage the dream of an inner-city school without any discipline or rules had not turned out to be quite the utopia everyone hoped.

Our rival was now more like something from *The Warriors* or the alternative *Back to the Future Part II* where Biff is in charge. In the face of declining standards and increasing violence the supply of upper-middle-class progressives willing to send their kids there had dried up, and the school had morphed into a dystopian sink where teachers were terrified of the pupils, and on one occasion were pelted with gravel-filled condoms during a fully fledged riot (at least according to the rumour mill – the story may have grown in the telling). It turned out that the educational progressives of the 1970s were on the wrong side of history and the experiment was abandoned. Today, with homework, discipline, and all those things that came back to fashion in the 2000s, Holland Park is oversubscribed and has fantastic GCSE results. (Although, since nearby Ladbroke Grove has a large North African population no fewer than five of its alumni have been killed fighting for ISIS – a few more and they would have been able to put up their own First World War-style memorial wall for jihadis.[9])

Upbringing moulds our worldview just as it does our character (although, as I'll get to later on, not as much as we think). No doubt the combination of a very relaxed home environment and a strict and even authoritarian inner London comprehensive shaped mine, since I never felt any need to rebel against authority at home while authority at school seemed preferable to the alternative. The 1960s ethic was and is still very strong, and adolescence was supposed to be all about rebellion against the older generation and the Man, yet things had changed a lot since that earlier decade's glorious explosion of youthful energy and music.

Conservatives certainly have a tendency towards moral panic, and yet society *had* got considerably less safe and my adolescence coincided with the most violent period in modern British history. The Hollard Park kids would regularly prey on their neighbours on the way home, and muggings were common; indeed, street robbery, which numbered around 400 a year in England and Wales during the 1930s, was so bad by the end of the century that there were 8000 in just one London borough in a single year.[10] Violence had hugely increased and one of the boys in our year, out of about a hundred, was murdered when we were in our teens. My part of London obviously wasn't the South Bronx, to put it mildly, but it's harder to stick it to the Man when you need him for protection from the Adolescent.

I always felt a sense of jealousy towards liberal baby boomers who had grown up in the far safer post-war period and got a chance to rebel because they had something to rebel against. Most of the teachers at our school seemed pretty decent and fair, despite huge provocation from some of the ingrates. Even the religious element, the forced Masses once a week and additional prayers at morning assembly, didn't strike me as overly oppressive. Sure, nobody actually believed it and were just mouthing these mantras, but religion had by this stage already retreated so far from public life that no one, at least my friends, felt constrained by it. And throughout my adult life I've listened to people repeat slogans that I'm sure most of them don't believe, slogans they had better claim to believe in if they wanted a career, so I presume it's just an aspect of human nature. Religion certainly didn't prevent anyone I know doing what they wanted, or make me feel especially guilty about sex; I'm sure if I'd grown up in 1950s Limerick I'd feel differently, but then if I'd grown up in 1950s Limerick I wouldn't have worried about being mugged on the way home from school.

And even in this rather antediluvian school the old faith was seamlessly blending into the new; outside of the inner circle of the headmaster and his deputy many of our teachers were quite obviously Left-wing. (I remember years later watching a documentary about the Young National Front leader who had made a list of teachers at his school who were 'Reds' and thinking,

'Wouldn't it just be easier to make a list of those who aren't?') Certainly, contrary to what humanist campaigners believe about faith schools, ours had a much better record of churning out young liberals than young Catholics; almost no one I kept in contact with remained a churchgoer, except remarkably those living near top-scoring religious schools who found themselves returning to the faith when their children turned three.

As kids we had trotted off to church each Sunday, where my brother and I used to sit at the back, bored senseless, until it dawned on us that Mum rarely spoke to the priest and we could just bunk off and go to the park instead. That was the upside to living in a pretty atomised area of a big city where most people didn't know each other's business, and where even the Church lacked any sort of community. The church itself was an ugly post-war building with bad acoustics, plain in style although with a slightly futuristic influence that a lot of religious buildings of the time went in for. It was also a pretty joyless place. The strain of Catholicism we grew up with was essentially Irish, and therefore influenced by Jansenism, an especially miserable interpretation of the religion that arose in the Counter Reformation. Its main aim was to suck the happiness out of everything, to be as dismal as the Calvinists but without any of the redeeming aspects of Protestantism, such as good singing and charismatic preachers.

What we hated above everything else, even more than the boredom and nonsensical Latin, was the sanctimony of the people we saw at Mass. Everyone seemed determined to look as miserable as possible in order to show how holy they were, and therefore better, as if it was a competition to be more sour-faced than the person next to you. And when I grew up I was instinctively repulsed by that same sort of self-righteousness in people's politics, which I saw in the Left far more than among conservatives. As the atheists say, if heaven means being surrounded by you people, I'd rather be in hell.

I'm not sure many people my age feared God but they feared the institutions behind Him, in particular the headmaster, although occasionally cracks would appear even in this iron authority. One night during a school trip in the third year (we were all fourteen, when adult physical strength in males coincides with complete moral immaturity) the teachers gave the boys a night off and allowed us all to camp out alone, so that they could have a night off from us and presumably get pissed. The result was predictably *Lord of the Flies*-like, with one slightly chubby and effeminate kid bullied so intensely for being a 'batty boy' that he wandered off into the Northumbrian night along the coast (luckily he came back). On another occasion towards the end of term, the headmaster's authority began to slip during assembly and he seemed unable to control the noise and instil fear. It was a bit like the moment when Ceauşecu addresses the crowd in Romania and everyone starts booing, and the television suddenly goes blank and plays patriotic music, to the sound of gunfire in the background. I distinctly recall feeling surprised and disturbed that I wasn't at all excited by this, as others clearly were, but felt rather anxious about the whole thing. There's no way someone like me is coming out of a riot or revolution in better shape than they started it.

That's probably not healthy, since a small amount of youthful rebellion is no doubt a good thing, perhaps a sign of emotional health. I really envy former Leftists, the ex-smokers of politics; cooler than conservatives, but smarter than liberals, devil-may-care in their youth but knowing when to pack it all in. The poet William Wordsworth was one of the earliest examples of this type, a radical angry young man who welcomed the French Revolution but later concluded it was a bit of a mistake; likewise his contemporary Robert Southey, whose early play on the Peasants' Revolt leader Wat Tyler he later tried to suppress when he became a reactionary. Lots of rock musicians famously become more conservative as they mature, although this does tend to coincide with them being in the highest income-tax bracket.

Likewise the most successful conservative newspaper columnists began on the Left, among them Malcolm Muggeridge, Janet Daley, Melanie Phillips, Paul Johnson and Peter Hitchens. But then they probably had something to rebel against. As former *Prospect* editor David Goodhart once recalled, his was a typical story in that 'as a Left-wing student, I was in rebellion against a bourgeois background'. Goodhart was a 1970s radical, and remembered that 'after breaking with the assumptions of my own upper-class background (my late father was a Tory MP) I became an old Etonian Marxist in my late teens and early twenties. Yes, how ridiculous, especially as my disaffection was probably triggered less by empathy for the wretched of the earth than by the setback of failing to reclaim my place in the 1st XI football team after an illness and failing to get into the 1st XI cricket team at all.'[11] Indeed, as he pointed out, this was the same motive for the 1930s Marxist politician John Strachey, who ended up serving in the post-war Labour government, a political journey that started because he failed to make the Eton team.

Likewise, actor Peter Ustinov once recalled that he was instinctively a Liberal because the Tories reminded him of the prefects at boarding school. I remember watching that interview in my late teens and feeling it was something I really could not relate to in any way; in our school, prefects didn't have any particular power, especially faced with lippy fourteen-year-olds from Harlesden half a foot taller who would happily punch them on the way home if they exercised any typically Tory-like authority over them. I really wished I could have had Ustinov's liberal aversion to Toryism.

And historically there was one ex-Leftie more significant than any other. Towards the end of A-levels our inspired and much-loved history teacher, a dear old man called Mr Brennan who was so ancient he remembered watching Chelsea at Stamford Bridge when a V-1 flew overhead, concluded the year by comparing each of his pupils to a figure from the course we'd just done on early modern European history (he did this at the end of every year). I was desperate to be compared to France's Henri IV, which, considering he was a famously brave and handsome womaniser, was a somewhat optimistic and deluded hope on my part. Instead, much to my disappointment, Mr Brennan likened me to some dreary politician from the era of the French Revolution. And that man's name – Edmund Burke.

4

REVOLUTION (DON'T YOU KNOW THAT YOU CAN COUNT ME OUT)

Around the time that Philip Stubbes was making his dire warnings about sumptuous clothing, King Henry VIII initiated the historic split with Rome, declaring himself head of the Church of England. Later, when Henry's morbidly obese, syphilis-ridden body finally gave out, the government of his sickly son Edward VI fell under the control of radical Protestants influenced by Reformation leaders such as Jean Calvin.

The great division in Western Christianity had begun in 1517 with the German priest Martin Luther proposing modest reforms but it had soon spiralled out of control as ever more insane elements turned up, pushing the revolution further. This led in turn to a Counter Reformation in which the Catholic Church adopted some aspects of Protestantism but also became far more belligerent and intolerant in fighting them, and both sides grew more polarised and unreasonable, much to the sorrow of those caught in the middle. After Edward VI died in 1553 his half-sister Mary acceded to the throne, as fanatically Catholic as her brother was Protestant, but she came to lose initial sympathy after burning three hundred Protestants to death, which rather alienated the middle ground of public opinion. Mary died miserably prematurely and was succeeded by her half-sister Elizabeth, who restored Protestantism and in turn persecuted and hunted down various Catholics, although doing so with a better PR team (and also doing much to blacken the name of her sister, who later became known as 'Bloody Mary').

Elizabeth had tried to steer a sort of middle course in which the Church of England still resembled Catholicism in many ways, but there emerged a radical wing unhappy at this halfway measure, a group who hoped to bring it closer to Calvinism. This strain of Protestantism had become dominant in the Netherlands, Scotland and Switzerland, where Jean Calvin had created a sort of Christian fundamentalist state in Geneva. Here people were forced by law to attend church and listen to Calvin's long, rambling sermons, while dancing, singing, feasting, 'indecent or irreligious' songs, theatre, jewellery, make-up and immodest clothes were all banned, as were Catholic practices such as having statues and relics.

In England this extreme Protestant movement was most concentrated in the eastern counties along the North Sea, which had historically been heavily influenced by the Dutch across the water. They came to call themselves the Godly but we know them better as the Puritans, since they wished to 'purify' the Church of Catholicism and sin. The Puritans comprised no more than 15 per cent of the English population but were disproportionately well educated and prominent in London as well as other southern and eastern cities such as Cambridge, and heavily represented in influential professions such as the law.

Marginalised under Elizabeth and her successor James I, large numbers of these Puritan dissenters had given up on England and began to head first for the Netherlands, but didn't like their children growing up speaking Dutch, and so instead set upon establishing a new colony across the ocean. Some thirty-thousand people left eight eastern English counties in the 1620s and 1630s for New England, but as the kingdom's gentry increasingly fell into conflict with James's son Charles I so the Puritans came to the fore with the advent of the Civil War in 1642. The Parliamentary forces fell under the control of the Godly and in particular the New Model Army led by Cambridgeshire MP Oliver Cromwell. When Charles was executed in 1649 a Puritan-led dictatorship came to rule England, among other excesses banning Christmas and theatre. They weren't tremendously popular, unsurprisingly.

Puritans were against the doctrine of the Divine Right of Kings espoused by ultra-royalists, the idea that God had chosen the monarch to rule his subjects; they instead believed that political power belonged only to the virtuous and Godly, and that the country should be ruled by an 'elect' guided by the Bible. This was the first real religious–political movement in England, and British conservatism emerged partly in opposition to it. The eighteenth-century philosopher David Hume, considered the leading light of the Scottish Enlightenment, was in particular critical of religious 'enthusiasm', as this form of Puritan politics was termed. As historian Jerry Z. Muller put it: 'Conservatism arose in good part out of the need to defend existing institutions from the threat posed by "enthusiasm", that is, religious inspiration which seeks to overturn the social order. The critique of religious enthusiasm, which was central to Hume's conservatism, was later extended . . . into a critique of political radicalism.'[1]

Religious division was at the core when during the later seventeenth century English MPs began to divide into political parties for the first time. On the one hand there were the Whigs, successors to the Parliamentarian side in the Civil War and supporters of the House of Commons, London commercial interests and Low Church Protestantism. Opposed to them were the Tories, associated with Catholic-leaning High Church Anglicanism, the landed aristocracy and the authoritarian Stuart dynasty. Both names were originally insults, *whiggamore* being a (Presbyterian) Scottish cattle rustler and *toraidhe* a (Catholic) Irish highwayman, and these two groups much later evolved into the Liberal and Conservative parties (although the latter contained the more conservative Whigs, also). They represented cultural divisions, too, Tories being attached to established religion, the monarchy, tradition and a more pessimistic view of human nature. Whigs were more likely to be merchants than landed aristocracy, had the overwhelming support of Dissenters – Protestants too radical for the Church of England – and tended to believe in progress, so that the 'Whig theory of history' came to be one in which things slowly but steadily go from bad to good.

These partisan splits could be intense. Today geographic polarisation is increasingly an issue in the United States, as people move into overwhelmingly Republican or Democrat areas to be around others like them, but this is not a new phenomenon. Many of London's grand Georgian squares were designed to be politically segregated, built by rival Whigs and Tories to live in enclaves. Hanover Square in Mayfair was a Whig stronghold while further south St James's Square was heavily Tory, close to the party's unofficial headquarters, the Cocoa Tree coffee house in Pall Mall; both English parties originally began in coffee shops, although Tories also met in taverns, perhaps because drinking has been found to make us more Right-wing. The Whigs were politically ascendant for most of the eighteenth century and their rivals were viewed as dubiously loyal and even ready to restore the Catholic Stuart monarchy, which had been deposed in 1688; indeed, workmen in the 1930s found a bolthole under the Cocoa Tree where Tories could escape if the law ever arrived. Thankfully our unpopularity in London today hasn't quite reached that terrible a level.

Although the Whigs dominated commerce and politics, most of the population throughout the later seventeenth and eighteenth centuries had more sympathy for the Tories, whose attachment to tradition found favour outside of elite circles. The Tories claimed to represent the 'Country Party' of the common people against a corrupt metropolitan elite, which always went down well.

Political divisions had emerged out of theological disputes, and there remained a religious element to English political divisions until relatively recently, with High Church Anglicans traditionally voting Conservative and Dissenters voting Liberal. That this sectarianism declined was partly because, after all the violence of the Reformation, one philosopher concluded that the only way to prevent permanent bloodshed was to allow religious tolerance.

John Locke's father had served as a captain with the Parliamentary forces during the Civil War and in the 1660s the son had found a patron in the Whig Lord Shaftesbury, who had come to London seeking help for a liver infection. Locke convinced him to have surgery, at the time an absurdly dangerous operation but which he survived. Shaftesbury afterwards gratefully supported Locke in his philosophy writing; his most famous work, *Two Treatises on Government*, was written just before the 1688 Glorious Revolution in which the Whigs conspired to remove the Catholic James II and replace him with the Dutchman William III, thus introducing a century of domination. He followed it up with *A Letter Concerning Toleration*.

Locke was inspired by a visit to the Netherlands where he saw tolerance in action, at a time where there was persecution and religious war in France, Spain and England. This was a dangerous idea, and his fellow Whig Algernon Sidney had been executed only in 1683 after his *Discourses Concerning Government* had argued that governments required popular consent and that the people had the right to remove corrupt rulers.

Locke is credited with the concept of empiricism, that human beliefs come from experience and our senses rather than divine action. He is best known, however, for arguing for pluralism in politics, a novel idea when it was previously believed that a nation could not function without religious uniformity. Although a sectarian civil war in France and a semi-sectarian one in England might suggest this pessimism to be correct, Locke argued that conflict came from attempts to force uniformity on people and that peace could only be established by allowing them to choose their own church. Religion, indeed, should step back from politics, because otherwise there would be permanent, ceaseless fighting – and so came the birth of pluralism and liberalism.

Religious liberty was an alien idea, in fact a concept so unpopular that leading Protestant Dissenters rejected Charles II's offer of tolerance because it also meant the hated Catholics being free, too. Because of this Dissenters ended up losing many civil rights, including the right to graduate from Oxford or Cambridge, for another century and a half – all to own the Papists, as they might say now. Even Locke's tolerance did not extend to Catholics, who by following a foreign sovereign in the form of the Pope could not be loyal to the realm; likewise atheists, who, it was largely believed, couldn't take part in the contractual nature of society because they could not be held to oaths. Locke did later question whether non-believers might be allowed some toleration, although atheists would remain discriminated against for long after.

Locke died in 1704, not especially respected at the time, and he was largely ignored for the next half-century; it was only with the discontent and unrest growing in the American colonies during the 1760s that his work began to have a profound influence. In particular his argument for the 'preservation of the life, the liberty, health, limb, or goods of another' became the philosophical bedrock of the new nation established by British rebels across the ocean.[2] When their ideological leader Thomas Jefferson wrote the American constitution, he basically copied and pasted huge chunks of Locke's text. (Jefferson also introduced full tolerance into his home state of Virginia with the Statute of Religious Freedom.)

These Whiggish, liberal ideas were hugely important to the British colonists as they began to protest against what they saw as an increasingly tyrannical London government. Indeed, the conflict between the British crown and the colonials was in some ways a second civil war, with large numbers of 'Tory' Loyalists in America – up to a third – opposing independence and many British Whigs supporting the colonies, with petitions showing widespread sympathy. (The American Civil War, between a north heavily settled by Puritans and a southern aristocracy descended from Cavaliers, was the big-budget third part of the trilogy.[3]) Among those British MPs sympathetic to the Americans was one Whig, Edmund Burke, who would become the spiritual godfather of British conservatism.

The Prophet

If conservatives went in for big parades each May where we carried Communist Party-style banners, then Edmund Burke's face would definitely be on one of them, maybe with Benjamin Disraeli alongside, inciting the workers to rise up and get a mortgage, a car and one foreign holiday a year.

The godfather of British conservatism, Burke was actually Irish, had grown up in the Whig tradition, and had he died a decade before he did would be remembered as something of a liberal. His father was Protestant and his mother Catholic and, though he felt British, this background gave young Edmund a sense of empathy with the Irish Catholic underclass. Burke's mixed background influenced his pragmatic view of the world, so 'The experience of seeing differences of dogma made moot in practice by the bonds of family affection and neighbourly respect was formative for him,' in the words of his biographer Jesse Norman: 'It seemed to leave him with a lasting sense that life was more complicated in practice than in theory – and that this was a good thing.'[4] This upbringing helped shape the young Burke's politics, compassion tempered by realistic notions about what is achievable in light of our flawed and complex nature.

His first major work was *A Philosophical Enquiry into the Origin of Our Ideas of the Sublime and Beautiful*, published in 1757, which contained many future Burkean themes, in the words of his biographer: 'Humans have a distinctive nature ... they are social animals heavily driven by instinct and emotion. The testimony of ordinary people is often of greater value than that of experts.'[5] His next, *An Account of the European Settlement in America*, also contained several ideas that would become central to conservativism: 'We have a common human nature. Peoples differ crucially in their history, character and manners; what institutions and culture they develop make a huge difference to their well-being and success; the Christian religion is generally a civilizing force.'[6]

An essential Burkean idea was that we must base our policies on how the world is, not how we wish it be, for as he wrote: 'A man full of warm, speculative benevolence may wish his society otherwise constituted than he finds it, but a good patriot and a true politician always considers how he shall make the most of the existing materials of his country.'[7] Another was that governments should limit themselves to governing, so that: 'It is for the satirist to expose the ridiculous; it is for the moralist to censure the vicious; it is for the sympathetic heart to reprobate the hard and cruel; it is for the Judge to animadvert on the fraud, the extortion, and the oppression.'[8] This opposition to government activism did not mean that Burke lacked compassion about the relentless grinding poverty around him, and he fretted about 'the innumerable servile, degrading, unseemly, unmanly, and often most unwholesome and pestiferous occupation, to which by the social economy so many wretches are inevitably doomed'.[9] Poverty always exists, though – it is the essential human condition, not a departure from it.

Burke had supported the American colonists in the build-up to the final split with the mother country, for what the New Englanders and Virginians were fighting for was continuity and constitutional government; their rebellion against the British government, as with their forefathers' fight against King Charles I, was viewed as essentially conservative. However, when a new, far more radical revolution shook the world a decade later Burke's place in the conservative pantheon of pessimism became assured.

'Bliss was it in that dawn to be alive, but to be young was very heaven!' as William Wordsworth said at the start of a political upheaval that would leave millions dead.[10] The French Revolution was the beginning of the modern era proper: a conflict of ideology rather than religion that introduced the concepts still at the core of our politics. At the National Convention in Paris it became custom that the king's supporters sat on his right and his opponents the left, after which the divide between tradition and radicalism would always be defined along those lines.

At first the uprising against Louis XVI's authoritarian and corrupt rule delighted people in England, and not just the radical fringe. After the Bastille was stormed London theatres re-enacted the event and the House of Commons proposed a 'day of thanksgiving for the French Revolution'. Leading Whig politician Charles James Fox said, 'How much the greatest event it is that ever happened in the world! and how much the best.'[11] The young poet Samuel Taylor Coleridge, meanwhile, burned 'liberty' and 'equality' with gunpowder onto the college lawns at St John's and Trinity colleges, Cambridge.

Despite the revolution being a secular event and partly inspired by resentment towards the privileged clergy, the Revd Richard Pryce saw events in Paris as a sign of end times when all injustice would end. Dr Price, a member of the radical Unitarian sect that denied Jesus was the son of God, said he awaited after the revolution the arrival of the Messiah, while his fellow Unitarian, the chemist Joseph Priestley, confidently predicted that the British Establishment would soon fall, too. He reckoned it would be twenty years at most. Priestley went on to discover oxygen, but his genius for science did not necessarily confer political wisdom.

Yet despite fashionable London opinion-formers seeing the French Revolution as a triumph for freedom, progress and perhaps even the everlasting kingdom, the naturally gloomy Burke grew increasingly concerned about events across the Channel. The Irishman was going against the grain in this, as his fellow Whig Charles James Fox had called the revolutionary constitution 'the most stupendous and glorious edifice of liberty, which had been erected on the foundation of human integrity in any time or country'.[12] Naturally Fox expected his old friend and comrade to be as enthusiastic as all the other liberty-loving folk, and so there was shock when in November 1790 Burke produced his most famous work, *Reflections on the Revolution in France*, warning that it would end in violence, anarchy and, inevitably, dictatorship.

Burke lost many friends over this, and his book also triggered a great pamphlet war in London, with the most high-profile and famous response coming from the celebrated radical essayist Thomas Paine. In a sense their great debate would become the opening round of the Left v. Right conflict in Britain. Paine had already made a name for himself with *Common Sense*, written in 1776 during the American crisis and which became a bestseller. He actually coined the phrase 'The United States of America' and rather foolishly allowed the Continental Congress, the embryonic American government, to keep the royalties from his book – which turned out to be a much bigger seller than anyone imagined. Poor Paine ended up living in poverty and squalor.

While Burke came from a mixed Catholic–Anglican background, his main opponent was raised in the Society of Friends, or Quakers, a politically radical Protestant sect that emerged in the north of England in the seventeenth century. Paine was heavily influenced by his religious background, although he criticised their austerity, and joked that if God had consulted the Quakers during creation all the flowers would be grey. Despite being small in number and mostly from modest backgrounds, the Quakers have arguably been one of the most influential groups in history. Disapproving of alcohol and in favour of social reform, the Friends were in many ways proto-liberal-Lefties, so that as well as being scolds they were also very good at getting rich.[13] The Puritans of Massachusetts had a saying that the 'Quakers pray for you one day a week and prey on you the other six.' Many of the main Left-leaning charities in Britain were founded in the nineteenth century by Friends, who were dominant in business and, since they didn't drink, couldn't fritter away the profits on more enjoyable pursuits than social justice.

And yet for all that the Quaker sanctity grated on their neighbours they put their money where their mouth was when given their own colony, Pennsylvania. The Puritans who fled to New England didn't want an end to religious persecution, they just wanted to be the ones doing the persecuting; they ruthlessly drove out heretics in their new home, and nearby Rhode Island was founded by one such bad-thinker (in fact, in the mid-seventeenth century the New Englanders executed more Dissenters than the Cavaliers did). In contrast, the Friends allowed anyone to come to their colony, established by William Penn in 1681, and Philadelphia became the one city in the British Empire where Catholics and Jews could worship freely and even take part in politics. They also received huge numbers of German refugees and within a short while Quakers were a small minority there, although they still remained economically dominant. Quaker political ideology has also come to have an outsized influence on American liberalism, most prominently with the anti-slavery movement but even with twenty-first-century ideas such as open borders.

Paine had a chaotic life, was frequently in debt and drunk, and often fell out with people, especially supporters. But he had a natural flourish when it came to making an argument, and had almost unparalleled talents as a polemicist. 'These are the times that try men's souls,' he wrote of America in 1776: 'The summer soldier and the sunshine patriot will, in this crisis, shrink from the service of their country; but he that stands by it now, deserves the love and thanks of man and woman.'[14] The French revolution was, Paine said, 'a renovation of the natural order of things, a system of principles as universal as truth and the existence of man, and combining moral with political happiness and natural prosperity'[15]. He wrote that 'the system of government now called the new is the most ancient in principle of all that have existed, being founded on the original, inherent Rights of Man'.[16]

Burke disagreed, believing that abstract ideas and 'rights' are essentially pointless, because they cannot be enforced and therefore merely make the person proclaiming them feel good about themselves, while only leading to tyranny. Hostility to abstract ideas is a core conservative principle, for as Burke wrote: 'what is the use of discussing a man's abstract right to food or medicine? The question is upon the method of procuring them and administering them . . . I shall always advise to call in aid of the farmer and the physician, rather than the professor of metaphysics.'[17]

Paine showed many signs of the radical thinking that would mark later, even more violent revolutions: that anyone who opposed it must have a devious private motive, that resistance should be violently crushed for the greater good, and that one day an earthly paradise will be created and the reactionaries swept away. Paine saw himself as being on the moral high ground, contrasting himself with the conservatives – 'the one encourages national prejudices; the other promotes universal society'.[18] Burke, in fact, believed prejudice a good thing, by which he meant 'received wisdom'; life would become impossible if we tried to think through every new situation from first principles, rather than our experiences and the collected knowledge of the past. Prejudice can be bad when it is used without evidence or reason but, says biographer Yuval Levin, 'since no individual can hope to reconsider every question from scratch, there must be some received opinions, but the best of these are formed by large communities over time'.[19] Revolutionaries just replace old prejudices with new ones of their own, based on first principles about human nature. Paine tended to judge systems on grounds of principle rather than pragmatism, and that Burke represented the old and oppressive way of doings things was reason enough to suggest he was wrong.

Paine's book was very popular with the sorts of people who read, and everyone who was anyone had a copy – he far outsold his rival. In contrast the 'people', or to be more precise the semi-literate mobs who represented many of them, were not so approving of these middle-class radicals, and in one notorious incident in Birmingham attacked a dinner to celebrate the anniversary of Bastille Day, smashing up three Unitarian and one Baptist chapels. There was widespread hostility to the revolution among all social classes in England, and Loyalist societies were formed with rather Right-wing-sounding names such as 'the Preservation of Liberty and Property against Republicans and Levellers'.

But by now the moderate French revolution of 1789 had indeed given way to a far more extreme and violent eruption in 1792. The execution of King Louis XVI, along with his wife Marie Antoinette, was followed by the Terror, in which the revolutionaries turned on each other, as squabbling revolutionaries inevitably do over matters of doctrinal purity. There was conflict between the more moderate Girondins and the extreme Jacobins; and inevitably, as would happen in later revolutions, the more crazed group came out on top. In September 1792 over 1200 people were murdered in a revolutionary frenzy, including more than 200 priests who had refused to swear loyalty to the new state. By this stage the revolution had fallen under the control of men such as Jean-Paul Marat, a radical journalist who ran a newspaper called *L'Ami du peuple* although he loathed the people in private. Marat had suggested the problem of counter-revolutionaries could be solved by cutting off 'five or six hundred heads', which would restore society's 'repose, freedom and happiness',[20] although his definition of 'counter-revolutionary' was pretty broad, and his main focus soon turned towards the Girondins.

Indeed, Pierre Victurnien Vergniaud, a deputy for the Girondin faction, had warned that 'it is to be feared that the Revolution, like Saturn, will end by devouring its own children'.[21] Vergniaud was right – he was executed in 1793, along with almost all the remaining Girondins. Before long the Jacobins turned on each other, and over the course of that year sixteen thousand people were slaughtered by the guillotine.

The leading Jacobin, Georges Danton, had said the way to prevent a repeat of the September massacre was to set up a Revolutionary tribunal, saying, 'Let us be terrible so that we can prevent the people from being terrible.' Danton was eventually outflanked in his lunacy by Maximilien Robespierre, 'a small, thin, dogmatic man of thirty-two with thick, carefully brushed and powdered hair and a slightly pock-marked skin of a deathly greenish pallor'.[22] Robespierre was the son, grandson and great-grandson of lawyers, which should have been warning enough, but he seemed to be fairly normal until he read Rousseau at college. Under his direction the revolution, for all its lofty claims arguing for the rights of man, turned into an orgy of bloodshed across France. Most of the worst revolutionaries were indeed lawyers or journalists although in Lyon over two thousand were killed on the order of local deputy Jean-Marie Collot d'Herbois, an actor and playwright.

During the height of the Terror some 1500 people were beheaded in eight weeks, about 6 per cent of them clergy. While the revolutionaries had a strong anti-clerical dint, in their own way they also sought to imitate the Church, so that religious buildings were vandalised and 'any kinds of superstitious jugglery' were forbidden by law, with statues of the Virgin Mary replaced by busts of Marat. Meanwhile, theatres offered parodies of Mass such as *L'Inauguration du Temple de la Vérité*, biting satire against an institution that was already powerless.

Some revolutionaries explored ideas to the limit, among them one called François-Noël Babeuf, a political journalist and a 'compulsive, tedious writer' who 'the more often he was derided the more sure he was that his theories constituted the answer to the problems of mankind'.[23] Babeuf concluded that 'perfect equality' and 'common happiness' could only be achieved by suppression of private property. There would be a common storage of food and 'a simple administration for food supplies', which would 'take note of all individuals and all provisions and have the latter divided up according to the most scrupulous equality'. Way ahead of his time, his ideas would later be taken up across much of the world – with hilarious results.

And yet many of England's radical thinkers continued to support the revolution even after it was clearly going wrong, among them radical writer William Godwin, author of *Enquiry Concerning Political Justice, and Its Influence on General Virtue and Happiness*. William Wordsworth's original enthusiasm had now faded and he expressed grudging support for England after France invaded Switzerland in 1798: 'Oh grief that Earth's best hopes rest all with thee!' he lamented of his home country.[24] Even with the advent of war between Britain and France, some Dissenters *still* supported the enemy, and a Unitarian minister, Ebenezer Aldred, said Britain was the real Beast of Revelation, 'guilty of imperialism, slave trading and sodomy'.[25] No doubt today he'd end up a talking head on Press TV blaming the CIA for every misfortune befalling the world.

Paine had enthusiastically travelled to France but ended up being imprisoned by the revolutionaries for being insufficiently crazed, and only escaped death because the chalk mark stating he was to be executed was accidentally put on the wrong side of the door. You would think that would have knocked some sense into him, but no. By this stage Paine had also managed to alienate the Americans, partly because of his kooky religious views but also snobbery from the rather upper-class Revolutionary leaders, with only Thomas Jefferson standing by him. He ended up broke and living in squalor and, to add final insult to injury, when some supporters brought his body back home to England it was stolen.

And while poor Edmund Burke had been proved right about dictatorship emerging in France, he had unfortunately died before being vindicated.

Instead, in his final years he was derided and laughed at and became increasingly depressed and paranoid; people even accused him of being a Catholic, which was as damaging as accusing someone of racism is today. He wasn't believed, despite being right – just like Cassandra. Burke wrote to Lord Fitzwilliam in 1793 in rather downbeat mood suggesting that: 'I cannot proceed, as if things went on in the beaten circle of events, such as I have known them for half a century. The moral state of mankind fills me with dismay and horrors. The abyss of Hell itself seems to yawn before me.'[26] Conservatives – we're such great fun.

5

THESE THINGS I BELIEVE

The argument between Burke and Paine has in some ways come to define our political debate to this day — one that Burke's side have been losing heavily of late. The term 'conservative' was first used in 1818, and like many of our political references was originally made in French, in a journal called *Le Conservateur*. It stated that it 'upholds religion, the King, liberty, the Charter and respectable people' — *les honnêtes gens*. But from the start the philosophy varied across different countries. Liberalism is by definition universal, since it seeks to guide society under a set of principles, and so it tends to be quite alike around the world, while conservatism varies more from culture to culture, since it seeks to defend specific traditions. Or as Tolstoy famously put it in *Anna Karenina*, 'Happy families are all alike; every unhappy family is unhappy in its own way.'

Each conservative tradition is slightly different, although the closer two cultures are, the more we can reasonably make a fit. France has historically lacked the more moderate English form of conservatism, and it's arguably the greatest drawback of that country, although they got the wine, the food, the weather and the sex appeal, so it's swings and roundabouts. In contrast America, it was said, lacked a 'conservative' movement in the European sense, its Right-wing philosophy largely descending from the English Whig tradition, since Toryism was all but dead there and there was no established Church or landed aristocracy to defend. American conservatism was therefore always more enthusiastic about trade and capitalism than its Old World equivalents, which were about defending the king and whichever Church was established.

In England conservatism – and the party that came to represent it – was strongly associated with Anglicanism, since politics originally began as sectarianism by other means, with the proto-Left originating from radical Protestant beliefs. The Puritans believed in the 'Elect', an oligarchy of Godly people destined for heaven. Although hardly egalitarian, this Calvinist idea was subversive, and meant people could be the equals of their social superiors just for being more righteous. Many Puritans were driven by a determined belief that God was on their side, and that they were bringing about a glorious future when they would defeat the Antichrist. They were quite progressive in some ways; the poet John Milton was among many who argued for legalised divorce, as well as 'the Liberty of Unlicenc'd Printing', although he only meant among the Godly, i.e. freedom of speech for people with whom he agreed.

Although the Puritans were fairly conservative, other more radical Protestant sects went even further, arguing that not just the 'elect' but many – indeed most – people could be saved. Even these radical Protestant sects, however, excluded the non-Godly from this salvation, which meant Catholics and Anglican Royalists – who were as good as Catholic – and who could expect no political rights if by any chance these radicals came to power.

Such was the link between Church and party that Samuel Johnson's 1755 *Dictionary* defined Tory as 'One who adheres to the ancient constitution of the State, and the apostolic hierarchy of the Church of England'. It was once famously said that the Church of England was 'the Tory party at prayer', and for long after the Civil War English politics 'was a branch of theology rather as twenty-first-century politics is a branch of economics',[1] with the Whigs having the support of low-church Protestants including the Calvinists, independents and later Methodists. Among the most radical were the Unitarians, who by denying Christ's divinity were accused of 'Judaising', bringing Christianity close to its parent religion. Unitarians were at the heart of English political radicalism in the later eighteenth century, and in the 1820s a group of Unitarian businessmen in the north of England started a newspaper, the *Manchester Guardian*.

The Victorian Liberal Party was heavily influenced by Nonconformism and a religious 'popular front of moral outrage' fed Liberal politics.[2] (So what's new?) Indeed, these Nonconformists were behind most of the typically Victorian moral campaigns, such as the movements against slavery and animal cruelty, but also the sort of sexual moralising that twentieth-century people would look down upon.

As time went on the more conservative Whigs moved towards the Conservative Party, as the Tories became known, and a core of beliefs began to become associated with conservatism. These can be summed up by the idea that 'humans are flawed, fallible creatures; reason is powerful, but prone to error; and tradition and prejudice are often good guides to social policy'.[3]

Perhaps the biggest confusion people have involves mixing up conservatism with what Jerry Z. Muller called 'orthodoxy', a belief that things should always stay the same because of ancient traditions that cannot be broken, sacred texts or a 'transcendent moral order, to which we ought to try to conform the ways of society'.[4] Conservatism originated as a very different philosophy altogether, indeed conservatism came partly as a defence *against* religion in politics, the dreaded 'enthusiasm'. Conservatives don't believe that things should stay the same, for as Burke said, 'a society without the means of some change is without the means of its conservation'.[5] Conservatives also see themselves as the conservers of civilisation against barbarism – which is after all the most 'orthodox' state of all.

According to Muller, religious fundamentalists are not conservatives in that 'they want their society to match an externally ordained moral order, so they advocate change, sometimes radical change. This can put them at odds with true conservatives, who see radical change as dangerous.' This was the case with the Puritans, whose radical ideas about rule by the Godly upset moderate Anglicans enough that they formulated a political critique of them. Likewise with 'radical' Islamists, who tend to oppose the conservative social mores of their parents and wish to replace tradition with a literal Koran-based order. Islamists are often against arranged marriages, which are more ethnic and cultural than Islamic, as well as traditional dress, replacing colourful south Asian saris with dour black Arabian clothing. It might be fair to call their philosophy 'radical conservatism', since I'm trying to avoid that annoying polemical habit of just assigning every bad thing in one's own tribe to the other, in an effort to be more generous and so more fruitfully engage with the libtards.

According to Muller: 'While the orthodox defence of institutions depends on belief in their correspondence of some ultimate truth, the conservative tends more sceptically to avoid justifying institutions on the basis of their ultimate foundations.' Yet conservatives might themselves downplay these subtle differences between conservatism and orthodoxy because it's useful that people believe an institution to have some mystical importance. In other words, they fake it to some extent, the most obvious example being with the royal family, who ultimately only owe their supposedly God-given position to their ancestors who were good at fighting (or of the right religion).

Conservatives support traditions but largely because their continued existence implies they serve some useful function, and, as Muller wrote, 'because eliminating them may lead to harmful, unintended consequences', or that the veneration felt by people makes them useful. All authority was originally won at the point of the sword, the institutions of today created by early medieval warlords, but the fact that institutions such as the monarchy have evolved and served a useful function makes their shady origins less important. Burke said that governments originate from barbarism and crime, but 'mellow into legality'.[6]

Conservatives believe in 'historical consequentialism', that is they judge institutions by their record, not the motive of their founders. The first kings were bullies who came to the throne through violence but that does not negate the importance of monarchy, nor need we stop believing in its mystical link with the other ancient institution, the Church, again an organisation that owes its creation and prestige to some seriously flawed men. Nation-states arose out of the greed of kings who were able to force their rule over a patch of land and help create a semi-fictional national identity. That these homelands were often created artificially and have invented traditions to some extent does not make them meaningless, since they have come to create a shared story among a group of people. The emotions people attach to them are real, and the communal benefits of that attachment tangible.

Once something comes to be believed and so celebrated by a group of people, that gives the institution its validity. As the French reactionary thinker Joseph de Maistre wrote: 'custom is the mother of legitimacy'.[7]

Older bodies come to be sacralised, linked to eternal divine approval, even if the institutions themselves have adapted down the years. The monarchs of England are anointed by the Archbishop of Canterbury, signifying that they have been chosen by God, in a ceremony that dates back to the tenth century and which has changed little since the fourteenth. Although most people might not literally believe that God has chosen the Queen, it reflects the powerful social proof the institution has come to develop. In other words, it's survived all this time so it must be doing something right.

This is called 'historical utilitarianism' – if something has survived several hundred years, then this suggests it serves some human need. German philosopher Hans Blumenberg argued that 'Where an institution exists, the question of its rational foundation is not, of itself, urgent, and the burden of proof always lies on the person who objects to the arrangement the institution carries with it.' Or as the eighteenth-century jurist Justus Möser put it: 'When I come across some old custom or old habit which simply will not fit into modern ways of reasoning, I keep turning around in my head the idea that "after all, our forefathers were no fools either", until I find some sensible reason for it.'[8]

And so conservatism is built around institutions, the framework of social organisation – monarchy, church, family, voluntary groups, legal and government bodies, even sports clubs. All institutions change and evolve but, as Muller wrote: 'Rather than representing the self-satisfied and complacent acceptance of the institutional status quo, ideological conservatism arises from the anxiety that valuable institutions are endangered by contemporary developments or by proposed reforms.' And so 'conservatism is the politics of delay', as Roger Scruton said; or in William F. Buckley's famous phrase, it's about standing 'athwart history, yelling "Stop"'.[9]

Support for institutions also entails support for traditions, which likewise carry social proof indicating they serve some function. Twentieth-century philosopher Russell Kirk argued that conservatives are marked by their 'distrust of those calculating men who would reconstruct all of society according to their own abstract designs. A conservative believes things are the way they are for a good reason: past generations have passed on customs and conventions that stood the test of time. Customs serve as a check on anarchy and the lust for power.' Kirk suggested that 'Tradition enables men to live together with some degree of peace; it manages to direct consciences and check the appetites.'[10]

Obviously conservatives don't support all traditions unquestionably. Human sacrifice was a pretty solid convention in many parts of the world but most of us would admit its useful function is probably quite limited.

Conservatism is also a belief in social relationships that don't necessarily include the state, which is why they're keen on volunteering, especially, it has to be said, if that volunteering helps reduce their taxes. They also tend to be in favour of religion as serving a useful social function, even if traditionally no conservative thinkers 'base their social and political arguments primarily on conformity with ultimate religious truth'.[11] If religion can make people act more morally then that is better than the alternative, which is more authoritarian government and interference. Self-restraint is therefore an important part of the philosophy, for as Burke put it, 'Somewhere there must be a control upon will and the appetite; and the less of it there is within, the more of it there must be without.'[12] We also believe that religion's function will simply be taken up by something else, often dangerous political messianism, and agree with the famous quip apparently made by G. K. Chesterton that when men stop believing in God they don't believe in nothing, they believe in anything.

Conservative reverence for institutions is linked to a core belief that people are inherently imperfect and are prone to act badly without the law or other threats of getting caught. It doesn't matter that most people are good because it only takes a few bad guys to ruin everything, or as the Russian proverb goes, an idiot can throw a rock into a well that a hundred clever men cannot shift. This was the idea in the 1980s behind 'broken windows', the theory of social scientists James Q. Wilson and George L. Kelling that tolerating petty crime and minor anti-social behaviour leads to more serious offences, an idea most famously adopted in New York. Likewise in schools or on the streets, when the authorities fail to keep order then violence can escalate rapidly through the actions of a very small number of people. Even in the most horrifically murderous central American cities, with homicide rates fifty or a hundred times the European average, most killings are committed by a tiny minority of men.

Muller identified human imperfection as a core conservative principle, and that 'More than any other animal, man is dependent upon other members of his species, and hence upon social institutions for guidance and direction.' Conservatives, therefore, are sceptical of 'liberation' and believe that 'liberals fail to consider the social conditions that make autonomous individuals possible and freedom desirable'. In other words, real human freedom is limited by our own moral weaknesses and poor decision-making, and by the cues we pick up from society. We are morally imperfect, and out of 'the crooked timber of humanity no straight thing could be ever made', as Immanuel Kant said.[13]

The French revolutionaries made a god of 'reason', but conservatives believe that humans are often if not mostly irrational, and that ideologies stating otherwise will end up inspiring people to commit terrible atrocities in the name of the end goal, which is never achieved anyway. Oxford historian Keith Feiling wrote that every Tory 'knows that there are great forces in heaven and earth that man's philosophy cannot plumb or fathom

. . . we do not trust human reason: we do not and we may not. Human reason set up a cross on Calvary, human reason set up the cup of hemlock, human reason was canonised in Notre Dame.'[14]

Humans are, of course, capable of reason, but most people are better at finding the faults in other people's arguments and often support political positions for irrational reasons, sometimes backing a candidate who doesn't actually share their policies because they feel like he or she's on their side. They'll vote against their own economic interests, choose the obviously bad policy idea, and even completely change their positions on major issues for partisan reasons.

Conservatives are therefore hostile to any project based on natural 'rights', or on any theory which claims to be applicable to people everywhere – Edmund Burke dismissed abstract ideas as 'the fairy land of philosophy'.[15] They are sceptical about solutions to social problems that are often entrenched and lasting, and prefer to focus on what works in practice rather than in theory (although everyone would claim that).

Conservatives are also opposed to excessive law making, and would rather that cultural and moral norms were held together by a system of unwritten enforcement. During their time in power the Puritans outlawed adultery, but most conservatives dislike making sins a crime, even if they disapprove of them; they believe that 'many of the norms that hold society together are unwritten, informally enforced, and possess power chiefly insofar as they impel psychological obedience'. These are things such as 'good manners, charity, duty and decency', which are not the concern of the law.[16] It is far better, for the conservative, that norms are maintained by social conformity of some sort, and weakening the norms that cause people to be better behaved will inevitably mean that laws come to replace manners.

Humans, conservatives believe, are prone to tribalism and nepotism. We prefer what is familiar to the distant, we favour family members to strangers and, to a lesser extent, compatriots over foreigners, and are more concerned about friends and relations than 'humanity' in the abstract – and there's nothing wrong with that. Humans are capable of great empathy but it is constrained by place and context, and it cannot be infinitely projected. Therefore systems that expect people to share resources with complete strangers, rather than friends and family, neighbours and fellow believers, are doomed to struggle. We love our children more than our friend's children, just as they do theirs. We also tend to suspect that people proclaiming their love for 'humanity' are terrible to their fellow human beings in reality, and take barely concealed joy when all our worst instincts turn out to be true.

Conservative Victorian High Court judge James Fitzjames Stephen, the sort of man you didn't want to be up against for a second offence, rejected the radical idea of a 'brotherhood of man', stating that: 'It is not love that one wants from the great mass of mankind, but respect and justice.' Are we brothers, he asked? 'Are we even fiftieth cousins?' In his book *Liberty, Equality and Fraternity* – none of which he entirely approved of – Stephen argued that 'Humanity is only I writ large, and love for Humanity generally means zeal for MY notions as to what men should be and how they should live.'[17]

Likewise Burke and Paine had different ideas of the nation, which Burke thought of as timeless communities and carriers of tradition, writing that 'Our country is not a thing of mere physical locality. It consists, in a great measure, in the ancient order into which we are born.'[18] According to a biographer, Yuval Levin, he believed that:

> The nation is the means by which order is made and kept, and by which order is made beautiful. A nation builds upon its past accomplishments through prescription by looking to its common history and finding in this history both sources of pride and principles for reform and improvement. Family affections become community affections and, finally, national ties. Every individual thus finds himself enmeshed in multiple communities – his geographic neighbours, his fellow workers or merchants or nobles – and all of these point up toward the nation, and only from the nation and through it toward mankind as a whole.[19]

In contrast Paine was a universalist, arguing that our loyalty should be to all mankind, and if they just had freedom and justice every country would be in a similar condition. Today his adopted hometown of Lewes in Sussex has a pub and stationery shop dedicated to his memory, the latter prominently displaying his quote in the window: 'My country is the world, and my religion is to do good', a catchphrase which neatly encompasses the modern Left's worldview in just twelve short words. No catchphrase of Burke could ever be so neatly displayed in such a way, nor give the displayer such a feeling of warm-heartedness for doing so.

The French Revolution Paine supported was a universalist project, designed to spread beyond France's borders at the behest of fellow believers across the world; the conservatives opposing it wanted to maintain local traditions and customs.

Perhaps no one has defined the belief system better than philosopher Michael Oakeshott, who wrote that conservatism was 'to prefer the familiar to the unknown, to prefer the tried to the untried, fact to mystery, the actual to the possible, the limited to the unbounded, the near to the distant, the sufficient to the superabundant, the convenient to the perfect, present laughter to utopian bliss'.[20]

Central to conservatism is the idea that radical change is almost always bad. To use an analogy from evolution, large mutations tend to be detrimental and sometimes lead to debilitating illnesses, but small mutations are often advantageous. Richard Dawkins wrote in *The Blind Watchmaker* on natural selection that 'the smaller the movement of adjustment, in relation to the initial error, the closer will the chance of improvement approach one half'.[21] Radical change is almost always terrible in practice, however exciting it all seems at the time; small reforms are necessary and beneficial for adaptation, and as circumstances change – and societies must always change.

Reform is necessary, but limited by the law of diminishing returns. You can solve the worst injustices in society but after that it becomes increasingly hard as you try to make the world a more perfect place. For example, it's relatively easy in a poor country to immediately alleviate the most extreme poverty; all you have to do is provide clean water, birthing facilities and free basic education, and things such as infant mortality and other measures of absolute poverty will drastically fall. But once you move the bulk of people out of destitution those who remain will be harder to help, and increasingly people still left in poverty are there largely because of their inability to function or make good decisions. In the US absolutely poverty declined from 25 per cent in 1950 down to 19.5 per cent in 1963 and 14.7 per cent in 1966, after which the Democrats launched the 'War on Poverty'; in 2013, after $15 trillion had been spent on this war, the rate was 14.5 per cent.[22]

Diminishing returns are probably most keenly felt in attempts to achieve gender equality in employment, which conservatives believe to be literally impossible so long as people will keep having children. By allowing women freedom to work you will rapidly increase their share of the labour market from 0 per cent but that figure will increasingly slow down as it reaches 50 per cent, and in some professions will not get anywhere near that. Even allowing freedom, more women than men will choose to stay at home with children, and this is by far the largest factor explaining the difference in earnings.

The pay gap is also explained by different life choices; more women prefer to go into industries which pay less but have other advantages, including more flexibility about childcare. These life choices are also partly determined by biology, but no conservative thinks they are *entirely* determined by biology or that there is not great variation among both men and women, or that there are not plenty of gender atypical people – they are *partly* explained by biology and no government policy can ignore human nature. We also believe in trade-offs. Often a good thing (people being able to work) will clash with another good thing (being around their young children). Some sacrifice will have to be made, and how these are balanced 'is in normal times a matter of prudence, not absolute principle'.[23]

Conservatives also believe in 'epistemological modesty', that there are limits to human knowledge, especially in politics, as human society is too complex for any one person or group to understand. Because of this, rule by central planners or even liberal technocrats is of poor quality, since even the best-informed know far less about people's needs than they themselves do.

Finally, there is anti-humanitarianism, the natural conservative distrust of the overtly caring, the mawkish and schmaltzy, and the language of therapy and self-growth. Muller wrote: 'Time and again conservative analysts argue that humanitarian motivation, combined with abstraction from reality, lead reformers to policies that promote behaviour which is destructive of the institutions upon which human flourishing depends.' And humanitarianism, most of all, is what characterises our age.

6

MAGGIE AND MADIBA

Dad's wacky interpretation of conservatism came from a particular archaic strand that developed in the nineteenth century, largely in reaction to the Industrial Revolution. Many Tories at the time disliked the social change brought about by new technology, which was throwing everything into chaos. The great Victorian polymath Thomas Carlyle lamented 'the collapse of a system of caring and humanity' that resulted from the decline of older Church-led structures.[1] He described an old Irish widow in Edinburgh left to die and compared modern laws with old Catholic systems for looking after the destitute. No doubt these conservatives felt pity for the impoverished, but they were also alarmed that the rural poor, who tended to be conservative and religious, were becoming uprooted to the cities, and so prey to evils like godlessness, beastliness and socialism.

While Whigs, the predecessors of the Liberal Party, represented the interests of finance, many Tories could be almost socialistic in their economic views. The art critic John Ruskin described himself as both 'a violent Tory of the old type' but also the 'reddest of the red'.[2] He advocated a paternalistic, hierarchical society that would also be redistributive. Indeed, during the peak Dickensian squalor decade of the 1840s, not long after *Oliver Twist* was written and in which Karl Marx was penning *The Communist Manifesto*, a number of Tory aristocrats sought to improve the conditions of the workers in the face of industrial change. This Young England movement was comprised mostly of toffs but it was led by the charismatic and rather un-aristocratic Benjamin Disraeli, whose grand-parents had all been Italian Jews.

Young England types saw the appalling conditions of the urban poor and looked back nostalgically to the Middle Ages, where, Disraeli wrote: 'the country was not divided into two classes, masters and slaves. There was some resting place between luxury and misery.'[3] Carlyle's morally ideal economic order was the thirteenth-century Abbey of Bury St Edmunds, which is exactly the kind of crazy argument my father would come out with. In fairness even Dad never got quite around to advocating the return of serfdom, although I suppose maybe if he'd lived a few more years he might have got there eventually.

It's safe to say there was a certain amount of romanticising, since life for a medieval peasant was pretty awful; in fact, monasteries were among the most rapacious landlords and the last to abandon serfdom, which was why they were the first places to be attacked during the Peasants' Revolt of 1381. The Young England strain of conservatism was indeed slightly crankish. John Ruskin, for example, favoured 'anti-materialism' as the way forward for soci-ety and opposed the 'Britannia of the market', as he called the increasingly capitalist Victorian society.[4] Some romantic Toryism was also, no doubt, just snobbery, and born of a visceral dislike of the vulgar nouveau riche, and the fact that 'consumerism' makes popular culture more proletarian. I say con-sumerism in inverted commas because most people seem to be fine with consuming when it's them doing it, just not other people.[5]

Dad had some really reactionary ideas. He tried to stop Mum replacing the washing machine because he thought they were destructive to com-munity life, whereas once women all went to the stream together to chat. So, we had to take our clothes to the launderette, where surprisingly for a Zone 2 London main road there wasn't a huge sense of community banter and instead it was mainly comprised of transients. Dad's argument infuriated me because the only reason it was once the women spending hours cleaning stuff was clearly because the menfolk were busy dragging a plough across a field or trying to avoid being hit by a longbow or having their head caved in by Scots, none of which exactly applied to Dad. Then, in an early lesson on how people will try to justify their first prejudices with some spurious rationale, he argued that the launderette was cheaper, a claim which even my eleven-year-old self realised rested on the idea that launderettes were actually subsidising all our washing for some unfathomable reason.

So, as I grew up I came to see Dad as a bit of a political crank, and after I started economics at GCSE and then A-level I became more convinced that his visceral loathing for Thatcherism was just the luxury of someone from a comfortable, public-school background. Being 'anti-materialist' is great if you have a big house with servants, or in our case a flat in Holland Park; it's entirely useless in getting people out of poverty or allowing them to afford a home. Thatcher was right.

The Tories had first been referred to as the Conservative Party by John Wilson Croker in 1830 and they came to be officially known as such under Robert Peel, who wished to allow in more moderates, uniting the middle class and old landowners.

Unfortunately Peel's government was wrecked by the Corn Laws controversy, the big cut-across issue of the day; people living in the cities, including merchants and the urban poor, wanted these tariffs abolished because it would lower the cost of food, but the majority of Tories — with their agricultural base — supported them, as they protected farmers. Although the Corn Laws had been repealed by Peel, most of his MPs rebelled and so the free-trade Peelites joined former Whigs in forming the Liberal Party. They came to dominate the next few decades, the golden age of Victorian Liberalism, while Disraeli and the other romantic medievalists were roundly beaten, and on a demographic hiding to nothing, with the urban population rapidly rising each year and the rural Tory world disappearing.

At school our history curriculum focused a great deal on the grimness of the Industrial Revolution, which seemed to be populated by heartless mine owners in top hats, yet living standards massively improved during the period as people moved to the cities, and life for most in the countryside was endlessly gruelling and terrible. Go to any lovely French farmhouse and you're walking where people have endured utter misery, something it's easy to overlook when you're surrounded by beautiful nature, but we're only able to afford such luxurious living because of the money we earn living in less bucolic but otherwise far wealthier cities. Romanticism seems like a nice idea when you're half-cut drinking red wine in a converted cottage, but the reality for 99.99 per cent of people throughout history has been hard. On the other hand, people often become unhappy in cities, an idea spelled out in the late nineteenth century by French sociologist Émile Durkheim; understandably, since we have not evolved to live in such enormous groups. In his 1897 book *Suicide* Durkheim popularised the idea of *anomie*, the idea that modern urban life leads to atomisation and so a breakdown of social norms and values.

Both Tories and socialists, who disliked Victorian capitalism for different reasons, went for this pre-modern romanticism, liking to imagine that industrialisation and globalisation are led by evil capitalist bastards forcing people into sweatshops. There must have been some comforting aspects of traditional village life, being around your friends and family and knowing that things would never change, but it's not a life I would jump at the chance to swap for my own. Even the (to me, bizarre) opening ceremony of the 2012 Olympics played on this notion, presenting a rural idyll destroyed by the evils of industrialisation.

Conservative romanticism also developed in opposition to the utilitarianism of early nineteenth-century liberal philosopher Jeremy Bentham, who argued that the only aim of politics should be to maximise the amount of happiness for the largest number of people, whatever traditions dictate. Bentham also thought that actions not harming others should not be considered a crime and, wildly ahead of his time, believed in decriminalising homosexual acts. Conservatives felt that utilitarianism was a threat to tradition and custom, and the poet Samuel Taylor Coleridge, among the most prominent of romantics, feared it would undermine religion and so destroy the moral order; that people would become materialists and thus miserable. Coleridge advocated a paternalistic society, led by a clerisy of thinking individuals who would provide moral leadership, taking care of the less fortunate while also effectively pressuring them into conforming to Christian (and Anglican) norms.

The Conservative Party's internal battle between old-fashioned traditionalists and economic liberals had shifted decidedly towards the latter with the election of Margaret Thatcher in 1979. Dad was not especially keen on the whole thing, and to him the Tory party of the 1980s was epitomised by Westminster Council leader Dame Shirley Porter, who famously sold three graveyards for 5p each. That was one of the first things I remember him ranting about, a scandal that was very close to home and confirmed his view that Tories didn't care about heritage.

No one loved the Thatcher government, and it seemed to me that only real weirdos idolised Mrs T, who lacked the hopey-changey-feely qualities that liberal or Left-wing politicians often possess. The Tories didn't inspire devotion even from fans, let alone the hostile intelligentsia, but it just became accepted that they were necessary in order to sort out the economy, because the 1970s had been terrible. That was the impression I got growing up, a cultural memory that hardened when Tony Blair ultimately accepted the Thatcher settlement.

After all, the relative cost of government borrowing had been higher in 1974 than in 1797, when we were years into a war with France. Inflation was running at 27 per cent in 1975, and in September 1976 sterling fell in value by 7 per cent in one go. That year Britain had to borrow $3.9 billion from the International Monetary Fund, the biggest loan to any industrialised country, 'cap in hand' as Tory partisans liked to describe it. And then there were the endless strikes by angry men in donkey jackets, culminating with the Winter of Discontent of 1978–9, arguably the worst social disruption since the early Victorian period. Although Conservatives aren't good at capturing the past, the Winter of Discontent stuck in the consciousness; certainly this must have all soaked into my mind, along with the other tenets of orthodox Chicago school economics.

And yet even during this period my parents saw the powers that be, and the organs of the state, as essentially Leftist. The collective consciousness of the 1980s is now dominated by the miners' strike, symbolic of class conflict between Hooray Henrys in Annabel's on the one hand and pitiful northerners facing deindustrialisation and ruin. Yet a lot of political conflict is obviously motivated by intraclass, not interclass, hatred. The most bitter enemies of Thatcher, the ones who viscerally loathed her, were only around the corner from us, in Campden Hill, where Harold Pinter used to invite his literary circle around and presumably swear a lot while talking about the Tories.

Likewise, my parents' main political hostility was towards Grandee Lefties, rich members of west and north London's social elite who, they believed, espoused all the most fashionable – and idiotic – ideas. Many had been sympathetic towards communism, long after it had been decent to do so, and for which there was virtually no social sanction or opprobrium. This naive sympathy for political mass murder was particularly common among writers, journalists and members of other artistic professions that attracted extreme narcissists, and George Orwell famously wrote of the 'masochism of the English Left' and its readiness to side with any cause, as long as it was anti-British.[6]

Numerous useful idiots, like the Fabian leaders Sidney and Beatrice Webb, had disgraced themselves with pro-Soviet propaganda. They were long dead by the time I was growing up, but the historian Eric Hobsbawm was still a leading light in British academia even though he maintained his loyalty to the Soviet Union throughout, even after the crushing of the Hungarian Uprising in 1956 and the Prague Spring twelve years later, and always thought Stalin was on the right track, basically. Hobsbawm was made a Companion of Honour by the British government, naturally, since being even literally an enemy of Britain is no bar to rising up the establishment. In comparison, when I was growing up Oxford University refused to grant an honorary degree to former student Margaret Thatcher.

Notting Hill, with its slightly bohemian and occasionally squalid atmosphere, had a long history of rich Leftists. Among those who believed wholesale the Webbs' Soviet propaganda was local resident, pro-communist publisher Victor Gollancz, who lived in a big mansion nearby along with ten servants, when he wasn't at his country house in Berkshire. He had a chauffeur-driven car, smoked big cigars and drank vintage champagne, had daily lunch at the Savoy, and published books extolling the Soviet Union during its most insanely murderous years. He was hugely influential doing PR work for the Soviets and nominated Stalin as Man of the Year and, years later, was knighted – of course. Yet even as far back as the French Revolution the country's wealthy radicals used to hang out in nearby Holland House, owned by Charles James Fox's nephew Lord Holland. These Whigs of Holland House so looked down on Britain that from here Lady Holland even sent Napoleon Bonaparte books after he was exiled to St Helena.

The progressive establishment, in Dad's view, had been responsible for a number of ills, especially in education and judicial reform, but worst of all was its destruction of city centres in the name of 'progress', ripping out old terraced streets and building tower blocks and motorways. Although he said the Tories shared the blame for this, driven by their misguided love of cars, their main motivation was greed, while progressives actually had an ideological hatred of the past. On this issue, as with many others, it was the intellectual elite who espoused radical change and 'the people' who opposed it, but then, as with comprehensive education or reduced prison sentences, it was the people who mostly had to suffer the consequences: Grandee Lefties always ended up living in the sorts of traditional houses they supposedly despised, just as they usually sent their own kids to the best schools.

It was mainly the hypocrisy that really annoyed people such as Dad. Famously CND founder Bertrand Russell, grandson of the Liberal prime minister and one of the most prominent atheist philosophers of the twentieth century, was asked why as a socialist he or his friend didn't give some of their vast fortunes away, Russell replied: 'I'm afraid you've got it wrong. [We] are socialists. We don't pretend to be Christians.'

Even if the Conservatives were in power, they were mainly focused on the economy and did little to win what Marxist philosophers refer to as 'hegemony', of controlling the narrative. Indeed, throughout the era there was a strong undercurrent of dislike for the Tories. By the time I became aware of politics, Thatcher was in her later, mildly deranged stage, the country was going into recession, the poll tax was hated and everyone was a bit sick of her.

The Tories made no effort to ensure that history was kind to them, as Churchill put it, by ensuring that they wrote it. The real great figure of the era, the one who captured the public imagination, was not in Downing Street but rotting in a jail cell some 11,000 miles away. And today Nelson Mandela is the one with a statue in Parliament Square, while a similar proposal for one of Margaret Thatcher can't be built because it would be vandalised.

An idea developed that Thatcher had created a more selfish society where the vulnerable are preyed upon, mirrored in the US with the Republicans under Reagan. Today only 5 per cent of Americans believe the Republicans are 'compassionate', and as Arthur Brooks said, 'If you take elected Republicans, paid staff, and blood relatives out of that [5 per cent] it probably rounds to about zero.'[7] Indeed, even a majority of American conservatives believe the Republicans are uncompassionate, and I'd be amazed if the same wasn't true of Tories.[8]

Neil Kinnock said in a famous speech in 1983 that if the Tories won: 'I warn you not to be ordinary. I warn you not to be young. I warn you not to fall ill. And I warn you not to grow old.'[9] I knew that Thatcher's famous quote 'there is no such thing as society' was sort of misinterpreted, that she meant society was not one composite whole but made up of a number of smaller networks of clubs, communities and 'little platoons' in Burke's words. But while homelessness and unemployment rose and general social dislocation continued to increase, it seemed understandable that some interpreted it that way. Indeed, the journalist to whom she gave that quote is a very good but quite Left-wing friend of my parents, and once called me a 'Thatcherite gimp' – in a friendly way. I think.

One of the recurring patterns of being a political ideologue is realising that the opposition think of you exactly how you think of them. So the Left believe we're responsible for a more selfish society, yet we associate that sort of self-centred worldview with the 1960s, with baby boomers obsessed with their own personal pleasure, rolling around in the mud on acid rather than going to work in a bowler hat. When the rot all set in, the sexual revolution of 1968 or the Thatcher revolution of 1979 depending on your political orientation, and both sides see in their opponents their own supposed worst traits.

Dad grew more hostile to the Tories as the 1980s went on, especially as he became one of those contradictory and perverse socialist reactionaries. He especially disliked the New Right's love of cars, believing railways were more civilised and better for society; in fact, he never learned to drive, which he considered endearingly eccentric but when you have children is basically just annoying. But while he was psychologically quite egalitarian – he hated anything that reeked of snootiness – he had come to loathe the Left even more. Dad had started his journalistic career with the *Manchester Guardian* and still considered it the best newspaper; he had a love–hate relationship with the *Guardian* although as time went on there was more focus on the latter than the former, as tends to happen in complex relationships.

Because they were in journalism my parents always had the *Times*, *Telegraph*, *Guardian* and *Daily Mail* in the flat, and so I naturally read the latter as it had the shortest words and most pictures. Mainly pictures of cellulite, and of underclass teenage mums scrounging off the taxpayer, but pictures nonetheless. Looking back on it I wonder what effect that must have had, and whether it probably warped my young mind and made me more neurotic and fearful. Focusing on all the dangers and threats from crime and other terrible things in the world probably has a bad impact on mental health, giving an unrealistic impression of how common such incidents are.

The paper has an important role in English psychology, part of a pack of tabloids that are overwhelmingly culturally conservative while also having a prurient interest in other people's sex lives and bodies. The *Mail* has a particular formula for covering sex scandals with just enough information to titillate and disgust at the same time, a dose of moralising and outrage, before concluding with a description of the property in which the filthy sordid actions took place and an estimated market value. ('MP's sordid sex sessions with rent boy in £600,000 maisonette'.)

The *Daily Mail* was not exactly the conscience of middle England, but it was certainly a guiding spirit, a collection of all its fears and hopes, although more of the former to be fair, a conservative horcrux. (I haven't read the Harry Potter series, by the way, I've just added that analogy to make the book appealing to Left-leaning millennials. I'm not even sure if that reference makes sense.)

If the entire intellectual elite was Leftist, as it had been for several decades, then conservatism had come to be defined by its anti-intellectualism, led by the tabloids, with complaints about health and safety, human rights, speed cameras and compensation payouts.[10]

The *Mail*'s overarching theme was of social breakdown, what was later termed 'broken Britain' or the 'broken society', the anxiety that social norms were falling apart, people were becoming coarser and less civilised, and that the underclass was growing as a result of an overgenerous benefits system; and that, given a chance, they would turn on you or at the very least ruin your area and the value of your home. (I don't mean that in a sneering way, since a house is a home and also often people's main investment and pension, and having a problem family move into the street can be a nightmare.) There was an underlying fear of barbarism at the door, an idea that forms a central part of conservative psychology. And yet it was not a totally irrational fear – crime *had* hugely increased from the 1960s to the 1980s.

Britain's crime rise was nothing like the rapid explosion of violence in America from the 1960s, which was by now reaching its nadir with the crack wars. The British have a sort of psychological awareness of 1960s America as being the era of civil rights and freedom, yet this social change went hand in hand with an enormous rise in murder in urban America, unprecedented anywhere in modern times. The homicide rate trebled or quadrupled in less than a decade in some cities, leading to an exodus of millions to the suburbs, a huge psychological shock to a lot of people that made 'liberal' a dirty word. For many people the experience of desegregation wasn't the image of a stoic Martin Luther King leading a dignified protest – he was largely unpopular at the time of his death – but shocking incidents of violent crime in their neighbourhoods.

Britain's crime explosion was not so extreme, but it was considerable nonetheless, and tabloids appealed to a demographic for whom the horrific violence of the 1980s and 1990s was inconceivable in the readers' childhoods. The Thatcher era saw many more extreme pathologies that reasonably scared people, the explosion of heroin and increased homelessness, and the growth of sink estates. Again, who was to blame was open to debate, but fear tends to push people to the Right.

The biggest sign of decline, as far as tabloids were concerned, was the rapid increase in unmarried teenage mums, which became a political issue as the levels skyrocketed in the late 1970s. Part of this was due to a change in social housing rules, the sort of bright idea thought up by well-meaning socialist theorists but which infuriates working-class people. The housing lists had been literally that, a queue, in which people waited their turn, with good behaviour and reputation a bonus. It changed to one of 'need', which put more needy people such as single mothers or immigrants – as well as people with various pathologies – ahead of locals who had queued, and who often had deep roots in the area. In doing so the welfare state obviously rubbed up against people's sense of fairness, but to conservatives it represented the problem of moral hazard, that financial rewards for poor life choices can encourage more people to make them. Like all political controversies it's far older than people realise, and as far back as the 1770s there were debates about the social sanctions against illegitimacy, with German social theorist Justus Möser arguing they were necessary because there needed to be incentives to marry.

During my secondary school years the country was labouring under the limp Major government and everyone either hated the Tories, or at the very least was just sick of them after so long. It was partly for economic reasons, being to do with the recession of the early 1990s, but there was also the tremendous stink of moral hypocrisy. George Bush the First, realising the growing strength of evangelical Christians within the Republican Party, began going on about 'family values'. He even had a go at *The Simpsons*, comparing the family unfavourably with the Waltons and just proving how lame social conservatives were.

John Major started his own campaign of moral renewal with 'back to basics', and this sort of became part of a folk memory in which the rich, wicked Tories picked on single mothers while getting up to all sorts of sexual depravity in their own spare time. Numerous MPs were discovered to have had affairs, often of a kinky variety, and it reached a nadir when one Tory MP died of auto-erotic asphyxiation, which barely even caused that much of a shock as people just expected it by then. The whole campaign soon became lampooned with the *Viz* character Baxter Basics, a Tory MP obsessed with getting his end away. The Tories were right, in a way, in that the existence of government subsidies do influence people's decisions in regards to having children and sexual partners, and this affects the life outcomes of children. Things like marriage, divorce and separation are also contagious, so that incentives can tip the norms within communities. But that kind of analysis never happened: all that we remember is loads of Tories getting caught shagging or with an orange in their mouth in a stranglewank gone wrong.

One of the big problems was that the Tories had been steadily losing what was now called the 'culture war', the battle of values. And so, despite the fall of the Berlin Wall in 1989 and the end of the Soviet Union two years later, things actually got worse for the Right.

7

ARE WE THE BADDIES?

There's an episode of *Peep Show* in which Mark, the downtrodden cultural conservative who feels desperately out of touch with the modern world, befriends a new workmate who seems just like him. They get on well, have a similar worldview, and Mark is overjoyed to have a fast friend in Daryl. His new pal is a war re-enactment fan and Mark does find it a bit odd that during the mock battles Daryl insists on only playing German soldiers, never one of the Allies, but he brushes it aside. He does also find it concerning that their Right-of-centre banter rather pushes the envelope somewhat, until eventually it dawns on Mark that, rather than being a fellow Jeremy Clarkson fan who likes to moan about 'political correctness' or 'health and safety', his new friend is actually a Nazi. It was just too good to be true, he concluded, that someone with his interests and worldview would turn out to be normal.[1]

Conservatism's modern failure has much to do with the events of the early twentieth century and the rise of an offshoot of reactionary conservatism that mixed socialist economics with a love of violence and some history role play thrown in. It wasn't entirely successful, obviously, or as Nick Griffin of the British National Party once apparently conceded, 'Adolf went a bit too far.'[2]

Nazism forms the main cultural memory of our world. I don't trust my own memories entirely because I sometimes wonder if I've absorbed a sort of *Daily Mail* interpretation of my childhood, but we studied the Nazis *a lot* at school. Whether or not children learned many basic facts, no one could have failed to digest the central lesson from history, which was 'whatever you do, don't do this again, and look for even the smallest of pointers that it's happening'.

The popular culture of my childhood also presented the Nazis as archetypal baddies, whether representative of actual Nazis such as in *Raiders of the Lost Ark* or fictional villains stylistically influenced by them, such as in *Star Wars*. But then, of course, they *were* archetypal villains and revelled in it. In their sketch show *That Mitchell and Webb Look*, the *Peep Show* actors have a scene in which two German officers are on the eastern front. One of them turns to the other and says 'Have you noticed that our caps actually have little pictures of skulls on them?' and then asks 'Hans . . . are we the baddies? I mean, what do skulls make you think of? Death . . . cannibals . . . beheading . . . pirates . . .'[3] The sketch has since become popular as a mini-critique of conservatives generally, cited whenever Right-wing politicians do or say something particularly outrageous.

The horrors committed by the Third Reich were exceptionally evil, even by the twentieth century's high benchmark of evil, and done in the name of ideas that were in certain ways linked to conservatism. It is impossible to separate these uniquely appalling crimes from the intellectual hinterland from which they came, like school bullies and their enablers who share responsibility for the misery of their victims. Even if Nazism was in the dock from 1945, conservatism left the courtroom with its reputation in tatters. As Michael Burleigh wrote in *Moral Combat*: 'Nazi crimes against the Jews drew on ancient mulch of Christian Judeaophobia that gives the Nazi crimes psychological traction among Western audiences, because its modern mutation of anti-Semitism is part of their more or less conscious heritage. The evocation of Nazi crimes rubs a collective scar in Western societies', while other crimes, committed in far-off cultures by one group against another, do not resonate.[4]

At the core of Nazi ideology was an extreme idea of exclusivity and the division of people into ingroups and outgroups based on ancestry, a revulsion to which has since gone deep into our collective subconscious. It was emphasised and articulated in one of the most powerful films of my childhood, *Au Revoir les Enfants*, in which the Jewish children are separated from the 'Aryans', this forced division a prelude to the most revolting and unforgiveable of crimes – the murder of infants. Mum took me to the cinema to watch it and it must have had some effect as I remember it pretty well, although to be honest I mainly remember being angry beforehand at being forced to watch a foreign film that obviously was going to offer little in the way of explosions or Bond-style derring-do.

The Nazi atrocities were also tied up in the collective imagination with the other great racial dramas, the US civil rights movement and apartheid South Africa, which frequently appeared on the news in the 1980s as black townships rose up in protest. We didn't quite have 'Jail Nelson Mandela' T-shirts at home, like Alan B'Stard in *The New Statesman*, but having listened to my father and read his *Spectator* articles I obviously digested his pessimism about ANC rule. Why couldn't I just enjoy watching the anti-apartheid Wembley Stadium gig like everyone else and pretend everything would be OK if we all just accepted how terrible racism is? All of these cultural conflicts helped to reinforce the divide between progressives and conservatives as a great moral battle between good and evil, but it wouldn't have been possible without the horrors of Nazism.

The intellectual origins of the far Right go back as far as the French Revolution. Although Burke was the most high-profile critic of events, he did so from an essentially liberal and secular standpoint, while in contrast the Frenchman Joseph de Maistre attacked it from an altogether different perspective, and his ideas helped to shape a different strand of conservatism. De Maistre was an ardent royalist and opposed many of the revolution's fundamental principles; he believed that some people don't want liberty and equality because they're quite happy with their status in the hierarchy. He approved of the first part of the revolution and admired Burke's book but his own work, *Considerations sur la France*, 'set out a violent and apocalyptic account of what had happened'.[5]

Although the violence of the Paris mob shocked many people, de Maistre observed that we don't blame the tiger for its actions but the keeper who slips the leash. By this, he blamed intellectuals for inciting the violence, just as later there was widespread hostility to American liberals in the 1960s as crime and public disorder shot up.

While Burke used secular arguments, de Maistre saw the revolution as divine punishment, a pretty reactionary interpretation even then. When asked what exactly they were being punished for, he replied 'that it did not much matter what, since mankind was so wicked that God might properly punish us at any time he choose and we would have no grounds for complaint'.[6] Great banter. Indeed, Voltaire had asked why God had struck Lisbon with an earthquake in 1755 when there was plenty of dancing, lechery and sin in Paris, to which de Maistre suggested that Paris should have been destroyed too.

Burke had a theatrical image of authority, believing that the show-business quality of royalty, the glamour and majesty, held society together; for de Maistre it was the executioner who was 'the horror and the bond of human society', and on whom order is built. Authority must be unchallengeable to de Maistre, for whom 'God is an absolute ruler whose decrees are inscrutable and whose operations are terrifying. This is the essence of authority. France needed an absolute monarch supported by an infallible Pope.'[7]

One of the essential themes of reactionary thought is that of civilisational decline and collapse, the most famous example being Oswald Spengler's 1918 work *The Decline of the West*, which foresaw the tragic fall of European civilisation and which also tied culture to race. The following year the Harvard lecturer Henry Adams, 'the most irritating man in American letters',[8] published *The Degradation of the Democratic Dogma*, which used the Second Law of Thermodynamics as an analogy – total entropy increases over time and as everything dissipates, energy is lost and everything goes downhill. Adams argued that human activity had peaked with the building of medieval cathedrals and the crusades and since then it's all been steadily in decline.

Russell Kirk wrote that Adams's conservatism was 'the view of a man who sees before him a steep and terrible declivity, from which there can be no returning.'[9] It should also be noted that Adams, the grandson and great-grandson of presidents, had political ambitions of his own, which went nowhere, and he was a very bitter man.

Why were these reactionaries so fearful? Many believed that the industrial workers would become a revolutionary force, disconnected from the land, overwhelming the established order. And yet to start with at least most of the recruits for new radical movements were skilled artisans whose livelihoods were threatened by change – the Luddites, for example – and so radicalism was often, paradoxically, quite reactionary, too.[10] But others began to take up a new idea called 'socialism'. .

Utopianism and Socialism

Back in 1794 the romantic poet Samuel Taylor Coleridge, along with another wordsmith, Robert Southey, came up with the brilliant idea of an egalitarian community in which all ruled equally. They settled on the name 'Pantisocracy', from the Greek for 'equal government for all', although rather unsurprisingly this has never quite taken off as an ideological slogan. The aim was that everyone would labour for the common good and only have to work two hours a day, all of these happy people governed by the 'dictates of rational benevolence'.

Sadly, if you want an infrastructure project built, having two romantic poets in large frilly shirts in charge is probably not ideal, and neither of them knew anything about farming, which was pretty important for an isolated rural community in Wales. Unsurprisingly, the whole thing collapsed, although happily the two poets remained friends and four years later were among the first men to experiment with laughing gas at the behest of their scientist pal, Humphry Davy. Southey later became Poet Laureate although perhaps his most lasting contribution is to have written the first 'Goldilocks and the Three Bears' story.

Coleridge and Southey were inspired in their utopian experiment by

Plato, one of the great Classical Greek philosophers but also the great-grandfather of almost every terrible political idea ever. Plato wanted people to raise their children communally, among other things, and have a team of experts run the country. His ideas took little account of what human nature is like, that people might care for their children more than those of non-relatives, that a technocracy would inevitably lead to corruption and be self-serving; or that experts can be biased, especially in groups. The ideas set out in his *Republic* became the starting point for the utopian tradition, a term later coined by Thomas More to describe an ideal city (literally 'no place').

The Protestant Reformation had led to a huge number of utopian movements, perhaps the most insane being in the Rhineland city of Münster over the winter of 1534–5 when some demented missionaries tried to turn the German city into a biblical paradise (it ended in almost everyone getting killed). With the decline of religion, however, utopianism became ever more popular, with numerous schemes launched at achieving a perfect or near-perfect society in which everything is shared. None of them succeeded, since egalitarian utopias overlook people's natural instinct to better themselves, while twentieth-century sexual utopias ignored the failures, disappointments and injustices that characterise human relationships, and in particular our natural tendency towards jealousy. Sorry if this narrative is starting to sound a bit depressing, by the way.

A few years after Coleridge's experiment a more concrete utopian community was established by Robert Owen, a Welsh-born textile manufacturer and social reformer.[11] Owen was supported by Jeremy Bentham as well as a Quaker philanthropist called William Allen who had campaigned for prison reform and against slavery (bloody Leftie). Although Owen had once shared Bentham's liberal view that free markets and freedom would empower workers, he came to believe in a new philosophy that disputed this and urged the intervention of the state; he became the first thinker to be called by the relatively new term 'socialist'. Owen had also broken out of the Left's historic Nonconformism and was hostile to organised religion. Furthermore, and also ahead of the time, he believed that human character was largely formed by social circumstances over which an individual has no control. If people in their earliest years were given a happy, healthy environment to live in then they would grow up to be healthy, happy and law-abiding human beings. He also argued for things that are pretty standard today – an eight-hour day and universal primary-school education, for instance.

Owen's solution to the misery of industrial life was to build utopian settlements in which children would be raised in a shared environment, this 'New Moral World' overseen by experts. Over a dozen Owenite communities were established in the USA, the most famous being New Harmony in Indiana, but even that fell apart after two years, one former member lamenting that 'our "united interests" were directly at war with the individualities of persons and circumstances and the instinct of self-preservation'.[12]

Still, if a group of two hundred or so friends can't successfully share things without falling out, then it's bound to work with an entire country, right? That was the genius idea thought up by German intellectual layabout Karl Marx, who had come to England to flee various continental authorities upset at his apocalyptic political vision of class conflict. Here he spent the next miserable, impoverished couple of decades formulating a theory of history that gave his name to a new religion, a grand theory of economic evolution from primitive communism to feudalism to capitalism. In his view this would inevitably lead to a revolution, then a dictatorship of the proletariat, which would then slowly wither into an egalitarian economic system, communism. Helpfully he was rather short on details about how *exactly* this paradise would be enforced without, say, 100 million people dying as a result, but this theory he called 'scientific' was in fact quasi-religious. He saw the working class as the Christ-like redeemers of society, something obviously influenced by Christianity and Judaism.

Marx's works *Capital* and *The Communist Manifesto* were hugely influential but they distorted the truth, falsifying quotations and using out-of-date sources to suit his grand narrative.[13] Marx's ideas failed to take off in

England but found more fertile ground in Russia, where due to a long history of serfdom, only recently abolished, collectivism was far more ingrained and individualism weaker, and where autocracy was the norm. And what happened next will blow your mind.

The eruption of communism, and the terror it inspired among the middle class, helped give birth to a socialist heresy that mixed nationalism, the extreme cultural pessimism of the Right and a thirst for heroic violence. There has always been a strain of conservatism that hates the mundane and longs for the romantic, transcendent and heroic. 'Happy those who with a glowing faith in one embrace clasped death and victory' – so go the words below a mural by John Singer Sargent on the Harvard First World War memorial, which as a conservative I like the sound of more in theory than in reality.[14] Religious movements once provided an outlet for this desire, the life of a Templar offering the sense of brotherhood and sacrifice for a greater goal (although, of course, the reality was grim). But as the nineteenth century went on many young men in particular were drawn to a heroic ideal, especially as civilian life seemed to them boring and meaningless, the decline of religion perhaps felt sharply in some. This feeling was most common in Germany, where there was a philosophical tradition opposed to liberalism and capitalism, those superficial Anglo-Saxon ideas. Mixed with a militaristic tradition, and the influence of various crackpots extolling the glories of the Germanic past, and millions of angry men who've just lost a war . . . well, it didn't have a happy ending.

This branch of reaction mutated into something altogether different from de Maistre's vision, an idea that came to become known as fascism, although 'idea' might be pushing it. Fascism had few real intellectual thoughts behind it, which makes it hard to define, and also easier to use as an insult, especially when it's incorrectly conflated with racism. In fact, the original fascist movement in Italy wasn't especially racist (there were anti-Semites in Mussolini's movement, but there were also Jewish members), while most democrats and even liberals of the period were by today's standards extremely so.

Communists revere political texts and ideas, just as Abrahamic religions do, and indeed the communists were doctrinally obsessed to a tedious degree; as with Christianity, countless people would die over small differences of textual interpretation that to non-believers seem utterly arcane. Fascism, in contrast, had no central texts or ideas and was mostly thuggish street theatre. What ideas it did have were an incoherent jumble, less a series of beliefs than a collection of things to which they were opposed – chiefly communism, capitalism and liberalism. In Germany, it fused with ultra-nationalistic movements that linked all three of these threats with one group in particular – Jews.

Fascism was formulated by a radical Italian journalist, Benito Mussolini, although he would be better described as a polemicist or, to use an anachronism, a troll, the type of man who writes long-winded posts below the line on comment pieces. Mussolini had been a socialist and obsessively and tediously anti-clerical, before the experience of the First World War converted him to the idea of extreme nationalism, and captured in his mind the need for the heroic ideal. The Polish-Israeli scholar Zeev Sternhell argued in *The Birth of Fascist Ideology* that fascism was a revolutionary movement, emerging from the radical Left but 'which became fused with "blood and soil nationalism"'.[15]

The intellectual forefathers of fascism, however, were mostly French, among them men such as Charles Maurras and Maurice Barrès. The latter coined the term *déraciné*, 'deracinated', to denote someone who had lost contact with their ancestors. One fascist 'thinker', Giovanni Gentile, argued that fascism gave the individual genuine freedom, which seems pretty torturous logic. In 'The Doctrine of Fascism' Gentile wrote: 'Political doctrines pass; nations remain. We are free to believe that this is the century of authority, a Fascist century. If the 19th century was the century of the individual (liberalism implies individualism) we are free to believe that this is the "collective" century, and therefore the century of the State.'[16]

This state-worship aspect of fascism has given many conservatives the comforting idea that the philosophy was 'Left-wing', because true

Right-wingers believe in a small state. In his entertaining book *Liberal Fascism*, Jonah Goldberg made a spirited attempt to show the extent to which Italian fascism and German national socialism had some common roots with the Left, especially Fabianism, Franklin D. Roosevelt's New Deal, and the obsession with public health (the Nazis did ban smoking, as pro-tobacco cranks often like to point out). And yet fascism only really shared with these philosophies a belief that the state was the solution to modern problems, reflecting simply the growing capability of a modern bureaucracy. Philosophically they were a world away.

Certainly the Nazis had some radical ideas, indeed they were environmentalists and pro-animal rights way before it was cool; and it's also true that the Left's role in some of the things now agreed to be bad – eugenics, for example – has been forgotten down some memory hole. But the Nazis were psychologically Right-wing in their attitude to art, sex, women and other social issues, and politics is not just about economics or the role of the state, but emotional responses and worldviews, our attitudes to social norms and threats. To call the Nazis Left-wing is tenuous.

Belief in the free market is strongest in the centre and centre-Right. The standard model used to define politics is the economic axis going from left to right, with a liberal and conservative (or libertarian/authoritarian) axis on the vertical axis. So a communist will be in the very top-left corner in the authoritarian/economically left area while a Nazi will be at the very top slightly to the right, with social liberals in the bottom left and libertarians in the bottom right. Alternatively one might measure politics like a clockface, with six or seven o'clock being the home of classical liberalism, socialism at three or two o'clock, conservatism at eight or nine and fascism eleven. Communism and fascism, diametrically opposed in one sense, do of course eventually meet at some point, according to 'horseshoe theory' – they both like killing lots of people, for one.

Free-market conservatives have grown used to the media employing the term Right-wing in a pejorative sense and their socialist opponents unfairly comparing them with fascists, so in response it's become a cliché of below-the-line arguments that 'dur, actually, Hitler was a socialist. They called themselves National SOCIALISTS' – this being the 'checkmate, Leftists' killer move. Yes, they indeed called themselves socialists, just as North Korea calls itself 'democratic' and China is a 'people's republic'. Maybe the Nazis were lying?

Among the first uses of the word 'socialist' in English was in 1835 in reference to the 'Association of All Classes of All Nations' founded by Robert Owen. Socialism is by definition internationalist, aimed at uniting workers of all countries, so 'national socialism' is as contradictory as national Christianity – love thy neighbour, as long as he's not a foreigner. (There are national churches, of course, but, like socialism, the principles of Christianity are universal.) Certainly both socialists and fascists were motivated by a disgust for liberalism, but the political philosophy of Nazism stems from the reactionary tradition, even if it is heavily mutated (and de Maistre no doubt would have regarded the Nazis as monsters and pagan deviants, possibly punishment by God for some sexual wrongdoing).

Nazism's political origins lay with that part of the Right supporting rigid hierarchy, authoritarianism, ultra-nationalism and opposition to the Enlightenment, modernism and liberalism. This extreme wing of conservatism opposed not just revolution and socialism but also novelties that mainstream conservatives came to accept, such as religious tolerance, the removal of God from everyday politics, women's emancipation, the widening of the franchise, free trade and laissez-faire capitalism. Ultra-conservatives dislike capitalism since it brings urbanisation and with it the mingling of different races and religions, the rise of a liberal bourgeoisie, social democratic politics and sexual licence – this was what disgusted the young Adolf Hitler when he lived in Vienna. Glorious death fighting the eternal racial enemy doesn't seem quite so attractive when you have a widescreen television, a comfortable sofa and a sexy, exotic girlfriend with whom to share it.

Hitler was an example of the extreme conservative mindset found in some young men, incredibly rigid in his routine and with very conservative

– and quite odd – attitudes towards women, while also being unduly obsessed in his writing with syphilis, prostitution and degrading sexual practices. While communists encouraged women to work and promoted sexual freedom and such practices as legalised abortion, Hitler set aside a special day to pay homage to childbearing, 12 August, his own mother's birthday, as part of his not-at-all-weird obsession with his mum.

Hitler was also deeply conservative in his moral, artistic, social and sexual outlook, and had all 'perverted' artwork removed from galleries, and even set up a *Degenerate Art Exhibition*, which ended up being hugely popular. To be fair, 'degenerate' art in the 1930s meant Picasso and Piet Mondrian, rather than degenerate art today, which is literally a pile of elephant dung or a huge statue of arse cheeks.

With the end of the Second World War, and the barely conceivable evidence of what the Nazis had done, there were concerted efforts not just to push forward the Western Allies' war aims but also to attack the very roots of the ideas that led to Auschwitz. Nazism was, in Allan Bloom's phrase, the Right's 'ugly last gasp' – and the entire conservative movement was tainted by that ugliness. When the Russian soldier raised the Soviet flag over the Reichstag it represented the start of the age of the Left.

Since then successive generations of children have become well attuned to anything that even vaguely resembles Nazism, and in particular the crimes it committed against Jews, uniquely evil even for that century. But then it's hard to avoid when conservative philosophy by its very nature does share some common ancestry with fascism. Conservativism is parochial, and drawn to attachments that are local and national rather than global. By definition these sorts of relationships must be exclusive, and any sort of immigration policy that distinguishes between citizens and non-citizens can be recast as *Au Revoir les Enfants*. Any national identity can become so, unless it's one so loosely defined as to be meaningless.

In the most influential series of children's books of the twenty-first century, the bad guys are defined by their outgroup philosophy, by which certain people are excluded based on blood. In contrast, the good people have an inclusive worldview, the only membership criteria of which are virtue and kindness.

The limits of people's collective memory and imagination are such that the minute any politician strays from the path of universalism, commentators reach for the most shocking (and only) historical comparison they can think of. The same mental reflex doesn't occur on the other side of politics when Left-wingers use the same language employed by Stalin or Mao, part of a sort of 'asymmetry of indulgence', as Ferdinand Mount called it. We often hear the argument that Tories want to turn people against migrants by dividing people between 'us' and 'them', followed by a very unsubtle 'let me tell you about another bunch of guys who believed in "us" and "them" – the Nazis', to paraphrase the salesman in *Clerks*. To take just one example, in 2016 there was controversy when asylum seekers were made to wear red wristbands in order to receive meals, a haunting echo of Hitler's Third Reich, as many people commented.[17] Except that it's more convenient than asking someone with a not especially good grasp of English to walk around with a form for his entire family; wristbands just have a logistical use, as they do at a festival. On the same day as that story broke Amnesty International put out an advert in the *New York Times* calling on European leaders to take in more refugees. The picture showed families behind barbed wire with the phrase 'Leaders of Europe, it's not the polls you should worry about. It's the history books.'[18] Chilling, once again, except for the fact that Germany's behaviour of recent years is as far from Nazism as it is possible to get; they had just let in 2 million refugees from the Middle East, which is not exactly a policy with terrifying echoes of Nazi Germany.

With history the most dominant subjects tend to crowd out all others, just as in any artistic sphere the most celebrated musician, writer or artist tends to become remembered at the expense of almost-as-good contemporaries. The Nazis, because of the fascination that they exert over the public, and the revulsion for their crimes, have come to crowd out other historical areas, just as knowledge of large areas of the past has become confined to a few enthusiasts. But one reason for Nazism's ubiquity is that the past has become a weapon in the culture war, a stick with which to beat conservatism. It remains a useful warning case of what happens when conservatism goes too far and when patriotism in particular is turned towards evil ends. Communism and the Left generally have never suffered the same stigma for the crimes committed in their name, partly because the Holocaust was so uniquely terrible and partly because communist crimes were far out of mind in the Soviet tundra. But there is also the fact that communism, although the more anti-clerical, drew on the Western Christian tradition of universal brotherhood and progress, and so in a sense its crimes were treated as unfortunate by-products of an otherwise well-intentioned idea. Nazism was an aberration from the moral norm, overtly revelling in its monstrosity; indeed, they acted out their part as the bad guys with relish.

And so when I was growing up the stalls of Kensington Market and Portobello all sold fashionable Che T-shirts, and markets still sell clothes with the hammer and sickle, a symbol that goes on display each May in London parades. The pass given to communism is one of those subjects that conservatives become really boring about, frustrated that most young people see it as an essentially noble idea. This asymmetry of indulgence filters out into how we treat the entire spectrum of conservative thought, though, so almost any proposal that has even the slightest of resemblance to Nazi Germany immediately sets off people's political memories like oversensitive 1980s car alarms.

The Second World War effectively meant the end of conservatism as a credible moral force. Nazism was seen as its more extreme cousin, but essentially part of the same family – just the worst of a terrible bunch. We were the baddies.

8

THIS COUNTRY IS GOING
STRAIGHT TO HELL

I often think it's comical
That nature always does contrive
That every boy and every gal
That's born into this world alive
Is either a little Liberal
Or else a little Conservative

Iolanthe, an opera by
W. S. Gilbert and Arthur Sullivan

For my fifteenth birthday one of my brother's friends gave me a poster from a record store in Portobello, featuring a scene from the poll tax riots three years earlier in Trafalgar Square. It showed a young female rioter, who was apparently the daughter of a duke or lord, launching some sort of a missile at a policeman, with the words 'Disarm authority, arm your desires' in bold red letters. It was literally the opposite of my worldview, even then, and though I put it on my wall I secretly thought myself ridiculous every time I glanced at it. If authority were disarmed I would be beaten to death within about fifteen minutes by the kids in the remedial class at school. This sat next to a poster of the Clash, a band that sung about rebellion, riot and solidarity with black youth against the authorities; led by a singer who, like me, was a middle-class man putting on an affected cockney and sometimes 'Jafaican' accent.

As a teenager you're supposed to be rebellious, an old idea that features in Shakespeare's *Henry IV*, in which the young Hal spends his evenings in a squalid pub with some cackling imbeciles while his father tries to run the country. Centuries later, adolescence meant immersion into a world of slogans extolling rebellion against the authorities, buying black T-shirts in Kensington Market and listening to vaguely socialist music mostly pumped out by giant entertainment businesses.

My favourite group around the time, Bad Religion, was led by a singer who was also a college professor, and sang songs about nonconformity and the evils of the corporations; one of their albums was called *Against the Grain*. In retrospect, he was vocalising sentiments with which not a single person I ever came across would ever disagree.

Adolescence is radical, so juvenile conservatives come across as strange, a sign that something isn't quite right in the head. In the Woody Allen film *Everyone Says I Love You* it's the subject of a comical subplot in which the young teenaged son starts advocating Second Amendment Rights and tax cuts, to the horror of his liberal New York father; eventually it turns out he has some medical problem that means his brain isn't getting enough oxygen, which doctors soon fix. Young Tories are vaguely amusing in the same way a five-year-old dressed up in a bow tie is, or else they provoke pity as objects of derision. Everyone remembered William Hague, aged sixteen at the Conservative conference, telling the old audience about how they'd all be dead in thirty years, something that probably hurt his future career because most people remember being that age and the last thing they would have imagined doing was turning up at a Tory party conference. Young conservatism is weird in the same way as that antiques dealer boy with curly blond hair who turned up on television in the eighties.

Youthful rebelliousness is linked with independent mindedness, or as Walt Whitman put it over a century earlier in his poem 'To the States': 'Resist much, obey little.'[1] Yet in reality teenagers are the most conformist demographic on earth, desperate to fit in with the prevailing orthodoxy, even when 'rebellion' is itself one. We only buy the anti-authority T-shirts because we're copying our friends or celebrities. Teens are also quite intolerant, on average, and love persecuting anyone who's vaguely odd or different. In real life the young Henry V was not the tearaway portrayed by Shakespeare but a religious fanatic who went around enthusiastically burning heretics. This youthful intolerance is why a lot of people really hate school.

I wasn't politically active as a teenager, but then conservatives tend to become politically conscious later than progressives, on average by around two years. The only occasion I remember was aged fourteen, at the time of the 1992 Tory victory, having a class 'election' where I represented the Conservative Party along with two other boys. We must have seemed like a trio of freaks, and I have no idea what my arguments were; probably parroted and regurgitated from my parents and the *Daily Mail*, but I had an overriding, conscious sense that being a young Tory was lame. Strangely enough, although I haven't seen either of the other two in years, the last couple of times I opened Facebook they were there furiously arguing over Brexit, each now a passionate partisan in that interminable debate.

One deterrent to political activism in the young is a low embarrassment threshold, which is far more extreme in those awkward teenage years. I'm very easily embarrassed, can't bear making a scene or being the centre of attention, and the idea of political protests always struck me as deeply cringeworthy. I understand people protesting about issues close to their heart, for instance if their ancestral homeland has yet to win independence, but teenagers shouting slogans from the Spanish Civil War in protest against a far-Right movement that consists of about five pathetic football hooligans is incredibly embarrassing. But then, as they are for all of us, my politics are shaped by my personality type.

Among the many people Hitler kicked out of Germany – he was quite intolerant, being a Leftie – was a group of academics collectively known as the Frankfurt School. The phrase 'Frankfurt School', along with 'Cultural Marxism', is normally an early warning alarm that the person writing a comment or article is not entirely well in the head, or at best is extremely tedious. When I became a blogger for the *Daily Telegraph* in my early thirties you normally wouldn't get as far as the fourth comment below the line before someone brought up the Frankfurt School, whatever the subject of the actual article. 'Will McIlroy win the PGA this year?' and right below it will be SwordofOdin giving us the full history of Jewish Leftist influence. It was usually cited along with 'Common Purpose', a British organisation that ran leadership conferences but also obsessed commenters because almost everyone in government had some connection to it. It sounded like a really dull Blairite masonic lodge where instead of hitting each other with chickens they sit around talking management-speak phrases such as 'synergy' and 'dynamic learning cultures'. But the Frankfurt School was behind everything in some people's minds.

Indeed, a couple of the philosophers associated with the group were very culturally influential, in particular fusing the ideas of Karl Marx and Sigmund Freud to create the quite effective idea that conservatives are mostly weirdos and losers. They popularised a Freudian idea that people's political stances are mostly formed by deep-seated psychological insecurities, so, for example, if you're anti-gay, then you must be gay.

Pro-law and order = your daddy beat you up, and you probably have strange, deviant sexual desires.

Pro-marriage = want to control women, and are probably strangely repulsed by them too.

Pro-authority = sadist or masochist; obsessed with Dad; tiny penis.

Worried about immigration = racist; fearful of the world; living in an imagined past.

This is an obviously caricatured summary of the highly influential book *The Authoritarian Personality*, written by the Frankfurt School's Theodor Adorno, along with three fellow Stanford academics.[2] The book came out soon after the war, when everyone was trying to come to terms with how the otherwise civilised Germans could have done such terrible things. Adorno's theory outlined why people had authoritarian political views, and in the Freudian lingo of the day the writers concluded that 'intrapsychic conflicts cause personal insecurities, resulting in that person's superego to adhere to externally imposed conventional norms, and to the authorities who impose these norms'. Projection is then used as an ego defence mechanism by displacing their own fears of authority and parents onto 'inferior' minority groups.

People with an authoritarian personality have 'a cynical view of humanity and a need for power and toughness resulting from the anxieties produced by perceived lapses in society's conventional norms'. They also have 'a general tendency to focus upon those who violate conventional values', a lack of imagination as well as a superstitious nature and 'an exaggerated concern with promiscuity'. According to the theory this sort of personality develops because of a 'hierarchical, authoritarian, exploitative' parent–child relationship and parents preoccupied with status, which leads to suppressed resentment against parents.

The researchers came up with the F (for fascism) Scale to measure authoritarianism, which they claimed was latent all over the US among people with 'ethnocentric' and 'conventional' attitudes.[3] Adorno warned that fascism was the real danger to America, a strange idea when communists then ruled half of humanity, but he was convinced the ideology was finding 'a new home' in the country. This was on the eve of the flower power and civil rights movements when, of course, America famously turned to fascism.

There were other writers making similar arguments. Back in 1941 Erich Fromm's *Escape from Freedom*, seen as 'an attempt to marry Marx with Freud', identified the authoritarian or sadomasochistic personality as those which 'respect the strong and loathe the weak'.[4] Another psychologist and refugee from Nazism, Else Frenkel-Brunswik, argued that 'intolerance of ambiguity' was related to prejudice, since some people could not handle atypical gender roles and needed more 'rigid categorization of cultural norms'.[5] This was all down to home discipline apparently. But long before this, German psychiatrists of the late nineteenth century such as Richard von Krafft-Ebing had first suggested that great Christian saints known for their extreme aesthetic self-punishment may have been motivated by masochistic urges.

The Authoritarian Personality argued that all Right-wing people, basically everyone ranging from Churchill to Hitler, were scared, uptight, awkward, sexually repressed weirdoes. And while most people may not have heard of the book, it was hugely influential in the culture at large, framing perceptions about conservatives and so making it harder to justify conservative ideas. Politics is often about the singer, not the song; it doesn't matter what point a person is arguing, if you think they spend their spare time whipping themselves or dressing in their dead mother's wig, you're not going to be receptive to their ideas.

Films and novels have long come to disseminate this theme of conservatives having deep psychological problems. *American Beauty* is a good example, a multiple Oscar-winning drama that features an uptight, military-type neighbour next door, who makes his son call him 'sir' and take regular drugs test, and mutters that 'this country is going straight to hell'.[6] The neighbour is obsessed with the idea that his son may be gay, and so becomes paranoid about the protagonist hanging out with him. Inevitably, of course, the neighbour turns out be a massive closet case himself. This conservative-as-repressed-weirdo has become such a successful meme that if a character in a book or film is very religious or upright, a viewer is surprised if they don't turn out to be some sort of sadist or self-hating sexual deviant. This meme really took off from the 1970s and 1980s, with Stephen King's *Carrie* a famous example, another being *Goodnight Mister Tom* by Michelle Magorian, a hugely popular book from my childhood about a London boy sent away from his demented, sex-hating Christian mum who gets pregnant and blames it on demons and sin.

Certainly many people believe that conservative dysfunction owes something to upbringing. An article in *Psychology Today* suggested that liberals by the age of three had 'developed close relationships with peers and were rated by their teachers as self-reliant, energetic, impulsive, and resilient', while conservatives were already 'easily victimised, easily offended, indecisive, fearful, rigid, inhibited, and vulnerable'.[7] They therefore needed 'the reassurance of tradition and authority'.

Another study found that conservatives were high on 'neatness, orderliness, duty, and rule-following' but 'have less tolerance for ambiguity', while liberals rate highly 'on openness, intellectual curiosity, excitement-seeking, novelty, creativity for its own sake, and a craving for stimulation like travel, colour, art, music, and literature', and are also 'more likely to see grey areas and reconcile seemingly conflicting information'.[8] A study by Berkeley psychology professors argued that people on the Right are marked by 'fear and aggression, dogmatism, and intolerance of ambiguity'.[9]

The annoying thing about the authoritarian personality theory is that there is some truth in it, as with lots of pop psychology. For example, there is one oft-quoted study showing that people with avowed anti-gay views are more likely to be sexually aroused by homoerotic imagery, although as yet the experiment has not been replicated.[10] Of course, these patterns won't apply to every conservative; I thought *Brokeback Mountain* absolutely disgusting, but I needed to watch it seven times for an article I was writing. Likewise, one study found that conservatives were more likely than liberals to use the adultery website Ashley Madison, the results being 'perhaps the strongest evidence yet that people with more sexually conservative values, although they claim to act accordingly, are more sexually deviant in practice than their more sexually liberal peers'.[11]

Adorno's theory was further developed in 1981 by Canadian academic Bob Altemeyer, who refined it with his measurement of 'Right-wing authoritarianism' in particular. Altemeyer's personality test consisted of thirty controversial statements, measuring tribalism, tolerance of inequality and perceptions of human nature, about whether humans should be more cooperative or competitive, egalitarian or hierarchical, as well as issues of submission to authorities and social conventions.[12] Altemeyer's test, like Adorno's work, is quoted in hundreds of social science textbooks, and a dogmatism scale created by social scientist Milton Rokeach found that authoritarianism did indeed correlate with conservatism.

Politics and the Big Five Personality Traits

Political outlook is very closely linked to personality. Psychologists talk of the 'Big Five' personality traits – openness, conscientiousness, extroversion, agreeableness and neuroticism, which you can remember as OCEAN,[13] and these correlate with political views, and to some extent with party affiliation, too. Tory voters 'tend to be antagonistic, conscientious, and even-tempered' while Labour voters are more likely to be neurotic and open to experience.[14] Indeed, studies across many different countries have linked higher agreeableness, openness and neuroticism with Left-wing parties and higher conscientiousness with the Right.[15]

People with flair, bohemian charm and artistic talent therefore tend to be found more on the Left, but they aren't the types who will turn up on time or pay you back without having to be reminded. Conservatives are also by nature neater and it's possible to guess an individual's 'political leanings at better-than-chance levels just from photographs of their desks'.[16] I'm not sure how to best describe the table I'm writing this on – 'anal', I suppose, would probably do it.

People scoring high in agreeableness 'are more likely to have co-operative tendencies' and enjoy a sense of belonging in politics, and so join the Labour Party. Labour members are also 'open to new experiences and ideas, but they are more anxious, tense and discontented and less prone to goal-directed behaviour'.[17] According to one in-depth study of personality and politics, 'Liberals and conservatives consistently differ in everything from occupational preferences to leisure pursuits to sensitivity to disgust, as well as personality traits, moral foundations, personal values, culinary choices, and preferences for music, art, cars, humor, poetry, fiction, and neatness.'[18] Conservatives even use more words related to the inhibition of behaviour in their text messages, according to three separate studies, as well as words related to resistance to change.[19]

Of course, we don't always take up the politics that our psychological leanings might drive us towards because we follow our class or ethnic interests, or for other social reasons. Many very Left-wing working-class leaders of the past have been pretty conservative, for instance, but they joined the Labour Party because it supported their people. People might also just follow the party of their parents, even if goes against their natural inclinations, yet the personality psychology of ideology still plays a big part.[20]

Conservatives are generally less open to experience, and are less likely to volunteer for psychology experiments that require it, while being just as open to those that require decision making or humour.[21] They are also 'less likely than others to value broad-mindedness, imagination, and "having an exciting life"' and score lower on 'Openness to Theoretical or Hypothetical Ideas, Indulgence in Fantasy, and Openness to Unconventional Views of Reality'. Right-wingers are also more uncomfortable with ideas evoking disgust, and anything that turns the moral order on its head. When asked, they were more likely to object to slapping their father in the face, even with his permission, for a comedy sketch, or to refuse to take part in an experiment to 'attend a short avant-garde play in which the actors acted like animals, crawling around naked and grunting like chimpanzees'. ('Avant-garde play' would be enough for me.) Likewise, Americans who felt sensitive to sexual disgust are much more likely to support the Republican Party and to have voted for Trump in 2016, despite his sexual record not being entirely squeaky clean.[22]

This is not entirely new knowledge. Long before Freud or Marx, Thomas Jefferson commented on how the Tory–Whig split reflected personality types, writing in a letter of 1802 to Joel Barlow, 'The division into Whig and Tory is founded in the nature of man; the weakly and nerveless, the rich and the corrupt, seeing more safety and accessibility in a strong executive; the healthy, firm, and virtuous, feeling confidence in their physical and moral resources, and willing to part with only so much power as is necessary for their good government.'

Certainly there are personality 'types' that tend to be found more on the Left and Right, and high openness helps explain why liberals dominate the arts, and also tend to have wider and better artistic interests. My musical tastes are admittedly dreadful and emotionally stunted, and have remained so since I first got into hard rock aged eleven; they have barely developed since the age of fifteen. My Spotify history would probably be indistinguishable to that of a spree killer, a mixture of angry heavy metal and low-IQ popular classical music, including lots of film scores.

Conservatives are also cautious by nature, and in experimental strategy games are more risk averse.[23] Meanwhile, according to a 2003 paper, 'Political Conservatism as Motivated Social Cognition', conservatism correlates with lower desire to learn through other's emotions, and increased 'motives to overcome fear, threat, and uncertainty'.[24]

According to the 'tough–tender' axis theory of politics, conservatism and liberalism are basically different parenting strategies, reflected in St Augustine's idea of the state being a stern father and Rousseau's hatred of his own cruel dad. Conservatives tend to dislike the state mollycoddling or acting as a nanny while liberals are more concerned about brute oppression, the authorities as parental abuser.

Again, it's easy to see why this makes the other side attractive. No one liked the friend's mum who would never let them out and scolded you when you came over; everyone liked the dad who had leather seats in the car and let you put on Guns N' Roses, even the songs with swearing. If you were in the army would you rather be in Willem Dafoe's platoon smoking weed and listening to the Rolling Stones or Tom Berenger's psychos setting fire to Vietnamese villages? Likewise, who wouldn't want to be in Animal House rather than the sadomasochistic military-obsessed squares in Omega Theta Pi next door?

When I was a teenager there were the cool people, and I mean cool in the non-pejorative sense of being relaxed and tolerant, and there were the idiots, and a foolproof barometer of telling the two apart was someone's attitude to gay people. At fifteen I knew that if someone expressed strong anti-gay comments, rather than a live-and-let-live attitude, they were almost certainly an idiot. It was a useful indicator because it correlated with kindness and compassion, or maybe just social nous, since if you didn't realise by then that being anti-gay repulsed most girls you were probably a moron. I learned this – valuable lesson of tolerance – from my older brother's friends, as most teens do with their social attitudes.

George Lakoff argued in *Moral Politics: How Liberals and Conservatives Think* that liberals speak the language of 'nurturant parent morality' and conservatives that of 'strict father morality'.[25] Nurturing parents think each child is inherently good, or as one of my teachers explained it, liberals see conservative morality as a bit like Victorian Dad from *Viz*, the discipline-obsessed religious nut who can't control his sexual urges after seeing a naked table leg and has to take a hansom cab to Whitechapel to 'clean up the streets'.

And, indeed, Right-wing parents are more likely to be punitive in demanding manners and neat dress, 'whereas egalitarian parents are more likely to use warmth in stressing values relating to being considerate of others'.[26] The same study also suggested that conservative parents are less likely to be emotionally close to their children. My dad was certainly distant, older and out of touch, although he was the opposite of a disciplinarian. But that's an anecdote, while overall liberals and conservatives do tend to follow different methods in raising kids. Although both think it's important to teach hard work and helping others, only 41 per cent of conservatives think teaching tolerance is important compared to 88 per of liberals, while for obedience it's 67 v. 35 per cent. Liberal parents also place more importance on empathy for others, curiosity and creativity.[27]

Richard Reeves of the think-tank Demos once said of the psychological make-up of conservatives and what motivated them: 'Anger at different things: modernity, Europe, immigration – fear of modernity, of social breakdown, of difference – wistfulness for an age that has passed – pride in Britain, in history, in certain institutions. Then again, perhaps conservatism is a less intrinsically emotional enterprise; perhaps it is more pragmatic, more accepting, more relaxed about the way things are.'[28]

Conservatism is certainly tied in to the just-world hypothesis, a belief that the world is essentially as fair as it could be. This might explain why more attractive individuals are more likely to identify as Republicans, and conservative politicians also tend to be better-looking.[29] In US local elections being attractive is more important for Republican politicians than it is for Democrats, and their attractiveness correlates with a 20 per cent increase in votes, compared to just 8 per cent for opposition candidates.[30] Likewise taller people are also more likely to vote Conservative, every inch increasing support for the party by 0.6 per cent.[31] (Apparently rich women prefer Right-wing men, and even three-quarters of wealthy Democrat women preferred to date a conservative man. And of the women surveyed, 85 per cent apparently agreed that conservative men are better in bed, because they have 'masculine energy'.[32] I'm not entirely sure I believe that one.)

If you're good-looking, of course you're going to see the world as fair, and so gravitate towards the party of the status quo. In American teen films such as *Heathers* it's always the jocks who are Republicans by nature, as are the good-looking blonde Queen Bitches, while the geeky outsider who listens to weird British indie music is obviously going to turn out liberal.

Conservatives are more likely to desire certainty and strict definitions and boundaries, and in one study were 'much less likely than liberals to say that an almost circular shape was in fact a circle'. We have higher 'cognitive rigidity', that is seeing the world in more strictly defined categories, and feel uncomfortable about things that can't be put in boxes.[33]

And we are in some ways more basic. One metaphor used is 'to picture the political-social mind as a machine: we might say that it is not necessarily that liberals' mental machines have more moving parts – it is that the bolts are not tightened as much: for liberals, there is more "give".'[34] (Or to put it another way, they have a screw loose.) This might be why political psychology studies show that people who express no interest in politics tend to be similar to conservatives, in the sense that apolitical people are basically conservative. Indeed, there is also some evidence 'that conservative ideologues are generally less integratively complex than their liberal or moderate counterparts'.[35]

This may explain why alcohol makes us more Right-wing, stripping away 'complex reasoning to reveal the default state of the mind' and drunkenness therefore encourages 'low-effort, automatic thought' and so promotes political conservatism.[36] Personally this jars with my own experience; because conservatism is associated with higher levels of fear, I think I tend to become more liberal as I drink more and everything in the world seems better, although of course in the morning, when I wake up in bed still wearing all my clothes and my mouth feeling like sandpaper, I'm basically Mussolini. The alcohol effect may also perhaps be because social liberalism is more acceptable in polite society, and many of us are more Right-wing than we let on. Or that away from female company perhaps men adopt more socially conservative views as a form of bonding, which alcohol sessions tend to be focused on. Or maybe liberalism is such a recent innovation that its thin veneer comes off just as easily as those centuries of Latin civilisation rub off the Germans and English after a few drinks. After all, progressivism, like its grandfather Christianity, is a revolutionary idea that goes against all human tradition and instincts, while conservatism, in contrast, is quite basic.

Another way of looking at it is to see conservativism as our default setting, because conservatism is an idea that sees the world as a dangerous place, and for millions of years the world has indeed been dangerous, only becoming safe for a small number of people in the last few hundred. That's because the difference between conservatives and liberals comes down to one key psychological factor, something Thomas Hobbes understood well – fear.

9

ZOMBIE APOCALYPSE

Republican voters prefer candidates with deeper voices in comparison to their opponents, while more generally conservatives like 'politicians who look physically strong and masculine; liberal voters prefer those who have less dominant features and seem more accommodating, perhaps even slightly feminine'.[1] The reason is that conservatives believe the world is a more dangerous place. (Rather depressingly, the same research also suggests that people choose between two candidates after looking at them for about one-tenth of a second.)

Some Right-wing commentators have this self-image of us as independent tough guys, cowboys out on the prairies who don't need no government to protect us. Even British politicians, who obviously don't have much experience rearing cattle, use similar language when talking about entrepreneurs or other independent spirits. And indeed conservative men are far more likely than liberal men to see themselves as 'very masculine' – 32 per cent compared to just 5 per cent – just as conservative women are much more likely to identify as 'very feminine'.[2]

It's probably not just self-perception, since upper-body strength might predict political leanings. A vaguely amusing Right-wing meme is that progressive men drink a lot of soy, which supposedly has a feminising effect on the body, turning them into what Arnold Schwarzenegger called 'girly men'. Yet men with more muscles are more supportive of inequality generally.[3]

Conversely, conservatives are more fearful, one of the key findings of psychological differences in politics. That's why I'm a conservative, at least. My *Guardian*-reading neighbours will see a group of teenagers and think how wonderful to have a vibrant youth scene in the neighbourhood; my reaction is 'oh no, some hoodies' and to worry they'll throw rocks at me and shout 'paedo!' Fear and conservatism are linked, and you can even make liberals more conservative by scaring them; at least according to Yale psychology professor John Bargh.[4] Studies show that when social scientists get liberals to think about their own deaths, or to otherwise make them frightened, they adopt more Right-wing views. After 9/11, for instance, there was a 'very strong conservative shift' in the US, and even liberals favoured more military spending.[5]

This may explain why the wealthy tend to become more liberal, for according to one paper, 'the disadvantaged might embrace right-wing ideologies under some circumstances to reduce fear, anxiety, dissonance, uncertainty, or instability, whereas the advantaged might gravitate toward conservatism for reasons of self-interest or social dominance'.[6] This makes sense, conservatism being both a way of dealing with anxiety and fear, and of orchestrating a hierarchy. Certainly this has long been a popular liberal explanation for why the poor vote for conservative politicians – that fear is spread by the rich and powerful to trick their prole followers into granting them tax cuts in return for protecting them from dangerous unknowns, an argument made by Thomas Frank in *What's the Matter with Kansas?*

One theory is that conservativism is a form of terror management, to cope with existential fear of oblivion.[7] This idea was influenced by Ernest Becker's Pulitzer Prize-winning *The Denial of Death*, which suggested that social institutions were devised as a way of helping us deal with our own impending doom. You may die but the Marine Corps lives forever, therefore you live forever. Naturally, therefore, during hard times people develop more conservative views. During the Depression years of the 1930s more people deserted liberal churches such as the Episcopalians and joined more authoritarian congregations such as the Southern Baptists and Seventh

Day Adventists who promised some real fire-and-brimstone old-time religion, compared to good years such as the 1920s. A similar trend was found in the 1960s in Seattle where periods of high unemployment led to more conversions to the Catholic Church and fewer for the liberal United Presbyterian Church.[8]

Four studies also showed 'stronger obsessive-compulsive symptoms' to be associated with social conservatism, which causes the paradox that 'right-wing ideology can function to reduce insecurity while people on the right still have higher levels of insecurity'.[9] Yet these attitudes might at least make us happier, according to research from two Canadian universities, which found a 'significant association' between authoritarian attitudes and well-being, and that conservative ideology 'may promote positive psychological outcomes'.[10] This is counterintuitive when one considers the link between conservatism and threat,[11] but perhaps, the authors conclude, 'the notion that everyone has their place . . . can arguably provide a coherent structure that makes the world seem less chaotic', which 'could, in turn, promote a sense of well-being'. Indeed, this is what Joseph de Maistre argued.

In another experiment a group of liberals and conservatives were shown 'a series of collages, each comprised of a mixture of positive images (cute bunnies, smiling children) and negative ones (wounds, a person eating worms). Test subjects were fitted with eye-tracker devices that measured where they looked, and for how long'. The results were 'stark', conservatives fixing their eyes much longer on the negative images and the disgusting but engrossing lure of death.[12]

The causes of these differences, contrary to what many Freudians of the mid-twentieth century believed, are probably less to do with our childhood and more simply the way our brains are comprised. People with liberal views have 'increased grey matter volume in the anterior cingulate cortex, whereas greater conservatism was associated with increased volume of the right amygdala', the part of the organ responsible for threat perception.[13] Large-scale analysis of conservatives and liberals has shown marked difference in genes that relate to neurotransmitter functioning, particularly glutamate and serotonin, both of which are involved in the brain's response to threat and fear.[14]

Conservatives react more strongly to signs of danger, including the threat of germs and contamination, and even white noise. Liberals, in contrast, have more genes implicated in receptors for dopamine, which is associated with sensation-seeking and openness to experiences.[15] That might be why actors, rock stars and basically everyone who's remotely cool or sexually magnetic votes Democrat or Labour, while conservatives tend to be, on average, more fearful, unimaginative and unadventurous, which makes us less attractive as dates – although we will at least turn up for the date on time.

Fear can be linked to anxiety about different kinds of people, and conservatives on average have higher levels of racial fear, so are more likely to feel discomfort when they are around large numbers of people from different ethnic or cultural backgrounds. With identity politics becoming so dominant some conservatives have accused the Left of being almost proprietorial about minorities, and holding non-whites to lower standards, called 'the soft bigotry of low expectations'; this leads some Right-wing pundits to argue that 'the Democrats are the real racists' – but this is clearly not true.

One theory is that xenophobia is an evolutionary response to pathogens, since strangers are more likely to carry diseases to which the ingroup has no immunity, and that's why conservatives respond more strongly to disgust and value purity and cleanliness.[16] Hitler's psychological ramblings encompassed ideas about Jews and Slavs but he also had an obsessive fear of germs and disease, and from the very start the Nazis passed laws ensuring workplaces were clean. (Yes, typical nanny-state Leftists, etc.) And so, the argument goes, the world has become more liberal since 1945 because infectious diseases have been gradually wiped out, causing people's conservative instincts to be switched off. The one problem with this idea is that it would make doctors super Right-wing, and anyone who's gone on social media will know that's not true.

It might also explain why poorer people, living in more overcrowded areas filled with germs and more vulnerable to epidemics, are more socially conservative; liberalism, however, also correlates with higher human density, so this would contradict the theory.[17] (I'm going to suggest some theories in this book I don't necessarily agree with, and which might contradict others, because I don't really believe in grand overarching theories of the world, which is unfortunate as they do tend to sell well.) Avi Tuschman argued in *Our Political Nature* that conservatism and liberalism may be different mating strategies, one of which is to keep sexual reproduction within a relatively small group and the other to expand the gene pool by marrying out, both of which have their advantages. Liberals have a wider circle of trust, and are prepared to display altruism outside their immediate family and group; they are more instinctively universalist.

People high on Right-wing authoritarianism are scared, then, viewing the world as a dangerous place. And so, according to Californian psychologist Scott Alexander's 'Thrive/Survive' theory of the political spectrum 'rightism is what happens when you're optimizing for surviving an unsafe environment, leftism is what happens when you're optimized for thriving in a safe environment'.[18] Alexander suggested that 'the best way for leftists to get themselves in a rightist frame of mind is to imagine there is a zombie apocalypse tomorrow. It is a very big zombie apocalypse and it doesn't look like it's going to be one of those ones where a plucky band just has to keep themselves alive until the cavalry ride in and restore order.' What would you want in such an environment? Well, guns to start with.

The fear factor explains why attitudes to crime are probably the best and most timeless way of measuring Left–Right politics. As teenagers, I remember, most of us got mugged or beaten up on the way home from school, or at weekends, at least once. We were attacked by other boys, sometimes for money and sometimes just for fun. It seemed pretty standard and unavoidable if you were a young male in London, and I was aware, through reading fiction or talking to older people or maybe just the *Daily Mail* again, that this was rare a generation earlier. (I should point out I didn't read the *Mail* all the time, or even much. Usually I read quite normal things for a twelve-year-old like *Spider-Man*, *Detective Comics* and Oswald Spengler's *The Decline of the West*.)

As I entered my teens England's homicide rate edged towards eight hundred a year, close to three times what it had been in the early 1960s, despite huge advances by paramedics in saving the lives of many more. It would peak at over a thousand in 2002, while the increase in recorded crime in Britain between 1990 and 1991 was more than the total of *all* crime in 1950.[19] To me, at least, London seemed quite a dangerous place, and there were a number of crimes that stuck in the imagination; a friend of a friend was murdered by a gang on Hungerford Bridge for no reason; another group of teens, operating only a mile from my home, committed a horrific gang rape on the Regent's Canal. One or two crews became notorious for tube muggings, and occasional stories of innocent people being murdered in public, either a result of youthful bravado or by schizophrenics failed by the care system, lodged in my mind.

One of the most disturbing incidents I remember was in Turnham Green – a nice part of suburban west London – where in my late teens I saw two boys, aged maybe eleven, shouting at an elderly Polish lady who must have been well into her eighties. She had told them off for throwing stones at a shop and so one of them fronted up to her with his chest as if he was confronting a young male his age. I just couldn't even comprehend it; I walked her back to her front door but I dread to think what horrors those boys went on to commit. I suppose, like de Maistre, I felt less anger towards criminals than the people who allowed them to behave that way, who made excuses for them, ensured they received 'community punishments' rather than prison sentences that kept them away from us. I always got the impression that those working in the system would be far more interested in the well-being of the eleven-year-old boys than the old lady; maybe an unfair idea, but I could never muster any sympathy for people who committed violence, even though, I guess, their home lives were probably horrific.

After a while I wondered if liberals sympathised with offenders due to some sort of animal magnetism, because they're charismatic in a brutal, Darwinian playground sort of way. In contrast, the actual victims of crime are just nobodies, too proud or ashamed to admit their fear. Perhaps the same power and glamour that allow criminals to intimidate followers and victims have an effect on people working in social services and the justice system. A certain type of middle-class person loves the glamour of criminality, which is how millions are made in music and cinema. There is also naivety, and the willingness to believe comforting ideas; I remember at school being told that bullies are low on self-esteem, even though the opposite is apparently true, as it is with violent criminals generally. And yet criminology had by this stage developed 'social theories of punitiveness', which 'typically portray punitiveness as a form of scapegoating in which offenders are just a stand-in population, masking more abstract anxieties'.[20] I have lots of transcendental anxieties but getting punched in the head as a teenager certainly didn't feel abstract.

Liberals tend to be less fearful of the world, and when ascendant support shorter prison sentences. In the 1960s there was a great wave of reform in both the US and Britain with a radical shake-up of sentencing guidelines, moving away from long jail sentences and towards probation and early release. The results were . . . predictable.

At the core of progressive philosophy is the belief that few people are inherently bad, and therefore if you give them enough carrots there is no need for the stick, or at least only a very small stick. Conversely it was once said that a conservative was 'a liberal who's been mugged', adapted by Irving Kristol to 'mugged by reality'. In fact, this has been found to be untrue, at least by one academic paper, which suggested that 'victimization experiences . . . do not appear to be strong predictors of punitiveness'.[21] Perhaps it's down to subtle modern status signals, since fear of crime is low-status (both cowardly and poor), and no one wishes to admit to being scared in their homes or streets. Perhaps this has skewed people's instinctive sympathy for the vulnerable, and convinced them that those who they fear must really be the victims. Or maybe liberals are just braver people. Alternatively it may just be more comforting to believe that the guy who mugged you is a victim of the system pushed to desperation to commit a crime, rather than that he victimised you because you're weak and he's strong, and he enjoyed it.

But then plenty of high-profile people on the Left have had a soft spot for criminals. Jean-Paul Sartre took up the cause of one criminal, a thief called Jean Genet, and wrote a 700-page book about him which also doubled, according to Paul Johnson, as 'a celebration of . . . anarchy and sexual incoherence'.[22] Likewise Norman Mailer had an obsession with jailbirds, even to the point of getting a killer called Jack Abbott released early. Abbott became a darling of the literary scene in New York until one day in July 1981 when he stabbed to death a complete stranger. Then there was author William Styron, who got the death-row convict Benjamin Reid paroled and then in 1970, upon Reid's release, arranged to have him live at his house and accepted into college. Reid then abducted a woman and her two children before raping her.

Around the time that Mailer and Sartre were portraying 'criminals as existential heroes in revolt against a heartless, inauthentic world',[23] psychiatrist Karl Menninger published *The Crime of Punishment*. Menninger wrote, 'It is easy to look with proud disdain upon "those people" who get caught – the stupid ones, the unlucky ones, the blatant ones. But who does not get nervous when a police car follows closely? We squirm over our income tax statements and make some "adjustments." We tell the customs official we have nothing to declare – well, practically nothing . . . Over a billion dollars was embezzled by employees last year.'"[24] Indeed, who is the *real* criminal, you ask? The man who brings back too many bottles of duty-free wine from holiday or the guy who sticks an axe into a stranger's head? Really makes you think.

I arrived late for school one morning in the upper sixth. It meant a £2 fine because that's how our headmaster dealt with people failing to turn up on time; if you couldn't afford the fine, then you'd have to come in on Saturday. Our classics teacher Mr Stubbings, an eloquent skinhead who was popular with the boys despite being feared (or because of it), took my name down nonchalantly and without any anger, explaining that assembly was going over a bit as the headmaster was addressing the upper school. Is it about what happened on Friday, I asked? Yes, he said, with a sad 'what is the world coming to?' expression.

At the end of the previous week, at another Catholic secondary less than three miles away in Maida Vale, headmaster Philip Lawrence was outside his school, St George's, when a gang arrived to attack one of the pupils there over some grudge. The father of four placed himself in front of the boy to protect him and so a teenager stabbed him; he died on the spot. Even for the standards of the day it was shocking, and our headmaster had used his assembly to pay tribute to Mr Lawrence and his selfless devotion, a man who had raised a sink school up from the nadir of the 1980s and was turning it around. (Years later, Lawrence's killer Learco Chindamo successfully avoided deportation to his native Philippines using human rights legislation because his family were mostly here. Of course, only low-status *Daily Mail* readers would think this is a bad thing and I'm sure some lawyer on Twitter can explain why.)

Perhaps older people felt that teenagers were out of control, 'feral' being the overused word, but it was other teenagers – especially teenage boys – who hated this sort of violence most, since we were overwhelmingly most likely to be its victims. There was definitely a noticeable shift to a more hyper-masculine street culture from around 1992, somewhere between the launch of Dr Dre's first album and Snoop Dogg's *Doggystyle*. Popular culture became much more open in glorifying violence and casual misogyny, but then if teenage boys have no prevailing culture or direction, some form of warrior ethos will become the default, since young males respect strength most of all ('being hard' was and always will be the number-one skill of any school hierarchy). I found it funnier later learning that Dr Dre's former NWA bandmate Eazy-E was a Republican Party sympathiser because I suppose the consumerism of 1990s popular culture was a grotesque parody of Reaganomics.

It's weird that, in one sense, men at the time were being pushed towards a more gentle, sensitive way of thinking and on the other there was this increasingly aggressive get-rich-or-die-trying subculture. Of course, what was happening was that society was becoming freer and more uncon-strained, and therefore more stratified; there was a place for men who wanted to be more androgynous, feminine and/or gay; and there was also more space for men who wanted to be complete bell-ends.

Freed from restraint, cinema also became noticeably more violent in that decade, starting with *Goodfellas* in 1990. There was more focus on things such as torture or rape. The bright new star was Quentin Tarantino, whose movies took great pleasure in extreme and horrific violence, always with an ironic soundtrack aimed at making it more horrendous. I went along with it but I was also secretly horrified, something I didn't want to admit to. I mean, do we really need to watch a guy's ears being cut off like that? Does he have to use the N-word, which is so unpleasant and dehumanising? I looked around at my friends, all laughing at the horrendous violence, and wondered if I was a bit weird or sensitive.

Soon after watching *Reservoir Dogs* for the first time I also happened to see *It's a Wonderful Life*, Frank Capra's 1946 tale of community life in a small American town. It was set in a society where people trust their neighbours and, when things get thin and frightening, they know their loved ones will support them and that life is worth living. I absolutely loved it. In the fictional Bedford Falls people relied on and helped each other, and having grown up in central London, where no one knew their neighbours and where violent crime felt always somewhere in the background, I longed to live somewhere like that (back when I was eight or nine there had also been two murders in my street within a month, which obviously never happened in Bedford Falls). But I just felt like a weirdo because I couldn't help wishing I lived in James Stewart's world rather than the horrific reality of modern Hollywood. This was aged sixteen or seventeen – I mean, that's not normal is it? Being prudish about these things just seemed low-status, the mark of a losing side as these issues of cinematic violence and pornography became part of a culture war that began to heat up in the last decade of the twentieth century.

10

THE SIXTIES, MAN

Look, Jez . . . for better or for worse the '60s happened
and now sex is fine. But can't we take the best of that, the
nice music, the colours, the "I have a dream", etcetera,
but not have to face the . . . squalor?

Mark Corrigan, *Peep Show*[1]

As a conservative I obviously hate the sixties and everything they stand for,
although I openly admit it's jealousy. They got free love, we had to worry
about Aids. They got the hippy trail in Afghanistan, we got al-Qaida. They
were raised in conditions of relative poverty but ended up with massive
houses and retirement cruises, while we grew up indulged and spoilt and
came of age in an economic system insanely built on runaway housing costs.

In the reactionary mind, in the words of political scientist Mark Lilla,
the 'story begins with a happy, well-ordered state where people who know
their place live in harmony and submit to tradition and their God. Then
alien ideas promoted by intellectuals – writers, journalists, professors –
challenge this harmony and the will to maintain order weakens at the top.'
He adds, 'The betrayal of elites is the linchpin of every reactionary story . . .
A false consciousness soon descends on the society as a whole as it willingly,
even joyfully, heads for destruction.'[2] This is the kind of thing I think
about when I take my kids to Malmesbury Abbey to visit the tomb of

tenth-century King Athelstan only to find the interior is being used as a skateboarding rink and hip-hop music is blaring out. One word: decline.

Lilla's summary is a fair one. People often dismiss conservatives by snorting that 'oh you just want to return to the 1950s', but as Peter Hitchens argued in not so many words, the 1950s were an age of jittery sexual energy and licence – we want to return to the 1900s. The conservative golden age was the Belle Époque era before the First World War when life was just one big *Mary Poppins*-style adventure, a crime-free paradise with happy house-wives carrying elegant umbrellas and Post-Impressionist artists drinking themselves to death with absinthe. If conservatives were to build a *Matrix*-style virtual reality where civilisation peaked it would be around the year 1911, before the First World War, modernist art and architecture, psychoanalysis, feminism, and the horrors of socialism and communism.

What went wrong? Intellectuals, of course.

As well as the members of the Frankfurt School, another hugely influential thinker who turns up a lot on below-the-line comments by angry conservative men is Antonio Gramsci, an Italian communist who was unfortunate to live under Mussolini. Gramsci had been imprisoned in 1928, an ordeal that eventually killed him, but his *Prison Notebooks* were smuggled out by his sister-in-law and published after the war, and in the 1970s were translated into English, French and German. Gramsci's great theory was that of hegemony, ideological domination that extends beyond politics and into culture, which is far more important. The Russian revolutionaries had taken control of the state but they failed to appeal to the people's hearts – emphasised a few years later when Stalin revived Russian nationalism to combat the Nazis because the people certainly weren't going to fight for Bolshevism. In the West there was very little appetite for communism, especially not among the workers, for whom traditional attachments to their homelands proved strong (as 1914 showed). It was no point seizing control of the state and its industries if you failed to infiltrate people's minds too. This was something Margaret Thatcher herself remarked upon in 1981 when she said: 'Economics are the method;

the object is to change the soul.' In a sense she achieved that wish, although not how she imagined or hoped.

But then, although Gramsci is seen as some Svengali-like manipulator-genius by conservative opponents, in reality progressive domination was something that mainly happened because of rising living standards, technology, education and greater freedom – the latter, of course, partly thanks to Tory and Republican governments.

Gramsci's ideas have often been called 'cultural Marxism', although since the term has become very popular with the extreme Right, using it is bad optics, to say the least. The idea is that economic Marxism is based on the idea that all history is determined by who owns the means of production; the capitalists own it, and therefore they exploit the workers, who are the victims. Cultural Marxism simply transposes this into the cultural sphere, and views history as a question of power and privilege. What people mean by 'cultural Marxism' might be simplistically surmised as opposition to tradition and hierarchy; radical gender politics; the Marxist theory of race in which whites are the bourgeoisie and non-whites the proletariat; intolerance towards non-orthodox thinkers; the necessity of changing the language; and the ideas that criminals are victims of society, marriage is oppressive and exploitative, and nations are artificial, imagined communities. It's roughly synonymous with progressive politics, then, perhaps just a slightly crankier way of saying 'progressivism'.

Until the war there was little doubt that conservatism had hegemony but the 1950s saw an increasing shift, the first rock 'n' roll music and use of the word teenager, as well as more radical artistic movements such as beatnik poetry (the 1950s had sort of been happening since the 1920s but had been confined to small groups). Young people had growing independence, thanks to the car and part-time service-sector jobs, and the spread of radio and television allowed the creation of a youth culture for the first time. Sexual habits changed, and in the US the percentage of couples who remained virgins until marriage fell from about 40 per cent in the mid-1940s to just over 10 per cent in 1961, the year the pill arrived.[3] Until then shotgun marriages were also common, one study in Denmark showing that 50 per cent of brides in the early 1960s were pregnant.[4]

Some recall the 1950s as a decade of great conservatism, one of the key cultural memories being McCarthyism, the campaign to exclude suspected communists from public life led by Wisconsin Senator Joseph McCarthy. We all know about it because there have been various films about the subject, as well as books and articles, and most influentially a play, Arthur Miller's *The Crucible*, which used the historical parallel of the Salem witch trials to show just how irrational the whole thing was.

It became a divisive issue, one that McCarthy lost, but it may have been less about communism than hegemony.[5] McCarthyite conservatives were trying not just to fight Marxism but assert their dominance by making communist-sympathising progressives beyond the pale of decency. Conservatives were trying to establish their views as orthodoxy, but liberals and progressives won the right to share the public space – and years later would repeat the same behaviour.

1968

Conservativism is 'more basic and fundamental', suited to the idea the world is nasty, brutish and short: 'Being defensive, risk aversive, hierarchical, and tribal makes sense when the threats around you are very real and immediate.'[6] And since life has become far less threatening in recent decades, liberalism has become an 'evolutionary luxury' we can afford. During the thirty years after the war living standards in the West vastly increased – and during a period when the state had unprecedented spending power for welfare programmes – and so, inevitably, this conservative worldview shrunk and the culture shifted Left.

Progressives are naturally better suited to good times, and since things have been getting better over the past seventy years, so the world has become more liberal. Their politics are annoying to me and cause unnecessary problems, but they're nothing like the terrible political systems that have dominated human life for the majority of our history. Medieval or early modern political systems, from the feudal anarchy of the eleventh century to the absolutism of the eighteenth, were the equivalent of small-pox or famine, while modern liberalism is more like Type-2 diabetes, the side effect of a society with too much good stuff. It's obviously not pleasant, but it's much better to live in a society where obesity is a problem than one where people are dragging down the corpses of hanged felons to have something to eat. It's a sign of our success.

The post-war economic boom also saw the further growth of a middle class, as large numbers of workers were finally able to afford homes, household appliances, cars and holidays. Many went to university for the first time, and accents began to level. Most radically of all, far more women were able to go into higher education, and to work, reflecting and accelerating changing social attitudes.

There was also a corresponding decline in industrial labour, made obsolete by new technology; Harold Wilson closed more mines than Thatcher, not that you'll hear any radio plays about that; dockers were made obsolete by technology, as were many fishermen. Socialist politics catering to working-class families therefore declined in importance, while progressive movements aimed at individual liberation and sexual freedom in particular became far stronger. Liberalism replaced socialism as the dominant creed, except it wasn't liberalism in the classical sense but what Americans call liberalism; devoted to both liberty *and* equality, but with a particular emphasis on sexual liberation being sacred, along with group rights. It was the start of what would become identity politics.

Another huge change was the decline of religion, which altered how we viewed human nature. Previously it had been assumed, as David Hume put it in 'Of the Independency of Parliament' 'that, in contriving any system of government, and fixing the several checks and controls of the constitution, every man ought to be supposed a knave, and to have no other end, in all his actions, than private interest'. Even Bertrand Russell, an atheist, said no one should run a school who didn't have a deep conviction of original sin.

That all changed in the 1960s, and there was a huge growth in what American conservative legend Thomas Sowell called 'the Unconstrained Vision' of human nature in which we could be 'improved, perfected even, if social conditions are improved', and that 'anything would be possible if artificial constraints placed on human beings' were removed. In contrast, conservatives believed in the Constrained Vision, that 'humans need external structures constraining them to behave well, including laws, institutions, customs, traditions, religion and nations. These constraints are built up slowly and organically by communities, but they can be destroyed quickly by radical reformers who don't understand their value.'[7]

Successful belief systems, as well as being better suited to the climate of the day, are also better adapted to the means of communications available. A key conservative plank of thought is that human beings are inherently sinful, which is a really bad message for the television age, since it's hard to make the claim without seeming unpleasant or unforgiving, the sort of person who probably believes period pains are a punishment from God. Progressivism, in contrast, holds that everyone is essentially good, a positive message people are keen to believe. Today 86 per cent of progressive activists believe that 'people's outcomes in life are determined largely by forces outside of their control', whereas 98 per cent of devoted conservatives believed 'people are largely responsible for their own outcomes in life'.[8] In a sense, they're both wrong.

This changing view of human nature was reflected in the growing popularity of Rousseau's idea of the noble savage. At primary school I was taught something to this effect about Native Americans, that their society was peaceful and egalitarian, when the reality was something more like Mel Gibson's *Apocalypto* with noble savages ripping out the hearts of equally noble, but somewhat weaker, savages and kicking their heads like footballs down a pyramid. It's something I remember clearly because I went through a brief stage of being fascinated by Native American culture. (I would say 'we still called them Red Indians' at the time, which was probably just about true in the 1980s but I would inevitably sound like Grandpa Simpson or Gareth from *The Office*.) This idea found expression in 1991 with *Dances with Wolves*, starring perhaps the most PC matinee idol of all, Kevin Costner, and later in *Avatar*.

The noble savage has often been a popular way to criticise modern men by shining a light on our faults, a literary device that goes back to the Roman Tacitus's lionising of the barbarian Germans. There's nothing wrong with that, but in doing so it helped spread a false idea about human nature. Countless studies of pre-agricultural societies indicate that they were almost uniformly extremely violent, and showed a willingness to inflict extraordinary cruelty to those outside of the tribe, most of whom weren't viewed with any empathy. (That does not make the genocide of Native Americans any less wrong, of course.) One study of the Inuit found that 40 per cent of girls were put to death at birth, while of 15 hunter-gatherer societies studied, 11 had homicide rates higher than the most violent nations today, and 14 were worse than the US in 2016, the exception being a group called the Batek who lived in Malaysia and whose survival strategy was to run away from rival tribes (which seems eminently sensible).[9]

Many of the ideas of this period resulted from a great groundswell of discontent among young people, the baby boomers, in particular a sense that wealth had not given life meaning and was also constricting.[10] This discontent and desire for change would erupt in 1968, often seen as the start of the progressive era. The year began with Vietnam peace talks in Paris, and then in April Martin Luther King Jr was assassinated, causing riots that led to dozens of deaths and further triggering the huge exodus of whites from America's cities to its suburbs. The violence partly inspired politician Enoch Powell to warn that month in a speech that immigration risked turning England's green and pleasant land into 'the haunting tragedy of the United States'.

In May, students in Paris erupted. Graffiti from Paris that year stated that 'It is forbidden to forbid', 'Never work' and 'I take my desire for reality, because I believe in the reality of my desires', heralding the age of the vacuous, pseudo-profound political slogan, many of which would appear on T-shirts and posters by the time I was a teen.

For those at the time it was about personal liberation, but it also marked what Christopher Lasch later called the 'Revolt of the Elites', an uprising by the middle class against the constraints that held everyone together. During the protest Sartre went to a Renault factory to meet some genuine proletarians, where his existential ideas went down like a turd in a swimming pool. The socialist paper *L'Aurore* recalled: 'The workers were not having it. Sartre's congregation consisted entirely of the few Maoists he had brought with him.'[11] That year the workers of Paris did not join the students, or the *Les fils à papa* as they called the privileged young people.

Among those in the French capital at the time was a young English student, Roger Scruton, who read various attacks on bourgeois civilisation 'with a growing sense that if there is anything half decent in the way of life so freely available in the world's greatest city, the word "bourgeois" is the proper name for it'. The *soixante-huitards* were the inheritors of that bourgeois way of life they attacked, the beneficiaries, and Scruton recalled his horror at their politics as 'an English reaction to continental posturing' and 'mumbo-jumbo'.

Yet, as Scruton wrote, he was brought up in an age when 'almost all English intellectuals regarded the term "conservative" as a term of abuse. To be a conservative, I was told, was to be on the side of age against youth, the past against the future, authority against innovation, the "structures" against spontaneity and life . . . The choice remaining was between reform and revolution. Do we improve society bit by bit, or do we rub it out and start again?' As he realised that summer, most of his contemporaries favoured the latter.[12]

11

REALITY IS A SOCIAL CONSTRUCT

At sixth form it was expected that most people would go on to another three years of education. University attendance had hugely expanded in the preceding years, most of all under Margaret Thatcher, with many former polytechnics becoming universities, the assumed thinking being that increased university attendance would boost national IQ or wealth. From the time I started secondary school to the time I left, the number of university students in England had trebled.[1]

And so after doing A-levels I left a fairly authoritarian institution and was now like a bee released from the hive, pretty clueless about what I wanted to do, a very undeveloped, emotionally immature eighteen-year-old. I started politics and philosophy at Manchester, which entailed six hours a week hard study and the excessive spare time I filled with drinking instead, eventually making myself ill and dropping out. The inability to handle freedom is the hallmark of the narrow conservative mind, after all, which is why we like to stop other people enjoying themselves.

Along with my main subjects I signed up to social anthropology because I'd been told it included a documentary about Papuan tribes fighting over Coke bottles and I found this funny. Our course began with a discussion of Franz Boas, the early twentieth-century giant of anthropology who did so much to influence the discipline, previously the preserve of northern European men with a somewhat unhealthy interest in measuring the body parts of brown-skinned people. Under Boas's influence the field had become less confident in the supremacy of Western civilisation, quite reasonably, although this opened the paradox that cultural relativism was itself a Western idea. It also became far more Left-leaning; Boas's apprentice Margaret Mead had gone to the South Pacific where she found a pre-agricultural society that didn't have sexual jealousy and everyone just happily shagged each other without it descending into murderous arguments. Mead's 1928 book *Coming of Age in Samoa* is viewed as a sea-change in anthropology, but also a pointer to where uptight Western society could do things differently. She had also been elaborately hoaxed by the natives and no such sexual utopia existed; in fact, Samoa had horrific levels of rape, and adultery had been punishable by death before the Europeans arrived.[2]

Ever since then anthropologists have searched for societies in which everything is shared equally, or in which women have power, and occasionally a progressive publication will publish a piece about such a tribe. Then you read around the tribespeople a little bit more and learn that they use enemy skulls as a currency and eight-year-old girls are married off to septuagenarians . . . and so the hunt for the lost City of Egalitaria continues. Perhaps more significantly, Mead and others in her field moved away from biological explanations for human behaviour, which were instead seen as a product of social structures.[3] This would have a huge impact on wider society.

In our first anthropology seminar the tutor told us that our Western idea about the heart pumping blood around the body was not 'objectively' true, no more so than the indigenous Papuan belief that it was a magic gateway to another dimension or some shite (my paraphrasing, not the tutor's, I should add). They were just as correct, 'objectively', and our notions were merely subjective, our cultural interpretation. What we called Western science was only a culturally specific form of ethnoscience, not a universally valid form of verification.

I had spent a decade in Catholic schools and appreciated that you were supposed to listen to a lot of stuff that didn't make any sense and just nod along and repeat it. I edged my eyes around the room to see what facial expression everyone else was making, if they look confused and sceptical, too. Was this one of those things we were meant to go along with, like prayers during Mass, or were we supposed to genuinely believe this? I mean, the heart *does* pump blood around the body, we all know this, right? I didn't understand why a university would teach something patently untrue.

My brother had gone off to study history three years earlier and I remember seeing some of the stuff he had to read, the strange, confusing form of English that was used, riddled with jargon and gibberish. By the 1990s the social sciences had already become overwhelmed with impenetrable writing, but I think it took me a while to realise that maybe the whole point was not to understand it. In retrospect I obviously had an anti-intellectual streak, but I also think that quite basic people have a pretty good sense of the difference between something that is incomprehensible because it's complex (astrophysics) and something that's incomprehensible because it's bollocks (cultural studies).

High levels of bullshit went with high levels of politicisation, it seemed, and under the expansion of the university system entire fields of progressive ideas had grown, funded by taxpayers and supported by Conservative governments. Universities had especially been influenced by Herbert Marcuse and Theodore Adorno's critical theory, the idea that education should be aimed at liberating people from oppression rather than just finding the truth, as traditional academic subjects had aimed for. Or as Karl Marx put it: 'Philosophers have hitherto only interpreted the world in various ways; the point is to change it.'

Critical theory was influenced by Marx's idea of ideology; because the bourgeoisie control the means of production, they also control the culture, and all the laws and morality reflect their class interests. So the powers that be try to convince everyone that there are these things called 'truth and values', which were in fact all bourgeois constructs all along. When people realised the distorting influence of power structures then they could see the world more accurately, and be liberated.

The British-Czech philosopher Ernest Gellner argued that the expansion of higher education from the 1960s led to increased demand for social theory and with it the growth of postmodernism. More people went away for three years to study theory, and so more theory was produced in order to satisfy demand. Since more people are hired so 'there simply must be the appearance of both profundity and originality. It is all intended to resemble scientific growth. But what if there isn't any? May this lead to a setting up of artificial obsolescence and rotation of fashion, characteristic of the consumer goods industry?'[4] Unfalsifiable, unintelligible ideas as luxury goods – the academic industry demands crap, and so more crap is produced. This led to the development of various schools of thought, many pushing the progressive arguments in more extreme directions.

In 1996, the year I'd left school, Alan Sokal, a physics professor at University College London, had submitted an article to a postmodern cultural studies academic journal to see if they would 'publish an article liberally salted with nonsense if (a) it sounded good and (b) it flattered the editors' ideological preconceptions'.[5] This they did, publishing an argument that quantum gravity is a social construct. A reasonable person in the mid-1990s might have thought this kind of insanity would wear off, but more than two decades later it seems as strong as ever. But then Sokal's spoof sounds barely any crazier than much of what gets published.

Some whole areas of academia had become activism-driven by this stage. Subjects such as race and cultural studies, women's studies, gender studies – pretty much anything with 'studies' in the title, in fact – are quite explicitly about promoting social justice on principle. Gender studies looks at the 'social and cultural constructions' of masculinity and femininity, aimed at analysing how social forces influence gender, based on the idea that masculinity and femininity are 'performative' and separated from the idea of biological sex. This seems to me quite obviously untrue, and yet fourteen thousand Americans take a degree in gender studies every year, each spending tens or hundreds of thousands of dollars for the privilege.[6] Gender studies has also been responsible for such breakthroughs in human knowledge as the claim that '$E = mc^2$ is a "sexed question" which belongs in "masculine physics" and "privileges" rigid over fluid entities'.[7] Likewise subjects such as criminology are heavily politicised,[8] as is sociology, so that graduates entering the realms of social policy are primed with a progressive approach.

To a conservative this is like having a widely funded educational system that teaches the Catechism of the Catholic Church, funded by the taxpayer and taking in the top 50 per cent of each school year. And it's not even like the faith school system, where many of the teachers clearly don't believe it and the students are expected to grow up leaving the religion because the outside world is secular – here they believe the literal truth of the faith.

The growth of universities clearly helped push the cultural norms Leftwards, and for a number of reasons. University is sociable, and sociability seems to make people more liberal, especially if they already have a predisposition to novelty seeking. More intelligent and open-minded people are also more likely to be socially liberal, and to attend college, but it's also true that attendance itself pushes people to the Left. There may be some influence from lecturers, who heavily lean Left, with just 12 per cent of British academics supporting Right-wing parties, compared to 50 per cent of the population, this disparity being far larger in the social sciences and humanities.[9]

Academics tend to lean Left because the personal traits most associated with liberalism – novelty seeking and openness – also direct people towards areas such as academia or the arts. Another reason is 'political typing', which is a tendency for certain industries to get a reputation for being suitable for certain people, and so attracting more of them. Artsy, bohemian folk are more likely to enter academia rather than, say, the Parachute Regiment. Another cause is 'social homophily', which just means wanting to work with similar types, since most people enjoy being around people like them. If you're in an office and all your colleagues are nice progressives the last thing you want is some weirdo opening up Breitbart articles about Muslims blowing themselves up when you're trying to discuss last night's Scandi noir drama or that Netflix documentary about racism in the US prison system.

But there is some evidence that academics become more progressive simply because the atmosphere is overwhelmingly Left-wing, and even conservative individuals 'reorient their views toward the left-liberal majority viewpoint due to some combination of concerns over funding and promotion, peer pressure from colleagues, or simply a willingness to conform'.[10] Professors may also become more Left-wing because they are relatively poor members of the elite, high in prestige but not in income, and so naturally favour more redistribution. Or at least they want a society that prizes money less and intellectualism (i.e. them) more; in contrast, the more that prestige is tied to wealth, the lower the status of academics. There is also the argument that academics adopt non-traditional attitudes towards things such as sex and marriage as a status symbol, which probably has some effect.

The Blank Slate

The expansion of universities also helped change our idea of human nature, advancing 'the Standard Social Science Model' or 'blank slate', the idea that humans are born completely devoid of pre-existing ideas, qualities or abilities. In this worldview we are entirely, or almost entirely, shaped by our cultural surroundings and upbringing, something that until the twentieth century most people would have found obviously absurd. Long before genetics was understood, it was assumed that people had a 'nature', that this ran in families and was explained by something being 'in the blood'. 'She didn't lick it off a tree', as my relatives in Ireland would say.

A lot of this changing worldview was down to Sigmund Freud, who was one of the most influential thinkers of the century, but who believed some absolutely insane things, some of which have had terrible consequences. Because of Freudianism, for example, autism was until very recently treated in France as the result of 'refrigerator mothers', with children cruelly being sent away to institutions as a result.[11] Freud also thought asthma was caused by people witnessing their parents having sex as kids, and believed that erotic problems were linked to the nose; he had one of his patients undergo a botched cauterisation of the nose to cure her of hysteria. It just gave her nosebleeds.

As the philosopher Todd Dufresne wrote: 'Arguably no other notable figure in history was so fantastically wrong about nearly every important thing he had to say.'[12]

And yet in the twentieth century we came to believe all sorts of strange things about human nature, propagated through the university system just as surely as madrassas spread the word of the Prophet. This was partly influenced by the shock and shame that followed Nazi Germany, after which any talk of biological determinism gave people the heebie-jeebies, and the word 'eugenics' still elicits a strong and negative reaction. Quite understandably, and yet there were plenty of murderers who believed the opposite. Chairman Mao was probably the most enthusiastic believer in the power of nurture, writing that China's people were 'a blank sheet of paper free from any mark [on which] the freshest and most beautiful characters can be written, the freshest and most beautiful pictures can be painted'.[13]

But in the post-war world there developed a widespread acceptance that human character was caused by the environment and socialisation – one is not born a woman, one becomes one, as Simone de Beauvoir said. This quite obviously boosted the progressive worldview, which rests on the belief that human beings are malleable creatures and so, with enough money and effort, social injustices can be ended and equality achieved.

The popularity of this worldview may have had something to do with growing urbanisation, and an environment completely cut off from the natural world. People who live around animals probably have a more realistic grasp of human nature, because it's obvious that if you breed two intelligent animals, or two placid ones, their children will mostly share those characteristics, and it would be odd if the same wasn't true for people. Indeed, the vast area of twin studies has shown the variation in human intelligence to be around 50 per cent heritable, as are the five major personality traits. As for sex, there are vast amounts of evidence showing that average differences in temperament between men and women across cultures are the product of biology, something also obvious to people who live closer to animals. I'm not sure anyone who had to walk regularly through fields of cows, and avoid those with bulls, would swallow the idea that masculinity is 'performative' or that gender is not binary, although it would be interesting to take such a walk with a gender studies professor.

Urbanisation also leads to fewer children, which again makes this idea easier to believe, and indeed parents have an overall better estimate of human nature, while educated mothers with more than one child are 'particularly accurate in their estimates of the genetic contribution to these traits'.[14] Men with no children have the least accurate view. It is probably not coincidence that the first modern proponent of the blank slate, John Locke, was childless.[15]

The blank-slate model is not explicitly mentioned but its assumptions lie behind most mainstream political discourse. When, for example, quotas for women in politics are discussed on the radio it's taken as a starting premise that, given true equality of opportunity, most industries would move towards a fifty–fifty gender balance, because differences between men and women must be socially constructed.[16] This is certainly untrue, but anyone who said so on radio would be cast as wildly extreme, almost deranged.

It's partly that the Left's vision of human nature is also a better selling point, a more optimistic story. Steven Pinker famously observed in his book *The Blank Slate* that 'Sophisticated people sneer at feel-good comedies and saccharine romances in which all loose ends are tied and everyone lives happily ever after. Yet when it comes to the science of human beings, this same audience says: Give us schmaltz.' People want stories of individuals overcoming the odds, and hate discussing depressing, but more useful, overall patterns. It's uplifting, but then the converse is that people are also scared of voicing their opinions, because beneath the Left's narrative of liberation is a darker, more authoritarian undercurrent. If you read the conservative media you might better know it as Political Correctness Gone Mad.

12

PC GONE MAD

When I was around ten our class had a session on the school's state-of-the-art BBC Micros. It was rare we got to use computers those days. (This is one of those stories through which I explain to my kids about 1980s technology and how you couldn't just pause the television and I may as well be saying, 'Now, to take the ferry cost a nickel, and in those days, nickels had pictures of bumblebees on 'em . . . blah blah blah.')

We all had to choose a username by which the archaic personal computer would continue to address us in that Bold Sans font, so for example 'You scored x points, Congratulations xxx'. I decided on the username 'Spastic', which I thought hilarious. Our science teacher Mr Brown was less impressed when he saw this, and in a fury berated me in front of the whole class, raging that making fun of the disabled was against everything the school stood for, the Christian principles of compassion and love. That word should never be used, he said – NEVER – and if I ever whispered it in the playground he would hear it up on the third floor and I'd be in trouble. I tried to rescue my damaged ego by afterwards making fun of how ridiculous that claim was, but I felt humiliated. Rightfully, of course.

The 1980s were a cruel era in some ways. Kids called each other 'Spacker' or 'Joey', after Joey Deacon, the tragic cerebral palsy sufferer portrayed in a documentary at the time. Later in the decade there was a famous *QED* episode about a Scottish teenager with Tourette syndrome, 'John's Not Mad', which was met with great hilarity in playgrounds because he kept swearing over and over again. Years later, in my early twenties, I watched the follow-up and realised how terribly sad it was, and felt ashamed.

On one occasion our geography teacher, the fiercely passionate and inspiring Mr Davies, pointed at disabled access stickers on a school outing and explained how such things were unknown thirty years ago and how much better things had got. I suspect he was very Leftie, in a Catholic sort of way. (Aren't all geography teachers in particular very Left-wing?) Now my children are at the same age, it would be inconceivable for their contemporaries to laugh at the disabled in the same way, and they comfortably watch TV presenters with disabilities. This change in attitude has occurred in tandem with a change in the language, a move towards greater sensitivity often called 'political correctness'.

As a child I remember mentally linking the phrase with the *Daily Mail* in particular, and 'PC' soon attached itself to lots of semi-mythical tabloid stories such as 'the war on Christmas'. I think my earliest recollection of the concept was the political puppet show *Spitting Image*, which ran a sketch featuring a bunch of middle-aged Tory activists getting heated about some minor linguistic change and muttering 'it's political correctness gone mad' while clutching their pearls, working themselves into a tizzy until eventually exploding. Political correctness usually had the words 'gone mad' attached, although I never understood why tabloids used that phrase, since if you're conservative it's mad to start with; it's like saying 'communism gone mad'.

'Political correctness gone mad' stories usually involved some term being banned because it had the word 'black' or 'man' in it, like the one about 'Baa baa black sheep' being removed for being insufficiently racially sensitive. PC, from what I understood, was about some well-meaning changes made to the language so as not to offend anyone; it was undoubtedly silly, but the people who got riled by it were obviously numpties. Personally I have an extremely low embarrassment threshold, so that every social encounter is like an episode of the *Office* in my head. If there's only one black person in a situation and someone lacking in tact or social nous starts raising awkward racial subjects that might make them feel self-conscious, I have the urge to be swallowed by the ground. Trying to use delicate language is something I completely understand, as is anything to do with good manners.

Political correctness could be, therefore, part of what Norbert Elias called the 'civilising process'; at some point men stopped fighting duels, watching animals rip each other to pieces, or urinating in the fireplace, and as these changes took place there must have been people – people like me, I suppose – who wondered why do-gooders had to go around changing things. After all, I used to watch human sacrifice victims having their hearts ripped out to appease the sun god when I was a kid and it never did me any harm. Perhaps more compassionate language towards the less advantaged was just another stage of the process, widening the circle of empathy to make society more inclusive. Indeed PC could be called 'political politeness', since in the popular imagination it is associated with euphemisms about race, sexuality, disability or any other perceived disadvantage, and as a consequence 'politically incorrect' has come to mean the same as rudeness.

Except that wasn't really the purpose of political correctness in policing the language. The aim in many cases was not to pressure opponents into being polite, but to stop them expressing their ideas altogether. PC, for want of a better expression, describes a set of acceptable beliefs, outside of which it is not permitted to step. And yet by focusing on articles about 'follicly challenged' replacing 'bald', newspapers probably made it easier for PC's real purpose – of censoring and controlling – to go unchallenged.

At the time *The Authoritarian Personality* came out, warning of a fascist takeover, another author was trying to find a publisher for his book about Soviet communism. Such was the high esteem that Uncle Joe held in the Western mind, despite the murderous insanity of the 1930s, that George Orwell struggled to get *Animal Farm* published at all. Indeed, when his allegory for Soviet communism was finally brought out he included a preface attacking those who had rejected it, accusing them of censorship.

It turned out to be a bestseller, but Orwell's final work, *Nineteen Eighty-Four*, would be his prophetic masterpiece.

Orwell is today rather over-cited, often by people making hysterical comparisons about their local council. The more obviously totalitarian aspects of the book are continually evoked as technology has made Orwell's world seem more real, although the counter-argument is that intrusive technology is now in the hands of private individuals and companies, not just the authorities (although China is increasingly looking actually Orwellian). But Orwell also came accurately to foresee the authoritarian confinement of beliefs and ideas behind political correctness, among them the branding of dissident thinkers as having *thoughtcrime*, attempts to change the language to change politics – *Newspeak* – and *crimestop*, the process of deliberately not thinking in the direction of anything that might lead to thoughtcrime, to build a wall of protective ignorance. The system wins in Orwell's world when opponents are forced to make statements that are plainly untrue, and precisely because they are untrue.

Theodore Dalrymple once recalled that

> the purpose of communist propaganda was not to persuade or convince, not to inform, but to humiliate; and therefore, the less it corresponded to reality the better. When people are forced to remain silent when they are being told the most obvious lies, or even worse when they are forced to repeat the lies themselves, they lose once and for all their sense of probity ... A society of emasculated liars is easy to control. I think if you examine political correctness, it has the same effect and is intended to.[1]

One characteristic of Soviet politics was the exclusion of bad-thinkers, it being a country where only ideologically correct views were permitted in academia, even when this led to the promotion of pseudoscience. The most notorious example was the biologist Trofim Lysenko who led the persecution of Mendelian geneticists, whose ideas offended the Marxist worldview in which humans could be perfected by their environment.

Communists were very good at destroying their enemies, not just by locking them up in Gulags – although that obviously helped – but by destroying their reputation, too. They were masters at popularising new terms to put their opponents beyond the pale in politics. 'From the beginning . . . labels were required that would stigmatize the enemy within and justify his expulsion: he was a revisionist, a deviationist, an infantile leftist, a utopian socialist, a social fascist and so on.'[2] This was a tactic that came to be used with increasing frequency among Western radicals in the 1960s, and the first signs of recognisably 'political' correctness could be seen then in communist student organisations on US campuses. PC was, in Dalrymple's words, 'Communist propaganda writ small'.

But political correctness also has a religious element to it, the focus being on protecting sacred groups, and is obviously influenced by US Protestantism. PC comes from a moralistic, sectarian tradition of American religious thinking applied to the Left-wing battles of the twentieth century. Seymour Martin Lipset explained in *American Exceptionalism* that 'private higher education largely began in church-affiliated schools. Most of these insisted that their faculty be denominationally correct' and 'Faculty who deviated from religious doctrine could be forced out. When particular institutions changed, and became less orthodox, the churches' right wings set up new schools.'[3] Harvard had begun as a Congregationalist (Puritan) college, but when it had moved away from doctrinal purity Yale was set up to offer religiously correct education; Brown University was Baptist, William and Mary was Episcopalian, as was Columbia, while Princeton was founded by Presbyterians. In England both Oxford and Cambridge were affiliated to the Church of England and no non-Anglicans could graduate anywhere until the establishment of University College London, in 1826.

After the Second World War, however, this sort of religious mindset became far more radical, and heavily influenced by Soviet politics, the USSR having won a great moral victory in the war in the eyes of American intellectuals. They also began imitating Soviet political tactics, especially the exclusion and persecution of bad-thinkers. As Lipset wrote: 'This moralistic stance led them to try to prevent supporters of the [Vietnam] war from speaking on campuses, to end all forms of collaboration by universities with the warmaking government, and to politicize discipline organisations like the Modern Language Association and the American Sociological Association.'

Despite the fact that McCarthyism is etched into the memory, Lipset pointed out that in the 1950s, at the height of the 'witch hunt', conservatives were still more likely to be ostracised on American campuses than Trotskyites. In 1956, twenty-six-year-old Yale student Tom Wolfe wrote a letter to a friend lamenting that an essay of his had been denounced as 'reactionary', and 'which means I must go through with a blue pencil and strike out all the laughs and anti-Red passages and slip in a little liberal merde, so to speak, just to sweeten it'.[4] He reflected, also, on how academics saw how Left-wing they could be as a status game, an idea Wolfe would return to in his writings.

In the 1960s many academic organisations became more politicised, and major scholars lost out on honours and prizes because of their conservatism. Some academics had horrible experiences with radical Leftists on campus and were disgusted by the fanaticism of the New Left, as the intellectuals of the 1960s were termed.

Protests against dissenting academics became far more organised – and intimidating. Many of these controversies were over the issue of human nature, since radicals opposed any biological explanations for social conditions, which was tantamount to justifying them. Psychologist Paul Ekman provoked huge hostility and protest when he suggested that facial expressions were universal and so most likely genetic. Anthropologist Alan Lomax denounced Ekman at an American Anthropological Association meeting and said he shouldn't be allowed to speak because his ideas were fascist. Harvard's Richard Herrnstein was called a racist for arguing, in 1971, that, because intelligence is partly inherited, then the tendency of clever people to marry other clever people will lead to stratification.[5] He wasn't even talking about race, but he received death threats and his lecture halls were filled with chanting mobs. Herrnstein and another academic, Arthur Jensen, were forced not just to cancel lectures but also to hire guards, because of their IQ research.

Then there was E. O. Wilson, whose *Sociobiology* concluded that some universal human attributes, including our moral sense, may be shaped by natural selection. The aim of the book was to explain human behaviour such as violence and altruism through evolution, yet a widely circulated article by a group of academics accused him of promoting theories that 'led to the establishment of gas chambers in Nazi Germany'.[6] Wilson 'became a target of vilification and harassment',[7] but unfortunately intimidation does work, and other academics and institutions were deterred from exploring similar questions.

Napoleon Chagnon was another victim. A renowned anthropologist who spent years studying the Yanomamö, a tribe in the Amazon rainforest, his 1968 book on the subject had sold a million copies. Yet many anthropologists were upset by his claim that the tribe's behaviour was partly explained by evolution, and for the less than Rousseauian way he portrayed them (the book was called *The Fierce People*). The world he wrote about featured men fighting each other over women, violence in the home, drug use and a lack of care for the environment, the complete opposite of what I was still being taught in the 1980s.[8] Chagnon was accused of fabricating his data and, worse still, stirring up inter-tribal violence himself and even deliberately spreading measles; the campaign hugely damaged his career.

By the early 1980s British biologist William Hamilton wrote in his diaries of a wish to return home because the academic atmosphere in the US was becoming stifling due to the self-appointed ideology enforcers. Since then countless others have lost jobs or livelihoods, or otherwise suffered harassment or threats, not because they had used offensive words, but because they had made arguments people found offensive.[9]

The student protestors of the late 1960s always had an authoritarian streak, often quite deliberately and consciously illiberal, and went against long-established liberal ideas of what the university meant. Herrnstein's thesis that meritocracy leads to IQ stratification can be either correct or incorrect, but whether it strikes people as morally wrong should not prevent its author being able peacefully to make his case. Charles Darwin might have struggled to find a publisher in the late twentieth century because his views would be politically incorrect; whether the great Huxley–Wilberforce debate would have been allowed on modern campuses is an interesting hypothetical. Many liberals have always vehemently opposed such intellectual straitjacketing, and indeed 'political correctness' was originally a pejorative and satirical term used by people on the Left 'as a guard against their own orthodoxy in social change efforts', in academic Debra Schultz's words.[10]

Although American politics became less radical in the 1970s and 1980s, with election victories for Richard Nixon and Ronald Reagan, academia became more so, especially when the students of 1968 returned as professors; and this radicalism fanned out into the wider culture of media and politics.

One interpretation of PC is that it is the 'paradox of tolerance', promoting tolerance of historically disadvantaged or persecuted groups to such an extreme that it becomes itself another form of intolerance.[11] The Left would argue that PC is used to fight injustices or hate speech, although what defines hate speech is the big question. Of course, whoever is in control tends to censor what their opponents do; in my glorious pre-1968 golden age theatre was still censored and comedians were prohibited from mocking politicians on television. Some comparisons are made between the PC enforcers and McCarthyites but it's worth bearing in mind that people were actually jailed by the latter.

Yet today the boot is clearly on the other foot and almost no one is going to get in trouble for saying something that upsets the Right, which at least suggests something about who has hegemony. No Left-wing journalist or academic or comedian is going to lose their livelihood, be barred from the

BBC or banned from speaking on campus, however extreme or bad taste a belief or joke. The Right flank of what is acceptable speech is far more strictly monitored and punished, and because of this the point at which acceptable speech ends tends to shift over time.

Political correctness is not about politeness, although that might be an instinct for some people who adapt their language. The motivation of radical social-science undergraduates storming debates and harassing professors accused of thought crimes was to crush dissent. They did so because they believed the political ideas of their opponents are dangerous or evil, and because it's fun to crush dissent.

And yet in the popular imagination people came to associate PC with euphemisms about race, sexuality, disability or any other real or perceived disadvantage, and as a consequence they began to see being 'politically incorrect' as the same as rudeness. By that definition, comedians who make outrageous jokes about the disabled or women are being 'un-PC': but actually, they're just being rude or tasteless, which is a different thing altogether. Likewise making jokes about Pakistanis or gay people doesn't make you 'politically incorrect', it just makes you an arsehole. (The joke could still be funny, but that's another point.) What does make you politically incorrect is asking uncomfortable questions that risk your career.

Most of all PC is about control; accepting opposing views and the marketplace of ideas is not natural to our species, and in only a small number of societies have people over many centuries of violence been able to reach a political settlement where this is done. Much more instinctive is the urge to control and repress, desires that are strongest in the young, who are the least tolerant and accepting of nuance and therefore the most attracted to authoritarian ideologies. In fact, part of the attraction of being a young politically correct activist is that you get to be the orthodoxy police and 'call out' people who are ideologically impure.

So when politically correct activists change the language, it's not mostly for the sake of kindness but to ruin their opponents. Political correctness is about controlling dialogue, and so altering the meaning of words so that it becomes harder to articulate particular viewpoints; and without anyone being able to do so, a political viewpoint becomes unorthodox, controversial, offensive and even illegal. If you cannot articulate ideas because the language has made them appear extreme or dangerous, then those ideas cannot be justified or given due weight in the political arena. One of the arguments made by supporters of political correctness is that the 'transformational nature of language' has the power to change beliefs and shape our world, and they are certainly right. So one way a political group can come to dominate the culture is by dominating the language, creating neologisms that imply acceptance of their worldview and making other terms unfashionable or unsayable. By forcing upon the English language novelties, with new implications and subtleties, progressives force English speakers to accept their beliefs or expose themselves as bad-thinkers. If I use a non-PC term I'll spend the rest of the day getting angry, abusive messages on the internet; if I just accept the politicised new term my life will be easier. In nature a mutation that carries only a 0.1 per cent reproductive advantage will soon become dominant in any population, and so with language.

Words can be ideologically neutral or partisan, so that two terms can convey the same essential meaning but with different political implications. Many academic subjects use highly politicised language, so in sociology

> terms used to describe features of society that liberals tend to oppose, but which conservatives might support, typically have negative connotations. Sociologists speak of constraints, as though people were physically fenced in; they speak of social controls, as though some entity manipulated people; and they speak of social structure, as though people could be located inside a physical edifice . . . What if we described society as comprehensible (constrained) rather than overwhelming (unconstrained), as shaped (structured) rather than formless (unstructured), as predictable (with social control) rather than volatile (without social control), and as ordered (hierarchical) rather than anarchic (equal)?[12]

A conservative friend in social work once described to me how everything in his workplace is so heavily expressed in the language of the Left that after a while it became almost impossible even to articulate the problems he saw in people's lives without using progressive language and therefore accepting progressive beliefs.

It's impossible to discuss this subject without sounding like one of those old people who used to write to the *Daily Telegraph* complaining that the word 'gay' had been hijacked by homosexuals. But many terms have come to change either their meaning or their tone. 'Elitism', once a good thing, now usually implies discrimination by the wealthy, privileged and unfairly advantaged. It makes you think of the Bullingdon Club or Draco Malfoy or whatever, and journalists even go on about elitism when politics is full of Oxbridge graduates, even though Oxford and Cambridge are literally the best universities in Britain. After all, we generally like the best people to be in charge of most things; we'd prefer if the guy flying our plane had gone to whatever is the flight-school equivalent of Oxbridge.

'Controversial' used to be a good thing, at least in art. Now it's a pejorative term in politics to mean 'beyond the pale' or 'thing we think is bad and you shouldn't support'. In theatre it's still occasionally used but nothing in theatre is actually that controversial. 'Diversity' has come to mean almost the opposite of what it once did, its former definition roughly being 'inequality', that is the variation between people in terms of ability, intellect and other qualities. 'Discriminate' was once simply about observing difference, and being able to choose between two options and calling someone 'a woman of discrimination' was praise. It obviously now means something entirely negative, a change that has had quite major consequences, making it harder to argue against greater government control of our lives.

Perhaps more importantly than the language, the rise of political correctness coincided with a wider problem to do with radicalism; in philosophy there is the 'principle of charity', an old rule that means interpreting other people's statements in the most reasonable and inoffensive way, and not to make second guesses about people's real intentions.

Christian-run colleges have often made this an important starting point because it makes the smooth running of society much easier and without it debating turns poisonous. In contrast, PC is the 'principle of injury', a key theme being to interpret conservative opponents' views in the worst possible light, and to look for ulterior motives.

When the aim of political debate is to detect bad-thinkers, people whose views make them morally deviant, then inevitably people interpret statements in the worst possible way, which is especially uncharitable when the person making it might be older and lacking the same generational sensitivity. It encourages bad-faith arguments, the idea that while someone is arguing for X, their real intention is to encourage the far more extreme and sinister Y. Another is the common employment of guilt by association – never mind what someone is proposing, look at who supports them. Similarly, one of the common tactics of online debate is the lumping together of hugely different individuals, so that someone will say, 'I can't believe you're allowing people such as Steven Bannon and Jordan Peterson', or 'Charles Murray and Milo Yiannopoulos', conservatives with very different politics, very different styles, manners and approaches to political opponents, the obvious intention being that the audience will associate the less offensive one with the more.

This change of attitude, and the growing conviction that conservatives had base hidden motives, would have a huge, poisonous impact on political culture as time went on.

13

'I WANT TO SEE HOW A CULTURE WAR
IS FOUGHT, SO BADLY'[1]

I suppose the great era of ideological conflict ended in August 1991 when a heavily inebriated Boris Yeltsin stood on top of a tank in front of Moscow's White House and brought a surprisingly speedy end to the Soviet Union. Communism's fall came after a decade of Reaganomics and Thatcherism, and soon Labour would vote away Clause 4, seeming to turn its back on socialism. With Bill Clinton increasing economic deregulation, it seemed that the Right had won all the economic arguments, which was epitomised to some Labour people by cabinet minister Peter Mandelson's suggestion that they were 'intensely relaxed about people getting filthy rich' (as long as they paid their taxes). So it's easy to see that from a socialist economic point of view the 1990s were a terrible failure and the Right was triumphant. Yet, on social issues, the story was very different, and New Labour's 1997 landslide was more than just a political victory; it was the culmination of an overwhelming cultural victory over what Blair would later call the 'forces of conservatism'.

The late 1960s was a period of overt radicalism but it ended up backfiring in many ways, the violence of student protestors alienating most Americans and Nixon winning a landslide in 1968, then followed by Reagan twelve years later. Meanwhile, the explosion in crime also led to 'liberal' being permanently tarnished in many people's eyes, with New York going from the glamorous city of *Breakfast at Tiffany's* to the crime-ridden hellhole of

Death Wish. Violence tends to push people to the Right, especially if Left-wing radicals are committing it, and over 1969 and 1970 they were responsible for 370 bombings just in New York City and over the next two years 'at least 2,500 bombs blew up across the country'.[2] For the first time, the Republicans started talking about 'coastal elites', with Nixon's vice president, Spiro Agnew, calling the media 'effete snobs' and 'nattering nabobs of negativism'.

But when the students of 1968 came to power in the 1990s, they were much more successful at winning the culture war through peaceful means than some of their contemporaries had tried to do by shock and awe in their youth. The year after the Soviet Union fell saw the election of centrist Bill Clinton while in Britain the Tories became wildly unpopular following Black Wednesday, a state they would never really escape. Clinton and Blair both pretty much abandoned any socialist principles their parties once held, but in return for this they won the cultural sphere. The one exception to this was the issue of crime, which had now spiralled so out of control that even liberal New Yorkers were prepared to elect a Republican; under Clinton the number of people in jail increased to 1.3 million, his 1994 Violent Crime Control Act being especially tough.[3]

During this period great strides were made in academia and the arts, as well as public opinion, all of which became far more progressive over the decade; universities saw campaigns such as the 'Canon Wars' to remove 'dead white males' from reading lists and replace them with women and minorities. The was the start of 'the culture war', a term first used in the modern sense in 1991 by University of Virginia academic James Davison Hunter in a book of the same name, but hugely popularised the following year after Pat Buchanan's run for US president. His 'culture wars speech', as it was termed, was a sort of last hurrah for a particular vision of America.

'There is a religious war going on in our country for the soul of America,' the presidential candidate said: 'It is a cultural war.' And it has gone not entirely to our advantage, for Buchanan's vision of his country – Christian, European, conservative and basically 1950s-like – has not just been defeated as an idea but made completely unacceptable, beyond the realms of decency. Benjamin Disraeli once said of protectionism that it was 'not only dead but damned' after the great nineteenth-century Corn Law dispute was finally resolved, and the same could be said of many conservative ideas by the 1990s; conservatives were not only losing, but holding these ideas put you beyond the norms of society. It made you a bad person.

After Buchanan's famous address journalist Molly Ivins made the cutting remark that it sounded better in the original German; it was a brilliant put-down making a rather unfair point in a memorable and clever way – if you're a conservative in the Buchanan mould you're basically a Nazi. And, generally speaking, people don't want to be compared to Nazis, who even the most ardent Right-winger will admit rather overstepped some moral boundaries.

During the Clinton era liberal values continued to gain strength in the US, while there was simultaneously 'the backlash', the radicalisation of some Republicans on moral issues, particularly abortion and evolution. In Thomas Frank's words, 'Unlike Ronald Reagan, they became absolutists on tax cuts, gun control, and abortion, and purged from their ranks any who dared dissent.'[4] Yet issues such as anti-abortion and even the anti-evolution movement gained strength just as, or perhaps because, popular culture and wider social attitudes on both sides of the Atlantic were becoming far more liberal, irreligious and sexualised. Someone once said that 'conservatives start culture wars and liberals win them'. I don't know about that; maybe conservatives start useless offensives away from their strong points, but it seems a bit like saying 'Catholics start Reformations and Protestants win them'.

The 1990s saw a change in values because baby boomers brought their cultural traits with them; the original 'teenagers' were now in power, the first politicians to have played in rock bands, experimented with drugs and taken the pill. They were also the first generation with that baby-boomer self-obsession, which fed the new politics, especially the therapy talk Bill Clinton used whenever he was caught knobbing some woman. Clinton, having defeated the old-style WASP grandee George Bush Sr, represented a new emotional culture, crying in public and using the language of self-discovery rather than stoicism, which seemed like a suspiciously convenient way to defend his obviously predatory attitude to women. (As the *Onion*'s 1999 book *Our Dumb Century* put it, 'New president feels the nation's pain, breasts'.) The idea that a politician caught doing something naughty might resign and quietly spend the rest of their lives helping a charity for homeless people, like poor John Profumo, was obviously alien to this insufferably narcissistic generation.

The 1990s radicals were also far more effective at getting their way by co-opting big business, and big business, once socialism was out of the way, found that they could love radicalism after all. And so in cultural terms America and Britain went heavily Left during the decade, with huge sea-changes in attitudes to issues such as immigration, diversity and gay rights.

In Britain there wasn't really a culture war as such, unless by war you mean one of those nineteenth-century colonial skirmishes where one of our dreadnoughts turned up at an African palace defended by guards with curly swords. It was far more seamless, accelerating from 1997 with Tony Blair, the first prime minister to have played the guitar in a band; he called himself 'a modern man from the rock and roll generation', sometimes wore a shirt without a tie and claimed to like football, which had now become fashionable among the middle classes following Italia '90 and *Fever Pitch*.

New Labour came to power soon after Britpop was at its peak and London's media was going through an orgy of coke-fuelled self-indulgence called 'Cool Britannia'. It began with the much-hyped rivalry between Oasis and Blur over the hot summer of 1995, followed by the arrival of the Spice Girls and then Euro '96. In November 1996 *Newsweek* had on its front cover the headline 'London Rules: inside the world's coolest city'. England indeed seemed to be cool again, or at least London and Manchester did, and Blair somehow managed to have himself inserted into the zeitgeist, which is not something that could ever be said of a Conservative politician.

Many people genuinely believed the election of New Labour would be Year Zero and everything would change for the better, and even at the time I felt baffled and alienated by such optimism. Everyone seemed to have great hope in this new man who would make Britain more modern and tolerant; everyone except the miserable readers of the *Mail*, *Express* and *Telegraph*, for whom everything in politics was a series of disasters. While Blair shone, we appeared like the brooding, bull-faced Afrikaans watching the smiling black people's dignified walk to the polling booth, cast as baddies in a morality play in which we would obviously end up the losers. Later, the same people who thought Blair would have a transformative effect on the country came to hate him with a passion, something I also found completely weird. He did a few things with which I disagreed, but in retrospect Labour did some good things, too; the endless spin probably increased cynicism about politics but that was how they had to win after four straight defeats and press hostility.

I was one of few nineteen-year-olds who voted Conservative (although 27 per cent of young people did vote Tory that year, and they would kill for those figures now). Everyone else I know either voted Labour, didn't vote at all, or just put their x by the silliest-sounding party for the LOLs. (Predictably, I think the voting age should be twenty-one, except for Our Boys in uniform, obviously; since you wouldn't allow an eighteen-year-old to take out a mortgage, why would you allow them to decide the fate of the country?)

My candidate was the insanely Right-wing Alan Clark, a historian who lived in a castle in Kent, who was also a notorious womaniser and rogue; he had once had an affair with the wife of a judge and also slept with *both* their daughters, and even his own wife referred to him as a 'shit'. In an age when people use all sorts of euphemisms to downplay how Right-wing they are, Clark described himself as a 'Nazi', although as with many reactionaries no one was really sure if it was a joke, or a joke masking deadly seriousness.[5] He did name his pet Rottweiler after Eva Braun, though, which I suppose the 'PC brigade' would get on their high horses about today. Clark had on various occasions raised eyebrows due to his somewhat controversial opinions, including his view that peace could be brought to Northern Ireland by simply shooting six hundred people. On another occasion, after the 1998 World Cup, when loads of England fans had fought running battles with Arabs in Marseilles, Clark spoke out in their defence on the grounds that they were just brave Englishmen continuing our military traditions. But he was a shoo-in for the super-wealthy constituency of Kensington and Chelsea – a seat the Tories could not possibly lose – winning over half the vote.

I didn't feel particularly bad about the Tories going. I was rather sick of the same old faces, and even though I supported them, I never felt that sense of familial, tribal loyalty Labour people have towards their party. The next day Blair turned up in Downing Street, surrounded by adoring members of the public who – surprise, surprise – turned out to be stage-managed supporters. It was completely disingenuous, just like so much of what New Labour did. The whole thing was so obviously going to end in bitterness and disappointment, because the Left always place too much hope in leaders in the mistaken belief that their goals are achievable. The only liberals who don't disappoint are those who get killed, and imagine how hated JFK would have been in 1969 after a second term where they were still stuck in Vietnam and the country had endured race riots and various other horrors. I know it makes me sound awful but I was absolutely terrified Obama would be killed by a white supremacist because the media would have just been insufferable, and I'd have had to go and live on a remote Scottish island forever to escape the gazillion films, books and newspaper comment pieces about it.

Soon enough the new rulers proved themselves to be just as arrogant as the last, and there was something about the new elite that really grated. In *The Leopard*, Giuseppe Tomasi di Lampedusa's pessimistic Catholic novel about the fading aristocracy of Sicily, the protagonist comments cynically that if his class were to vanish, 'an equivalent one would be formed straight away with the same qualities and the same defects; it might not be based on blood any more, but possibly on . . . on, say, length of time in a place, or pretended knowledge of some text presumed sacred.'[6]

Or as the Who put it: 'meet the new boss, same as the old boss'.[7]

In fact, the new bosses had far more arrogance, because they saw themselves as products of merit, more deserving than the lords they disenfranchised or the aristocratic Tories they had kicked out. This was epitomised by Lord Derry — one of countless lawyers in the new administration — who had his official residence redecorated at the cost of £650,000, almost a tenth of that being spent just on wallpaper, then rather put his foot in it by saying he couldn't just get something from B&Q.

Blair wanted to get rid of the archaic position of lord chancellor, although like with full reform of the House of Lords, the complications got the better of him. The English constitution is intrinsically conservative because, unlike almost any other political system, it's a mess and a jumble, the product of centuries of precedent. There's no central planning involved, and the utilitarian tradition, of which New Labour was certainly part, loves planning. As Michael Oakeshott put it, the genius of the utilitarian 'is a genius for rationalization, for making life and the business of life rational rather than for seeing the reason for it, for inculcating precise order, no matter at what expense, rather than for apprehending the existence of a subtle order in what appears to be chaotic'.[8] They hadn't thought through the actual mechanics of change, they just wanted something 'modern', one of the many buzzwords Blair liked to throw around. New Labour loved change, almost for its own sake, something horrific to conservatives, who see civilisation as being held together by what Burke called the 'crust' of prejudice. If people just changed things whenever they felt like it, then people would have no link with the past and so 'men would become no better than the flies of a summer'.

The prime minister spoke of Labour being the 'political wing of the British people', which sounded pretty demented, but they were unassailable. At the 1999 party conference Blair spoke of 'Today's Tory party — the party of fox hunting, Pinochet and hereditary peers: the uneatable, the unspeakable and the unelectable.' Faced against Peter Mandelson and Alistair Campbell's PR machine the Tories seemed hopeless, like cavalry charges against Panzer divisions, old, grey-haired men facing the youthful Blair and his sharp-suited managerial sidekicks. The Tory vision of the country just seemed laughably outdated and low-status, because New Labour represented not just a political but also a big emotional–cultural change too – they had hegemony. Looking back, some of the restrictions still in place when Blair took charge seem incredibly archaic. Hardcore pornography was still illegal; the age of consent for gay men was twenty-one; treason was still a capital offence, at least technically. Things changed a lot in that decade.

I suppose my childhood ended in August 1997 when we emptied our childhood home, going through shelves and shelves of books. There must have been thousands in the flat, including at least a dozen doubles, and such was the genius of my parents' categorising system that they had *four* copies of at least three different books. (One of those was in French, the sort of detail best left out if I was ever to stand for public office and pretend to understand 'real people'.) My brother and I had both left for university and Dad had endured enough of London, having suffered a stroke the previous year, and so they sold up. We spent that weekend packing away everything from our childhood, which is always sad, and as we did so the radio served as the melancholy background soundtrack, with non-stop coverage of the death of Princess Diana. Mainly, to be fair, non-stop drivel.

It was obviously tragic and I felt sorry for her sons, but the reaction from the drooling imbeciles who took over the country that week was bizarre. It was how I imagined things would be if a hostile intelligence agency had poisoned the water supply with acid or ketamine. We were only a mile from Kensington Palace and on the Sunday, just hours after Diana's death, Mum and I strolled down to watch the crowds, dozens of people already, most in tears. Soon those dozens would be hundreds and then thousands, growing angry that the royal family weren't sharing in their grief at the death of a woman they had never even met. I seem to remember one moron punching some poor Slovakian tourist who had dared to take one of the People's Teddy Bears left by the palace gates.

The death and the insanity that followed signified to some conservatives how our culture had changed, and for the worse. Mum was now at the *Daily Express* and her colleague Peter Hitchens made it the starting point of his book *The Abolition of Britain* (a seminal work, and of course totally normal reading material for someone aged twenty-one). He compared and contrasted the funeral of Winston Churchill in 1965, dignified and stoical, with the days following Diana's death when a bunch of gibbering, hysterical nincompoops bullied the Queen into grieving publicly, with Blair in the thick of it.

Politics is not unconnected to emotional temperament, and if you're conservative then by nature you're much more likely to favour emotional repression. 'Need for effect' is the term used to describe our tendency to approach or avoid emotion-inducing situations, and one theory is that liberals behave more emotionally because they score considerably higher on this need for effect.[9]

I'm emotionally quite restrained, although I suppose 'emotionally crippled' might be slightly more accurate, which I got from Dad. He would get annoyed if people showed emotions at funerals; too much wailing and he'd mutter that people 'were making a scene'. He actually said that once. Dad had been sent to boarding school at the age of seven and three years later to Canada, part of a government scheme to move British children abroad to escape the expected Nazi invasion. The boat directly behind them in the convoy was sunk, killing seventy-seven children. At the time, personal suffering was so ubiquitous that if people started blubbing about everything that went wrong it would become unbearable for everyone.

Now the culture of therapy had become so all-encompassing that people were expected to talk about themselves and express their feelings, all of which was obviously a reaction to previous norms. Yet this didn't suit everyone, and I was very much with Tony Soprano in wishing that people would just bottle it up a bit and be more like Gary Cooper, the strong silent type. Years later, I found *The Crown* deeply saddening because I couldn't help lamenting the era it portrayed, for all its faults and drabness. The sense of putting duty over personal happiness seems to jar with our modern notions of choice and individual fulfilment, yet I think I'd rather be in that world (obviously living in a palace would be a plus). Why can't we just go back to the days of *Brief Encounter* when everyone was reticent and chose to stay in their passionless marriages to asexual Englishmen, or *A Night to Remember*, where just because you're on the sinking *Titanic* and are going to drown that's no excuse to start embarrassing everyone around you with emotions?

There is something appealing about repression. Dorothy Sayers, in writing about the medieval poem *The Song of Roland*, observed that 'The idea that a strong man should react to great personal and national calamities by a slight compression of the lips and by silently throwing his cigarette in the fireplace is of very recent origin.'[10] Men in the Middle Ages were impulsive and almost childlike in their behaviour; when something went badly, they cried; when someone made them upset, they stabbed them. Rather than being modern-looking by putting behind us that Victorian stuffiness, we were returning to an older ideal of emotional incontinence. It did not seem a coincidence that this emotional change took place while violent crime was reaching a peak, with violence that often seemed to be over the most childish of causes (one, I seemed to remember, started over a water-pistol fight which escalated into actual pistols). Rather than these kids growing up too soon, they weren't growing up fast enough, never learning the concept of deferred gratification or self-control.

People who favour visible displays of emotion forget that some people find it uncomfortable, even threatening. The *Telegraph*'s Mark Steyn – at the time King of the Jungle of Right-wing columnists – observed that there was something menacing in this very new British sort of public display of emotion. Indeed, the new therapeutic culture seemed to be most embraced by the most violent, something chronicled in Theodore Dalrymple's prison diaries in the *Spectator*, the hilarious weekly litany of *Untermensch* scum; men who justified their appalling actions using the cant and pretend remorse of the therapy industry, blaming everyone but themselves and wallowing in self-pity. Indeed, this was the premise behind *The Sopranos*, the best television show of this period – perhaps of all time – in which the mobster Tony explores his feelings of unease and guilt in therapy. Eventually, however, we realise that he has not 'grown' as a person, and is indeed just a selfish sociopath who uses therapy to justify his own grotesque behaviour. Therapy isn't going to make him a better human being, it's just another form of manipulation. We believed him for so long because we wanted to be tricked.

New Labour's social liberalism went hand in hand with a weirdly authoritarian streak. They introduced anti-social behaviour orders, or ASBOs, meaning that people could go to jail for walking in a particular area or playing loud music, things that were in themselves not a crime. The number of people in jail increased, from just over sixty thousand when Blair took over to more than eighty thousand when the Tories returned. The Labour government created three thousand new offences, many completely pointless or overlapping, signalling how tough they were on crime. Edmund Burke believed that the root of social evil 'lay in the meddling instinct',[11] and New Labour *loved* to meddle. Indeed, the most terrifying phrase you hear from people on the Left is not 'I'm from the government and I'm here to help', as Reagan said, but 'there is still much work to be done'. Meanwhile, actual crime went up after a decline under the Tory Home Secretary Michael Howard, with homicide peaking in 2002.[12] A lot of this crime involved urban gangs shooting at each other, around the corner from streets which were becoming the most expensive in the world but where people learned to zone out what was happening nearby.

Much of the difference between the liberal and conservative worldview comes down to our preference for the city v. the countryside. Cities attract certain types of people but they also affect our behaviour; those living in dense environments are on average more creative, more sexually promiscuous, more likely to be mentally unstable, and also more extremely different to the people around them. London has long been like this but these vast disparities, of wealth, background and behaviour, became more extreme under Labour, not least because Blair hugely increased immigration and actively liked the idea of cultural diversity. Most of my contemporaries found it exciting and liberating, while I just thought we were going to end up like Brazil, a *Blade Runner*-like dystopia with walls separating luxury villas from hellish slums.

Because the City money flowed in, Labour could avoid reforming the benefit system and push more people into low-paid jobs, which instead went to less troublesome and keener migrants. It was certainly the easier thing to do; welfare fraud in the greater scheme of things accounts for only a small total, and a wealthy country can easily handle it. For Conservatives it's more the principle that people should work rather than have something for free, for their own sake as well as general societal fairness, even if small-c conservatives accept that society isn't fair.

The old idea that Puritans are people who can't stand the thought of someone having fun is not quite true; conservatives don't like the idea of having to pay for someone else's fun. In *The Selfish Gene*, Richard Dawkins wrote about how birds would pick lice out of each other's hair, a reciprocal system that depended on everyone making the effort to do so. Unfortunately, some couldn't be bothered and never returned the favour – 'cheats', he called them. Of the others, some would always reciprocate even to cheats – 'suckers' – while others would return the favour but not to cheats – 'grudgers'. The relative size of the three population types would go through an endless cycle where cheats would grow at the expense of suckers, until the sucker population fell so much that the cheats would start to die out, until domination by the grudgers would allow the suckers to grow; and so the cycle would begin again. I remember reading that book when I was about fourteen and understanding I was one of nature's grudgers; I'm happy to contribute and help, but I hate the thought of helping freeloaders, which reflects an essentially mean-spirited, begrudging nature.

That characterises many conservatives, which is their problem with the welfare state, a system set up by suckers which by nature will benefit cheats;

I suppose liberals would say that's a small price to pay to help the needy. Conservatives don't like the idea they're being taken for a ride, forced to pay for other people's fun and the consequences. It's why the growing number of single mums, or welfare queens as Americans called them, really angered people in the way that the reckless rich getting away with their behaviour didn't. We're not paying for the rich's mistakes – well, we weren't then at least.

Yet there also seemed to be a growing sense that the privileged felt no obligation to use their wealth to help others; tax avoidance by the rich dwarfed benefit fraud by the poor, and still does, but tax avoiders were still knighted and feted. British society had come to worship conspicuous wealth, and the fashion trends of the late 1990s and 2000s were all about bling, gold and champagne. The behaviour of Premiership footballers, now paid a fortune, was especially galling, while the wealth-worshipping genre hip-hop became the most dominant musical genre; nine hip-hop albums went platinum in 1992; in 1998 it was thirty.[13] Labour ministers did not seem exactly to shy away from the company of rich men, who were no longer class enemies but almost heroes. But I suppose it didn't matter that there was a serious social malaise underneath and several million people festered in unemployment or disguised unemployment, so long as the Treasury was paying for the increased spending in public services, and the City money flowed in.

Sex People

In my childhood mind the world had almost literally come to colour in the 1960s, before which no one really had any fun, or swore, or had sex. The past was represented by Mary Whitehouse, the elderly housewife from Wolverhampton who had become Britain's most famous killjoy with her continuous letters to the BBC's permissive liberal director-general, Hugh Greene. For young men she personified the scolding great-aunt who wouldn't let you do anything fun. She stood for all the old people who ensured that even the slightest rude word on TV had to be bleeped out.

While Whitehouse came from a lower-middle-class background and had a funny West Midlands accent, her nemesis Sir Hugh Carleton Greene – brother of novelist Graham – had gone to private school and Oxford (obviously), and epitomised the new ruling class of the 1960s who wanted liberation from the stuffiness of the past, to be able to poke fun at the powerful and make light of things. Greene became director-general in 1960 and three years later Britain apparently stumbled on sex. That year the Beatles released their first LP while the woolly liberal Bishop of Woolwich John Robinson published *Honest to God*, a criticism of organised religion and its attitudes to sex in which he stated that 'nothing can of itself always be labelled as "wrong" . . . the only intrinsic evil is lack of love'.[14]

There was also the Profumo affair and the *Lady Chatterley's Lover* obscenity case, the most famous moment being when the prosecutor asked whether members of the jury would be comfortable with their servants reading the book. How laughably out of touch they seemed. After the trial Bishop Robinson argued that 'what Lawrence is trying to do is to portray the sex relationship as something essentially sacred . . . in a real sense an act of holy communion'.[15] And so was born that staple of liberal-Left Britain, the infuriating *Thought for the Day* slot in which wet religious types express the most inoffensively progressive views imaginable in a desperate attempt to seem relevant to a Godless society, and for an institution they must realise utterly despises them. (I'm not a huge fan, you might have guessed.)

What followed with Harold Wilson's 1964 election victory was the 'permissive society', a term originally used as a criticism. Homosexual acts were legalised in 1966, abortion the following year, theatre censorship was abandoned and divorce liberalised in 1969. Labour had become the party of social liberalism, and although little commented upon, it was at this point that the huge class divisions in British politics began to decline. It was a sign of things to come.

'You can't turn the clock back' has been the phrase used since, although the people making it obviously mean 'you shouldn't', and, while this sounds incredibly petty, as an analogy it doesn't really make sense, as clocks are cyclical. Besides, very few conservatives would argue that everything in the sexual revolution was wrong, just as they wouldn't argue that the French Revolution was all bad. Revolution throws lots of new ideas into the mix and inevitably some turn out to be worth keeping, often because technology and improved living standards mean that some ancient restraints can be eased.

Britain was quite late catching on with this whole 'sex' business, the Russians having got there forty-five years earlier in 1918. Among the first communist decrees were 'On the abolition of marriage' and 'On civil partnership, children and ownership', removing the differences between legitimate and illegitimate children, downgrading marriage and encouraging sexual freedom. There were 'anti-shame' demonstrations involving a mixture of exhibitionists and people whose main focus was intense hatred of Christian traditionalists. Young men loved it, obviously, and within a short space of time the country had three hundred thousand *bezprizorni*, homeless children abandoned by parents and forced to live in Russian state institutions – which, you'll be surprised to learn, weren't huge fun.[16] Eventually, however, the Soviets decided to turn the clock back, sexual shame returned, homosexuality was recriminalised in 1934 and abortion banned again two years later. It wasn't that Stalin was 'pro-life', as such, rather that the Soviets were by then worried about population decline – but then mass murder will have that demographic side effect.

Likewise in the eighteenth century illegitimacy was common but the Victorians reined in the excesses of Georgian society, while way back sexual matters became more conservative in the high Middle Ages as births outside marriage became less common. Clocks do come around again.

The sexual revolution of the 1960s had a second wave in the 1990s as I was going through my teens. The Blair government liberalised laws governing pornography and alcohol, but there was also a deeper cultural shift; indeed, for a while even bankers from respectable firms took clients to strip bars – completely unthinkable just twenty years later. Prostitution became far more normalised and porn ubiquitous, and it was obviously seeping into mainstream culture, with advertisers using more hardcore-influenced imagery, aided by fashion designers who always have deep respect for women.

The difficulties of trying to find something even vaguely pornographic on TV before the internet came along is something kids these days really wouldn't appreciate. We had to stay up watching tedious Channel 4 foreign art films just because there was apparently a lesbian scene halfway through. In fact, even the German porn that arrived in the 1990s with cable, which was then incredibly filthy, is by today's standards quaintly innocent, almost like a Robin Asquith sex comedy.

The Soviets had 'Down with Shame' days but in our sexual revolution absence of sexual shame went alongside lack of shame about wealth. There were even popular dating websites that excluded poor men and women not deemed attractive enough, while others helped husbands and wives to enjoy extra-marital affairs. I don't think you need to be a character from *The Handmaid's Tale* to find a lot of these things squalid. Likewise at one point 13 per cent of British teenagers had chlamydia, while there were eighty-three thousand children in care, more than before the Abortion Act, which, it was hoped, would lead to a big fall in the number of unwanted children.[17] Being prudish is seen as low-status or sometimes unkind, but sexual liberation always has its *bezprizorni*.

Sexual freedom also fed the sense of a growing divide between the successful and the rest. Sexual liberalisation, like economic liberalisation, frees some people to realise their dreams but leaves others envious and miserable. Average men could now enjoy more sexual variety, while also feeling still inadequate, since more successful men had enjoyed a far bigger share; for women it meant the beauty arms race going nuclear. Would we have been happier back in the old repressed days of black and white and *Brief Encounter*? Some would and some wouldn't, I suppose. I'd probably have ended up losing my virginity in a brothel in Tanganyika and catching syphilis, left untreated because I was too scared to confess my wickedness to the doctor. But unrestrained sexual competition can feel stressful to many people.

After university I wrote to a number of magazines asking if I could do work experience, that route by which the middle class come to dominate the media. Only one replied, a men's magazine, and I ended up in that industry for five years. It was a strange, unintentional career trajectory because I'm naturally quite shy and prudish. I blush easily, something the glamour model Lauren Pope brought up in front of the whole *Nuts* office once, asking 'Why is your face so red?' Which made me go more red. Like most of the people who worked in that industry I saw it as a route to more serious or at least less pornographic work, but instead it became more and more seedy. I think most of my colleagues thought it quite liberating or harmless, or at least said so, although I was never sure if this was just one of those mantras people repeated. Certainly the prevailing atmosphere in the *Nuts* office was very Left-liberal, but then that's the norm in pretty much all media companies. Of thirty-five people or so in the editorial team there was one other Toryish person, an Irish libertarian, who by the standards of the office was the closest thing to being Right-wing. Everyone else read the *Guardian* or *Independent* and aspired to work for the former. One day we were vaguely discussing politics and a colleague from the West Midlands was stunned when I mentioned that I had voted Conservative at the last election. 'You're a Tory? Seriously?' It was like I had announced I was a Scientologist or went dogging. I had often made outrageous Right-wing comments in the office to get a laugh but presumably he thought it was an act.

I had started reading *Loaded* and *FHM* in my teens mostly because of the humour, which was similar to *Viz*, but the general hedonism appealed to me as a teenager (I mean, the attractive women didn't hurt, but the laughs were definitely a big part of it). But then, as the market became ever more intense and then struggled with declining sales, the wit gave way to a more straightforward sales pitch; IPC media, of which *Nuts* was a part, had hired some marketing experts who were paid a fortune to organise focus groups and who came back with the revelation that young men liked looking at tits. An amazing, counterintuitive insight. It became far more cynically marketed, the boob count went up and it eventually dawned on me one day that I was a pornographer.

None of the women I knew objected to men's magazines, but only much later did I realise many felt uncomfortable but were worried about appearing prudish. Low-status signals deter a lot of people from expressing their views, and when I was growing up there was already a negative image of feminists being ugly and bitter. I remember learning about Andrea Dworkin, who was basically the real-life Millie Tant from *Viz*, and who said all sex was rape (or something to that effect). The fact that she didn't exactly look like she was likely to hugely inflame men's lust probably didn't help. Then there was Clare Short, the Labour MP who campaigned against the *Sun*'s Page 3 on the pretty reasonable grounds that having topless women in the country's biggest selling newspaper is really odd. The red tops in turn attacked her for her looks, sort of implying she was just bitter because she couldn't be a Page 3 girl and instead only got to be a stupid old Member of Parliament making actual laws.

But in the 1990s feminism got new energy. With the good times rolling there was emphasis on freedom rather than equality, and freedom included the freedom to sell sex or give it away without being judged. Sexual attitudes hugely changed in that quietly revolutionary decade. In 1987, 74 per cent of British people had said same-sex relationships 'were always or mostly wrong'; by 2016 only 16 per cent believed this, and we can assume a lot of them are called Violet or Ethel (yes, I know those names barely exist any more but old people now don't have very comically old-sounding names). In 1983, 'only 41% thought it was right for a homosexual to teach in a school' and just over half for one 'to hold a responsible position in public life', which by 2012 were 83 and 90 per cent respectively.[18]

Likewise views about sexual roles changed a great deal. In 1987 half of the population agreed that it was 'a man's job is to earn money' and 'the woman's job is to look after the home and family'; by 2012 only 13 per cent took this view, and any politician who suggested otherwise would be 'cancelled', as the kids now say.[19] By 2015 large majorities 'agreed that gender equality was desirable; that it had not been achieved; and that more needed to be done to rectify this'. Yet while feminism had achieved its goals, it hadn't really got any credit for it (so what's new, women might say), and while two-thirds of people say they are sympathetic to feminism, only 9 per cent of women identify as a feminist. The biggest reason, I'd imagine, is that it's seen as unattractive and therefore low-status.

14

ALL THE GOOD SONGS

In the late 1990s, with the therapy culture intensifying, there was a craze for misery memoirs portraying abusive childhoods, set in a very bleak mid-twentieth century. The most popular was probably Frank McCourt's *Angela's Ashes*, all about the miseries of auld Oireland in the days when it was nothing but rain and pneumonia and the drink and abusive priests. This publishing phenomenon reflected a culture that saw the past darkly but also one obsessed with victimhood; in fact, many of the bestselling mis-lit books turned out to be frauds, including a whole sub-genre of fake Holocaust memoirs with implausible stories of children escaping Nazis with the help of wolves.

We didn't always see the past this way. Until the eighteenth century most societies had a golden age myth about a time long ago when everyone was better off, more innocent or wealthy. The most obvious reason is that for the majority of people life was pretty terrible and so they reasoned there *had* to have been something better once. People also tend to cherish the memory of their youth, when they were healthier and happier, and so look at the old days fondly, even if they suffered great hardship at the time. That we don't take golden ages seriously now is partly because we have historical records, including data; I have fond memories of my childhood in the early 1980s, but even then infant mortality was three times what it is now.[1]

But the death of the golden-age myth is also a recognition we have undergone cultural revolution. In Arabic the period before Islam is called

Jahiliyyah, 'Age of Ignorance', and Muslim writers naturally played up how backwards and violent this culture was before their ancestors adopted the new religion. Likewise, Christians in Europe emphasised the negative aspects of the polytheistic societies preceding, focusing especially on 'pagan' treatment of the faithful, even though Roman oppression of Christians was nothing like as bad as Christian persecution of other Christians. And so, in a similar way, since the cultural revolution of the 1960s is viewed as the start of a new way of thinking, everything before that is a sort of conservative *Jahiliyyah*.

How someone regards the past and future correlates well with how conservative or liberal they are; the way British people voted in the 2016 referendum can be very accurately predicted by a question to that effect, both Labour and Tory Remainers being much less likely to think things were better in bygone days.[2] As Émile Durkheim said, socialism 'is wholly oriented toward the future . . . It concerns itself much less with what is or was than with what ought to be.'[3] In contrast, as Mark Lilla put it: 'The reactionary mind is a shipwrecked mind. Where other see the river of time flowing as it always has, the reactionary sees the debris of paradise drifting past his eyes.'[4] The past, therefore, becomes another front in the culture war, and our vision of it is viewed through the lens of those who tell it best, artists and writers and filmmakers – most of whom tend to come from the Left.

For example, our image of the Victorian era as one of neglect, child illness and sexual hypocrisy is heavily influenced by Left-leaning early twentieth-century historians such as Arnold Toynbee, who was in turn influenced by Friedrich Engels's *Condition of the English Working Class*, all helping to create the common idea of Victorian callousness. In fact, Engels's work was full of mistakes; his sources were up to forty years out of date, and he also cited evidence from the Factories Enquiry Commission of 1833 without mentioning the Factory Act had been passed that year to get rid of those same conditions. Likewise, he quoted an inquiry about the condition of cotton workers in Manchester without stating that the inquiry had helped eliminate many of the problems.

His confederate Marx was even more successful at shaping our idea of Victorian capitalists being ruthless, heartless bastards, and the Industrial Revolution an era of relentless misery. Marx borrowed from very dubious sources, among them Peter Gaskell's *Manufacturing Population of England*, 'a work of romantic mythology which attempted to show that the eighteenth century had been a golden age for English yeomen and craftsmen'.[5] This was conservative rural idyll mythmaking feeding a socialist worldview. Later, in the twentieth century, liberal socialists Barbara and John Lawrence Hammond popularised a vision of a Victorian 'bleak era' with the poor trapped in 'smoke and squalor'.[6]

Historians arguably have less influence than artists, and our vision of Victorian poverty is most heavily influenced by Charles Dickens. Industrial poverty has entered the collective consciousness because by Dickens's time there was now a middle class large enough to care, but the rural poverty that preceded it was far grimmer; it was just too remote for anyone to do anything about, and it was the norm for most of human history. I often see people on Facebook posting an inspirational Nelson Mandela quote: 'Overcoming poverty is not a task of charity, it is an act of justice. Like Slavery and Apartheid, poverty is not natural. It is man-made and it can be overcome and eradicated by the actions of human beings.' Which is pretty much the stupidest thing ever said by anyone – poverty is the most natural thing in the world, and until the nineteenth century the vast majority of people lived in it.

Wages had barely improved for British workers from 1760 to 1820 but by Marx's time things were rapidly getting better, with rising living standards, as well as improvements in working conditions. There were also welfare schemes introduced to stave off revolution, and yet Marx still helped to create the popular idea of a world of urchins starved and worked to death by a callous squirearchy. At my school the Industrial Revolution was largely presented as an endless litany of poverty and misery, rather than the greatest breakthrough in living standards in history. And, what happened in Britain in the years following, between 1840 and 1900, was something of a miracle, when a country with a rapidly growing population managed massively to reduce poverty, crime, disease and illiteracy, a time of unparalleled improvement in most people's lives. Likewise the most recent thirty years have seen an incredible reduction in world poverty, with billions lifted out of poverty, something of which 84 per cent of Americans are completely unaware of (and I'm sure the British are the same).[7]

The Victorian era is the only one judged by the situation it inherited – the grinding poverty of the *Oliver Twist* age – rather than the one it left, the much wealthier and healthier Belle Époque period. The Victorian values we deride didn't cause that squalor but were a response to it, and were pretty successful too; every measure of misery had gone down significantly by 1900 and this was not just due to economic forces, either; for example, the reduction of illegitimacy went hand in hand with declining infant mortality.

An irony of modern hostility to 'Victorian values' is that it was the ancestral Left who were the most prudish and sanctimonious. The Chartists campaigning for universal suffrage banned even 'suggestive hugging' in their clubs, while in one Owenite socialist community in the 1840s married members were supposed not to have sex 'more than once in two or three years'.

The role played by voluntary organisations and Christian charities in enacting reform is also somewhat forgotten, because in our minds everything is the work of the state. We all learned about the 1870 Education Act at school, but there had been vast improvements in literacy rates long before that, mostly due to cheap private schools, and by 1851 two-thirds of primary-school-age children were attending school in England and Wales, entirely voluntarily.[8] Similarly a voluntary welfare state had long been in existence before Labour came along; by 1901 friendly societies had 5.47 million members, over half of adult men, and provided benefits for 40 per cent of adult males. Clement Attlee's government didn't create the British welfare state, it nationalised it. As for housing, more homes were built during the 1930s under the private sector than by local authorities in the

1960s, and the latter were on average of far lower quality, often hated by residents and since torn down.

We all know Victorians obviously had funny ideas about women, and when some made the argument that they should be allowed to vote, they were told they were too hysterical and ruled by their hormones. Or at least that was how we were taught about the female suffrage movement at school, and we weren't alone; American writer Helen Andrews recalled the argument that 'the burden of deciding whom to vote for would cause infertility by diverting blood from the uterus to the brain . . . was the only anti-suffrage argument ever mentioned in any of my public school American history classes'.[9] In fact, opponents did not see voting as a fundamental human right, and as Andrews wrote, 'No one in the Edwardian era put suffrage in the same category as freedom of opinion, the right to a fair trial, or the right to property.' The main concern was that, since most women did not vote – and where local elections had been opened to females in the US and Britain turnout had been very low – during periods of crisis these elections would be decided by inexperienced voters who had previously taken little interest in politics. Furthermore, since women were (and are) more religious than men, Frenchmen in particular worried they would use their vote to reverse secularisation and instal a Catholic king, while in America it was feared that women would push for prohibition. There was a large female anti-suffrage movement, too, who like many people regarded the suffragettes as extremists.

In fact, many of the suffrage campaigners were equally as ridiculous as their reactionary opponents, believing that it would lead to free love or an end to war, although we were certainly never taught about that: all lost in the historical memory.

Alas our conservative golden age ended with the catastrophe of the First World War, which was seen as a gigantic error made by a stupid, blundering upper class. At school we were taught that the war was basically everyone's fault and a calamity brought about by our imbecile leaders, rather than, primarily, due to German aggression. Most common myths about that are wrong, too. No one said it was going to be over by Christmas at the time. No one cheered at the outbreak of war, and the *New York Times* recorded in early August 1914 that there 'no flag waving, no demonstrations, no music-hall patriotism'. My English grandmother's memoirs, which conclude as her childhood ended in 1914, recalled that her parents were in tears at the table because the politicians had failed. Their misery was further compounded when her older brother returned home in uniform, having joined up not because he wanted to – he was terrified – but because he felt England was endangered by an aggressive Germany and didn't want to appear a coward to his friends. He survived, but suffered horrific shellshock.

That war ended our golden age. Yet it's not quite true to say that conservatives are stuck in the past, since nothing really compares with having antibiotics and modern dentistry. It's not like we long for the return of rickets, as one historian once mockingly suggested – we just think that social liberalism is an unwelcome by-product of our improving lives, not the cause of it. And as we are fonder of the past, we are also less judgemental about it. 'Conservatives are moral relativists when viewing the past but moral absolutists when viewing other cultures,' in the words of the Cato Institute's Alex Nowrasteh: 'Liberals are moral relativists when viewing other cultures but moral absolutists when viewing the past.'[10] We appreciate that there are reasons why people behaved as they did, even if to us their actions seem strange or harsh.

Perhaps people tend to be nostalgic about any period when they were winning. Old socialists idolise the Attlee era because it meant the NHS and huge council house building. More recently social liberals have turned the London Olympic Games, seen as the high point of multicultural liberalism, into a nostalgic golden age and get weepy about it (even though, post-Brexit, Britain has continued to get more diverse and public opinion towards immigrants is much warmer than it was back in the good old days of 2012).

The progressive idea of *Jahiliyyah* goes up to the 1960s, the period of Awakening, and so the decade immediately before that is seen through a particularly negative lens, stultifyingly dull and conformist, or in the case of 1990s film *Pleasantville*, literally black and white. Racial attitudes are a huge aspect of this, with great attention focused on the American South, a part of the English-speaking world as anomalous to Western civilisation as Sparta was to ancient Greece. The battles of this unusual subculture have come to dominate the psychology of the cultural war in the northern US, Britain and Canada to a strange extent. It's easier to remember the injustices of an *ancien régime* (and an odd one at that, formed by a peculiar historic institution) than think about how the wider solutions to racial inequality are harder to fix, and remain unsolved even after sixty years of liberal dominance.

Such is the need to turn history into a narrative of good v. evil that conspiracy theories try to make the story neater. In the third year of school, a history teacher gave us all a talk on why JFK, Robert Kennedy, Martin Luther King and Malcolm X were all killed by conspiracies, this being a pretty popular view in the early 1990s. He was a senior teacher at the school and so I naturally believed him; I suppose everyone did. Years later and it's pretty obvious that JFK was shot by Lee Harvey Oswald, and Oliver Stone's grand conspiracy is the preserve of cranks. And yet the cultural memory still refuses to budge; on the fiftieth anniversary of JFK's death the *New York Times* ran an article on how Dallas 'grappling with the assassination means reckoning with its own legacy as the "city of hate," the city that willed the death of the president.'[11] From the tone of the article you'd get the impression Kennedy was killed by Right-wing 'hate', rather than someone who was literally a communist.

Perhaps it is because the Left has always been better at mythmaking and story-telling. Marie Antoinette never said 'let them eat brioche', and the phrase was first written down by Rousseau when she was an infant, but people still remember it. As Tom Lehrer sung of the Spanish Civil War: 'Remember the war against Franco/That's the kind where each of us belongs . . . Though he may have won all the battles/We had all the good songs!'[12] Indeed, the Spanish war helped create a powerful story for the Left, a unifying cause of good v. evil, even while the Soviets were murdering huge numbers of their own people at home (which is not to deny the terrible atrocities committed by Franco).

The Spanish Civil War also had a galvanising effect on making art more Leftist. Its most famous artwork, Picasso's *Guernica*, highlighted the atrocities of the Nationalists' Nazi allies. A number of British writers headed to Spain to defend the Republic, including Laurie Lee and George Orwell, so a war the fascists won played a big part in further entrenching Leftist control of the arts.

15

GRYFFINDOR V. SLYTHERIN

When we go to bed our sleep is divided into two sections; the first few hours are called NREM (non rapid eye movement) and during this period our minds digest the day's events in an organised way. Afterwards, during the latter part of sleep, REM, we make sense of these episodes by interpreting them – and that's when we dream, sometimes in surreal or nonsensical ways that may also seem meaningful.

Likewise there is news and current affairs, on the one hand, and art on the other. Films, plays and television drama tend to reflect on historical episodes a few years after events, when our brains have spent time adding meaning to dry historical accounts. Our view of the First World War is heavily influenced by a series of plays, including *Journey's End*, that came out in the late 1920s, when the horror first became digestible, which all showed it as a needless and futile waste, and likewise films about Vietnam made it to the screen in the late 1970s and early 1980s.

The most influential novels, films and plays shape our political world-view far more than even bestselling polemics, and since liberals are more skilled at telling stories, as they are gifted with a better imagination, therefore events tend to be crystallised through a progressive lens. So while the Left arguably lost the political battles of the 1960s, they still got to write the story, and we remember events mostly through the films of the era; racial dramas such as *Guess Who's Coming to Dinner* and *In the Heat of the Night*, or tales of personal liberation and small-town prejudice such as *Easy Rider*. There are far fewer films about the urban homicide explosion of the 1960s, except perhaps the Dirty Harry series (which avoids the racial angle by showing murderous hippies running around San Francisco).

As American blogger Andrew Breitbart once said, politics is downstream from culture, and this has been the case since people first wrote down stories, which after all pre-date political tracts by several thousand years. Edmund Burke's great book on the French Revolution had far less influence on the wider worldview in the coming decades than those of Walter Scott, whose Waverley novels romanticising the past and medieval values of chivalry helped disseminate conservative ideas to a wider audience. But overall, and for at least two hundred years, artists, poets and novelists have tended towards the Left, influencing our culture as narratives inform our worldview far more than facts or even news stories. Artistic dominance has grown as the media has developed, in publishing, theatre and later films and television, which were able to create a truly shared cultural experience and control it. As Percy Bysshe Shelley wrote, 'Poets are the unacknowledged legislators of the world', and unfortunately it was one of the few sensible things he said.

Shelley was one of the first poets to have an influence on world politics and, like many artists, he had quite infantile Leftist views. As Paul Johnson put it, he 'believed that society was totally rotten and should be transformed, and that enlightened man, through his own unaided intellect, had the moral right and duty to reconstruct it from first principles. He also argued that intellectuals, and especially poets – whom he saw as the leaders of the intellectual community – occupied a privileged position in this process.'[1] A scrounger to his rich family and heartless to women in particular, Shelley 'put ideas before people and his life is a testament to how heartless ideas can be'.[2] Sounding like a modern-day actor, full of strident but incoherent views about how the world should work, he had the contradictory idea that the 'people' were just, but also that everything should be ruled by a select group of rational individuals such as himself. He called for action by the 'people', writing 'You are many, they are few'. On another occasion he proposed an alliance of 'enlightened, unprejudiced' people to resist 'the coalition of the enemies of liberty'. He would have *loved* Twitter.

Although people on the Left are naturally better at art, its political importance has also been better grasped by socialists. The Soviet authorities were so concerned with the importance of manipulating art that in October 1932 Stalin invited forty 'Soviet literary megastars' to Maxim Gorky's Moscow mansion where he instructed them that 'Our tanks are worthless if the souls who must steer them are made of clay. This is why I say: the production of souls is more important than that of tanks . . . Man is reshaped by life itself, and those of you here must assist in reshaping his soul . . . And that is why I raise my glass to you, writers, to the engineers of the human soul.' This they did, helping to create the wildly unrealistic style of fiction called 'socialist realism', although it wasn't entirely rewarding for the authors involved – Stalin later murdered eleven of them.

You cannot win in politics unless you win culture; most people don't have deeply thought-out political views, and often express and hold the opinions that will impress others, or react on some emotional level based on whom they trust. It's not because they are stupid, simply that forming an opinion is time-consuming and it makes more sense to subcontract it out. Most people aren't hugely obsessed with politics, and don't spend their time doing political things, while almost everyone enjoys cultural and sociable activities, whether it's watching films or reading books, or spending time with friends, from whom they pick up their views and signals.[3]

Perhaps the most effective forms of political communication are feature-length documentaries, which tend to have the same ability to entertain as films, while also giving the impression they are politically informative. They're also the most manipulative of art forms, polemics that are able to use edited footage and incidental music to create a highly simplistic and distorted view of an issue.

But novels arguably still shape the culture as much as any art form, as they are consumed by elites, and the truly influential ones introduce memorable archetypes and ideas. Among the most powerful of post-war novels are *The Handmaid's Tale* and *To Kill a Mockingbird*, one about the sexist patriarchy and the other a powerful tale about racism in the Deep South. But probably the most influential book of recent years came out just a month after Blair's election, both reflecting and magnifying progressive cultural ideas. It told the story of a boy born to bohemian parents who has the bad luck to be brought up in a stultifying conservative Surrey suburb by his dully conventional uncle and aunt. After the geeky, open-minded protagonist is allowed to go to wizard school, what follows is a battle between two worldviews: the snake-like house Slytherin, which favours only the pure-blooded and aristocratic, and the inclusive house Gryffindor, kind-hearted and open to people of all backgrounds.

Harry Potter's uncle Vernon is an archetypal *Daily Mail* reader – an uptight, intolerant and cultureless golf-club bore who is scared of anyone different to him, which in this case is wizards but might as well be asylum seekers or travellers. (It was not exactly a surprise when author J. K. Rowling said that Uncle Vernon would have voted Leave in the 2016 referendum.) Vernon is just unpleasant rather than malignant; Harry's rival at school, Draco Malfoy, represents aristocratic evil, and starts off by suggesting he's better than Harry's friend Ron Weasley because he's from a more noble-born family, and also contemptuous of people such as Harry who come from only half-wizard families, a very clear allegory for snobbery and racism. Of course, the story is itself quite hereditarian and elitist, featuring a hero who earns his place in a neo-Gothic boarding school through powers he inherited from his father, but then hereditarian stories are as timeless as wizards and magic.

In fact, drama schools often teach that the basic forms of storytelling remain conservative, because most stories tend to be boy meets girl, or other variations of these basic tropes. But men and women falling in love and getting married is not a uniquely conservative theme, nor is the idea of claiming one's rightful inheritance – it's human nature and liberals do it, too. They are basic and universal concepts, but most modern films tend to be progressive in that there are white hats and black hats, groups with whom one should sympathise and those that are deemed powerful and oppressive. White hats are women, ethnic minorities, especially black people, and other disadvantaged or disempowered groups. Black hats are corporations, white men or Christian bigots.

Most films have a basic liberal narrative of fighting oppression, because it makes for a better tale. Jonathan Haidt wrote that the 'heroic liberation narrative' works best because 'Authority, hierarchy, power, and tradition are the chains that must be broken to free the "noble aspirations" of the victims'. The conservative narrative 'is a heroic narrative of defence' and so 'rather than the visually striking images of crowds storming the Bastille and freeing the prisoners, this narrative looks more like a family reclaiming its home from termites and then repairing the joists'.[4]

Films have archetypes and stereotypes, so when big business turns up it is inevitably engaged in something evil, such as harming the environment or exploiting Africans, rather than helping to take a million people out of poverty every day. Which would indeed make a very boring film. One of the reasons for conservative failure is that simple archetypes work as memes. As Mark Lilla wrote: 'The retrograde, sexually repressed cleric, the sadistic right-wing thug, the authoritarian father or husband are familiar cartoons in our literature and visual culture. Their ubiquity is a sign of imaginative laziness of the B-movie kind that puts sheriffs in white hats and bandits in black ones.'[5]

Hollywood films were, until the late 1960s, governed by strict codes about sex and violence. That began to change pretty rapidly, and to many it was disconcerting; by the late 1980s there was quite active opposition by social conservatives who believed that Hollywood was attacking their values. And, inevitably, many of those campaigning against the film industry sounded insane, with talk of 'the gay agenda'. This liberal bias speeded up in the 1990s, even in films that weren't overtly political. While *American Beauty* featured the psycho military-obsessed conservative dad who hates gays and turns out to be one, *Titanic* was full of fin-de-millennium prejudice about the ruling class of the Belle Époque era, selfish and snobbish and cowardly, when in reality far more first-class men died, proportionally, than third-class women (although first-class women did the best).[6]

There are some conservative films, namely *Falling Down*, which chronicled the frustrations of the white middle class in the 1990s, the protagonist living in a squalid city full of Hispanic gangs and polyglot people from whom he feels alienated. It was written in America's second most violent year, 1991, and filmed during the LA riots the following spring, and so appeared when American audiences felt an acute sense of threat. But, as with many good films, its political message is ambiguous, while the only straightforward conservative films tend to be action movies aimed at adolescent men, such as *Red Dawn*, which has Colorado teenagers resisting a commie invasion, or perhaps *Death Wish*, which came out at a time when urban squalor was alarming; but then these kinds of films have very limited impact establishing clichés. Even *Falling Down* featured the trope of a Right-wing extremist who was really into leather and domination for a different reason altogether.

These tropes became more universal as the revolution of the 1960s grew more established, since a film that didn't feature them might have seemed subversive in a bad way. When zombies take over in *28 Days Later* it is the multiracial underclass that heroically struggles to save society, not the vicious soldiers led by Christopher Ecclestone's demented army officer. In *Four Lions* the jihadis are basically sympathetic characters, if a little stupid – at least apart from the fanatical white convert – while the only truly callous figure is the policeman at the end. Films that reversed those portions of sympathy would be genuinely controversial. Pre-revolutionary institutions and establishments are the ultimate black hats, perhaps best illustrated by *Mad Men*, a damning attack on the old New York Wasp elite who were apparently sexually incontinent, drunk, corrupt and, worst of all, tediously miserable and solipsistic.

It helps, of course, that the acting profession also veers Left. The fact that the club of Hollywood conservatives, Friends of Abe, 'keeps a low profile and fiercely protects its membership list, to avoid what it presumes would result in a sort of 21st-century blacklist', says something about where the incentives and deterrents lie.[7] The same is not the case for the far bigger liberal version, People for the American Way, which spends large amounts raising money for the usual causes and whose members are well known.

It's annoying that, as a general rule, the better an actor is, the worse their opinions seem to be. As a conservative you inevitably face the sad disappointment that most of your favourite people on the screen will believe in completely infantile and idiotic things. Twitter has obviously made this far, far worse, a hellish vortex where every childhood and adolescent memory is besmirched, where the footballer you idolised as an eight-year-old drones on about Brexit and your favourite novelist from your teens turns into a fourteen-year-old having a meltdown over Trump. Or you find a new favourite comic actor and look him up to see the most recently thing is a retweet of James O'Brien or David Lammy. And you just think – why, God, did you make me this way? Even possibly my favourite comedy of all time, *Father Ted*, has been ruined by politics, its co-writer Graham Linehan in my opinion becoming, for a while, one of the worst people on the site, and that's with some fierce competition.

Linehan once declared on Twitter in one of his characteristic political tirades that 'Writers tend to the left because writers tend to have compassion. The nasty party has none so the BBC will never be just right for them.'[8] He added that 'reality has a left-wing bias, and writers tend to deal with the real world'.[9] It was a strange thing to say, since some of the best novelists and artists in history have been terrible human beings: John Lennon, Hunter S. Thompson, Ernest Hemingway and Bertolt Brecht were awful people, and you could make a giant list of similarly selfish, appalling creative bastards. To go further back, the fifteenth-century Gilles de Rais, arguably the first man ever to put on a proper modern theatrical production, was literally a serial killer.

What writers are good at is using their imagination to understand the views and motives of other people – except, for some strange reason, when it comes to conservatives. But rather than living in the real world, artistic people have unusual personalities, and one study of 214 professional actors showed that 'Both male and female actors scored significantly higher than non-actors on Antisocial, Narcissism, Histrionic, Borderline, and Obsessive–Compulsive personality disorder scales . . . Male actors scored significantly higher than the male comparison group on Schizotypal, Avoidant, and Dependent personality disorder scales.'[10] Perhaps a society in which actors are given high status is one in which social order is going to be fairly chaotic.

Conservative commentators often sound tedious with claims that certain professions or institutions are dominated by the Left but I don't think anyone would disagree that the theatre is. When a *Daily Telegraph* columnist asked 'Why do so few of today's plays challenge the left–liberal consensus?' Lisa Goldman, artistic director of the Soho Theatre, suggested in response, 'What would a right-wing play have to offer? Anti-democracy, misogyny, bigotry, nostalgia of all kinds? Let's get back to a white Britain? That the slave trade had a civilising influence? That women should stay in the home?'[11] It seems odd that highly intelligent and educated people could really have such a basic view of a major political philosophy, especially when their entire craft is about exploring other people's emotions and motives. It's a cliché to talk of liberals living in bubbles, but then theatre people tend to be quite interesting and fun, so it's probably easier to fall into one.

Theatre wasn't always like this. Surviving works from Euripides to Shakespeare demonstrate quite a conservative mindset, going back to the birth of Western civilisation and the *Iliad*. Yet there is something about acting and the imagination that is radical and threatening to the status quo. In ancient Rome, actors were considered dangerous because they upstaged the very social order, and so Seneca, 'watching a play in which a slave played Agamemnon and imperiously threw his weight around, had been prompted to reflect on the illusory nature of rank itself. "Who is the 'Lord of Argos?'" he mused. "Why, only a slave!"'[12] This is exciting to a few, but disconcerting to others.

The arts, however, only became recognisably Left-wing in the nine-teenth century with the growth of an urbanised upper-middle class, and of literary circles large enough to develop a Left-wing culture. And as the artistic medium has grown through literacy, urbanisation and technology, so has the influence of artists. In the late nineteenth century came the development of modern theatre, the most influential playwright being the neurotic Norwegian Henrik Ibsen, who helped create many of the familiar clichés we see in theatre and cinema, in particular that married life is always repressed and claustrophobic. If a play set in the 1950s shows a white-bread husband saying, 'Hi honey, I'm home,' he will almost certainly be knobbing the secretary or hanging around men's toilets while his wife downs gin to drown her existential anguish. (Ibsen's own views were suitably idiotic: 'Abolish the concept of the state, establish the principle of free will.' He argued that 'the minority is always right', by which he meant what might today be called a liberal elite.[13])

According to Paul Johnson, Ibsen was the first playwright who 'deliberately and systematically, and with stunning success, used the stage to bring about a revolution in social attitudes'. The Norwegian was also the first writer 'to persuade a conservative state to subsidize a literary life devoted to attacking everything it held dear'.[14] From the 1950s every country in western Europe accepted the principle of state-funded theatre, although the subsidy was never enough, and most playwrights and actors continued to live in poverty, and always will. (And we spend nothing like as much as other countries – just one Berlin theatre gets as much funding as all British theatres combined.[15]) Although the meanly subsidised US theatre has a similar political bent, it seems unlikely this has no effect. Back in the days when the Church paid for great works of art, artists gave glory to God; now that it is paid for by the taxpayer, they sing the hymns of the state – equality, fairness and social justice.

In 1968 the old system of theatre censorship was abolished, and British theatre figure Kenneth Tynan, who argued that socialism meant 'progress towards pleasure', became the first man to use the F-word on television in 1965. Today there is no censorship in theatre but it rarely tackles any really taboo subjects, by which I mean something that could imperil the careers of those involved, such as making a blasphemous or homoerotic play might have once done. While British arts folk love to break taboos, the highest praise, they only like breaking the taboos of fifty years ago, not the sort of ones that today will actually lose you friends. So the Pinter Prize, awarded annually to a British author who 'casts an unflinching, unswerving gaze upon the world', is given to artists such as David Hare, soon after his television play, *Page Eight*, which featured American torturers, extraordinary rendition and Israelis killing unarmed protesters, was broadcast. Other plays of his had taken the controversial lines that Tony Blair was too close to the City of London, or that the Iraq War was not brilliantly well thought out, or that pre-sexual-revolution boarding schools were stuffy. Whether or not Hare is a great talent, are these positions going to cost someone anything among people of influence in the arts?

In contrast, you won't see many productions about sex scandals and hypocrisy in charities, or of the violence of ANC-run South Africa, or a play about immigration to Britain from the point of view of a white kid growing up in inner-city London, something far more relevant to most people's experience than endless rehashes of *To Kill a Mockingbird*. Maybe those perspectives just don't interest playwrights or producers, but I suspect that if they ever thought about them, they would soon put the idea away, aware that it just wouldn't be made. Theatres might put on a play by an Asian writer criticising traditional cultural practices, and think they're super-edgy for tackling a taboo subject, but I can't imagine that anti-censorship campaigners in the 1960s would have expected that in half a century's time performances daring to criticise forced marriage were on the border of what is acceptable to discuss.

Most theatre is more interested in attacking the old institutions from the Age of Ignorance – the Church, the family and the nation. As composer James MacMillan once put it, we have a 'cultural regime which adjudicates artists and their work on the basis of how they contribute to the remodelling, indeed the overthrow of society's core institutions and ethics'.[16] What replaces those institutions? The same one that just happens to fund theatre – the state.

Burke criticised the tendency of people to bravely attack dead tyrannies, while exalting modern ones. 'The sophistic tyrants of Paris are loud in their declamations against the departed regal tyrants, who in former ages have vexed the world. They are thus bold, because they are safe from the dungeons and iron cages of their old masters. Shall we be more tender of the tyrants of our own time, when we see them acting worse tragedies under our eyes?'[17] As with theatre, television people like to think they're taboo-breaking and controversial, yet they're generally timid about upsetting the established ideas of today. Even taking aside the issue of Islam, and the de facto ban on blaspheming it, there are huge areas ripe for satire and criticism, from the wilder shores of the transgender movement to the many ridiculous figures in multiculturalism, but no theatre director or TV producer would ever make fun of them. Like Parisian theatres in 1793 mocking the Church, they generally feel much more comfortable attacking the taboos of yesterday.

The same is true of comedy, which is especially supposed to feed off social taboos because taboo-breaking is funny. The last time I went to the Edinburgh Festival was 2004 and every other stand-up routine started with a joke along the lines of 'George Bush . . . what's up with that guy? What an idiot!' Many comedians had a pop at the government for not being Left-wing enough, despite it then being well on the way to building up a wartime level of debt last seen when Napoleon was around. There were jokes about 'the War on Terror' being stupid because you can't fight an emotion (perhaps because it's a deliberate euphemism for the 'war on Islamic extremism' designed not to alienate moderate Muslims). People's cultural windows tend to close off sometime between adolescence and middle age, and with it comes a sense-of-humour failure. For me, I think it started with really unfunny jokes about the *Daily Mail* on BBC panel shows. 'Single mothers! Immigrants! House prices! HA HA. Aren't the outgroup stupid??!' Isn't this just so . . . obvious?

Rod Liddle once observed that all the comedians of the 1970s were basically Right-wing, while today you'd struggle to find one not on the

Left. Comedy was once a working-class world, many radio and TV stars starting in music hall and working men's clubs, but from *Beyond the Fringe* and Monty Python onwards Oxbridge graduates began taking over, and Oxbridge graduates tend to be pretty good at things. They are also instinctively liberal. They weren't interested in making fun of their mother-in-law, but rather the cabinet ministers who went to their college. The BBC had once not even allowed mockery of politicians, seeing it as damaging to public institutions, but that all changed in the 1960s with shows such as *That Was the Week that Was.*

As it grew more middle-class, comedy became a lot more political from the early 1980s, but it also became politically uniform. Today almost all the top comedians in Britain are identifiably on the Left, many quite stridently so.

There aren't many Right-wing comics partly because conservative ideas are obviously stupid and irrational, on the face of it absurd, but they are also paradoxically logical, while liberal ones are obviously right, but in practice often don't work. The strongest conservative argument is the law of unintended consequences and that's quite hard to make in a comic skit. American think-tanker Arthur Brooks wrote that our arguments 'simply takes too long. We think we have thirty minutes to lead people into a logical conclusion. In reality, we have less than thirty seconds.'[18] Likewise Burke's ideas need some explaining, and they rely on the concept of paradox, and comedy is about timing. It's easy to point out the absurdities of, for example, religious dogma in a comedy sketch; quite hard to explain the importance of moral capital, or the unintended consequences of welfare.

Comedian Stewart Lee once suggested that there were no Right-wing members of his trade because comedy should be about 'punching upwards', and that 'It's a heroic little struggle. You can't be a right-wing clown without some character caveat, some vulnerability, some obvious flaw. You're on the right. You've already won. You have no tragedy. You're punching down . . . Who could be on a stage, crowing about their victory and ridiculing those less fortunate than them without any sense of irony, shame or self-knowledge?'[19] Yet I think of my conservatism as a symptom of my failure as a human being, of my fear and neurosis and crushed dreams. Isn't that also why all the great British tragicomic figures are conservative, at least since Basil Fawlty, the archetypal middle Englander desperate to ingratiate himself with his betters? Or Alan Partridge, the obviously UKIP-leaning Norwich DJ who has terrible taste in music and fashion, and fantasises about being part of the elite even though he will never be accepted by them. (In an early radio episode, Partridge congratulates the local Tory candidate for having 'got rid of the gypsies'.[20]) It's also probably true of David Brent, the middle manager who thinks business is cool in that modern managerial way; although he probably voted Blair, his natural instincts are with the Tories and he's awkward with women and ethnic minorities, making jokes in an attempt to ingratiate himself, which all backfire terribly. They're all frustrated, failed human beings who believe they ought to be higher up in a system they support, and that's before getting into more obviously conservative figures like Alf Garnett or Albert Steptoe.

All those great comic figures come from an institution with which conservatives have had a tortured relationship in my lifetime. It is an institution with such emotional power that British people living abroad sometimes become sentimental about the *Grandstand* or *Match of the Day* opening music, sounds evocative of home. The BBC is central to our identity that the corporation has come to be known by the familiar term Auntie. To my father, certain sounds evocative of wartime broadcasting would bring emotions flooding back to him – well, relatively – including the Dutch national anthem, played every night during the conflict. Peter Hitchens recalled of his suburban 1950s upbringing that 'To me the BBC is still utterly linked with good things of home and hearth. Till I die I will not be able to hear anyone say that the time is "a quarter to two" without being plunged into a Proustian reverie . . . It brought back memories of a sunny sitting-room with chintz-covered chairs, in which I am sitting, thumb quite possibly in mouth, at my mother's feet. Outside are many miles of suburban or rural peace spreading away in all directions.'[21]

For me it was a different world, perhaps a more cynical one, the BBC having changed in the 1960s to reflect and influence social attitudes, much to Mary Whitehouse's annoyance. I remember *Blue Peter* and *John Craven's Newsround* but not long after came anarchic and irreverent comedies such as *The Young Ones* and *Blackadder*. Lenny Henry was probably my earliest comedy hero; my first vague understanding of racism came when I was maybe eight or nine and someone told me what the Ku Klux Klan was and that they killed black people, and I was upset that someone might harm him. I don't follow him on Twitter, obviously, because it would be too painful. The BBC was a familiar, avuncular sound in the background of my childhood, a voice you could always trust. Benevolent, calm, well-spoken – just the sort of reassuring patrician voice you'd want in an airline pilot if you ever got into trouble at 30,000 feet.

Institutions are essential in the conservative mind, the bodies that provide continuity and stability in an otherwise hostile world. And there is a certain type of conservative man who attaches himself to such organisations, whether it be the golf club or military, or in times past groups such as the masons or guilds. Most of all there was the Church and, as many people have observed, since its creation in the early twentieth century the Beeb has acted as a replacement. Whereas once all Englishmen read from the same Book of Common Prayer each week, encoding a sense of national identity not found in Catholic countries, from the early twentieth century it was the BBC that served as our common font of rituals. The FA Cup final was something much of the country watched together, along with most major sporting or political events, as well as even more symbolic moments such as the Coronation or royal weddings.

And, just as many teenagers lose faith in the Church their parents worship in, conservative maturity brings with it feelings of disillusionment and even hostility towards beloved Auntie. Even if we feel that there's much good in the institution, we no longer believe its message or its values, no matter how much we might like some of the congregation and the nice hymns they sing.

Impartiality has always been a big concern and a controversy within the BBC, dating back to its coverage of the General Strike of 1926 (when it was seen as too pro-government). From the 1970s the corporation began to think about giving more of a diverse range of views, since social change had increased the variety of political and cultural opinions in the country.[22] But by the Thatcher era the corporation's relationship with the Conservatives was openly sour. Even by the time I was politically conscious the supposed bias of the Beeb was an old cliché. *Drop the Dead Donkey* featured a drunk government minister ranting about the Bolshevik Broadcasting Corporation, which is what a Tory MP, Peter Bruinvels, actually called it during the Falklands War – and Thatcher observed that she had fought three elections against the BBC.

In recent years numerous people who've worked there have admitted there was always a huge Left-wing bias among its staff, and in its reporting, especially on the issue of immigration – something that was not entirely a secret. The problem is that the anti-Beeb Right-wing headbanger has long become a tedious self-parody of a figure, and it's very hard to make the argument of bias without coming across as a crank or bore – and heaven knows I've tried. It is also that the bias is so slight, and therefore more effective; read a compass that is a tiny bit off and a few miles down the road you'll be far away from your intended destination; an obviously broken compass will warn you. Very few people watching Fox News could be in any doubt it has an obvious agenda, a very unsubtle one, but objecting to the Beeb's output involves largely complaining about small nuances of language or, perhaps more importantly, what it deems newsworthy and in what order. The people doing this complaining inevitably sound petty, but cultural shifts do not happen by crude tabloid use of rhetoric, but by subtle changes in language that within a relatively short period of time will shift opinion, putting some majority-held beliefs beyond the pale. So, when reporting on China or India the BBC uses the term 'illegal immigrants', but in the US they mostly use the term 'undocumented immigrants' or even 'dreamers'. It makes you an incredibly tedious person even to notice, of course, but these things effectively change the tone of debate.

Conservatives have for years made just these sorts of complaints of bias about the *Today* programme and other flagship shows. It was once a constant moan of Right-wing blogs that the panel on *Question Time* was skewed Left, which became worse once they started inviting comedians. The panel is bad enough, but the audience always seemed to be hugely unrepresentative of the public, obviously not on purpose but because the kind of person who volunteers to endure watching the show live has a bee in their bonnet about something. So you get some 'ordinary member of the public' who harangues the Conservative politician about cuts to the NHS and then – seemingly without fail – is revealed the next day to be a long-term Labour member and union activist. The Tory on *Question Time* was basically like that poor guy who used to dress up as an Iranian on WWE so he could get jeered at by all the crowd and beaten up by Hulk Hogan. (That's changed a lot now, apparently, and the audiences are full of angry, red-faced Brexit supporters, but I stopped watching ages ago so who knows.)

If you're a conservative you are almost perennially annoyed by Radio 4 but, like me, you may have some sort of compulsive, news-junkie urge to listen to it even though you know it's probably shortening your life. Until eventually you become just another boring, red-faced idiot shouting at Radio 4 – with the wife raising her eyes, thinking to herself, 'Here he goes again.' And yet the conflicting thing is that I love the BBC – I love the sound of David Attenborough and Stephen Fry, I love its high-mindedness, its comedy and its peerless documentary making. I like drinking wine in the kitchen while cooking, with *Front Row* playing, or the familiar figure of Gary Lineker sharing the nation's dreams during another World Cup adventure. As a conservative I like institutions – they provide the warm feeling of oxytocin that reminds me I'm not alone in this world – but what happens when they become captured by the other side?

16

CONQUEST'S LAW

The BBC's central importance to British identity dates to the Second World War, and the moral support it provided during an existential national crisis. It's a period with which we are obsessed in a slightly embarrassing way, the British remaining prisoners of the conflict long after its primary aggressors and victims have found inner peace. Although it was Our Finest Hour and everything, it's also where everything sort of went wrong for Britain in the conservative narrative. It led to a huge growth in the size and scope of the state in a country previously known for having very little government interference in everyday life, a situation we have never really reversed. It's been said before that previous to the First World War an Englishman's sole interaction with the state was posting a letter, which seems like a misty golden age for anyone turning on Radio 4 hearing about the Department for Health's latest initiative to micromanage our lives because we're all too fat.

During the war, with Churchill focused on the military, his Labour coalition partners effectively took over the running of the country, and by the time the conflict ended Britain had witnessed six years of full-on socialism, a war economy that was credited with defeating Nazism in alliance with a communist ally. Admittedly socialist war economies can be hugely productive, in terms of both innovation and output, but then people will tend to work quite hard if the alternative is slavery or death.

And once the state takes over things, it's very reluctant to let them go afterwards. During the war the establishment of the National Blood Service led to the creation of the National Health Service, whereas almost every continental country went for a different system afterwards, while also providing universal coverage. For some reason British people cannot fathom that there are more than two types of health systems in the world – our NHS which treated my gran, and the American one in which a paramedic rifles through your wallet to see if you have a credit card before bothering with CPR. Trying to explain the existence of the German or Dutch medical system to British people doesn't just meet with incredulity, it doesn't even register, the words popping like bubbles before they reach their ears. Likewise the Council for the Encouragement of Music and the Arts, which was set up to organise theatre and ballet in army camps and churches, led to the creation of the Arts Council, another government body I remember Dad used to rage about for being full of Leftists.

Marcus Chown, the scientist-cum-Twitter celebrity, once tweeted that 'If I had only 6 letters to encapsulate what makes Britain Britain, they would be NHS-BBC. The Tory government is destroying everything that makes us us.' As the German economist Kristian Niemietz dryly commented, paraphrasing Voltaire's quote about Prussia, Britain is not a state so much as a hospital service with a TV station attached.[1]

Britain was not just a dangerous wartime enemy because its economy could pump out Spitfires and Lancasters; it was a country high in what sociologists call social capital – trust, support for shared institutions and political moderation, freedom of assembly and private property, and most of all numerous independent associations collectively called 'civil society'. When the Nazis planned to invade Britain in 1940 they drew up a list of all the people and institutions they were to destroy once they got in power. The *Sonderfahndungsliste G.B.* named individuals who would be 'questioned' but also organisations that could be hostile to Nazi conquest, including the Boy Scouts, the Church of England and the Freemasons. All clubs independent of the state would be closed down, churches would be monitored and organisations such as the Mothers' Union or civil support groups such as the Friendly Societies placed under close surveillance.

All of these were independent, voluntary organisations that linked different members of society in a web of interconnecting relationships. Edmund Burke referred to the 'little platoons', the institutions and collectives that formed civil society, and these would be rivals to a Nazi regime in which everything outside of the state was a threat. Likewise when the communists did take over Hungary later that decade they closed down five thousand groups within a year, including 'brass bands, choirs, theatre groups, boy scouts, reading societies, walking clubs, private schools, church institutions, charities for the relief of poverty, discussion societies, libraries, wine festivals, hunting and fishing clubs'.[2] Independence from the state was intolerable to communists. As elsewhere, the Marxists set up their own ersatz versions of these organisations but even three decades after central Europe freed itself, the region struggles to revive the social capital lost under its imprisonment.

So if you compared the Britain of 1940 with that of today, how many institutions threatening to a totalitarian regime would be independent, compared to those either state run or heavily funded by the state? Not that many, I'd suggest. It would basically just be Mumsnet. Mumsnet v. the Nazis. Most of the others have either been taken over by the state or severely undermined by it, and so as a consequence falling to Conquest's Second Law, named after Robert Conquest, the great expert on communism.

Conquest famously argued that there were Three Laws of Politics:

> First, that everyone is conservative about what he knows best.
>
> Second, that any organisation not explicitly right-wing sooner or later becomes left-wing.
>
> And third, that the simplest way to explain the behaviour of any bureaucratic organisation is to assume that it is controlled by a cabal of its enemies.[3]

Conquest's Second Law could apply to almost any institution over the past fifty years, especially as even private, voluntary organisations have come to take more money from the state. No one likes turning down money, and once this happens it pushes organisations to the Left, because they rely on more public spending and so develop a belief that the state should expand more, and perhaps also because more Left-wing people enter these organisations. And so Leftism becomes the institutions' over-arching ethos, just as Catholicism once pervaded medieval government and universities.

Many charities founded by Christians eventually evolved to accept the new religion of the social gospel, which eventually dropped the 'gospel' bit. Some maintain a nod to the old faith while trying to avoid raising it too much to avoid the glare of the diversity industry, or just not to sound crazy. Some keep their Christian baggage, even though it's no more relevant to them than the Lancashire and Yorkshire railway depot is to Manchester United or Thames Ironworks to West Ham. Others drop it altogether: groups such as the former Young Women's Christian Association,[4] which in 2011 became 'Platform 51' because Christianity 'no longer stands for who we are'. The YWCA had been founded in 1855 with the aim of providing spiritual and moral support to young women against the physical and moral poverty of the new cities, and it did this, among other things, by running prayer groups. Its aim was to get people out of poverty by encouraging Christian virtues such as sobriety and abstinence. By the time it changed its name it was run by an equality quango chairman, and its brochure stated that 'We campaigned for the Equality Act to protect pregnant schoolgirls and teenage mums from discrimination, harassment and victimization' – pretty much the opposite of what its founders would have believed. This reflects a changing worldview, towards an Owenite belief that we are victims of social circumstances, or perhaps it was just that the tougher nineteenth century needed harsher policies.

Charities were once largely staffed by volunteers, often upper-middle-class women, and most had a Christian mission, especially a nonconformist one; today they are professional, employing humanities graduates and espousing what might be called a progressive political agenda. Where once these bodies relied on the Church, they now rely on the state; where once they were Christian, they are now statist. And so by the time New Labour left office, around twenty-five thousand British charities were receiving more than three-quarters of their income from the government, and many more enjoyed smaller but still significant payments.[5] At one point, twelve of the largest charities were getting £742 million a year from the taxpayer, and spending on average £400,000 each just 'managing' their relationship with government.[6]

Not coincidentally, pretty much all the major charitable organisations have become overtly political. Most of the large hunger charities campaigned for a 'Robin Hood tax' on the City of London, despite pretty much all of them taking large chunks of taxpayers' money and so clearly having a conflict of interest. There's no doubt they do a lot of good work, and are staffed by people more selfless than I am, but it is difficult for conservatives to support charitable institutions that are involved in progressive activism. In fact, trying to find a benevolent organisation that doesn't also act as a Leftist campaigning group is quite a challenge, which is why I suspect donkey charities are so popular. (After all, just how Leftist can they get?) Also, while there is nothing necessarily wrong with a charity working in partnership with the state and so receiving taxpayers' money to run a particular service, it rather stretches the definition of the word 'charity', since anyone who refuses to fund such operations goes to jail. It's also hard for a charity not to stray into advocacy, since if you're dealing with abused children or cancer victims you can hardly be expected to keep a polite silence about what you see causing those problems. What in effect happens is that the taxpayer ends up funding thousands of campaigning organisations – thousands of campaigning organisations that, because of the good work they do and the air of political neutrality, have a strong moral authority that no politician or public body can match.

Another grating thing about the charitable sector is that the same sort of people end up running them, and with vast salaries, usually human rights lawyers or some other genus of Leftie grandee. Progressives are just far better at getting their people into positions of power, ensuring that even when they leave office the machinery is still run by fellow believers. Conservatives almost never bother doing the same.

When he made his Second Law, Conquest cited two groups as particular examples, one of which was Amnesty International.[7] The human rights charity was started after the war with the particular aim of helping non-violent prisoners of conscience but has since got itself involved with pretty much every progressive cause imaginable.[8] Amnesty aimed to speak on behalf of people held without due process or trial, and didn't support anyone who committed or advocated violence. In 1964 they refused to take up the cause of Nelson Mandela, and later, although their leader Seán MacBride was the son of a famous Irish Republican and a former IRA chief of staff himself, they didn't support the Irish hunger strikers either. That's all gone, obviously, and more recently the group has campaigned for members of al-Qaida, which is not exactly a non-violent organisation.[9] In 2011 Amnesty also 'produced a 1,000-page legal brief aimed at persuading the authorities in Canada to arrest the former US president George W. Bush' for invading Iraq. The group were now heavily involved in the issue of gun control as well as 'LGBT rights; gender issues; migrant rights; surveillance; policing in Ferguson, Missouri; and access to emergency contraception.'[10]

Amnesty is now also involved in what it calls 'economic rights' so that, as a staff member said, they 'could assess whether a country has adequately mobilised resources for public services'. Naturally it's also entered the trans debate, issuing a press release complaining that government registrations only offer the options of male or female, and children are not allowed to change sex and so are 'completely excluded' because they have to wait until eighteen to have 'their true gender legally validated'.[11] I mean, it's not quite the same as being held in the Lubyanka is it? Likewise, the American Civil Liberties Union, once a strictly neutral group that sought to defend people's freedom, has inevitably become bogged down in culture war stuff, tweeting that 'We will continue to support survivors', by which it meant people who made rape claims, which perhaps goes against what a civil liberties organisation should stand for.[12]

Many of these charities had their origins in Christianity but as they have adopted the new faith they have turned against the parent religion. Amnesty was founded by two Catholics and had strong Christian underpinnings but in the 2000s it began more overtly to support abortion. And so, with a great sense of sadness, in 2007 the Bishop of East Anglia resigned from Amnesty, leading to an exodus of Catholics from the organisation.

The other organisation Conquest cited was the Church of England. Despite Anglican churchgoers historically being the core of the Tory party, the hierarchy itself has been heading Left since the start of the twentieth century. Today vicars, unless they're in the minority evangelical or to some extent Anglo-Catholic wings of the Church, are almost guaranteed to be ardent Lefties. A seminarian wrote in the *Spectator* magazine that of the sixty vicars-to-be at his college, around three are conservative and far more were Marxists:

> Any overtly Tory priest-in-training would quickly learn the error of his ways . . . We are fed a constant diet of propaganda which assumes that all Tories are evil and that they exist solely for the benefit of the rich . . . It is bad enough to be a Conservative – if you were to support UKIP or hold libertarian views, you would be putting yourself well beyond the pale; indeed, if word were to reach your bishop you might find yourself struggling to find a post after ordination. It is by such methods that the political orthodoxy of the church is maintained.[13]

In many ways this network of charities and other quasi-public-sector bodies has sort of become a new Church, in charge not just of the caring industry but also of public morality and educating the young. The 'neo-reactionary' blogger Curtis Yarvin coined the phrase 'the Cathedral' to describe a network of bodies that set the moral tone, and to which people were wise to conform if they wanted their careers to progress. The growth of the new church means that for a younger generation huge numbers of talented people work in areas where there is an institutional hostility to conservatism. This is partly because Tories do not believe their work should be professionalised and run by the state, but most of all that once a body has a critical mass of progressives it becomes institutionally progressive.

Thatcher, notoriously, destroyed thousands of working-class jobs, or at least stopped subsidising industries that provided them; but even with all the privatisations of her government the number of people working for the public sector went up considerably. There were more public-sector employees in the late 2000s than in 1979, when the state was in charge of electricity, gas, the railways, coal, steel, airlines and many other heavy manufacturing industries.[14] This is perhaps inevitable in a more complex state, but it certainly helps the Left; when Thatcher died there were loud cheers in my local council office, at least according to a friend who worked there.

During the Blair era, complaining about quasi-government bodies – 'quangos' – became another Right-wing newspaper cliché, with the number of bodies growing despite Gordon Brown in 1995 promising there would be a 'bonfire' of the things. By the time he left office spending on quangos was £64 billion a year,[15] and there were apparently 529 quangos that duplicated each other and quangos that had objectives directly working against another[16] – the £6 million British Potato Council existed to make us eat more spuds, while the £140 million Food Standards Agency was there to tell us to eat fewer. Conservatives sometimes call this group the *nomenklatura* (in reference to the Soviet Union's swollen bureaucracy), which all had a vested interest in promoting the ideology. And once this monstrosity is created, who is going to stop it?

A Lot of Layabouts with Nothing Better to Do . . .

As the Blair/Brown government went on, spending lots of money and interfering in every tiny aspect of our lives, I read more and more libertarian blogs. It just seemed that every time I turned on the radio in the morning there was a new initiative by a different government department wading into every aspect of our lives. The obvious problem was that there were too many people in government and so they just created work for themselves – and we were all paying for it.

Many public-sector workers are extremely badly paid, but by 2010 over twenty-six thousand NHS staff were getting over £100,000 a year. I grew agitated by that tabloid staple, the 'Council Fat Cat', especially as I now lived in a borough that in 2009 was listed among the worst in England with very high council taxes and with a 'Chief Executive' on £190,000 a year. I read about these people with dismay, all these 'change facilitators' and 'diversity champions', wondering what on earth made me think about a career in the media. I didn't care how tedious their jobs sounded, I'd got to the age where for that amount of money I'd be willing to do anything; evil things; the sort of things that normally only happen in Marseille prisons. As with much political conflict, intra-class rivalry drove my political agenda.

On top of this, some 39 per cent of the population were now receiving one or more of the forty state benefits on offer, up from 24 per cent in 1997, which required the Department of Work and Pensions to employ one hundred and thirty thousand staff, with HM Revenue & Customs needing another eight thousand just to deal with tax credits.[17] It made me nostalgic for the idea of a Victorian-sized state that almost never bothered you, and when tax was still tuppence in the pound, as it was in 1874 (admittedly there would have to be *some* public-sector cuts for this to happen). Many people felt that just as the state was unable to deal with basic problems such as crime and border control, so inevitably it became involved in various things that weren't really its business. Milton Friedman made this argument years back, that 'Government is failing at a lot of these things that it ought to be doing because it's involved in so many things it shouldn't be doing.'[18] He said this in an interview with *Playboy*, of all things, back when the gentleman's interest magazine/masturbation aid used to run improbable highbrow interviews between pictures of naked women.

After the bailout in 2008, and reading about the levels of debt we were in, I also became concerned about how much we were borrowing. I even attended a protest, I think maybe my second or third, the 'Rally against Debt', which must have got at least a hundred people, at a time when anti-cuts events attracted tens if not hundreds of thousands. It wasn't even that I thought I was getting taxed too harshly – being in journalism I never had to worry about that. But I suppose there is also that Middle England Man part of me, the 'why can't they just leave us alone?' bore who hates 'busybodies'. I think many Englishmen sympathise with Basil Fawlty that Nazi Germany began with 'A lot of layabouts with nothing better to do than to cause trouble.'[19]

That sort of Middle Englander also has a natural aversion to 'positive rights', the number of which have vastly increased in recent years, as have lawyers. Isaiah Berlin distinguished between negative liberty and positive liberty, the former being freedom *from* other people doing stuff to you, the latter the freedom to be granted things. The most important and most ancient right in English law is Magna Carta's Clause 39, still on the law-books, which guarantees freedom from arrest and imprisonment without 'lawful judgment of his peers'. Negative freedom is 'the cornerstone of classical liberalism' while positive freedom is a far more controversial area, encapsulated by the growth in 'human rights' legislation.[20]

Human rights are another great caricature tabloid obsession but there is a reason for that, and in the Blair years there were some outrageous cases brought about through this kind of legislation. It didn't help that his wife was a lawyer and her chambers made a fortune from human rights laws, including the case of the adolescent religious fanatic from Luton who was sent home from school because she refused to conform with their uniform policy and insisted on wearing full Saudi-style Islamic dress.

And so a natural place to migrate to, if you're young and don't like being bossed around, is libertarianism. For a while I even considered myself libertarian, like a lot of young conservative men who are basically confused and in denial about their conservatism.

'Most of the harm in the world is done by good people, and not by accident, lapse, or omission. It is the result of their deliberate actions, long persevered in, which they hold to be motivated by high ideals toward virtuous ends.'[21] So wrote Isabel Paterson in *The God of the Machine*. Paterson is considered the founding mother of libertarianism, and was so anti-state that in old age she even refused to receive benefits, keeping her Social Security card in an envelope with 'Social Security Swindle' written on it. Her philosophy emerged after the decline of 'Classical' liberalism, all-dominant in the mid-nineteenth century but later in Victoria's reign squeezed between conservatism and the Left, which might be described as social democracy, 'Left-liberalism' or progressivism. And so libertarianism, or 'Right-liberalism', is a sort of political relic, the equivalent of some weird salamander, which is basically a dinosaur that has somehow survived the asteroid and lives on in the jungle, unbeknown to anyone else.

Left-liberals believe that equality is a social good for which governments should strive, while Right-liberals believe in freedom above everything. Progressives tend to think that if something should be legalised then it should be accepted, too, and that the state should actively take part in that process. Libertarians take the more authentically 'liberal' stance that what people do in their bedroom is no one's business, but also that the person's neighbour is perfectly free to disapprove of that lifestyle. This made libertarianism quite Right-wing, because progressives of the 1968 type cannot tolerate that sort of conservative judgementalism about other people's lifestyles, which in turn makes them judgemental about people's beliefs. It also partly explains why libertarianism has such limited appeal, since people find moral neutrality off-putting.

Libertarianism is, I suppose, the purest form of liberalism. It stems from the likes of the great French philosopher Montesquieu, who argued that we were more likely to have peace if religion was taken out of politics, or Thomas Jefferson, who passed the Virginia Statute for Religious Freedom, arguing that 'the legitimate powers of government extend to such acts only as are injurious to others. But it does me no injury for me to say there are twenty gods, or no god. It neither picks my pocket nor breaks my leg.'[22] It comes down to a distinction between private and public, which again is an idea most people have trouble with, even if they pay lip service to it.

It's an oddball sub-genre of politics, and in the US attracts wacky young men who want to create artificial states on cruise ships with no income tax or legalise donkey porn or whatever crackpot ideas the annual Libertarian Party conference throws up. My parents had a journalist friend who believed drink driving should be legal because, so long as people were doing so safely, it was none of the state's business what they put in their bodies. I remember Mum explaining that he was a 'libertarian' as if this was some bizarre religious sect that believes the earth to be no older than the flood. I don't know if he still clings on to that belief; he has since had kids so I suspect not.

Libertarians tend to be bright, the most analytical thinkers in the American political spectrum, and are overall the cleverest political subgroup, much more so than progressives or social conservatives.[23] Libertarians share the tolerant and forgiving qualities of Left-liberals, but without the sanctimoniousness. They don't view politics in religious-like moral terms so don't see non-believers as sinners or heretics, because libertarians tend to be more cerebral than emotional.[24] They are more likely to have autism, too. Indeed, their arguments are too cerebral for most people, and therefore always remain unpopular.

For a while, as I became more intensely political in my twenties, libertarianism seemed to be a growing movement. The *Independent* called it 'a silent revolution happening on campuses across the world', although as it turned out so silent no one ever heard it.[25] It mainly consisted of Ron Paul, whose following was select, to put it kindly, and one article about the craze cited a libertarian gathering that featured a hundred people, tiny compared to any Leftist demonstration. Among the groups reacting to this state growth was UKIP, which at the time defined itself as 'libertarian'; when I went to one of their conferences years back their youth leader was in favour of legalising bestiality. But obviously as the party grew in size, they realised that the number of people who loved 'Our NHS' and didn't want more immigrants numbered in the millions, while the total of Ayn Rand fans could probably fit in a modestly sized hotel room.

And it was inevitable that some libertarians were just conservatives, but had only adopted the philosophy as an identity because it didn't have the baggage associated with the authoritarian Right, and the socially crushing effects of being a young conservative. Many of us also don't know what we are politically, and are looking for an identity, or at least a definition. Social conservativism extols a repressed, reserved culture of personal restraint, sacrifice and modesty, framed by Christianity in general – and that's obviously deeply off-putting to pretty much anyone under the age of fifty. In contrast, libertarianism is relatively cool, or at least by the extremely low standards of the Right generally.

My problem with the libertarians was that I thought they were deluded for believing they could get a Victorian-sized state without Victorian attitudes. Sure, we could have legalised heroin, if most people still went to church and celebrity role models didn't exist, but it's not really going to happen. Then, when I was twenty-nine, Labour banned smoking in pubs, which I was at first furious about. That very month I'd moved in with my girlfriend to a small 1970s flat with really low ceilings, which made the living room a bong if even two people were smoking in it. I had literally no indoor place left in Britain I could smoke in. But then the following spring she became pregnant so I was forced to give up anyway, as I'd always promised in a vague way that I would when I had kids, and now having that extra nudge was appreciated. Sometimes the nanny state *was* right. Sometimes freedom isn't all it's cracked up to be.[26] Sometimes meddling makes the world a better place.

And so, having turned thirty and with fatherhood approaching, I had come to accept that I was conservative and I was fine with that. I had always felt uncomfortable with the tag, because I didn't want to be seen as something like Harry Enfield's Tory Boy. But then the end of youth brings with it some liberation; you never, ever have to go to a nightclub again, for instance, something which I only did because our First World War-era statist licensing laws forced pubs to close. More fundamentally, maturity also brings with it the liberation of no longer having to pretend to be something you're not; within the space of a year I had become a father, joined the Conservative Party and started going to church.

17

RELIGIOTS

If men will not be governed by the Ten Commandments,
they shall be governed by the ten thousand commandments.

G. K. Chesterton[1]

As well as our local church, Mum sometimes took us to Mass at St
Etheldreda's in Holborn, which was popular with journalists on account of
its proximity to Fleet Street. Afterwards we would have lunch upstairs with
the priests, among them the elderly Frenchman Fr Jean-Marie Charles-
Roux, a man so reactionary that he made Dad look like a dangerous,
free-thinking radical.

The tall and slender French priest was devoted to the old Latin Mass,
wore a monocle and buckled shoes and, with his high cheekbones, looked
every bit the aristocrat. Fr Charles-Roux's great passion was a personal one-
man campaign to have Marie Antoinette canonised, a charmingly lost
cause if ever there was one, and he refused to even acknowledge the
legitimacy of the French Republic, or as he called it, 'the Regicide State';
even when he retired he wouldn't return to France because it was plagued
by an 'awful republican sickness'. My brother and I always saw him as a
kindly but slightly clownish figure, and only much later, after he'd died at
the age of ninety-nine, did I learn about his past; how he had heroically
served France in 1940 and after its surrender escaped Nazi occupation by

swimming to Spain in winter. He had then found his way to the Free French in London, eventually becoming Charles de Gaulle's translator. Despite his appearance he wasn't actually of noble blood, in fact descending from a guard at Versailles who was killed during the storming of the palace, one of the ordinary people of France willing to die for their king.

Conservative Catholic circles in London were often involved with anti-communist organisations in eastern Europe. I remember my uncontrollable rage around the age of nine when Mum gave our VHS copy of *Jaws* to a Polish Catholic charity. I just couldn't understand why people in Soviet-occupied central Europe might be more deserving than me, living in Holland Park.

My parents wore their Christianity pretty lightly, and we weren't that involved with the Church, although I was dragged along to a Lourdes pilgrimage when I was thirteen, which was ghastly – the tackiest place on earth and the most boring age to be on any sort of trip with loads of old and sick people. I could never really identify with people who grew up so entranced by priests that they would literally take everything they said to be true, because that wasn't our experience. On the English side, our family had been secularised for many generations, having mostly been Dissenters originally; I imagine many of my ancestors were on the wrong side during the Civil War. My grandmother was an atheist and Dad had become Anglican despite his own background, but it was partly a cultural thing to him; attending Church of England services was just what an Englishman did, in his view.

Although I had stopped going to church around nine, I had never turned against religion or Catholicism; in England in the 1990s it didn't seem powerful enough to really hate, almost irrelevant. I didn't believe in what it preached but I can't ever remember thinking of it as a force for bad. And after becoming a parent I was drawn to the idea of churchgoing because instinctively I saw it as carrying the flame, that link between ancestors and posterity. My family had been doing this for 1400 years, many had suffered great penalties to do so, and if someone was going to drop the baton it shouldn't be me. But because I hadn't been to church for a while, I was a bit stunned to find out just how Leftie it all was.

Mum had a column for the *Catholic Herald*, and so through sheer grit and persistence I had managed to get a commission to write for them, and had started regularly contributing articles while still at *Nuts*. The guy who sat next to me reviewed hardcore porn films as a freelance sideline, so we had a wealth of journalistic experience. I continued writing regularly and so, two years after leaving *Nuts*, I began full-time work at the *Herald*, the first and presumably last person to ever work for both a lad's mag and a Catholic newspaper. As I joined, the Catholic Church in England was finally severing its connections with Amnesty, with great sadness and bitterness. It was part of a losing culture war for many Christians, finding that charities they once ran had turned against them, that political parties inspired by Christian groups discarded their members, and in the clash between the old religion and the new faith of equality and diversity the enemy was winning on all fronts.

The *Catholic Herald* served a doubly declining demographic, churchgoers and newspaper readers, so it was testimony to editor Luke Coppen in particular that it had managed to survive and thrive. Christianity was in sharp decline in every Western country, a huge and unprecedented civilisational change, and Britain had long led the pack. Since the early 1980s the percentage of people in the country claiming no religion had increased from 31 to 53 per cent while the number attending church fell to half what it had been in the 1960s.[2] Among the generation born in the 1990s and beyond, churchgoing was on the verge of extinction except among immigrants.

Catholicism in England is politically contradictory. The Roman Church, almost by definition, is more conservative than the Anglican communion, having formed the original 'Right-wing' of the Christian political spectrum, and its views on sexual matters are still much more traditional than any other mainstream church. And yet, for ethnic and class reasons, its membership is historically on the Left; just as the Church of England was the Tory party at prayer, the Catholic Church had a long association with

Labour. Most Catholics came from Irish immigrant backgrounds, disproportionately working-class and living in the big cities of London, the north
and Midlands, as well as the west of Scotland. In the late nineteenth century Cardinal Manning had been a huge hero of London dockers, who
turned up in their tens of thousands for his funeral in 1892, the biggest
since Wellington's. In recent years the bishops had a particularly prickly
relationship with the Tories, and it was said that on the night of Blair's victory champagne corks could be heard at Ecclestone Square, the bureaucratic
headquarters of the bishops in Victoria. If true, then it was soon to turn
sour. Or flat, I suppose.

The *Herald* had once been the more Left-wing of the Catholic papers but
had since repositioned itself on the Right, a *Telegraph* to the rival *Tablet*,
which as the paper of quite posh liberal Catholics was more like the *Guardian*.
As Catholicism had declined, the Church had become less working class,
and there were fewer dockers in the pews and more *Brideshead Revisited* types
who liked wearing cravats and pretending they had been to Oxford. It had
also become less Irish, and more heavily African, Asian and eastern
European, another reason why on this subject the hierarchy was so progressive on immigration. And yet the Catholic Church was widely detested
on the Left, as it had been at least since Diderot supposedly suggested we
strangle the last king with the guts of the last priest. At the time I joined,
The Da Vinci Code, the film of Dan Brown's blockbuster novel, was all over
the news, portraying the Church as a secretive, reactionary organisation
that hated women. A terrible film, but a great meme processor, although
literally the opposite was true in reality – not only is the Catholic Church
overwhelmingly female dominated, but the hierarchy is pretty right on, at
least on some issues.

And so my many attempts to get back to churchgoing were severely
tried by the fact that whenever I stepped inside, now with a baby in tow, and
irrespective of whether it was Catholic or Anglican, the homily or sermon
was like having the *Guardian*'s 'Comment is Free' section read to you. The
language used was that of the centre-Left: please pray that we have 'social

justice' and a 'fair distribution of resources' and pray for farmers in the developing world who suffer because produce is being sold abroad as a cash crop. At our local church we were always being told to celebrate diversity, while the former local Anglican vicar used to go on about climate change (I mean, I agreed with him, but it wasn't the place). To make it worse, while I was to the Right of the Church on economics and immigration, I was a fair bit more liberal on issues to do with heterosexual shenanigans and far more liberal on the subject of homosexuality. Even when they were Right, they were wrong.

The nearby Anglican church was attached to a very popular primary school and lots of upper-middle-class urban liberals in my area ended up going every Sunday to get their kids into it. Many found they quite liked it, the sense of community and warmness, and at the very least it's an hour when the kids are quiet. The schools issue was a front in the broader culture war, with agitated atheists arguing that faith schools are indoctrinating (which they aren't) and selective (which they are). When I arrived the New Atheism Internet Wars were at their height, a gruelling five-year conflict in which thousands of lives were wasted typing below the line in pointless arguments about religion. It was, I think, the first taste Britain really had of a culture war, even if it was an obscure one fought away from most people – sort of like the Balkan Wars preceding the big conflict in 1914.

The year I joined, 2007, Christopher Hitchens's *God Is Not Great* was published, with its line 'religion poisons everything'.[3] Hitchens was a truly gifted writer but his central argument was basic, and whenever he found someone religious who was good (say, Martin Luther King) he'd just downplay their faith as being some broader humanism. When he saw a secular ideology that he didn't like, such as Stalinism or North Korean communism, he declared it was actually religious, rather than perhaps exploring the obvious explanation that human nature causes us to follow ideologies that have a quasi-religious nature. Likewise ethnic conflicts that had sectarian elements, such as Northern Ireland and Bosnia, he attributed to religion rather than nationalism or just basic human tribalism.

That sort of set the tone for the whole New Atheism wars. In one sense the atheists had the far more logical argument, that their whole premise wasn't based on an unproveable assumption, but their smugness irritated me; this was personified by Richard Dawkins, the biologist's diatribes against 'religiots' and his unbelievably self-satisfied followers. Then there was the argument mocking conservative Christians by pointing out the obvious contradictions between (a caricature) Thatcherism and what Jesus said about wealth, ignoring that Christianity is a long and complex body of work and beliefs, which can be reconciled with most political beliefs. Likewise 'Jesus never said anything about gays!' written as if it was a really clever point. He was a first-century rabbi – I think we can probably guess his views on the issue. He didn't say anything about internet copyright laws, either.

One group of 'sciencocrats', arguing for a public policy based on reason, called themselves 'the Brights', a terrible name that gave the impression they thought other people dim, even if that hadn't been the intention. As for the belief we could build a better world if people were more 'rational': the popular scientist Neil deGrasse Tyson came up with the brainwave of a state called 'Rationalia' in which all public policy should be based on evidence, an idea so stupid only a very clever person could think it up. I mean, this has been done before and the track record isn't great.

The below-the-line God Squad were probably even worse; I never understood their argument that atheists just 'hate God' or are angry at Him. They clearly *don't* hate something they literally don't believe exists, and are only angry at the people they think are making God up to gain power or put off the terrifying prospect of death. The Christian argument was the same one I couldn't stand in Lefties: you might be arguing x, but I know you actually believe y.

But then I also thought many New Atheists were being fundamentally dishonest. Lots of people claiming to be worried about growing political religion in the 2000s cited a supposed anti-evolution, anti-science movement in the arse end of nowhere in America. What they were really concerned about – quite reasonably – was one religion in particular, a faith quite clearly hostile to free speech, which had a terrible modern record regarding freedom for atheists and religious minorities, and some of whose adherents tended to behead people who committed blasphemy. And, unlike Christianity, it was a religion growing in strength and numbers across western Europe; if that was their fear, they should just say so, rather than focusing their ire on Anglican primary schools that taught a nice, soppy, universalist worldview almost indistinguishable from the secular Left.

The supposed threat of the 'religious Right' was a mirage, since even in America Christianity is in terrible demographic trouble. The percentage of Americans with no religion went from 5 per cent in 1972 to 25 per cent in the 2010s, including 39 per cent of Millennials, while the percentage of people who say they are atheist or agnostic rose from 10.3 per cent in 2007 to 15.8 per cent just seven years later.[4] England and France are way ahead on that one, but the rest of Europe is catching up, and in Italy the number of church marriages declined by over 10 per cent in just one year in the 2010s.[5]

But then politics just fills the void that religion leaves. And if any rational atheists think this has a happy ending, then they haven't been paying attention.

Equality

My time at the *Catholic Herald* coincided with many social reforms that were unsettling to some readers. Imagine being born in, say, 1935 and just seeing most of the moral values you grew up with turning on their heads, sometimes 180 degrees. But even worse, that this change is accelerating as you get older, just at the age where you really don't want to try new ideas. No moral issue has shifted so much in so little time as our attitudes to homosexuality, and most conservatives would think rightly so, since not every revolutionary change is bad. Even French Royalists in the 1820s would probably concede that centimetres are just easier, and exempting the aristocracy from tax is something we won't raise again. The massacres of priests and reign of terror – definitely a mistake though. But then all revolutions throw up some good ideas, almost by definition.

It's a thorny issue because Christianity from its start was hostile to same-sex relations, and yet at its heart it's about compassion and the dignity of the individual. It was always more comforting for bishops to talk about non-sexual issues where polite company was more accepting – about why the Tory cuts are bad and why we should welcome the immigrant into our community, rather than telling people to keep their knickers on. The ongoing, almost never-ending child abuse scandal had also seriously weakened their ability to lecture people about sex, understandably. Even if lots of Catholics wanted radically to alter doctrine about homosexuality, the Church is like a moral supertanker in that it's difficult to change direction quickly enough to compete with a culture that is rapidly shifting its attitudes. That's partly why the Catholic Church has survived for two thousand years, but moral change has speeded up much more quickly in the past half-century than in any previous era.

As well as losing support from potential waverers, this clash also means Christianity is at odds with the state, which sees equality and diversity as moral absolutes. In 2006 Labour passed the Equality Act, followed by a 2010 update, which Harriet Harman called an opportunity 'to fashion a new social order', the kind of thing that sounds terrifying to me.[6] Under British law public authorities were now required to 'promote equality in everything that they do, also making sure that other organisations meet their legal duties to promote equality while also doing so themselves'. Equality is a central part of the progressive religion, which itself stems from a Christian idea, yet the old religion and new inevitably come into conflict.

There had been disputes between state and Church before, the biggest over the question of abortion, but at the time of the Abortion Act it was not a Left/Right issue. This was not just about 'choice', since Catholic medical staff also wanted the freedom not to take part in abortions or help in any way, and increasingly this was under threat. (In one big case two Glasgow midwives in 2012 lost their right not to help staff in abortion procedures.[7])

There were also more complicated conscience issues, such as the morning-after pill, which the Church considers a form of abortion although this is heavily contested by experts. Many Catholic doctors warned that it was becoming hard for them to remain in the medical profession.

But there are very few areas where a state committed to 'equality' is not going to clash with Catholicism, partly because the followers of the new religion share with the old a belief that everyone should be saved. Perhaps the most sinister argument the New Atheists made was that religion is 'child abuse', which had real echoes of Soviet Russia, where religious people were 'free' to practise their religion as long as they did not 'indoctrinate' their children. One of Richard Dawkins's confederates, the psychologist Nicholas Humphrey, even said (much to Dawkins's approval) that 'parents have no God-given licence to enculturate their children in whatever ways they personally choose'.[8] Having just become a parent I felt that, well, I did have that licence – if I wanted to bring my children up to believe in my sky fairy that was up to me. Some issues are more visceral to us than others, in that they trigger a deep-seated response, and I suppose this was one such for me, the idea that schools could be overstepping parents on such personal matters. Indeed, for many Catholics one of the worst things was the state's policy of giving out contraception to underage girls without their parents' consent; I didn't have very Catholic views on contraception but this struck me as, well, paedo-enabling.[9]

Much of the paper's news content involved ongoing culture-war issues that the Catholic side was obviously losing, constantly retreating as secularists made headway. Public opinion, already hostile, was shifting further away from Christians, because once utilitarianism becomes accepted then Christian arguments stand no chance. It was interesting watching this culture war being played out from the defeated side, although a bit trying. Whenever I explained to people where I worked, they would raise the subject of a) homosexuality b) the child abuse scandals c) some *Da Vinci Code* bullshit d) controlling women's bodies and e) (yawn) Pope Benedict serving in the Hitler Youth.

But the clash between religious conscience and gay rights was the hardest circle to square. Our culture's strong hostility to homosexual relations arose out of Christianity's idea that sex should be an act of procreation and not dominance, as it was to the Greeks and Romans (and perhaps from a practical point of view homophobia makes sense for Bronze Age communities where underpopulation was a big threat). Conversely the modern idea of accepting gay people and allowing them to find happiness came from an ultimately Christian idea of the dignity of the individual. I sympathised with the latter; I even appreciated the argument that legal equality wasn't enough and that acceptance should be encouraged, I just didn't like the idea that the state was deciding what the agreed public morality should be, and prosecuting people for their views. There were increasing numbers of cases of religious preachers arrested for condemning Gay Pride, or elderly couples interrogated for saying the Bible condemns homosexuality. It became a regular generic story type in the *Herald*. It didn't help that a lot of the people in question seemed rather odd, or old, or just otherwise not the sort with whom you'd want to hang around. These traditionalist Christians seemed like a lost species descended from the Puritans, now being persecuted by another subspecies who had evolved different characteristics.

Some of these cases were appalling, such as the man in Trafford suspended from his job for a Facebook post opposed to gay marriage, who was thankfully supported by the ever-principled Peter Tatchell.[10] Then there was the incident in which police held a Christian preacher for fifteen hours without food or water after he was reported by a pair of boys, who sounded like the sort of kids the Soviets indoctrinated into grassing on their parents.[11] If someone declares 'God created Adam and Eve, not Adam and Steve', or whatever the lame argument, you are perfectly entitled to laugh at them, but what kind of person calls the police?

The Evangelical campaigners weren't my sort of people, but the increasing tendency for Christians to be punished for expressing views now considered beyond the pale seemed like a throwback to the days when subjects of the Crown were expected to attend Anglican Communion. It seemed that secularisation had not brought increased liberalism; rather it had replaced the authority of the Church of England and Christianity in general with the moral arm of the state, helped by the charities and campaigning groups it funded. It's a basic principle of liberalism that Church and state should remain separate, which requires that the Church should not make laws, but also that the state should not seek to become arbiter of morals either.

More importantly, the whole point of liberalism was that it was the only way in which lots of people with different worldviews could rub along, by agreeing to disagree. Now that we had hugely variant worldviews it seemed more necessary than ever, but instead we had equality activists harassing people they disagreed with, because they were strong and their opponents were weak. And, most tellingly, few people seemed to care.

18

THE RIGHT SIDE OF HISTORY

It used to be said that as you get older you get more Right-wing. Not any more. According to Pew Research, the percentage of US millennials who see themselves as liberal went from 41 per cent in 2004, when the youngest were eighteen, to 57 per cent in 2017, with just 15 per cent now calling themselves conservative. Among Generation Xers, born between 1965 and 1980, the number had increased from 29 per cent in 1994 to 43 per cent today.[1]

A big change is happening, and the reason is religion. Liberals tend to be less religious and, once large sections of the population abandon Christianity, liberalism becomes their default setting. Today just 16 per cent of American liberals think religious faith gives them a 'great deal' of meaning in life, compared to 62 per cent of 'very conservative' Americans. And yet into the void left by religion something else takes its place, and so 30 per cent of very liberal Americans find a 'great deal' of meaning in political causes, compared to just 9 per cent of conservatives.[2] Religion simply becomes replaced by ideology, a term first used during the French Revolution by the philosopher Antoine de Tracy. Politics seems to satisfy the same thirst as Christianity, a decaf version in some cases or a dangerous synthetic opiate in others.

But progressivism also seamlessly takes the place of faith because it is a heresy of Christianity, and its followers have inherited the Christian traditions of equality, universalism, individualism, free will and eschatology, the idea that we are moving towards an end time of triumph – 'the right side of history'. And yet perversely these secular believers lack any of the doubt that has been injected into modern mainstream Christianity and made it more tolerant.

The Left originated with Christianity, and in Britain descends from low-church Protestantism in particular. In the words of Robert Tombs, 'The Nonconformist tradition bequeaths campaigning militancy, a self-image of anti-Establishment rebellion, a view of politics as moral struggle (as opposed to "the art of the possible") . . . and sectarian suspicion of the motives of opponents.'[3] In the nineteenth century some referred to the Liberals as 'the party of Christ' because of their association with fervent nonconformism, while the parts of England with the strongest Anglican presence in 1851 still vote Tory in the twenty-first century; indeed, some 60 per cent of Anglicans voted Leave in 2016, compared to a slight minority of Catholics.[4] (Even when age was accounted for, Anglicans were heavily in favour of Brexit.[5]) And so it's likely that the decline of the Church of England will have large implications even for those of us who aren't members.

In his magisterial 2014 work *Inventing the Individual*, American-born philosopher Larry Siedentop argued that liberalism is 'a child of Christianity', which goes against the common assumption that the eighteenth-century Enlightenment brought liberalism into the world despite the best efforts of religion.[6] Siedentop argued that St Paul invented two radical ideas that shook the world – moral equality and human agency – and pointed out how different the Greek and Roman views of human dignity were. For Siedentop, 'St Paul was the greatest revolutionary in human history', a belief shared by quite a few Left-wing academics who in recent years have reclaimed the apostle.

The 'American Religion' in particular is a product of that, by which I mean that optimistic belief that history is an arc in which progress and justice are brought to a widening circle of people – women, black people, gays – and prejudice and bigotry conquered. The idea that two men should be allowed to marry and be treated as equals because of their *essential moral equality as individuals* is an idea that would have been completely incomprehensible to a Greek or

Roman, just as arguments for the abolition of slavery would have been. A medieval Christian would certainly disagree with gay liberation, but the basic arguments might have been intelligible, and indeed would have been not dissimilar to the Church's case against human bondage. It's why Christian campaigners struggled to articulate arguments against gay marriage – because from a Christian point of view it's sort of logical.

This Christian mindset extends towards things such as the trans debate and whether someone with a penis can be a woman. When Liberal Democrat MP Layla Moran argued that 'I see someone in their soul and as a person. I do not really care whether they have a male body', she was using an essentially Christian idea to argue for trans equality: a person born in a man's body is a woman because they possess a woman's soul.[7] And yet, perhaps once belief in God fades, then the principles of individual liberty and universal equality are simply self-explanatory.

Some philosophers talk of religion helping societies reach a certain stage of development, after which they are no longer needed; I suppose like thrusters attached to space modules. The logic of egalitarianism and individualism then goes on without the creed that helped start it – that's the theory.

Even my complaint that priests are Lefties is nothing new. William Graham Sumner, a Victorian proto-libertarian, argued in his 1883 book, *What Social Classes Owe to Each Other* that the 'ecclesiastical prejudice in favor of the poor and against the rich' would 'replunge Europe into barbarism'.[8] He complained that 'it is not uncommon to hear a clergyman utter from the pulpit all the old prejudice in favor of the poor and against the rich', and later concluded his career by writing, before his death in 1910: 'I have lived through the best period of this country's history. The next generations are going to see wars and social calamities.'[9] See, pessimists *are* worth listening to sometimes.

'Reason'

There are many terrible arguments levelled at the secularists, but the strongest is that, without religion, people still believe in irrational things. 'Rationalism' is a political idea that goes back to Jeremy Bentham's utilitarianism but it heavily influenced both Friedrich Engels's scientific socialism and Woodrow Wilson's 'scientific public administration' as well as various other terrible progressive ideas. Engels claimed his friend Marx had created a 'scientific' theory showing that class-bound societies would inevitably collapse, and it was Marxists' belief they were 'rational' that made them so dangerous. Indeed, non-believers can be terrifying in their certainty, especially if they think they're the good guys.

Yet reason is an illusion, and most research tends to support David Hume's idea that emotions are in charge of the brain when politics is concerned; we just use reason when we want to come up with good explanations for how we reached our prejudices.[10] The idea that one side of the political divide is 'rational' goes at least back to Shelley, and yet there is overwhelming evidence that bias is pretty evenly split between Left and Right. According to one meta-analysis of fifty-one experimental studies using eighteen thousand volunteers, liberals and conservatives 'were biased to very similar degrees'.[11] Both groups had the same 'tendency to evaluate otherwise identical information more favorably when it supports one's political beliefs or allegiances'. This backs up the symmetry hypothesis, the idea that Left and Right 'showed no difference in mean levels of bias across studies'.[12]

Likewise, while conservatives are more religious, Democrats are more likely than Republicans to believe in a number of irrational beliefs, such as that 'thought can influence the physical world', 'houses can be haunted by spirits', and that fortune telling and astrology are real. Republicans were in contrast more likely to believe that 'Satan is responsible for evil', by a margin of 15 per cent.[13] Only around 10 per cent of adults pass the Watson Test of rationality, the most popular tool for measuring bias.[14] And so the New Atheist argument that without religion we would behave rationally is itself so obviously irrational. All that happens when cultivated and philosophical religion declines is that dafter faiths take their place or people start to look for justice and paradise in this world through politics. Institutional religions also carry a body of work and wisdom, sort of the equivalent of a Common Law which can be used as a reference but also a constraint. Without that, people just come out with ever crazier ideas, and crackpot ideas also became status markers.

Humans have a tendency towards unifying belief systems, and many things have a vaguely religious bent. American conservatives arguably treat the constitution like a sacred text, and Ronald Reagan as a prophet. The environmental movement is often accused of resembling a religion, with its initial paradise and its warning of apocalypse, although in fairness to the greens if we do push the global temperature above 2 degrees then it will start to feel a bit Old Testament.

As Émile Durkheim wrote, it is 'a universal fact that, when a conviction of any strength is held by the same community of men, it inevitably takes on a religious character. It inspires in men's minds the same reverential respect as beliefs which are properly religious. It is, thus, very probable . . . that religion corresponds to an equally very central area of the conscience collective.'[15] Religion is defined by Wikipedia as 'a cultural system that creates powerful and long-lasting meaning by establishing symbols that relate humanity to beliefs and values . . . They tend to derive morality, ethics, religious laws or a preferred lifestyle from their ideas about the cosmos and human nature.' The etymology of *religio* in Latin is 'to bind', as in to form a society, and likewise for many people a political cause is about creating a community, although this is far stronger among socialists and progressives.

Left-wing people tend to see their political organisations the way Christians see their churches. It is much more a community of believers, which is partly why the other side are just far better organised; more social, more filled with belief, and dedicated to spreading that faith even if it entails humiliation. They are sometimes prepared to die for socialism, whereas I can't even tolerate the idea of being embarrassed by wearing a blue rosette in the street because someone will shout 'twat' at me. Outside of the upper-class horsey scene, where the Tory party is a social thing, conservatives aren't particularly passionate about the movement. Even people I know who've been Tory members for years and years literally cannot fathom the emotional attachment Labour folk have to their party, this mass movement and social organisation – this church.

Conservatives are not very good at organising, and 'when they do, right-wing activists tend to stay in their own lanes and not work together, share notes, or reach out to one another's followers', as one writer put it, illustrating how the supporters of one Leftist cause will often turn up to support the rally of another.[16] They will form a church of like-minded believers, and gain much more practice building political movements.[17] The only really successful Right-wing group in the culture war is the anti-abortion movement, which in the US has managed to keep public opinion fairly onside – largely because it is overwhelmingly a religious organisation and so highly social. Unless they're actually Church-run, conservative causes don't tend to have the same sort of oxytocin-inducing communal feeling as progressive ones.

Political movements often have a certain religious feeling, something that's been noticed since *The Old Regime and the Revolution*, where Alexis de Tocqueville wrote of 1789: 'It created an atmosphere of missionary fervor and, indeed, assumed all the aspects of a religious revival . . . It would perhaps be truer to say that it developed into a species of religion.'[18] The revolutionaries, hoping to 'possess the souls that the Church had recruited', demanded that priests swear an Oath to the Revolution, and those that didn't were either killed or hounded out of their villages.[19] So much for the tolerant Left.

Bertrand Russell called Bolshevism a 'religion' and spoke of the 'habit of militant certainty about objectively doubtful matters' while Albert Camus saw that communism brought all the worst excesses of faith.[20] Many communist regimes had obvious pseudo-religious elements such as the embalming of former leaders or North Korea's worship of the president, although none took it as far as Mao's China, where under the lunatic dictator 'there was the ubiquitous holy red book, the collective morning prayer before the icon, regular breaks for reading the scripture throughout the working day, public recitations of the sacred works, the confession of sins, and the blessing of food by pronouncing "Long Live Chairman Mao" or still longer recitations of good wishes for the Great Helmsman'.[21] Even mistaking paper with Mao's texts on it for toilet paper or speaking one of Mao's phrases with the wrong intonation could lead to prison or even execution.

Marxism inherited from Christianity the idea of eschatology, that history is going in a lineal direction towards a glorious end point, a view shared by progressivism. Martin Luther King is often credited with the phrase, 'History has a telos and it is one of liberal progress – the arc of history is long but it bends towards justice.', although it's far older.[22] For those who believe this idea, the date itself attracts some meaning, so that people argue that they 'can't believe this [terrible thing] is happening in [the current year]'. The irritatingly handsome Canadian prime minister and fancy-dress enthusiast Justin Trudeau was once asked once why it's important to have a gender balance in the cabinet, one which included 'immigrants, aboriginals, religious minorities, a quadriplegic and 15 women'.[23] The photogenic leader replied: 'Because it is 2015.'[24] A similar argument was made by Barack Obama the previous year when he said that 'One thing we can all agree on is that a group like Isil has no place in the twenty-first century', although it seemed like jihadists did have their own, niche place in the current century.

C. S. Lewis called this 'chronological snobbery', the idea that previous ages were always more backward simply because of the date. Conservatives are more likely to see history in terms of cycles, an older worldview that made sense when the only certainty was that spring would follow winter, and when society noticeably changed less in a lifetime. The seventeenth-century Nicolas Poussin painting *Dance to the Music of Time* illustrates this idea of life being a cycle, from rags to riches and back to rags again; on a larger scale, conservatives tend to believe that civilisations rise and fall, going from barbarism to decadence; liberals tend to think things will just get better and better and better.

Americans, influenced by the oddball sectarian groups that founded the country and more recently by Left-wing intellectuals, have long had the idea of history as a struggle between good and evil in which the former triumphs against bigotry and hatred, an explicitly Christian message. Around the time the arguments were being made for gay marriage Steven Spielberg's film about Abraham Lincoln came out, which culminates in a long scene where Congress debates ending slavery, in that schmaltzy way Americans love. It ended, obviously, with the bigots being defeated and the American dream of equality triumphing because humans are inherently good and the arc of history etc; just as it would do a hundred years later for the civil rights movement, and another half-century after that with gay rights, another example of the American Religion in action. Indeed, *Lincoln* seemed like an obvious analogy for same-sex marriage; or perhaps that was just me, so deep into culture war stuff that nothing was ever just a story.

This idea of linear progress is shared by progressivism and communism, 'twin children of the Enlightenment, raised in the same nursery of the Revolution'. Both believe that 'radical freedom for all is inevitable, the forces of History will sweep toward their ultimate victory – and *therefore* it is essential that every good citizen accept' the faith and promote it. Both progressives and communists are preparing for a glorious final victory, although 'the forces of irrationality, hatred, discrimination, and reaction are still strong – in the Vendée, among the kulaks of the Bible Belt who cling bitterly to their guns and their God, and even in the universities.'[25]

Like Christianity, liberalism is sacramental. According to Polish philosopher Ryszard Legutko: 'Public life is full of mandatory rituals in which every politician, artist, writer, celebrity, teacher or any public figure is willing to participate, all to prove that their liberal-democratic creed springs spontaneously from the depths of their hearts.'[26] This dates back to the 1793 Festival of Reason, where a woman dressed as the Goddess of Reason was placed on the holy altar in the Church of Our Lady in Paris. Or more recently, when Twitter boss Jack Dorsey apologised for having eaten from Chick-fil-A, a fast-food brand known for opposing same-sex marriage, during Pride month; he was forced to recant for violating the holy month, like some poor Muslim teenager shouted at by the religious police for daring to enjoy a cigarette during Ramadan. It is this belief in final, inevitable victory that gives progressivism its energy, and its determination to convert everyone.[27] Like any religion, it cannot stand heretics or apostates, which is why liberals are far more hostile to white Christian conservatives than authoritarian Muslims, who are merely infidels.

Nietzsche was one of many to draw comparisons between socialism and Christianity, and the old misery guts was a fan of neither. His compatriot Eric Voegelin, in his 1938 book *Die Politischen Religionen* (*The Political Religions*) had argued that totalitarian ideologies are similar to faiths; later, in his 1968 *Science, Politics, and Gnosticism*, Voegelin called all modern political movements 'ersatz religion'. He argued that after the Enlightenment people began to see their own activities as sacred, including their politics, and that 'When God has become invisible behind the world, the things of the world become new gods.'[28]

And so, as Christianity started seriously to haemorrhage support in the 1960s, so a new faith arose, progressivism as Christianity 2.0, with 'privilege' a form of original sin and vulnerable groups the new sacred. The old and new faiths have much in common: even the progressive tendency to repeat what children say as if they're great fonts of wisdom comes from the Bible, and the Gospel of Matthew. 'And Jesus saith unto them, Yea; have ye never read, Out of the mouth of babes and sucklings thou hast perfected praise?' This has become a media staple in recent years, my favourite being a *New York Times* report about a primary school in Boston in which a teacher asked some kids the question: 'What is gender?' And to which a second grader – i.e. aged seven to eight – replied: 'It's a thing people invented to put you in a category.'[29] That's sweet. I mean, it's completely untrue, but sweet. The 'Woke eight-year-old' who tells her progressive parent that Donald Trump is going to create the Fourth Reich – her thoughts being suspiciously like a Simple English version of the parent's own musings on the subject – is such a cliché on social media that more often than not it's done in jest. Yet supposedly highbrow newspapers make this comically unintelligent and twee argument with all seriousness. But then, perhaps once you take the supernatural out of the faith then what you're left with is paradoxically less rational.

Declining religion may make people think less, because they no longer have to train their mind to contemplate paradoxes; Catholicism is quite baffling sometimes but it involves a weighty appreciation of serious issues about what life is about. It also forces people to think about conflicting goals – 'justice' and 'mercy' are at the core of that inner conflict within Catholicism – and how we square them; by agonising over these things one might reduce the tendency towards moral absolutism. In contrast, some of the more vociferous social justice activists see the world in very binary terms, between good and evil, something I find a bit frightening. Burke's idea that things are complicated in reality is intelligible to a religious person; faith also lets them understand that there are limits to our abilities, and to what can be done.

People who do not believe in an all-powerful creator are more likely to believe that the state can move mountains. From Robespierre onwards people have believed that the state can perform any God-like function, something Jonah Goldberg called statolatry – worship of the state. Perhaps a belief in a supernatural deity acts as some form of vaccine for this idea; Scruton speculated that people who believed in paradise in the next world were perhaps less likely to go along with schemes to create it here, and maybe there's some truth in it.

Even institutions now take on a more sacred function. Famously Nigel Lawson once remarked that the NHS was 'the closest thing the English have to a religion',[30] and those who have dared to criticise this institution are met with fervent hostility. Sometimes Britain's NHS obsession strikes me as deeply weird, like something from China: there was an NHS-themed series of *Great British Menu* on BBC Two in which one chef cooked a dish to honour junior doctors, and another in tribute to health service founder Nye Bevan. Watching the opening ceremony of the 2012 Olympics, you would think that no other country in the developed world had free universal healthcare and, in most cases, better outcomes than us. On one occasion health unions even called for 'a National Vigil to save the NHS', people being encouraged to light candles in their home to sort of pray for it.

But what is most troubling about the progressive religion is the assumption by some on the Left that their side is moral, whereas genuinely moral people should never be comfortable in their righteousness. As Christopher Lasch observed in The Revolt of the Elites, 'For those who take religion seriously, belief is a burden, not a self-righteous claim to some privileged moral status. Self-righteousness, indeed, may well be more prevalent among sceptics than among believers. The spiritual discipline against self-righteousness is the very essence of religion.'[31] People in positions of moral authority should never feel content that they are the saved; they should feel confused, agonised even. I admit that I feel some jealousy when I read centrist, liberal writers, who seem to be so comfortable in their own moral skin, content that they are the good guys, untroubled by any other possibility. What's worse, maybe they're right.

Dr Tom Wright, a former Anglican bishop, once wrote about how journalists are obsessed with Catholic moralising and hypocrisy but largely because they are rivals: 'The media want to be the guardians of public morality, but some people still see the church that way. Very well, it must be pulled down from its perch to make way for its secular successor.'[32] His point was that the commentariat aren't anti-clerical – they just want to be the clerics, and they become more priest-like the more secular the country becomes. Others have argued that there is only a set level of moralising in each society so once the moral leaders stop lecturing us on sex outside marriage or drinking gin, they just replace those things with other forms of social deviancy, such as having bad opinions.

And just like the old priesthood, the new one has its hypocrites, the eco-activists who fly across oceans or the egalitarians who send their kids to private school. There are saints who really do live by their progressive values and make sacrifices for their beliefs – I've known many – but human nature and frailty never change. Hypocrisy is built into the human mind, and we also remember the hypocrites more than the Leftists who do send their kid to a challenging comprehensive. That humans are frail and temptation strong doesn't mean that we shouldn't strive for morality, whether it's suppressing lust, greed or racial hatred, just that we are all tempted, and the more idealistic and utopian the political system, the more such hypocrisy becomes overwhelming.

This clerisy's anti-Catholicism became much more intense over the summer of 2010 ahead of Pope Benedict's visit to Britain, which sadly meant I had to leave our rented chateau in the Loire valley early so I could get back to London, and perhaps get in a couple of *Telegraph* blogs attacking 'the metropolitan elite'. The *Guardian* and Channel 4 ran a series of articles and programmes attacking the Church for being a nest of bigots and child abusers. There was a march against the Pope, whose views apparently ran counter to British values, whatever the hell that means. The *Guardian* editorial on the day before the papal visit advised: 'A little less preaching and a bit more humility might help the next state visit of a pope.'[33] Also from the paper's online edition that day was one commentator writing about the evils of rape jokes, which have to be ended 'now', another on why wolf-whistling is wrong – 'it isn't fine, it shouldn't be socially acceptable, and that it must end'. There was a piece on why the theatre is too white and middle class, making 'a deeply flawed medium'. And, of course, Polly Toynbee was writing about poverty, calling it 'a man-made calamity, due to political decisions' and 'the great moral issue of our time'.

On the second day, still exhausted from the all-night drive across France, I watched the secularist demo walk up Piccadilly, a liberal crowd that looked like the demography of the Green Party: proclaiming their love of 'science', complete with that annoying modern habit of the twee, humorous banner, which I believe started with people using the *Father Ted*-inspired 'down with this sort of thing'. Afterwards I made the stupid point in a *Telegraph* blog post observing how this protest was 99.999 per cent white while the Catholic pilgrims inside the park just five minutes away were widely multiracial.

It was a disingenuous argument because I don't attach any moral weight to whether a crowd is diverse, and I think anyone who does is a simpleton. But it has always interested me how ultra-white the most progressive causes always are, and how hard they find it to interest others.

Which is certainly not a problem with the Catholic Church, which continues to grow enormously in Africa even while dying in Europe – on show that day in Hyde Park with the crowds waiting for Benedict XVI to appear on stage. I found it exhilarating, or at least fun considering religion was involved and alcohol wasn't. Why did I feel so rapturous and happy being in an enormous crowd full of energy, screaming with love as a German guy arrived on stage? I just don't know what it was. It was like a festival, except rather than bands there were lots of priests talking; and no booze or drugs, unless you count getting high on religion, which obviously is nothing like as good.

Before the main man arrived on stage there was a series of warm-up speeches. Standing there with a friend from the *Herald*, I watched as a number of clerics and other churchy types came on, becoming increasingly dismayed as they each bravely stood up to the orthodoxies of the day. A priest from the East End came on and started talking about global poverty and how corporations were responsible for starving the global south. Another had an attack on the free market and how it was selfish, or something. Then some other Church worthy came on, and started talking about diversity and welcoming the stranger, i.e. more immigration, and then we were all made to applaud Cafod, the Left-wing Church hunger charity, which makes Oxfam look like the Koch Foundation.

I stood there, starting to feel exasperated and needing a drink. Oh Lord – is *anyone* here not a communist?

19

THE CREED

Aged thirty-one, I finally joined the Conservative Party. I'm not really sure why, except that now that I was a father and at the higher end of youth, and mentally already about fifty-seven, it felt like the time. Going to a couple of Tory get-togethers in north London, it also felt quite pleasant if a bit weird to be at a social event where everyone vaguely agreed with me politically; rather than being, not just the most Right-wing person in the room, but a freakish outlier.

I got on well with some of the people but I've never felt being a Tory member a part of my identity, and couldn't really understand the sentimental attachment the other side felt. During the Labour Party's long meltdown following Jeremy Corbyn's election as leader, the emotional pain and anguish expressed by moderate members about their party were clearly heartfelt but to me just baffling. Some of the arguments people made for why they were staying in the party, because their great-grandfather joined it to fight for better wages in 1921 or something, just struck me as weird. Education campaigner Fiona Millar wrote that:

> For those of us who have spent decades (in my case more than 40 years) as members of Labour, these are not easy times. I grew up in a strictly atheist household, where the party was akin to religion. My parents were products of the trade union-sponsored Ruskin College; my father worked on *Tribune* in the 1950s. My childhood

> was punctuated by Labour events: Saturday mornings churning
> out newsletters on an ancient Gestetner copier, Labour bazaars,
> election campaigns and ward meetings.[1]

Some other party activist, devastated about its extremism, recalled how their father would respond to any good thing, even those unrelated to politics, as 'Labour win'.

For me that sort of tribal loyalty is completely incomprehensible. I saw the Tory party as simply an organisation of convenience to keep socialists out of power, not something we're all going to cry about if it outlives its purpose. (When reading this you have to imagine I'm speaking in a heartless-sounding aristocratic voice, perhaps Charles Dance as Tywin Lannister or Alan Rickman in *Robin Hood: Prince of Thieves*.) It's just a thing orientated towards a goal – if you're not religious and want the emotional attachment and hormonal high of a brotherhood sharing each other's agony and ecstasy, get a football team.

But Labour folk see things differently. Before the referendum threw British politics up in the air like the neural pathways of a long-term drug user, three times as many people identified as Labour supporters as Conservatives, even though the two parties tend to average a similar vote. The downside of this is that once you have a solid moral community then you're probably more likely to feel hostility towards the outgroup. For fervent religious believers it's often the case that their entire life is dominated by the faith, and they tend to develop quite a sectarian attitude to non-members. Jeremy Corbyn reportedly once said that he could not be friends with someone who isn't Left-wing, which for a potential prime minister struck me a red, flashing, warning light; a similar opinion has been voiced by a couple of Corbynite MPs.

There is certainly asymmetry of hatred. When the Tory party met in Manchester during the 2010s people entering the arena had to go through a baying mob shouting 'Tory scum', the protestors' faces contorted with hatred. When Left-wing polemicist Owen Jones turned up at the Tory conference in 2018 people asked to have selfies taken with him. Unsurprising, then, that Tory MPs get the most abuse on Twitter, men especially, with Labour women getting the least, and a lot of the abuse Labour MPs get is from party supporters who think they're insufficiently socialist.[2]

Some Leftists don't hate us, obviously. Labour blogger Hopi Sen once wrote a piece in which he pointed out the obvious fact that Tories do not want the poor to starve. 'Ultimately, I don't think being left-wing is morally better. I just think it's practically better,' he wrote. 'I think Social Democracy *works* – it produces better outcomes, it raises more human capability, it educates, heals and employs and it constantly tries to improve.'[3] Yet more common is the argument that conservatives cause suffering to the vulnerable out of indifference or active cruelty. People on the Left often have more of an imagination, yet novelists and screenwriters, when talking about conservatives, sometimes lose all nuance, that ability to see the good and evil in the same person, and we just become caricatures. If they wrote about a criminal or someone of the opposite sex with that lack of depth they would be panned, but instead we get 'Iain Duncan Smith wants to kick the poor to death' or 'George Bush is worse than Hitler squared'. I remember a friend of a friend, an artist who lived in Hoxton or Shoreditch or somewhere like that, declaring that George W. Bush was *literally* worse than Hitler.

This might explain why violence is more likely to be forgiven if it's done by the right people. Former members of terror group the Weather Underground ended up being welcomed back to society, and 'were so normalized that the 9/11 issue of the *New York Times* infamously ran a profile lauding Weatherman alumnus Bill Ayres'.[4] In Norway Lars Gule is regularly brought out on TV to opine on the Middle East despite once being caught with a bag of explosives that was destined to be let off in Israel, and had served time in jail for it; nowhere in a million years would an unrepentant Right-wing terrorist be allowed space as a media voice anywhere in western Europe or the US.

Some on the Left do genuinely think that conservatives are bad people, either selfish or heartless, but by many measurements those on the Right are more altruistic. Conservatives tend to give more money to charity, for instance, at least in the US, one study finding 'sizable differences in overall giving between partisans' and that this was explained by religiosity rather than economic status, or 'differences in beliefs about government spending'.[5] In his 2006 book *Who Really Cares*, Arthur Brooks looked at the figures and concluded that households headed by a conservative give 30 per cent more dollars to charity than those headed by a liberal, this despite liberal families earning on average 6 per cent more. Again, conservative generosity is mostly down to religion, which also explains why Americans give so much more than Europeans.[6] Likewise data from 2002 showed that people who identify as conservative or extremely conservative are one-fifth of the population but provide a quarter of all blood donations.[7]

I've read some quite respected commentators arguing that Right-wingers are actually 'evil'. Yet don't evil people think they are good? It's not like with the *Captain America* comics I used to read as a kid where the Nazi villain the Red Skull says 'and once my plan is complete evil shall triumph' before cackling. Once you realise that the other guy also thinks he's the goodie you're at least open to the possibility that you're the baddie.

One of the best days in recent British politics was the twenty-four hours following the 2015 election. Obviously, I was pleased the Tories had won and we avoided the 'years of chaos' we'd have got under Ed Miliband. Everything is going absolutely brilliantly, I thought, we'll have a smooth two terms of comfortable Conservative government. But the best part of it was the sheer schadenfreude, laughing at all the people having meltdowns, the best moment being a blogpost from a philosophy lecturer at Royal Holloway, with the post 'If you're a Conservative, I'm not your friend'.[8] Rebecca Roache began her blog post by writing: 'One of the first things I did after seeing the depressing election news this morning was check to see which of my Facebook friends "like" the pages of the Conservatives or David Cameron, and unfriend them.'[9]

This asymmetry of hatred is reflected in social media patterns. Democrats are three times more likely to unfriend someone on Facebook for their political views, and Remainers are far more likely to object to a family member marrying a Brexiteer than vice versa.[10] According to Pew, liberals block people they disagree with on Twitter more than conservatives do.[11] Right-wing Twitter users are also more likely to follow political pundits from the other side, and over a third of people following the top Left-wing political pundits were on the Right, compared to a quarter vice versa.[12] A 2016 study by the Public Religion Research Institute found that Democrats were more likely to have 'blocked, unfriended or stopped following someone they disagreed with on social networking sites'.[13]

Contradicting all this, and to give the false, illusionary impression that I'm not completely biased, there are also studies showing that liberals 'are somewhat more likely to share' content on social media posted by someone with a different ideology.[14] And a YouGov survey from 2015 found that Right-wing people are more likely to think they are morally better than the average person, 47 per cent compared to 39 per cent of Lefties.[15] Which is surprising, and either suggests that liberal guilt really does reflect lower self-esteem, or it's social desirability bias, with liberals having the nous to realise that thinking yourself morally better is not a good look.

Yet a YouGov survey also showed that Conservatives and Republicans were more relaxed about a child marrying a supporter of the opposite party than the other way around.[16] In fact, more Labour voters objected to a daughter marrying a UKIP voter than an actual criminal, a level of sectarianism reminiscent of the old Irish joke about a woman who goes to England and telling her mother she's become a prostitute. ('Phew, for a moment there I thought you said *Protestant*.') During the 2016 US presidential election Pew found Democrats more likely to say a friend voting for the other candidate would put a strain on their friendship.[17]

And politics can certainly put a strain on friendship. One night I had a bad falling out with a friend from *Nuts*, after we had ended up in a heated debate about whether the growth of Islam was a threat to the European way of life. I thought it was, or at least had the potential to be, but he argued that such multicultural states had been the norm before and people rub along. We didn't speak for years (although we've made up since), but it makes me feel ashamed that I lost a friend over politics. On the other hand, I remember my brother's two best friends having a much more bitter falling-out, one that went on for months and caused real lasting resentment, over an Arsenal v. Spurs game; one of them is a particle physicist and the other a senior figure in the education sector.

Roger Scruton once wrote that 'Left-wing people find it very hard to get on with Right-wing people, because they believe that they are evil. Whereas I have no problem getting on with Left-wing people, because I simply believe that they are mistaken.'[18] It's hard to make this point without sounding smug but it's obviously true, and not a recent phenomenon. Thomas Sowell cited this pattern going back to the eighteenth century, when Thomas Malthus said of his critics that 'I cannot doubt the talents of such men as Godwin and Condorcet. I am unwilling to doubt their candor.' In return the radical William Godwin called Malthus 'malignant' and questioned 'the humanity of the man . . . I profess myself at a loss to conceive of what earth the man was made.'

As Sowell pointed out:

> This asymmetry in responses to people with different opinions has been too persistent, for too many years, to be just a matter of individual personality differences. Although Charles Murray has been a major critic of the welfare state and of the assumptions behind it, he recalled that before writing his landmark book, *Losing Ground*, he had been 'working for years with people who ran social programs at street level, and knew the overwhelming majority of them to be good people trying hard to help.' Can you think of anyone on the left who has described Charles Murray as 'a good person trying hard to help'? He has been repeatedly denounced as virtually the devil incarnate – far more often than anyone has tried seriously to refute his facts.[19]

The American writer Shadi Hamid observed that 'the assumption of bad faith on the part of those you disagree with' was a commonality of political and religious sectarianism, calling it 'the absence of religion mimicking the certainty of religion'.[20] It's also the moral certainty that brings out the worst in people, the assumption that opponents must always be arguing from bad faith, and that criticism of the tribe's beliefs are personal attacks. People who think their belief system can make the world a better place often end up doing some terrible things; Jonathan Sacks used the phrase 'altruistic evil' to describe religious-based violence, which is easier to commit when you believe yourself to be righteous. Strong group identities also lead to distorted 'motive attribution', the belief that the other side are driven by dark impulses.

In some quarters there is real hostility to diversity of opinion, which again is linked to the *religio* aspect of politics. The tendency to fall out over issues of doctrinal purity and orthodoxy seems more common among Leftist groups, as it is with religious communities or communists of old; admittedly in the old days you'd get sent to a Gulag in Irkutsk and now you just get some people with blue hair picketing your speech, but the principle is the same.

This maybe explains why the Left is so much less diverse than the Right, which is by definition an alliance of everyone who's not on the orthodox Left, and who has been cast out for one reason or another – including such incongruous groups as libertarians, neoconservatives and Christian socialists. Indeed, a study of eighty thousand people across four hundred political issues found that liberals are more alike than conservatives are, agreeing more across a swathe of political arguments.[21]

Religions tend to have a series of credal points in which members are obliged to believe, so if you don't support a woman's right to choose, for example, you have no place on the Left, even if you might agree on 98 per cent of issues. Conservatives tend to be more idiosyncratic in their beliefs, although that same survey found that within smaller sub-groups, they were more in agreement with each other. Outside of those clusters, the

'Right' have little in common except that they're not on the approved Left. Lots of Catholics are very active in Left-wing causes, especially on the subjects of poverty, immigration and pacificism; you occasionally still get nuns trying to break into nuclear bases, for instance. Yet at the same time their views on things such as sex education and abortion evoke more hostility from their own side than any of their beliefs do on the Right. During my time at the *Herald* the government had the temerity to appoint a pro-life charity to a government health body, which the *Guardian* took as an outrageous attack on women and a return to the Victorian era. This government forum already included multiple pro-choice groups who all shared a *Guardian*-friendly worldview, including Brook, the Family Planning Association, the Sex Education Forum and Marie Stopes International. They got upset at the invitation of *one* organisation offering a different perspective. And many of these pro-life campaigners have otherwise very Left-of-centre views. More recently, the people behind the US Women's March excluded members of Christian women's groups who also wanted to protest against Donald Trump, because of their anti-abortion views. But then, if your political movement is an active community, rather than a loose alliance, it has to have a creed of sorts – a set of principles to which everyone must sign up. This continual drive for doctrinal purity keeps the Right more diverse, a loose collection of people who have failed that test of faith in some way and so are not welcome in the progressive communion.

All the signs are that this political sectarianism is rising. For years those in charge have made hostility towards racial outsiders a huge taboo – the Greatest Sin – but what if that sense of outgroup hostility was innate and so instead was merely projected elsewhere? Contact theory holds that, once exposed to different religious or racial groups, racists will become less bigoted and hateful. Conversely if your social network never allows you to meet a reasonably intelligent conservative you will probably develop a hostile attitude. And if, as the evidence suggests, conservatives are becoming far less common in certain professions or even geographical areas, won't hostility grow into full-blown hatred?

20

SEX AND THE SUBURBS

One November my wife and I were blessed with a beautiful daughter, after a long and exhausting twenty-four hours; technically Emma did the majority of the work but it was definitely a team effort. Having children is the most amazing thing in your life and for the first couple of weeks after your first child is born you feel the most incredible warmth and goodwill to the rest of humanity as you float on a cloud of oxytocin.

The love you feel towards your newborn baby will be so intense it will scare you, a hormonal response like no other; every aspect of life must be looked at in a slightly different way. Parental worry can become overwhelming, too much to bear, and everything else, even the fear of one's own premature death, pales compared to the investment in a child. Politically things change, too, and there is more of an urge to put down roots, and to invest in the neighbourhood. One's world shrinks.

A year earlier, just before I turned thirty, I had moved in with my girlfriend, who lived in Crouch End. The area, in suburban north London, had changed somewhat since Victorian misery chronicler George Gissing had described life as being 'insufferably drab even in the decent dullness of Crouch End'.[1] Stephen King, whose author friend Peter Straub lived in the area at the time he visited him in 1980, wrote a short story set there, and in which the place was described as being so far away from anything that policemen saw being stationed there as a career end. But thanks to the economic miracle of runaway housing inflation the area had become fashionable before my arrival, and despite my presence became even more so afterwards. It was already filled with actors, writers and open-minded artistic types, and so obviously I fitted right in politically.

A while back there was an American blog called Stuff White People Like (SWPL), which satirised a certain type of college-educated, early-middle-age urban liberal – bohemian and somewhat hipstery people who liked certain white-people things.[2] In London terms, Crouch End was SWPL central and indeed everyone here had *The Wire* box set, number one on the blog's list of Stuff White People Like. Likewise, with Scandi noir dramas, hipster coffee shops that advertised Japanese baby massage, or one of the countless yoga studios in the area. Being SWPL central made the area a really, really nice place to live in. White liberals *are* generally very nice, interesting, humorous and sharp – and with good taste in TV, too. They also tend to have fashionable, high-status opinions, and fashionable, high-status opinions in a largely visual culture with a quasi-Christian sentimentality are generally quite bad. The Anglo-American journalist John Derbyshire once described himself as a 'metrocon', a metropolitan conservative, confessing that: 'I dislike modern American liberalism very much, and believe it to be poisonous and destructive, as well as arrogant and false; yet I'm at ease in a roomful of New York liberals in a way that, to be truthful about it, I am not in a gathering of red-state Evangelicals.'[3] That summed me up too, and it can get annoying, although maybe being around people with different views is good for you. In the same way some Catholics believe beating yourself bloody with a whip is good for you, or living in a freezing cold cell on bread and water. I mean, I can't immediately see the benefit but maybe it's there somewhere.

My area voted 75 per cent Remain, while the constituency of Hornsey and Wood Green also usually comes in the top three of the list of areas signing those fatuous petitions against Donald Trump visiting Britain, or whatever; it's always there or thereabouts, along with your Brighton Pavilions, your Islington Norths, your Bristol Wests. In fact, even among those who voted Brexit around here, a few almost certainly did so for communistic reasons, and people selling hard-Left papers were not an unusual sight when I moved in. There used to be an old guy hawking a paper called the *Proletariat*, the organ of the Communist Party of Great Britain (Marxist-Leninist), which is not to be confused with the Communist Party of Great Britain (Provincial Central Committee), which seems to be less in favour of Stalin (and, yes, they are bitter enemies). I signed one of his petitions once, trying to save the local A & E department, and when I asked him if he was actually a communist he replied yes in a cheery way. On another occasion, I casually asked a neighbour if he'd seen the comedy *The Death of Stalin*, to which he replied there was nothing funny about it because Stalin was 'really up against it' and 'tried his best'.

Another word for SWPL might be 'Bobo' – bohemian bourgeois, the term coined by David Brooks for the new middle class who were immersed in a bohemian culture in their music and fashion tastes, while actually living pretty bourgeois lives. Among London Bobos, as with their American equivalents, most are in pretty conventional and usually married relationships; in most cases, the man commutes each day, while the wife more likely works in an office part time or at home, and this arrangement is still largely taken for granted. (In the US, very wealthy women are the least likely to work once they have children, even though few are socially conservative.) So while Bobos tend to have progressive political views their actual lifestyles are quite traditional; in many of our high street's 328 or so coffee shops you'll see mums from the local school discussing fundraising schemes, helping out on top of freelancing at home, looking after kids and all the other drudgery people in their forties have to do. There is a lot of social capital in these SWPL neighbourhoods.

I had started writing a blog for the *Telegraph* around the same time, which was originally called 'Culture Wars' and involved me ranting on about Leftists. I'd get wound up by reading the *Guardian* each morning, or listening to Radio 4, then write some equally partisan response, and inevitably come across as a bit of a prat. I didn't think this at the time, obviously, I just believed I was speaking sense and (puts on golf-club bore voice) telling the truth about the PC brigade. I'd feel a sort of unease whenever people in our local parent circle learned what I did, and swiftly change the subject, and actually felt relief when I learned that one of the other dads worked for a tobacco company; at least he wasn't going to look down on me as a bad guy.

Unlike the part of town I grew up in, my liberal north London suburb is absurdly friendly – or at least it is once your children enter the school system. It's a cliché but parenting really does make you less mobile, in a good way; it feels like you're actually laying down roots as you build friendship circles based around your children. This immediately begins with nursery school, where to my surprise they did actually sing 'Baa baa woolly lamb' there, rather than 'Baa baa black sheep', something I previously assumed was a tabloid myth. Chalk up another victory for the Frankfurt School, I thought.

We settled into an SWPL lifestyle of eating at somewhat expensive breakfast places, me with a baby in a Kari Me, trying to pretend that having children didn't entirely ruin lots of things we enjoyed beforehand. We watched boxsets, mostly HBO stuff but also Scandinavian dramas, starting with *The Killing* and moving on to *Borgen*, a television show that extols progressive values and frames a central liberal idea that conflict can be resolved (but it's resolved because the Left is always right). I loved it, but maybe because whenever someone said some pious prog-nonsense I could just smile indulgently and think, 'Oh the Scandis, bless them, they're like charmingly innocent Eloi'; while if an English person said the same thing in that irritatingly sanctimonious Radio 4 voice I'd throw the control at the wall.

I'd always wanted to live in an authentic local community, something I've craved and didn't get growing up in Tory Kensington, where most people were pretty unfriendly. I found it instead here in Lefty Haringey, a place where my political views are considered almost insane. It's my Bedford Falls, but Bedford Falls if everyone read the *Observer*. But then no wonder it's a trusting, friendly place because liberals are, on average, more trusting and open-minded, and so do indeed make the best neighbours.

The *Daily Mail* once claimed that being more Right-wing makes you happier, because people 'benefit from the belief that problems are a person's own making – which helps them deal better with whatever life throws at them'.[4] I can't say it has exactly worked for me, but what is probably making some people happier is living a conservative lifestyle, because the things that tend to make people content are companionship, meaning and a strong sense of community.[5] And paradoxically, just as we were immersing ourselves in an ever more liberal world in Crouch End our lifestyle was becoming far more conservative.

People's view of nuclear families, and traditional gender norms, heavily correlates with their place on the political spectrum. On the extreme Left the Bolsheviks saw the family as a 'bourgeois' institution and so set out to do what they normally do to things they don't like. In contrast, women in Hitler's Germany got medals when they produced six children, just as in Sparta women who birthed a certain number of healthy sons had the honour of an actual gravestone when they died.

After our eldest was born my wife stopped working, in order to look after the kids, and would do so for five years. Our income suffered, and her earnings will take some time to recover. And so the irony of living in progressive Nappy Valley is that liberals form tight communities just as they do the thing that pushes people to the Right more than any other event – having children. Many wealthy people on the Left live a conservative lifestyle, and sociologist Charles Murray had argued that America's cognitive elite should 'preach what they practise'. Of course, the problem is that having children is expensive, what the *Economist* rather strangely called the 'child penalty'.[6] Getting married increases both partners' long-term financial prospects, acting as a security against poverty, but having children vastly decreases a woman's income, and is the biggest factor explaining the gender pay gap. Various studies show this fairly conclusively, and that even maternity leave makes little difference, with evidence from several countries all producing the same results, including Denmark, Sweden and New Zealand.[7] Every time this issue comes up as a major national scandal a couple of free-market think-tanks will point this out, no one will pay attention, and people will keep on believing it's just sexism.

Child-rearing is made even more expensive because of property prices, though, and amazingly it turned out that Britain's economic model of runaway house-price inflation wasn't the greatest idea. House-price discussion was apparently a middle-class cliché but at some point people must have stopped talking about it, because it just became depressing (it's never come up at any dinner party I've been to, except as a general 'What the hell's going on?' lament). People found themselves not just priced out of the nice neighbourhoods in which their parents had bought, but even pretty crappy ones, and they were the lucky ones who could afford anything. Conservatives, traditionally the party of homeowners, had nothing to say as this social catastrophe unfolded in the 1990s and 2000s. When the coalition came to power in 2010 they just further inflated the market with a help-to-buy scheme, without really increasing supply. The Tories came to rely on older voters who own homes, who want those homes to increase in value, and don't want new homes built near them. This would prove disastrous for conservatism.

The Marriage Gap

In the early 2000s American blogger Steve Sailer observed something interesting about voting patterns in presidential elections – the more expensive housing was in a US state, the more people supported the Democrats. This trend had become more pronounced over time, and was also found in cities, with super-expensive San Francisco becoming ultra-progressive and Texas's relatively cheap urban districts remaining fairly mixed. This difference between cheap Right-wing areas and expensive Left-wing ones he termed the 'dirt gap', and the pattern has continued since – Trump won all twenty-two cheapest states, while Hillary Clinton carried fifteen of the sixteen with the priciest housing.[8] This, Sailer concluded, was linked to what he termed the 'marriage gap' – the huge difference in Republican Party support between married and single white women.

The theory was tested by George Hawley, a political science professor at the University of Houston, for the peer-reviewed journal *Party Politics*, who concluded that Sailer was correct.[9] Hawley's data found that every $10,000 increase in median home value in a county resulted in the Republican vote falling by 0.3 per cent, while increasing median income, despite correlating with house prices, had the opposite effect.

And the reason that expensive housing reduced support for the Republicans was that it reduced the rate at which people married and had children. Hawley ran the model looking at women in their late twenties, and found out their marriage status 'was a greater influence on vote choice than any other variable'. For every 1 percentage point rise in marriage, Bush gained 0.2 per cent more votes, and in areas with very large numbers of married people it increased by up to 5.5 per cent. Marriage was such a strong variable that it overwhelmed all others, Hawley concluded, calling it 'eye-popping'. It also completely countered the 'education effect' whereby more schooling tends to make people more liberal, since once marriage was taken into account 'education ceased to have any statistical significance in predicting votes'. And every $10,000 increase in house prices reduced the marriage rate by 0.3 per cent among the twenty-five to thirty-year-old cohort.

The same conclusions came in a 2016 paper entitled 'Residential Building Restrictions, Cost of Living, and Partisanship', with Dartmouth professor of government Jason Sorens stating that richer states had become more Democrat and poorer ones more Republican because of 'cost of living, driven by residential building restrictions'.[10]

At US elections media attention is often focused on the gender gap and yet there was a marriage voting gap of 20 points in the 2008 US election, compared to just a 7 per cent difference between men and women.[11] Married women tend to vote for conservative parties in huge numbers, and the marriage rate among white women remains one of the most reliable variables for predicting the Republican Party's support in any state.[12] This was most pronounced in the 2012 election featuring Mitt Romney, a very wholesome candidate who Charlie Brooker described as looking like a president in a 1960s comic book. The gap slightly declined in 2016 since Trump's support came from the social class most affected by divorce, and many women were – for some mysterious reason – repulsed by him.[13]

But while Trump lost many university-educated females, he still won 53 per cent of white women overall, despite making some appalling comments about grabbing genitalia and generally being an awful person. On top of this he was standing against a female candidate who made being a woman her main selling point. Hillary Clinton touched on the marriage gap when she argued that white women voted for Trump because 'of ongoing pressure to vote the way that your husband, your boss, your son, whoever, believes you should'. She was basing it on an Oregon State University study of female voting patterns, which argued that 'when you're married to a white man you get a lot more pressure to vote consistent with that ideology'.[14] But that seems questionable, since most of the evidence suggests that conservative women are *more* conservative than conservative men; it also goes against a great deal of historical precedents that women tend to influence their partners' belief systems.

So rising incomes don't have any political benefits for conservatives if they also come with rising land costs and other penalties to marriage. Even I feel bored and repulsed by politicians talking about 'families', especially if the dreaded word 'hard-working' is inserted beforehand, yet conservative politicians have an existential reason to support marriage. Progressives don't; they have a more individualistic worldview but that individualism also entails a closer bond to the state, something illustrated by Barack Obama's election campaign ad 'Life of Julia'. It was designed to illustrate how women's lives would be better under Obama than his rival Romney, but it also showed a woman whose closest and most important relationship was with the government.

Few conservatives want to stand up for traditional families because they would just sound lame, either a chauvinist who does nothing around the house or a pearl-clutching Stepford Wife. Or worse still, like someone from

Mad Men who wants their wife to have their bland evening meal on the table after they get home from a hard day's shagging the secretary. And when the Tories returned in 2010 Chancellor George Osborne gave the clear impression that he would rather well-educated, highly intelligent women were in the workplace generating tax revenue. Meanwhile, rising housing costs continued to light a bonfire underneath Tory electoral hopes, with Labour winning 51–31 among the growing number of renters in the 2017 election.[15]

And yet perhaps now it's too late anyway, and conservatism needs to reach a critical mass before it can turn an area blue (or red, in America). There is less evidence of a marriage gap in the UK; certainly marriage rates are high in my part of town, most people have kids and a mortgage, yet this doesn't make a huge difference to people's antipathy to conservatism, at least in the abstract. The surrounding culture is too deeply progressive.

Social life matters a great deal in political currents, and there is the fact that conservatism equals social death. I knew a guy who was a similar age and had a pretty similar middle-class social milieu; he worked for Migration Watch. At every social event he must have had this 'And what do you do?' terror hanging over him. Likewise an acquaintance who worked at an anti-abortion charity – and he's an actual man with a penis. There are certain issues that put you beyond the pale, and one of them I suppose is having 1950s ideas about family formation: very few big-C conservatives would ever say they would prefer more women to stay at home and raise children, yet conservatism as an idea depends on it.

Married people become conservative after they tie the knot, but a lot of evidence suggests this effect is stronger in women, having a big influence on views about gender roles in particular.[16] This effect is even more pronounced in more secular Britain than in the US, and contrary to what people might assume it has a greater impact on highly educated women and on those who planned to go back to work after having children. One interpretation is that of 'disappointed labour expectations', a sort of rationalisation whereby the declining career prospects brought about by having children makes women more in favour of being traditional homemakers. Alternatively, they might just have had enough of commuting and office politics.

Perhaps liberals might take comfort that there is something different about conservative women, that they lack female empathy – a charge often thrown at Thatcher – but this doesn't seem to be the case. Although women are on average more compassionate than men, Right-leaning females have the same levels of empathy and tenderness towards the less fortunate as liberal females do. Likewise caring for the vulnerable 'has no significant relationship with partisanship after accounting for gender differences'.[17]

But something about having a child triggers a change in attitude long before maternity leave ends. A Scandinavian study found that new mums adopt 'conservation values', which 'emphasize self-restriction, preservation of traditional practices, and protection of stability', and show decreasing support for 'openness to change values', which by definition means conservatism.[18] The study followed 292 Finnish couples entering parenthood from the first weeks of pregnancy to three months after their child was born, and found that both the mothers and their partners believed the women's views to have shifted. New mothers also perceived a similar shift in their partner's personal values, although strangely the men themselves didn't think so.

The difficulty for social scientists is that declining marriage rates are both cause and effect of liberalism, so they can't be entirely sure which way the arrow goes.[19] And, confusingly, the proportion of people getting married is declining in all social classes, but way faster at lower education and income levels, and yet it is the upper class who are moving Left, and the working-class pushing to the Right; many liberals in liberal areas are in stable marriages, in the wealthiest states where marriages are strongest.[20] Perhaps two contradictory trends could be going on at once, since very low marriage rates in Britain and the US mean that a large proportion of the university-educated remain single and liberal. Their contemporaries who marry and have children perhaps become more centrist, or at least tacitly accepting of some conservative values. Indeed the relatively small number of conservative graduates are much more likely to get married than liberal classmates. The problem for conservatives is that in this case demography is against us once again, as it is with everything.

Back in the nineties and noughties *Sex and the City* was the one show I recall female colleagues referencing a lot, and it reflected the new norm of economic independence – thanks in part to Reagan and Thatcher – as well as growing sexual freedom even compared to the 1980s (measured by the average number of sexual partners, as well as social attitudes to things such as promiscuity, births outside marriage and all the other things of which Mrs Whitehouse disapproved). But most of all *Sex and the City* reflected the fact that more people were delaying marriage and children, and that there was a far greater pool of single men and women, not just in their twenties but in their thirties and even forties. For millions of people in gentrifying areas of big cities life continued to be a bit of an adult's playground, a world free of children. This is a trend that has accelerated since.

In 2009 the proportion of American women who were married fell below 50 per cent for the first time in history, and the number of adults below thirty-four who had never wed jumped 12 points in less than a decade. Back in 1965 the percentage of never-married women aged thirty-six or below was 17 per cent; by 2017 it was 57 per cent.[21] 'It is a radical upheaval, a national reckoning with massive social and political implications,' as one analysis put it: 'We are living through the invention of independent female adulthood as a norm, not an aberration.'[22]

Not unrelatedly, American women have since the 1970s shifted massively to the Left, especially those with a degree.[23] Today around 40 per cent of young women identify as liberal or far-Left, twice the early 1980s figure, a trend that has accelerated in the 2000s.[24] Men used to be much more Left-wing than women but the reverse is now true, and females under the age of thirty-five today support the Democrats by a margin of 68 per cent to 24 per cent, while younger men are pretty much evenly divided.[25] In American politics the biggest gulf is the extreme chasm in voting between college-educated women, who have drastically moved Left, and non-graduate men, who have gone to the Right.[26]

This trend has gone hand in hand with declining marriage and birth rates, but has also coincided with the huge increase in women attending university, both in absolute numbers and in relation to men, especially in the humanities.[27] Between 1960 and 2008 the proportion of American women with degrees increased five times, and regression analysis suggests 'that females who were better educated, less religious and of higher social class were more Left-Wing'.[28] Merely attending university pushes people to the Left, immersing them in an environment that is overwhelmingly progressive, and in many cases teaching subjects that have an activist element. But another reason is that university attendance reduces women's likelihood of marriage and children.

And yet while women are more liberal, conservative women are more conservative than conservative men. Polls consistently show that more men than women are in favour of legal abortions, both in Britain and in America.[29] In Britain 59 per cent of women want to reduce the legal limit from twenty-four weeks, compared to just 35 per cent of men, and 10 per cent of British women would ban abortion outright, ten times the male figure.[30] The oft-repeated line that 'if men got pregnant abortion would be a sacrament' is so untrue I wonder if there must be some paradoxical truth in it, but I can't find it. The pro-life movement is overwhelmingly female, while in contrast pro-choice women tend to be much more pro-choice than their male comrades, since more men don't feel invested either way. Perhaps culture war issues are more polarised among women because women have to make bigger life choices and sacrifices, whether it be career or baby. Therefore the path she takes, whether to have a family or not, and in particular to be a stay-at-home mother, might influence the side to which she leans.

What's ominous for conservatism is that historically dominant belief systems begin with a big gender skew. Back in antiquity various Roman writers complained that ladies were easy prey for any 'foreign superstition', but one in particular was very successful at recruiting women in large numbers. Roman men, raised in the tough and unforgiving culture of their forefathers, could not understand the appeal of this strange new cult from the eastern Mediterranean with its obsessive focus on forgiveness and peace, and worshipping some sort of dead criminal. Indeed, they feared this subculture in which 'women enjoyed far higher status than did women in the Greco-Roman world at large', and which opposed infanticide, divorce and male homosexuality, making it appealing to females.[31]

This new cult's most successful propagandist, St Paul, wrote an Epistle to the Romans issuing 'personal greetings to 15 women and 18 men', and since men tend to predominate at the head of such movements, this large number of women even among the leadership suggests that the Roman Christian community was already heavily female. An inventory of property taken from a Christian church in Cirta, North Africa, during the Diocletian persecution of 303 found '16 men's tunics and 82 women's tunics as well as 47 pairs of female slippers'. Both Christian and pagan accounts mention a sex imbalance and 'ancient sources simply swarm with tales of how women of all ranks were converted in Rome and in the provinces . . . and that the percentage of Christian women, especially among the upper classes, was larger than that of men.'[32]

Early Christian man was far more likely to be a secondary convert, someone who joins a religion because a spouse had done so, whether out of zeal for life in the next world or an easy life in this one. European history is filled with examples of kings who adopted the new faith in order to placate their Christian wives, including Clovis, leader of the Franks, and Ethelbert of Kent, the first Christian kings in France and England respectively.

Christianity is not unique, and history suggests that if a lot of women are joining a religion or belief system then it will come to dominate, largely because the men will follow. As Pierre d'Avrigny, a French medieval priest, said of the hugely popular thirteenth-century heresy Catharism: 'Men may invent heresies but it is women who spread them and make them immortal.'[33] (Catharism might have spread further had it not been wiped out with

– rather masculine – genocidal violence.) In eighteenth-century England there were three Methodist women to every two men, at a time when that movement was rapidly growing in number, and females had important roles as lay preachers and organisers. The same is true of the immense wave of Protestant conversions taking place in Latin America, where 'a substantial proportion' of men have joined after their wives.[34]

Men tend outwardly to adopt a worldview that appeals to women; just as many in fourth-century Rome would have worn a cross to appear attractive, so today they become secondary converts to progressivism. Anecdotally a lot of previously quite Right-wing single men who partner up become more politically liberal, perhaps under female influence; or perhaps just because the Islamification of the West doesn't seem like such a pressing issue when you have an actual girlfriend. But then growing liberalism could be seen as social feminisation, since the traditional masculine qualities are not as necessary when society becomes less dangerous and less dependent on jobs and tasks involving physical strength. The 'Civilising Process' has in the past been heavily influenced by women, and things such as gay acceptance were certainly female-driven, just as with the abolition of duelling or animal cruelty or all the other screwed-up things men will get up to if left alone. And perhaps this is just the latest stage of the relentless drive towards our progressive future, and I'll be regarded by my descendants as being like the hell-bound pagans of Rome.

21

TINKER BELL AND THE GLOBALIST PLOT TO IMPOSE OPEN BORDERS

When they were around six and seven, my daughters started French classes at a library near us; French is no longer taught in many primary schools, and there's no way they're going to escape the misery I endured. Also, in a slightly reactionary way, I lament the fact that French is no longer the international language, as it was in the nineteenth century, when even British passports were in that more civilised tongue (I couldn't care less about blue passports – *this* is the hill I will die on).

At our local children's library the entire front desk area was made up of hagiographies of Barack Obama and Nelson Mandela, and hagiography is the most accurate term, rather like the little *Lives of the Saints* books I used to read at church. Among the children's history section, I picked up one book explaining the Chinese Revolution, in which Chairman Mao is described in bold letters as a 'social visionary', which is one way of looking at it, I suppose. The book made no mention of the millions who died under his visionary scheme, only a figure of thirty-five thousand attributed to conflict during the period. Every week while they learned French upstairs I would browse the children's section, looking for something to affirm my own prejudice that the kids were being brainwashed.

If you're a conservative, then once you become a parent, you're faced with the prospect of raising your children in a culture that is filled with simplistic, untrue messages about the world. I realise that I can spot bias on the side of a cereal packet, but all the media messages children are fed prepare them for life as a progressive. Sometimes I find it annoying, more often just boring; it's how it must feel in totalitarian regimes constantly being fed the party's drivel. Kid's books and television give an interesting insight into where prevailing beliefs come from, regularly hammering home the message that borders are bad, stereotypes are wrong, mankind is a menace to the planet and girls ought to be masculine. Humans are natural storytellers, and we seek out narratives to explain the world; from a very young age children are read books and shown films that teach them the message that we are all basically good and others are just like us, and then the more intelligent ones are sent off to universities where conservatism has been frozen out and the same message, in a slightly more complex form, is imparted.

Most of my children's favourite books contain essentially progressive themes, especially of people who are gender atypical, or about overcoming our fear of the Other because preconceived ideas are wrong. Stereotype inaccuracy is a common theme: to take one on our bookshelf, *The Pirates Next Door* is about how the entire neighbourhood fears these travelling 'pirates' moving in because they have loads of prejudices about how these 'pirates' live, and the local small-minded meanie said horrible things about them. But they turn out to be loveable free spirits who are a bit chaotic and don't play by the meanie's bourgeois rules but make lovely neighbours and don't in any way steal everything. It's a fun book, as is the very sweet *Library Lion*, about how it's unreasonable for an uptight librarian to refuse a lion in his library because this lion turns out to be a bookworm and has never eaten anyone, despite the harmful stereotype that lions tend to be ferocious carnivores. Or the charming *Moon Man*, about an interplanetary asylum seeker who's mistreated by authorities who fear him because he's different when in fact he's completely peace-loving.

And this is one of those moments where I'm sitting reading to a three-year-old, focusing my thoughts on how children's book are culture war meme processors, and wondering if politics is eating up my very humanity; I've become not just a monster, but a boring monster too – just enjoy the books, for God's sake, I remind myself, they're fun and sweet. And then I look at my iPhone – because I now have one and am addicted – and some idiot has said something annoying on Twitter and that inner conscience is ignored.

I think I snapped while reading Michael Morpurgo's version of *The Pied Piper of Hamelin*, in which a bunch of ruddy-faced toff kids live it up in luxury while some poor urban (and multiracial, because they're the goodies) urchins are left to starve, which is obviously an allegory of Thatcherism. At one point the Pied Piper refuses a large payment because, he says: 'When one man becomes rich, ten others become poor.'[1] I'm not an unswerving free-marketer by any means but I blurted out as I read this, 'That's just not true, you know that, right? That's the lump of Labour fallacy!' My daughters didn't seem that interested for some reason, although they were four and three at the time. Still fuming, I googled Morpurgo's net worth and found he'd made over £15 million in a decade![2] There must be dozens of people homeless as a result, the bastard.

Children's stories in the past weren't like this. My in-laws kept dozens of books from the 1970s and early 1980s, the time when their kids were young, and many of which I vaguely remember reading. The take-away messages in these books are not at all the same: *My Naughty Little Sister* is naughty simply because she's a bloody nuisance, and it's not really celebrated either as some non-conforming high-status trait; she's just annoying. (People kept on insisting that *The Tiger Who Came to Tea* [1968] must be some sort of metaphor for fascism, but author Judith Kerr, a refugee from the Third Reich, disappointed people by saying it's just about a tiger. Who comes to tea.)

The culture has changed, with increasing demand for stories that reflect progressive ideas. But does it actually matter? It's not like people are in a polling booth for the first time and think, 'I'll vote Labour because of that Morpurgo book that was read to me fourteen years ago.' Maybe not, but I think messages, especially ones repeatedly spoken by the powers that be, probably have an impact; people remember stories and archetypes far more than they do political arguments.

And books seem nothing like as obviously indoctrinating as films or TV. The girls went through a big fairy phase for a while, around the time they were into *Frozen*, especially with the Tinker Bell films. One day I sat down to watch the Tinker Bell film *The Secret of the Wings* with them, while trying to read John Julius Norwich's magisterial history of Byzantium. The film is about a world in which the sun fairies and winter fairies are kept apart by a wall, and good fairies on both sides (because obviously there are good fairies on both sides, and in fact they're basically all the same) have to break down these walls to live together in the face of opposition by some meanies who don't want them to mix. It could have been scripted by George Soros, I thought to myself as I was reading about Basil the Macedonian's rise to the imperial throne, sheer meme-processing propaganda that will prepare the pathways for later progressive arguments. Ditto *The Lego Movie*, which is about an authoritarian father figure who wants to control everything because he doesn't like alternative lifestyles or Lego people mixing or being able to travel around. Instead, he wants them literally glued to their place and stuck in his rigid hierarchical society. (I was able to enjoy the film while thinking this – I'm not a complete monster.)

Likewise children's television emphasises therapeutic ideas about self-esteem, which began with *Sesame Street*, 'conceived by a group of academics, psychologists and educationalists with the aim of promoting tolerance, politeness and racial harmony as well as teaching' subjects such as English and maths.[3] Henry Jeffreys observed in the *Spectator* that in older cartoons baddies tend to have what is coming to them while in contemporary stories the reckless avoid suffering for their stupidity because self-esteem is more important. He noted that the lesson of punishment, 'although not necessarily political, naturally leads to a conservative outlook in life, that is that authority has a role in taming our inner child and turning us into mature adults responsible for their actions and its consequences. The latter contains the message that misbehaviour is a product of unfortunate circumstances, in this case a lack of self-esteem, and it is one that naturally leads to a liberal outlook in life.'[4]

Maybe Lefty-ish ideas are easier for children to understand because they are in some ways childlike and naive. Children like to believe the world is a nice place and that people are at heart good, which is charming in a seven-year-old but it's not really what you want to hear from the people running the Ministry of Justice. Many political slogans of the Left focus on the concept of 'fairness', which, as any parent knows, is an obsession with children; if one child is seen as getting something more it's a source of great anger, and they end up more discontent than if no one got anything. I tested this by asking each of my children if they'd rather have one sweet and their siblings had two, or none of them got any sweets; all chose the latter option, something any psychologist could have predicted, since it's found to be very common until children reach maturity.[5]

One of the old books my in-laws kept, a selection of endearing things that kids say about life, could be a political manifesto for the anti-austerity movement; lots of things about why the world isn't fair because some people are rich, and why can't people just get rid of all guns and why can't they just give everyone in Africa enough money so no one starves? After an academic had suggested that six-year-olds be given the vote, the *Guardian* asked some children that age what laws they would pass.[6] Pretty much everything was either 'this should be free' or 'this should be banned', among them alcohol, tablet computers, swearing and buggies in schools.

And yet almost all fairy tales have a deeply conservative message: 'Little Red Riding Hood' is a warning to pubescent girls that the world is a dangerous place full of predators who will steal their innocence; 'The Emperor's New Clothes' explains an aspect of human nature so well – our tendency to be dazzled by innovation – that it has become the most overused cliché in political discourse. Go back further and 'The Ant and the Grasshopper', like all of *Aesop's Fables*, has a very conservative message: save or starve. It may also be that the modern mediums by which stories are told are better at conducting liberal ideas, or perhaps it is just the case that those stories that say something about human nature – which tend to be conservative – last the test of time. Or maybe the environment and culture in which we have grown up is more comfortable and, therefore, more favourable to progressive themes. The grasshopper will receive state aid to prevent starvation, which is anyway very rare in the developed world. Little Red Riding Hood doesn't have to worry about being deserted with a child because we have the pill and women don't need chaperones any more because violent crime is far lower than in the Middle Ages. The emperor's new tailors would have to undergo rigorous checks, as do all new ideas (and obviously we wouldn't have an emperor anyway, nor anyone in a position of absolute power).

I also wonder to what extent Christianity acted as a buffer against naive, progressive ideas about the world, as it brought with it a collection of folk wisdom that had a naturally conservative message, including original sin. My children's generation are much more cut off from that body of wisdom and so more receptive to novel ideas. But then once you realise that progressivism is essentially a replacement religion, this takeover of the children's media makes sense, since it is aimed at teaching the moral values of their tribe.

Likewise, with education. In Michel Houellebecq's *Submission*, the Muslim Brotherhood come to power in France in a coalition in which their only demand is that they are able to control education, since all that matters in the long term is raising a generation to share your beliefs. Famously the Jesuits had a saying – give me the boy at seven and I'll give you the man, which is grim news for us, since two generations have been almost inoculated to the fundamental ideas of conservatism. Children are easy to indoctrinate, which is why I find all those Woke eight-year-old quotes so insipid. Kids will repeat whatever grown-ups tell them, which is also partly why I'm wary of saying anything around them in case my eight-year-old tells someone at school, 'Daddy says all teachers are communists.' Personally, I'd cringe if one of my offspring came out with something that was clearly parroted from me, and I'd also be quite happy for them to be liberal while they're young and able to enjoy life, since conservatism is more of a burden than anything else.

Our children will inevitably be influenced by the school system anyway, and even more so by the wider culture, which has a progressive bent. All the music they listen to and the films they watch will have explicit or implicit anti-conservative messages, whether to do with equality or sexual expression or whatever, and that's even before we get onto their teachers. I was taught things in lessons which I know now to be almost entirely untrue, and I imagine the bias in London's state-school sector is even stronger now, progressivism being the de facto faith in secular education, and among the overwhelming majority of teachers.[7]

As with a lot of things, social media has made me more concerned about the issue because I'm made more aware of what people in positions of power think. When a teacher appeared at a Labour conference and declared that if everyone was educated properly no one would grow up to be a Tory, it did slightly worry me. In the same way I wouldn't want religious fanatics teaching my children, I don't want political zealots doing it either; no parent feels comfortable with the idea of their children growing up in a different faith to them, however you define it. I also don't want this sort of political sectarianism being normalised.

None of this would matter so much if education was just a business like any other, one where consumers and producers were able to sell the best product in the most efficient way. But it's not; the school is your community, your network of friends and trusted parents, you don't just pick and choose it like a gas supplier. And much of the stuff being taught at schools is concerning. The exam board Edexcel, 'on the subject of Conservative ideology' in a recent A-level Government and Politics syllabus, stated that conservatism was defined by support for 'social and state authoritarianism'. Conservatism sees people as 'limited, dependent and security-seeking creatures' and supports 'resurgent nationalism . . . insularity and xenophobia'. The entry on socialism described it as being about 'social stability and cohesion, social justice, happiness and personal development', and the worst thing that can be said about it is an allusion to 'conflict as a motor of history'.[8] And in the Soviet Union they had flowery meadows and rainbow skies and rivers made of chocolate, where the children danced and laughed and played with gumdrop smiles.

Perhaps because they view it in the way religious people see their faith, people on the Left are more likely to regard politics as something to be passed on to the children. The Corbynite group Momentum even launched something called Momentum Kids, which aimed to increase 'children's involvement in the movement by promoting political activity that is fun, engaging and child-friendly', while also providing childcare. The aim was to engage with children as young as three and with activities such as 'imagining the party your favourite toy might lead and creating placards for a mock protest'.[9] It sounds hellish.

Conservatives are more reluctant to share politics with their offspring, only one in ten thinking it appropriate for ten-year-old children to engage in politics, compared to a quarter of Labour and Lib Dem voters.[10] Left-wingers also become politically engaged earlier than Right-wingers, around the age of sixteen for Lib Dems and eighteen for Tories. In recent times, when schools have been threatened with cuts, many have actively encouraged the kids to take part in protests, which I found a bit weird, because they can't possibly understand the complexities – and involving children in politics seems like using them as human shields.

In some cases this might just be naked triumphalism, a way of expressing that 'we own the future'. But then there is also a certain sentimentalising of children, as well as a history of pandering to 'youth' that goes back to Chairman Mao, who loved young people, especially when they were beating up his enemies.

As mine reach the age where they start to develop an awareness of the world and ask questions, I struggle to answer a larger proportion of their questions fairly. At this point, how much does one hold back on giving them opinions when they're unable to form views themselves, and cannot see through their parents' ideological biases? My reluctance to offer my own views is partly shaped by seeing the way other people pass on their politics like a family religion. When people raise their children to be 'socialists' or 'feminists' it always brings out my inner Richard Dawkins, when he argued that children can't be 'Muslim' or 'Christian'. My counter to Professor Dawkins would be that religion is a tradition, it is inherited even if it can be abandoned later in life; to baptise a child is to bring him or her into your community. I suppose many people feel the same about their politics, and yet religion is about the Truth and at least until the recent modern era believers were supposed to hold that their faith alone contained it. Surely to raise a child in a political-faith community and to believe one's politics to be the Truth will lead to a new sort of religious sectarianism transferred into politics. I fear that's where we're heading.

22

THE BLOB

The whole modern world has divided itself into Conservatives
and Progressives. The business of Progressives is to go on
making mistakes. The business of the Conservatives is to
prevent the mistakes from being corrected.

G. K. Chesterton[1]

The inauguration of Barack Obama in 2009 was followed by eight years
without a single joke on any BBC comedy show about the president of the
United States (unless I missed one). Comedians tend to prefer when a
Right-winger is in power, for obvious reasons, and just over a year later the
British public obliged by kicking out Labour, replacing Gordon Brown with
an Old Etonian Tory. Finally, after thirteen long years, we were rid of them,
although there was nothing like the same sense of optimism felt among the
Left in 1997. As with New Labour, we'd had to abandon our principles, so
that after years of failure and being presented on the news as mad old guys
only interested in shooting foxes, the Conservatives had chosen a quasi-
Blair-like figure in the form of David Cameron.

There is the argument that one aspect of conservatism is realising when
to give up. The Victorian historian George Saintsbury advised that: 'We
can't always help things going to the Devil, but we can make them go
slowly.' Similarly Edwardian prime minister Arthur Balfour talked of

staving 'off the fighting by gradual and insignificant concessions where possible'.

The Cameron faction of the Tory party, who had mostly settled in that part of Notting Hill my friend Ben used to live in — now absurdly unaffordable — believed in staving off fighting by making significant concessions; pretty much everything but the economy. They seemed to concede that the culture war was over and had the surrender papers ready, although those of us writing the *Telegraph* blogs didn't seem aware. We were the culture war equivalent to Japanese soldiers still fighting in the Borneo jungle in the 1970s, refusing to accept that the fight was over.

Cameron was supposed to do for the Tories on social issues what Blair did for Labour on economic ones — bury the past and make the party truly modern. And so came all the hug-a-hoodie business and turning up in the Arctic Circle as part of some PR stunt. The new prime minister would also finally put to bed the issue of Europe, which had been driving everyone insane for so many years; as it turned out, not entirely successfully. And yet, unpopular as Labour now were, Cameron could not muster anything like the enthusiasm Blair did. The modernising appeared cynical, alienating some Tories while not seeming to attract many urban professionals either. They ended up in power only with the help of the Liberal Democrats.

After the 2010 election the departing Treasury secretary Liam Byrne left a note for his successor, the Lib Dem David Laws, with the message 'I'm afraid there is no money.' It was a joke, but one a bit close to the knuckle, since according to the Institute of Fiscal Studies there was indeed a £45 billion hole in public accounts. By 2010 the government deficit of £149 billion, or 10.1 per cent of GDP, was at Napoleonic wartime levels, and so for all the controversy about 'austerity' — the subject of most BBC political comedy for the next few years — one way or another that money had to be paid back.[2] By the time Labour left power, £156 billion was going on benefits every year, a third of all state spending; by 2017, after seven years of austerity, that figure was £264 billion, the exact same proportion of state spending. Even though I was still earning peanuts, and had no financial incentives to reduce tax, the amount of money being spent just struck me as reckless.

Yet despite this many were reluctant to go with the Conservatives, whose image had not much improved since the days of Baxter Basics and Tory Boy. It didn't help that the leaders were posher than ever and had mostly been members of something called the Bullingdon Club, a society for rich idiots who liked smashing up restaurants, which journalistic Oxford contemporaries cited as evidence of their elitism. I'd never heard of them but it all seemed like something from a Jonathan Coe novel, and the pictures of the Bullingdon Boys did rather make them look like they were in Slytherin, as one Radio 4 comic observed. (Okay, I do enjoy Radio 4 comedy sometimes.) Opening my computer and looking at the pictures of our new leaders dressed in dinner jackets with their noses raised with effortless privilege, I just felt this perennial frustration: 'Why are we *always* the baddies?' But I could also sense something within the party, that lurking class resentment felt by the Tory foot soldiers, the sullen, grumbling Saxons whose simmering anger will one day have them buzzing around like hornets against their Norman rulers.

The Cameron project was aimed at winning over the growing demographic of urban graduates who were economically liberal but also repulsed by the Tory party of old. Yet by marketing themselves as being indistinguishable from Blair the New Tories had a real problem Labour didn't, since if voters see two candidates as being pretty much the same, according to one study, 'the electorate breaks roughly 60 per cent to 40 per cent in favour' of the Left-wing party.[3] Supporting a Left-wing party feels better, more caring and more communal, and carries social proof because people around you are loudly declaring their support for the Left, too, while Tories are more likely to keep their head down. But the main problem is the empathy gap, with both Republicans and Conservatives failing to give the impression they care about others; the same study found that a Republican who can 'overcome the empathy gap' can win up to 65 per cent of the vote in a race with a very similar Democrat candidate because people regard them as more effective.

During the 2010 campaign I helped canvass for the first time alongside the prospective Tory candidate, a nice local businessman called Richard who faced an insurmountable challenge, with the Tories well behind in third place, barely in double figures. In typical style Haringey Council messed it up by sending out over seven hundred ballot papers asking voters to pick three candidates.[4] But it doesn't matter, since the council has been Labour longer than East Germany was communist and will remain so after the sun has undergone core hydrogen exhaustion and died.

A few of the people I doorstopped disliked Labour, but I remember just one guy being enthusiastic about the Tories, a suave-looking older Greek man. On one occasion our group were out campaigning in Muswell Hill and stopped for a drink in a pub. To my horror I saw sitting there the boyfriend of my wife's friend Lottie, a bloke called 'Gary' (I've changed his name to protect me, so he doesn't work out it's him and come and beat me up). He was much older than his girlfriend, who was young, beautiful and privately educated; in contrast, Gary came from a working-class background, had a child by another woman and loathed Thatcher and all Conservatives with a vengeance. He was one of those people who was good at charming women because he genuinely believed in stuff such as Tarot reading and the 'third eye'; he also thought the Tories were evil, big business was evil, America was evil and everything Michael Moore said was true. I had never responded to any of his political comments and he probably had no idea about my views.

As our little group of Tories sat down in the pub, all floppy-haired and soft-cheeked, Gary spotted me and must have seen the blue leaflets on the table. He looked at me quizzically – he had a certain instinctive cunning and noticed things – and got up to come towards us. I began to palpitate, readying myself for the most colossal of awkward moments, when his friend stood to leave and beckoned him to come. I mumbled something to the effect of seeing him the following weekend, encouraging him with all my psychic will to follow his pal, and breathed a heavy sigh of relief when he shifted to leave. He waved and walked out.

The party also strong-armed me into standing for the council in my ward, much to my reluctance. 'What if I win?' I asked. 'I can't think of anything worse than being a local councillor, having to spend my time sorting out other people's problems for very little money. I mean, I didn't get into politics to *help* people, I'm a Conservative.' 'Don't worry,' they reassured me, 'there is no chance of the Tories winning in Haringey,' and on the day we came in well behind Labour, the Lib Dems and even the Greens. I'm pretty sure my wife didn't even vote for me, if I'm honest. On the same day our candidate trailed in third in the general election, and having spent all our time bad-mouthing the local Lib Dem MP we were now in government with her and the rest of the sandal-wearers and fruit-juice drinkers.

The new government faced huge problems, their entire programme being aimed at reducing spending, which meant doing some bad things. They didn't actually cut spending – they reduced the rate of increase – but this alone meant some local authorities making harsh decisions. Inevitably the focus of debate was on the 'cuts' and 'austerity', and it seemed that every morning the *Today* programme would invite representatives of some large charity to blame government belt-tightening for worsening poverty. All of these charities, without exception, received funding from the state, and yet were always presented as disinterested bodies who profess these beliefs purely out of the goodness of their hearts. It would be like inviting on someone to wax lyrical about how the Catholic Church was the answer to society's ills without mentioning that he happened to be a bishop. This kind of thing would drive me nuts, shouting at the radio, 'He works for a government-funded charity!' while my toddler sprayed orange baby food on the floor, and the new baby dribbled breast milk. Then I would go off and write a *Telegraph* blog in an ill-thought-out fury, in order to make other people angry.

There was pain, as with any spending reduction, but the Notting Hill Tories did seem to focus the pain on areas that hurt the poor, such as local government. There was a perception that the very rich were doing very well while the rest were sort of stuck. Conservativism was supposed to be about helping the 'average man' – *l'homme moyen* as French statistician Adolphe Quetelet called it – yet for all their progressive language I suspect that Cameron and Osborne just didn't have that much experience of even 'average' people, let alone the actual poor.

That insulated background, in which they only met other high-status people, perhaps made them more liberal, too. The Cameron faction wanted us to accept social liberalism just as Blair accepted Thatcherite economic liberalism, but I wondered how much this was because of the wider electorate and how much because conservative elites now move in circles that are overwhelming liberal and they just want to be liked, or at least not hated. I understand, since most of my social network is Left-of-centre, and if I went into politics I would probably lose a lot of friends. It takes courage to stand out, and the Notting Hill set came from quite liberal cultural milieus, at least compared to previous Tory leaders. Boris Johnson's metropolitan background explains why his persona as a fun-loving multicultural mayor always seemed less false than his subsequent Brexit nationalist rebrand; indeed, one reason he agonised over the referendum was that it meant falling out with family and friends, something I could relate to on a smaller scale. Johnson's sister is a Remain campaigner, while his brother is married to a *Guardian* journalist who broke the Windrush scandal, a politically mixed marriage that is increasingly rare, especially on the other side of the Atlantic.

It's a good thing that the establishment of both parties mingle as one, because we know from the American experience that the alternative is worse. Back in the 1990s Newt Gingrich encouraged Republican politicians to get out of the Washington bubble by flying back to their states at weekends, something which only helped to further inflame partisan divisions. And yet a conservative elite that mixes in largely liberal social circles will find themselves like minority-language speakers, faced with the sheer weight and force of prevailing opinions. The temptation to abandon their followers becomes intense.

In chemistry there is something called Le Chatelier's principle whereby 'If to a system in equilibrium a constraint be applied, that system will move so as to oppose that constraint.' Because holding socially conservative views carries a cost in high-status circles, and since the same is not so true of the opposite, then elites will become more liberal. Most people want to be part of a cultural consensus, but as with any consensus the inevitable tendency is for it to drift towards the line of least resistance. Ancient historian Tom Holland compared social media's Leftward drift with the phenomenon in Classical Greece where, because soldiers were covered on their right by a comrade's shield, the phalanx would inevitably shift in that direction as soldiers looked for protection.

And the Tories face further problems in that, once the state grows in size, there develops that institutional network of people who have a vested interest in not allowing the government to reduce it. These aren't miners; they're educated, well-connected and have a disproportionate voice in media, and tend to develop a collective worldview. Some conservatives in the 2000s began talking about 'the Blob', especially in education, to describe this network of people ideologically committed to state power and a statist ideology. It was synonymous with what blogger Curtis Yarvin called 'the Cathedral' to describe a wider progressive network, encompassing the media and academia. The term relates to how much cultural power they had, resembling the medieval Church in its ability to shape public discourse (the etymology of cathedral is 'seat' or 'throne', and when a pope speaks *ex cathedra* he is pronouncing with the full authority of the Church).

Left to its own devices, the Blob just gets bigger and bigger, developing more departments and quangos, taking on more functions once done privately, so making it harder for any knight to slay it. (I know knights slay dragons, but I'm not sure what slays a Blob.) On top of this, the powerful state broadcaster is very much part of that Blob and so, with the best intentions in the world, shares its worldview. Conservative governments find it difficult to dismantle this network and more often further empower it, and there is rarely movement in the opposition direction; politically neutral or Leftist organisations do not become conservative. Labour also made sure not just to create more public bodies but to pack them with vocal supporters and sympathisers; over the entire course of the 2010s the Tories managed to appoint two genuine conservatives, Sir Roger Scruton and Toby Young, both of whom were forced out.

The Tory leadership seemed fairly relaxed about progressive domination, as long as the economy ticked over, yet it's a short-term strategy. Social liberalism requires a large state bureaucracy, while a population with low marriage rates and no religion naturally drifts Left. The Cameronian acceptance of social liberalism is also untenable because social liberalism cannot stay still. Progressive politics must, by its very nature, move towards more radical positions partly because people on the Left are in competition to outdo each other and so will push it further as part of the status competition – this is why social media hatefests are usually directed at other people on the Left. Many Tories would like to accept that, on social issues, liberals have won so that they could focus on economics instead, but progressivism is always changing, indeed perhaps accelerating. There are no surrender papers we can simply sign and get on with our lives.

The new government liked to talk a lot about 'hard-working families', but the sort of hard-working families they had in mind involved two working parents supporting the Treasury and hiring a nanny. They did almost nothing to reduce housing costs, and the proportion of home-owners went ever downwards while the Tory party busied themselves with their policy of social reform. Perhaps David Cameron thought that people would remember him chiefly as the man who legalised gay marriage, to which future historians of the twenty-first century will, I suppose, only conclude: 'LOL'.

And so under Cameron the social changes that stunned and confused older *Herald* readers sped up. They were especially bitter that the Tory front bench mostly voted into oblivion Catholic adoption agencies because they refused to place children with same-sex couples, a law to punish people for homophobia even at the expense of potentially allowing children to go into care. It seemed that all three major parties were chasing a metropolitan minority, at the expense of a socially conservative and economically egalitarian majority. This was inevitably going to lead to some sort of reaction.

In a sign of acceleration, gay marriage went from being something not considered by anyone in 2010 – even the Lib Dems didn't propose it – to 'anyone who doesn't support this should be purged from polite society'. Polly Toynbee described the Tory party as 'a nest of bigots' because it was divided over the issue.[5] It was disconcerting to people who hadn't even considered it a decade earlier, and to traditional Catholics for whom marriage is a sacrament, and so cannot be changed. I saw the logic of the pro- argument, and that the meaning of marriage had changed to one of recognising a partnership of love, but I also hoped that people could disagree without being called 'bigots'. The hatred on display was quite depressing, and mostly in one direction; the more hateful they were, the more they accused their opponents of being haters. What I found disconcerting was the moral absolutism of supporters, because people who see issues in such stark terms are unlikely to care about such things as freedom of conscience.

One of the recurrent social media memes around gay marriage was a list marking all the terrible things that do happen and might yet happen in the world, and pointing out that gay marriage would not change them one bit. And then, under 'things that will happen': gay people can marry the person they love. All very clever and everything, but it wasn't quite that simple. In fact, around this time, and for various reasons, the scent of victory drove progressives to become ever more intolerant of those who disagreed with them, heralding the start of the 'Great Awokening', and the decline of liberalism.

You Have No Brain

All the best people go from Left to Right as they lose their youthful naivety: Peter Hitchens, Paul Johnson, Melanie Phillips, Anakin Skywalker. It's seen as an inevitable part of the ageing process, as one gets wiser but also jaded and cynical. And yet it seems to be happening no longer; in the US the cohort behind the 'blue wave' of 2006, when young people turned out in large numbers to elect the Democrats, has not switched to the Republicans so far.[6]

'If you are a socialist at xxx you have no heart and if you're a socialist at xxx you have no brain' has been attributed to Victor Hugo, Benjamin Disraeli, George Bernard Shaw, Georges Clemenceau, Winston Churchill and Bob Dylan. The truism was probably first written down by nineteenth-century French political theorist Anselme Batbie, but he in turn attributed it to Edmund Burke. And it's no longer true, especially among the highly educated, who are now overwhelmingly liberal even as they hit forty. In the US more than half of people with postgraduate degrees have 'consistently or mostly liberal' values,' and there has been a sharp increase in highly educated Americans with 'across-the-board' liberal views, among postgrads an increase from 19 per cent in 2004 to 31 per cent in 2014, and among graduates a jump from 5 per cent in 1994 to 13 per cent a decade later to 31 per cent in 2014.[7] While in 1992 Republicans had a 7-point lead among the university-educated, by 2014 the Democrats were ahead by 12 points.[8]

But a lot of this shift is not down to obvious reasons. One study at the University of Leicester found that many middle-class, middle-aged people were more conservative than they think, still voting for centre-Left parties and identifying with liberalism even though their actual opinions had changed.[9] They misunderstood their own position on the spectrum because they were socialising in a largely progressive milieu: 'Detached from the broader electorate, they fail to notice that their views have become distinctly conservative.'

Thirty years ago, many educated people would have naturally come to identify as Conservative as they headed into their late thirties, aided by the social proof of friends and acquaintances doing the same; now they're much more likely to live in political deserts, a point where social networks become so liberal that conservatives effectively disappear. And social networks really matter: one research paper showed that people tend to reject established scientific findings not because of 'ignorance, irrationality or overconfidence' but because they believe what their peers, and those they trust, tell them.[10]

Likewise self-censorship begins to kick in when people feel they are in a minority or might attract disapproval from high-status individuals, and are 'less ready to express opinions which deviate from the perceived majority view'.[11] It is the fear of sanctions that causes 'a spiral of silence', while another experiment showed 'the expectation of being personally attacked can explain why people are more willing to voice a deviant opinion in offline rather than online environments'.[12] Meet a homeowner in their thirties or forties in London and you can guess with pretty reasonable accuracy their views on most social issues – they will be the same as those of their neighbours.

It also leads to ignorance about what the other side believe. The libertarian economist Bryan Caplan coined the term Ideological Turing Test to define the ability correctly to articulate what an opponent actually believes, named after Alan Turing's yardstick of a computer's ability to mimic a human. Ignorance means that minority opinions have to pass a tougher stress test, since as Caplan argues, 'If someone can correctly explain a position but continue to disagree with it, that position is less likely to be correct.'[13] US liberals have a less accurate view of conservative beliefs than the reverse.[14] Likewise when asked to rank the reasons why their opposite number voted in the 2016 referendum, Leave voters were more correct in characterising Remainers than vice versa.[15] My own theory for why liberals don't understand conservatives is that conservatives are lower-status, and people don't generally tend to pay attention to people lower down the pecking order (except to those at the very bottom, with the underclass, who exert a lurid fascination). It's become a cliché to talk of people who live in bubbles but that's because it's true.

It's hard to see how this could be reversed. Back in the fourth century Christianity reached a demographic tipping point and, following the

Emperor Constantine's legalisation, swiftly became the dominant and eventually only religion of the Roman Empire. Later that century the Emperor Theodosius had the Roman temples shut down, so the new religion quickly became as intolerant as the old. Roman temples shut down, so the new religion quickly became as intolerant as the old. Indeed, Christians were far more enthusiastic in killing Christians, those who had rival interpretations of the faith, than the old religion had been. This was not because Christians were bad people; in fact, in their attitude to slaves, women and children they were more compassionate than the pagans, probably in practice as well as theory, but the Christians were also vehement in their beliefs, and because of this they were determined to win.

And yet many people stubbornly hung onto the old gods even as it became apparent that they were the past. In 355 a pagan came to the throne for the first time since Constantine's conversion forty years earlier; a man known as Julian the Apostate because he had reverted to the old religion. Julian was a wise and benevolent ruler who, compared to most Roman emperors, murdered hardly anyone. He also tried to turn the tide by removing Christian influence root and branch, even banning Christians from teaching at schools, through which they had come to dominate Roman society; but it was too late and the new faith had become unstoppable. The clock could not be turned back and the Apostate was on the wrong side of history. Julian's supposed dying words, reflecting on how he had tried to own the Christians but they had indeed owned him, were 'Thou hast conquered, O Galilean.'

It has always been assumed that, as young liberals grow older, they will inevitably become more conservative as disappointment crushes their dreams, but among those born after around 1975 that is no longer the case. All the indicators are that their liberalism is permanent, and so most likely will be that of the generation that follows them, and perhaps those of us left on the Right will become the equivalent of the last pagan generation of Rome. Perhaps what we're witnessing is the start of a new culture entirely, as conservatism among the under-forties becomes a genuinely dying creed.

It's not that younger people are actively Left-wing but that being progressive is just a sort of default state, a replacement for Christianity as their moral anchor. If you're a decent, thoughtful person under a certain age then, unless you have some particular reason for being conservative, like an attachment to religion, the Left is your faith. People have been detached from conservative ideas in almost the same way as they have from religion, and once this is established it becomes very hard to reverse. And perhaps one day the last conservative will pass from this world, muttering some sad lament about being conquered by the Lefties.

23

MECHANICAL JACOBINS

Our thirties are the decade we become who we were destined to be, our true selves emerging as the pressure to conform reduces. The degree to which genetics plays a role in intelligence and personality increases as we get older, since we are no longer influenced by peer groups. We are free – to become our parents. Inevitably, as much as I resisted it, I was starting to think like my dad, in particular his belief that Conservatives aren't actually interested in conserving much. Nor, once they had cut down the state, did they have any ideas about what holds society together.

The *Guardian*'s environmentalist George Monbiot, who came from a Tory family but is firmly on the Left, once wrote:

> As a young man, I was amazed to see the burghers of middle England look the other way as their beautiful market towns were turned into car parks and the glorious countryside that surrounded them into chemical deserts. They claimed to love a national character exemplified by independent butchers, bakers and greengrocers, but shopped at Tesco . . . As a road-building programme driven by the demands of construction companies ripped through ancient monuments and nature reserves, they did nothing, leaving hippies and anarchists to defend our national heritage . . . Everything conservatism is supposed to defend – tradition, continuity, community, national character, the physical fabric of the

nation – is ripped apart by the demands of capital, whose permanent revolution the Conservative party assists and accelerates.[1]

Two centuries earlier Samuel Taylor Coleridge had complained that
'The ancient ideals of England were surrendered to the stock-jobber and
the modern political economist . . . to the class of persons intent on
denationalizing society, men who would dig up the charcoal foundations of
the temple of Ephesus to burn as fuel for a steam-engine.'[2] In my lifetime
there has been little Tory opposition to lending at high interest, for instance;
likewise with online gambling, or types of booze that are clearly marketed
at serious alcoholics, we leave control or opposition to Labour. These are
things conservatives should care about, and a cynic could hardly be blamed
for concluding that since the victims are mostly from lower social classes,
and the people selling the poison are from more Toryish sections of society,
they have little reason to care.[3] Whether there is a Conservative or Labour
mayor in London makes absolutely no difference to the spread of dystopian
glass-and-steel architecture straight out of *RoboCop*, buildings with
absolutely zero sympathy for surroundings or history; in fact, the Tories
were arguably worse.[4]

Just as with Monbiot's England, Rod Dreher recalled witnessing local
government meetings in America's heartlands where Republican officials
voted through big business-sponsored plans to destroy local high streets
and small, family-run shops to allow strip malls to take over.

The political community for Burke was shaped by 'the wisdom of unlet-
tered men' in a partnership of living, dead and yet unborn. In contrast,
liberalism was 'a system of letting loose all ties and bonds whatever, but
that of selfish interest', in the words of Victorian scientist and evangelist
Henry Drummond.[5] Plenty of Tories in the nineteenth century campaigned against rapacious capitalism, although admittedly some of them
were pretty eccentric. Matthew Arnold disliked the 'philistinism' of industrial society, and the new industrialists 'who most give their lives and their
thoughts to becoming rich'.[6] Snobbery plays a part in that tradition, of

course, but red Toryism also has its function within conservatism. It's now half-buried, like a Wren church surrounded by soulless glass-and-steel skyscrapers.

Individualistic Anglo-Saxon conservatism values freedom, yet it was always dependent on firmly established moral codes, and in particular Christianity; just as capitalism cannot survive without trust, so freedom cannot last without some internalised moral order. In contrast, the British Left now sees the state as the only vehicle for social progress, and to some of them almost every institution outside the state is viewed with suspicion, a potential hotbed of sexism, racism and homophobia.

The Thatcher era saw a growing contradiction between two aspects of conservatism, belief in the free market and support for tradition. John Gray once acutely observed that Thatcher had tragically created a society more in the image of her son Mark than her father Alderman Roberts, the upstanding Methodist shopkeeper. But then that is the conservative dilemma, in that free-market capitalism tends to destroy all things conservatives hold dear, especially the family. The Canadian commentator David Frum even argued that Edmund Burke would not recognise the sort of ideas now associated with the free-market Right, even though he and Adam Smith were politically aligned: 'The conservatism of recent days has been a conservatism of radical individualism: a politics that sees its job as protecting society's "makers" from society's "takers".'[7]

The post-Thatcher Conservative Party has taken it as an axiom that they stand for 'freedom' and the individual, and the essence of that is being able to hire an Uber or start a business – but 'freedom' is not what conservatism is about. Burke had argued for restraints on men since, like liberties, they are 'to be reckoned among their rights'. He thought that 'the inclinations of men should frequently be thwarted, their will controlled, and their passions brought into subjection'.[8] Some people are prone to making bad decisions, and 'freedom' without guidance and direction will cause them to ruin their lives – a tragedy for those around them, since no man is an island. During the American Revolution, when hot-headed radical Samuel Adams told his more moderate cousin John that love of liberty was within all of us, the future president replied that it's also within all wolves; and the two instincts were no different except when 'enlightened by experience, reflection, education, and civil and political institutions'.[9]

Tories also like to talk of 'the politics of envy', but what they really mean is the politics of resentment, which is not an entirely unreasonable emotion. As Scruton said, 'Resentment is not a good thing to feel, either for its subject or its object. But the business of society is to conduct our social life so that resentment does not occur: to live by mutual aid and shared rejoicing, not so as to be all alike and inoffensively mediocre, but so as to gain the co-operation of others.' Envy-avoiding is good, and people with money should be ashamed to show it off, since 'Resentment is the equilibrating device that keeps the society of strangers in balance, by punishing those who offend the laws of solidarity and rewarding, through its absence, those who contribute to the common good.'[10]

Many conservatives dislike confiscatory taxes but we still feel uncomfortable with people displaying grotesque levels of wealth, and the fact there is no stigma to it. During the Blair years this got much worse, the whole obsession with bling and footballers who thought they were in hip-hop videos. One IT girl, I seem to remember, spent a million pounds on a bath tub, and yet none of these rich idiots attracted the sort of public hostility that occasional high-profile tabloid scroungers did; you certainly never heard much from big-C conservatives on this issue. It was hard not to be a bit disgusted by the amount of money on display, but at least the taxes were rolling in, and people in the City seemed to know what they were doing.

Actually, of course, they didn't, and the great breakdown in trust towards major institutions dramatically spread to finance in 2007. In retrospect, thank the Lord that Gordon Brown was in charge and took action, although on the other hand reading about the numbers brought home just how much debt the country was already in. But you didn't have to be some raving Marxist to feel a bit angry at how unjust this all was, and that almost no one was punished for it, while since then wages have stagnated at the middle and bottom. After our third child reached toddlerhood my wife went back to work in a new career as a chef, always a difficult business, physically tough and badly paid. Sometimes the company she worked for didn't need her and so simply cancelled her work in the morning, without any compensation. My first thought was, 'What kind of Third World country do we live in?' and then after that, 'If only we had some sort of organisation for workers to get together to demand better wages. And perhaps some sort of political "party" to represent them?' To quote Homer Simpson, *That wasn't part of the deal, Blackheart! That wasn't part of the deal.*[11]

Even on the marriage issue I began to see that the Left had a point. The Conservative 'family values' thing is perhaps *the* most boring argument made by anyone on the Right, tedious and sanctimonious, but there is logic to it. Encouraging marriage is an insurance against poverty and leads to more social peace, and is obviously better for the children, and as a conservative it seemed obvious that tax systems should nudge people towards marriage, while at the same I didn't want MPs becoming preachy about it. (Especially since I imagine a number of them are privately engaging in 'unspeakable acts of degradation', as one tabloid once described some sex scandal, which took place in a £550,000 two-bedroom flat.) Yet money does play a part, since 'the relentless downward trend in men's median wages, the even more relentless downward trend in labor force participation' is 'undoubtedly' having an impact, according to one analysis.[12] Medium male income is declining, but even more so in relation to women, and one study found that 'within marriage markets, when a randomly chosen woman becomes more likely to earn more than a randomly chosen man, marriage rates decline'.[13]

There seemed a growing discontent among the Tory foot soldiers. Even former *Daily Telegraph* editor and Thatcher biographer Charles Moore was left to lament in 2011 that he had lost his faith in Thatcherism. 'When the banks that look after our money take it away, lose it and then, because of government guarantee, are not punished themselves, something much worse happens. It turns out – as the Left always claims – that a system purporting to advance the many has been perverted in order to enrich the few.'[14] This was a moral problem deep within conservatism, Moore wrote in response to the closure of the *News of the World*, a paper that had enjoyed a long and mutually beneficial relationship with the Conservative Party. And yet this organ of working-class Toryism published inconsequential rubbish and intrusive porn, spreading poison and sleaze and ruining many people's lives with their prurient intrusions into privacy. In Moore's words, the Tory press has come to be a 'disappointment to those of us who believe in free markets because they emancipate people. The Right has done itself harm by covering up for so much brutality.'[15]

Conservatism had also encouraged a moronic public culture. A survey of school children in the 1980s found their top choices for future careers were teaching, finance and medicine; a similar one by Sky Television in 2009 found the most popular to be sports star, pop star and actor. Left on its own, the free market completely lacks any high-mindedness, so that the things people admire and respect are money and sex appeal. The only men and women who could instil high culture, the types who run Radio 4, are crippled by a fear of appearing elitist or politically unsavoury, because most high culture is overwhelmingly white and male. But if conservatism is just about the free market and 'choice' then it is nothing, and it will be beaten.

All large parties are coalitions, and since the late nineteenth century, at least, the Tory party has been a pact between free-market liberals and conservatives; yet when I read MPs saying that we stand for 'freedom', I wonder what exactly I have in common with them.

Conservatism is individualistic only in a legal sense and in opposition to the state; conservatives are opposed to forced collectivism, and value economic freedom, especially when it comes to private property. But conservatism *is* communitarian in regards to informal duties, bonds and obligations; we don't believe in absolute freedom. The cowboy goes off onto the prairie only so that he can support his family when he gets back; his rugged individualism is only rugged in regards to state overstretch, not his community. Once you lose those social obligations, and the institutions that bind us, then what's left exactly? Conservativism is about institutions, but its fortunes are linked in particular to those of the nuclear family, just as liberalism is linked to the individual. Yet it became obvious that senior Tory politicians would rather we were all out pushing up the quarterly figures rather than raising children in financially secure, child-friendly environments.

Besides which, nothing in the culture war really matters if the experts are right about the biggest issue of all, because climate change could well plunge the world into catastrophe, with widespread dislocation and fighting over resources. But, to look on the bright side, a new dark age in which we're living in a skull-based economy, the surviving patches of inhabitable land controlled by *Mad Max*-style warlords – that will probably be bad for the Left, right?

We once owned this issue. In the early twentieth century Lady Eve Balfour effectively founded the organic food movement, and preserving the countryside, especially from urban intrusion, has always been a heavily conservative thing. Of course, that's partly because more Tories could afford the costly environmental options, and some green movements today remain upper-middle-class pursuits for that reason. Likewise, the restrictions they wish to place on consumption affect the poor hardest, which is why Right-wingers make the rather disingenuous argument that, say, restrictions on dirty old cars or cheap air travel are just 'snobbery', which ignores the fact that environmental catastrophe will inevitably hit the poor hardest.

Why did we cede the environment to the Left? Partly, I suppose, it is because some Tories care more about GDP than posterity, and also because of some Right-wing machismo, or a fear of the state-driven solutions; or conservatives just dislike the preachy Lefty-ness of environmental campaigners, something with which I certainly empathise. Political tribalism tends to eat up all sorts of issues, and with the environment that happened in the late twentieth century; following environment campaigns such as that against DDT, the green movement tended to become pro-big government and internationalist.[16]

Some conservative men also have some weird defensive thing about cars, the most un-conservative thing in the world. Just like Mark from *Peep Show*, I only learned to drive in my late twenties when my girlfriend gave me lessons for my birthday, just what I didn't want. It was a prerequisite of taking the relationship further that I finally make some steps towards leaving adolescence. Yet when I had children it just triggered off some weird hormonal response, which turned me into my own father in his intense hatred of these things. Dad was right about what a menace cars are, usually the most dangerous and disruptive thing in a child's life.

Cars were supposed to represent freedom and independence, in this adolescent interpretation of conservatism in which only Lefties care about the environment. In Britain, it was the Tories who came up with the Beeching Axe that unnecessarily destroyed so many railway lines, a day that will live in infamy; Euston Station was demolished under a Tory government and St Pancras would have gone the same way if it wasn't for John Betjeman's campaign. As Peter Hitchens says, railways are beautiful, civilised and ordered, the very epitome of conservative values, and give us an appreciation of the landscape that cars will never manage.[17] Also, as he doesn't mention, you can drink beer on them too.

Driving is obviously convenient, and I can appreciate the beauty of some older cars, but aside from the pollution and the huge numbers of deaths they cause, they also ruin cities and ruin childhood. I grew up on a main road and as a teenager I was conscious of how horrible the fumes were. The speed limit was 30 mph at the time, and there were virtually no speed cameras back then so even this was routinely broken. Yet the papers were full of opinion pieces about how traffic police were basically the Gestapo, how speed cameras were a government scam, and in my young mind car drivers were on our side because they read the *Mail*. Why the right of moronic men to speed is somehow more authentically conservative than the right of my kids to have safe streets is in retrospect quite baffling.

Likewise, I never saw how choking the atmosphere with pollution should be seen as a core conservative value.

I began to change my mind during an earlier aborted attempt at driving lessons in my early twenties when my instructor, a part-time fireman, recalled his past experiences on one particular stretch of road where his job used to involve pulling bodies out of cars. Since a speed camera had been installed here, he had been spared that horror. Indeed, from my childhood to the present day the number of road fatalities has dropped from five thousand a year to two thousand, despite an increase in vehicles and journeys, and each speed camera is associated with one fewer fatality every five years, saving two lives a decade.[18] All thanks to the nanny state and the Traffic Stasi.

It is not just a matter of needless deaths; one of the things that conservative analysis of the Good Old Days™ has ignored is the role played by cars in destroying street life, something that has become far more obvious to me now I have children. Just as crime affects thousands of scared people beyond the immediate victims by reducing non-victims' feelings of safety, so the car restricts people's liberty through fear. Eventually it dawned on me that cars are the enemy of conservatism; indeed, years ago philosopher Russell Kirk referred to them as 'mechanical Jacobin' and stated that motor cars 'could alter national character and morality more thoroughly than could the most absolute of tyrants'.[19]

Walkable, non-car-centred cities are happier, healthier and more civilised, the secret to Copenhagen's success, for instance.[20] This was really brought home to me one summer when our street was closed for works. For weeks the children played in the road with friends while our front door was left open, strangers instinctively smiling at kids being able to run around with the freedom of the city. It felt so much like the 1950s that I thought about sending my eight-year-old down to the shops to buy me some Woodbines. This was another area the Left had undeniably got right, while in the twentieth century conservatives both in Britain and especially in the States became enthralled to the car because of 'freedom'.

Liberalism is a product of urbanisation. 'Innovation comes from the cities, where man uprooted seeks to piece together a new world,' as Kirk put it: 'conservatism always has had its most loyal adherents in the country, where man is slow to break with the old ways that link him with his God in the infinity above and with his father in the grave at his feet.'[21] But personally I like cities; I enjoy the bucolic, romantic ideal of rural conservatism, on holiday, when drunk, but even my idea of small-town existence from watching *It's a Wonderful Life* is better found in London's Zone 3. Conservative urbanophiles are rare but, paradoxically, I think cities need us, because cities need to be civilised and beautiful, and progressives have terrible tastes in urban beauty and are psychologically incapable of dealing with crime. In return, we'll let the liberals run the coffee shops and theatre.

So yes, basically, I had reached that terrible landmark, that point that most men accept will inevitably come, when he will turn into his father. Only a matter of time before I'm sitting in my chair with a glass of whisky, holding forth on why everyone was happier in the fourteenth century, despite all the evidence to the contrary, and why the Beatles are just a fad.

24

SHOWN THE DOOR

When George Clooney said that 'liberals' are right, what did he mean by that? Americans and British people obviously have slightly different definitions of the term, but most of the 'liberal-Left' in both countries have little in common with historical liberalism, while still enjoying its positive associations (historically it meant both 'free' and 'generous').[1] Liberalism is chiefly about freedom, and John Locke, its godfather, articulated the principle of *curat Deus injuria Dei* – it was up to God to punish people who had offended him, not us. From the eighteenth century onwards liberalism was defined as a willingness to accept other people's ideas and beliefs, as well as an openness to new ideas. That tradition is dying, I think it's fair to say. The reason, as the great Enlightenment philosopher Montesquieu argued, was that a society would lose its liberty, even if it had separation of powers and a system of government set up, if the same ideas became uniform throughout its institutions, and subject to the 'tyranny of opinion'.[2]

A few years back a number of celebrities and high-profile commentators shared a cartoon from the *xkcd* webcomic, which had a character explaining that 'the right to free speech means the government can't arrest you for what you say', but 'if you're yelled at, boycotted, have your show cancelled, or get banned from an internet community, your free speech rights aren't being violated. It's just that the people listening think that you're an asshole, and they're showing you the door.'[3] Lots of smart people thought it very clever; I found it deeply sinister. And as the 2000s and 2010s went on increasing numbers of people were 'shown the door' – sacked, harassed, sometimes hassled by the police, publicly shamed and vilified, sometimes violently disrupted during speeches, all for their opinions. Perhaps the most high-profile case involved Brendan Eich, booted out by Mozilla after an internet campaign because he opposed same-sex marriage, while there was also the case of the Google worker sacked for expressing non-acceptable (but scientifically quite accurate) views on why there are relatively few women in tech. What seemed most disturbing was how many self-identified liberals thought this was all fine, because the men being sacked had bad opinions. As these campaigns of vilification were largely rewarded, so they escalated, with more intimi-dating and violent protests against unwelcome speakers. In one disturbing incident in 2017, students at the elite Middlebury College in Vermont attempted to shout down a speech by sociologist Charles Murray, and when organisers tried to move the talk next door they were jostled so aggressively that a female academic ended up in a neck brace. Protestors also pounded on the car Murray was in, rocking it and climbing on the bonnet, as he tried to escape.

Some conservative Christians have come to regard things such as the 2010 Equality Act as a sort of modern-day Test Act, the 1672 law that required people to take communion in the Church of England before they could enjoy certain civil rights. Of course, twenty-first-century Britain is far more tolerant than in the days before the Catholic Emancipation Act, and you don't have to sign up to the thirty-nine articles of Political Correctness before getting a degree. But membership of polite society does depend on adhering to a number of beliefs that conservatives do not share. The polling industry talks of the 'shy Tory' phenomenon, but I wonder how much it is influenced by a genuine fear that people will lose their jobs or be socially punished if they admit to being non-believers. As John Stuart Mill pointed out long ago, in *On Liberty*, social stigma is usually a far more serious threat to the free exchange of ideas than are legal penalties.

The call for censorship against people on the Right has grown apace. Crowdfunding platform Patreon has taken to defunding conservatives, some of whom are extreme and some of whom aren't, but the pressure has come from payment providers such as Mastercard, Visa and PayPal who wish financially to blacklist anyone seen as being on the 'alt Right', a very vague term.[4] The Left-leaning Electronic Frontier Foundation stated that banks have become 'de facto internet censors' by defunding conservatives. I know it gets tiresome when usually upper-middle-class conservative commentators say that Lefties are now the establishment, the same people students would have protested against in 1968, but if you're on the side of financial powerhouses blacklisting controversial political writers, then you probably are the establishment.

The basic principle of English liberalism has always been that people should try to engage with each other in the public square despite strongly held differences of belief. This did not arise because we are naturally drawn towards compromise and agreement, but the opposite – tolerance – is not the norm in human society. Pluralism took centuries of conflict to achieve, and it's more fragile than we think. Everyone wants 'freedom' for themselves, just as a wolf does, but what's more unusual, and harder work, is agreeing to freedom for others, for people you despise.

Nothing like the Test Act exists in modern Britain or America, but that does not mean that tolerance is not in retreat. All freedom, whether it's of speech or assembly or religion, is to some extent a spectrum; you can squeeze people's liberty without sending them to Gulags or having them burned in front of a screaming mob. Financial loss, job insecurity and public shaming are all effective deterrents to speaking freely. Having unpopular opinions can certainly lose you your job, and there is also plenty of evidence of discrimination against conservatives in employment.[5] If the government isn't arresting you for your views but mobs of organised protestors are putting pressure on companies to boycott you, then you aren't enjoying freedom. Indeed, historically not all religious intolerance involves burning at the stake, although that was certainly the most dramatic. When the sixth-century Eastern Roman Emperor Justinian wanted to drive the old pagan religion from Constantinople, he didn't need to set fire to anyone; he simply banned polytheist professors at the Academy in Athens from teaching philosophy in public. Justinian said they were 'diseased with the insanity of the unholy Hellenes' rather than 'bigots on the wrong side of history' but the essential idea was the same. St Augustine had a similar view of those following the old religion: 'As for pagans, they were simply told to "wake up" to the fact that they were a minority,' in the words of one historian.[6] They were shown the door, so to speak. And how many worshippers of Jupiter have you met recently?

Or perhaps what we're seeing is a re-run of the Reformation. When Elizabeth I came to power in 1558 the bulk of English people were certainly Catholic, while Protestantism had been the fixation of a small minority of people mostly in London and the south-east, a group who were disproportionately well-educated and opinionated, and convinced they were righteous. Outside of these circles most people found the idea of abolishing ancient aspects of the Mass, or destroying monasteries and artworks, extreme and off-putting. In 1564, the year of Shakespeare's birth, half of all Justices of the Peace had hesitated to swear the Oath of Supremacy recognising the monarch as head of the Church. By the time Elizabeth I died in 1603 Catholicism, very recently the majority religion, had become a mark of extremism, totally outside what we would now call the Overton Window of acceptable ideas. In just a few years the belief system that had dominated the country for almost a millennium was now seen as beyond the bounds of decency, even if a shrinking minority continued to cling to it.

The old faith provided the security, rituals and social cohesion most people craved; the new offered radical ideas about salvation and a war on sin, although for today's Godly it's the sins of racism, sexism and homophobia that must be driven out. And indeed there are parallels with our own time, where a highly motivated, disproportionately well-educated minority in London and some university towns are able to present the recently dominant culture as extreme. If you look at the present day, cultural changes that have occurred under the second Elizabeth have shifted the acceptable range of beliefs within a generation. The 'British values' now taught at schools would be baffling and alien to my grandparents when they were my age.

When campaigners talk of the 'persecution' of Christians who oppose same-sex marriage they are being hyperbolic and indeed a bit silly. Christians really are persecuted in places such as Pakistan or Iran, but what they mean is that the Anglican supremacy has been replaced by a progressive, atheist one, and that people who don't believe in its articles of faith, whether it be gay marriage or multiculturalism, face mild legal harassment and rather larger social handicaps. They are being shown the door.

Today's new puritans maintain that they are fighting for equality under the law rather than control of the public sphere, but this is untrue; people can have equality before the law but ideologies cannot, for one must be dominant. We could indeed have 'procedural' secularism, in which the state allows people to worship and does not favour any religion in particular, but when two sets of beliefs – sexual equality and traditional Christianity – have such opposing belief systems, the state has to favour one. That's what it did on things such as Catholic adoption agencies; it's not quite the same as being squashed underneath seven hundredweight of metal or having your guts cut out before a screaming mob of toothless Tudor cockneys, but we live in more peaceful times, and no one wants to lose their job or funding, especially when the state is so much larger today.

Although most people are quite moderate on culture war issues, just as in the sixteenth century the most fanatical are also the most vocal and determined; they understand the media of the day better than either moderate liberals or conservatives. Just as print triggered two centuries of ideological conflict on our continent, so digital is doing the same. Instead of pamphlets, blogs and social media now do the job of polarising debate, whipping up anger against the other side. During the Reformation excitable sectarian pamphlets sold in huge numbers, tracts such as Dr Henry Sacheverell's sermon against the Dissenters and their 'hellish principles of Fanaticism, Regicide and Anarchy', which shifted a hundred thousand copies in the early eighteenth century. Today, we have clickbait arguments peddling political sectarianism, or as they have might have said at the time, 'Watch John Calvin deftroy ye papists in one utterance.'

Perhaps the seeming Western liberal victory of the 1990s has made people complacent about how unusual it is for a society to tolerate wildly different viewpoints, and how much blood was spilled before we got there. Other people's opinions are annoying, even as individuals; as groups they are infuriatingly self-righteous. Freedom of speech and religion came about after a hundred and fifty years of religious violence, until people in western Europe realised there was no other choice – either reduce the role of religion in politics or endure continual violence. With the decline of Christianity, politics is becoming more like a faith and so Lockean tolerance is in decline, with old prejudices returning in mutated form; and with ideological sectarianism we now see increasing signs of the sort of intolerance and boycotting that once characterised politics in the past.

Humans haven't evolved to live with confrontational views being shoved in our faces; we have a deep-seated desire to be in communion with like-minded people, which is why we can't help judge people by their views. Four experiments using facial mimicry showed that our view of others' moral worth is influenced by knowledge of their political beliefs, and most 'perceived the moral character of other persons as much higher' if they shared the same worldview.[7] Another study, from Harvard, suggests that once a man or woman learns another person's political views, they feel less comfortable with them performing even non-political tasks, and will conclude that someone with similar views to them is better at the job – even when presented with evidence to the contrary. They were also more likely to be 'influenced by politically like-minded others, even when they had good reason not to be'.[8] In the US two-thirds of people using a shrink assumed the psychotherapist was politically on their side, even among Trump supporters who, considering the political make-up of psychologists, must be overwhelmingly incorrect.[9]

Since the conscious mind's job is to justify the choices it has made, we are prone to confirmation bias, seeing what we want to see, and treating contradictory evidence as a threat. Functional magnetic resonance imaging of partisan brains shows that when presented with bias-confirming knowledge the ventral striatum, the brain's pleasure point, start 'humming'. In contrast, areas of the brain associated with negative emotions and threat are activated when people are told of their side's hypocrisy. Naturally we discard the latter while trawling the internet for the dopamine hit provided by the former.

We also choose policies based on what our team believes. Stanford's Geoffrey Cohen conducted an experiment in which he presented 'self-described conservative and liberal Americans with two different welfare policy proposals', one of which was far more generous. Obviously, liberals preferred the generous one, but Cohen and his team then redid the experiment, assigning a policy either to the Republican or Democratic Party – and that made far more of an impact on people's opinions: 'Liberals liked extreme conservative policies in liberal clothing better than they liked extreme liberal policies in conservative clothing. The conservatives did the same thing.'[10] During the Reformation there would have been many Catholics and Protestants whose actual views on issues such as clerical celibacy, transubstantiation and the use of Latin were closer to the other side; many probably died in sectarian wars, fighting for a team cause in which they didn't even believe.

But then politics is also about who's your enemy. A study of atheists found that they were less likely to agree on an aphorism if it came from the Bible than if it were unattributed, yet there was no effect when it came from the Jewish Tanakh. For American and British atheists Christians represent a hostile outgroup, members of an opposing political tribe, while Jews do not, even conservative Jews whose religious beliefs are close to Christianity.[11]

That's because 'negative partisanship', who we define ourselves against, is almost as important as who we are. Likewise, people in Germany, Britain and the US found the same aphorism less true when it was attributed to a member of a rival ideological group.[12]

The Big Sort

This growing political divide, at least in the US, is coinciding with physical segregation, with people geographically sorting by politics and personality 'into communities of psychologically/ideologically similar people', according to Will Wilkinson of the Niskanen Center think-tank. Wilkinson says America 'may be dividing into two increasingly polarized cultures: an increasingly secular-rational and self-expression oriented "post-materialist" culture concentrated in big cities and the academic archipelago, and a largely rural and exurban culture that has been tilting in the opposite direction, toward zero-sum survival values, while trying to hold the line on traditional values'.[13] The same thing is happening in Britain, with Labour support increasingly being concentrated in big cities, huge swathes of which are now Tory-free, while Conservatives make gains in formerly red small towns.[14] This also intensifies the liberal tilt of most major media outlets, which are almost entirely staffed by people living in big cities.

Social commentator Bill Bishop coined the phrase 'The Big Sort' to describe Americans becoming more polarised by geography. While 27 per cent of Americans in 1976 lived in counties with at least a 20-point margin of victory for one candidate, in 2016 60 per cent did. More politicians coming from safe districts means more politicians whose main concern is to win over their base, which is more extreme, and not the more moderate general electorate. And the further that mainstream parties move away from any agreed middle ground, the more they'll hate each other.

Cities are, paradoxically, less tolerant. A 2019 study of the most and least politically intolerant counties in America found almost all to be Democrat, with Boston, Massachusetts, the most prejudiced and unforgiving to people with different views;[15] and so unfortunately William Buckley's famous quip that he'd rather be ruled by the first five hundred people in the Boston phonebook than the faculty of Harvard is rather out of date. Perhaps the growth of cities and megacities, while initially leading to the rise of liberal tolerance, eventually creates a less forgiving environment. Conservatism is rural, and liberalism is urban, yet people in cities are less open-minded in some ways, because they can find their clique or niche. If you live in a small town you're basically stuck with a group of people with whom you've got little in common and so you just learn to accept people's differences. If you're in a big city you might pass through areas filled with people from vastly different cultures, or subcultures, but you probably won't have much interaction with them. My mum lives in a town of twenty thousand people; I live in a city of 8 million, and her friendship circle is much more diverse in terms of background, education level and politics, if not nationality. Likewise, friends of ours who moved to rural Gloucestershire had a farmer in their National Childbirth Trust (NCT) class, which struck me as wildly exotic, where everyone in our NCT group had pretty much exactly the same socioeconomic background (and, I'd bet, very similar political views).

This geographical polarisation is intensified online, where social media gives us the freedom to form tribes of like-minded people. It may also help to drive polarisation in the US by giving Facebook users a 'blue feed' and 'red feed'.[16] Being a metropolitan conservative, more of my friends are liberal, so whenever I open Facebook my heart sinks when I see a good friend linking to a *Guardian* article by someone or other about how the Tories literally want to shit in poor people's mouths and the comment 'YES, HE NAILS IT'. Yes, he 'nails it', in the sense that the Revd Ian Paisley used to 'nail' Catholicism during his sermons every week, the ability to articulate all your tribe's worst prejudices against the other and distort what they believe in an amusing way. By that measure he does indeed 'nail it'.

Echo chambers are a cliché but they do exist, and have an effect; a study of Facebook and Twitter, using regression analysis, found that people in more politically homogenous environments were more likely to unfriend someone whose views annoyed them.[17] And partisanship pays in terms of popularity for Twitter users, according to one study from Aalto University in Finland.[18] When political tweets are broken down by political leanings, there are two quite separate lumps, conservatives tweeting conservative links and liberals doing the same for their tribe. One researcher found that 'a majority of users produce and consume content from the same ideology' in echo chambers where 'they aren't being exposed to the other side'. Not only that, but people who tweet more partisan content tend to have more influence, gain more followers and more retweets. The prime example of this system, of course, is King Troll himself, President Donald Trump.

As a medium, Facebook works better when people avoid contentious issues; it's a bit like a dinner party where you invite over lots of friends with different backgrounds, and braying about politics is perhaps not the best way to get everyone to enjoy themselves. And it does cause people to fall out. A Pew Research Study found that 18 per cent of social networking users had unfriended someone because of their political views, while 16 per cent of Americans stopped talking to a family member or close friend because of the 2016 election.[19] And yet there is an imbalance in who hates whom, with liberals more likely to unfriend friends over politics.[20] According to a CNN poll, around a quarter of Americans, but considerably more Democrats, have limited their interactions with friends or family because of politics.[21] Some 13 per cent of Americans have blocked friends on social media because of their politics, but 30 per cent of Democrat women have.[22] White women were 'significantly more likely' to report 'serious election-related stress' during the 2016 election, especially very liberal or very conservative women.[23] Liberal women are most likely overall to unfriend someone for political reasons.[24]

Even contact with the opposite tribe can make us more intolerant: Republicans 'paid to follow a liberal Twitter bot became substantially more conservative post-treatment', while Democrats in the same experiment went the other way.[25] That's part of the problem with social media, not that it doesn't expose us to the other side but that it tends to expose us to their worst and stupidest examples. Commentators also have the temptation of publicly arguing with a member of the opposing group deliberately chosen for their poor reasoning and bigotry, a tactic known as nutpicking.

The asymmetry in blocking and unfriending perhaps reflects the fact that the liberal-Left is the prestige, established faith, so its adherents are less likely to meet people their own age with different views. Perhaps it's also because liberals are more likely to believe opponents to be just fundamentally wrong and/or evil, or perhaps it's due to the greater coherence of the Left. Whereas conservatism is often eccentrically local and idiosyncratic, liberalism is more a worldwide body of beliefs and there is also far more of a sense of a community of believers, a sort of progressive *Ummah*. Liberals, for example, are pretty comfortable mingling with people from all around the world, but they feel less happy doing so with conservatives, even family members or neighbours. The liberal *Ummah* is their ingroup, and conservatives the 'other', as academics used to like saying.

The campaigning journalist Heather Brooke once wrote: 'Our printing press is the Internet. Our coffee houses are social networks.'[26] We're going through a second reformation and normal people who would be horrified by the idea of religious sectarianism fail to appreciate how similar political sectarianism can be, and how new media is accelerating it. On Twitter the competition to be purer-than-thou and to gain status in the moral community is the most tiresome aspect of the site; it turns comedians into bad preachers and writers into lazy partisans. This sense of moral superiority is also what drives so many high-status people with blue ticks to be so unpleasant and even violent-sounding. Social media encourages tribalism and gives a dopamine reward for the feeling of moral outrage, but there is also the theory that the algorithms drive people towards more intoxication through extreme ideas.[27] According to one *New York Times* article, a study in Germany found that towns with more Facebook activity also had more attacks on refugees.[28] The paper, which since 2016 has admittedly become a bit unhinged about Facebook, also links the site with violence in Sri Lanka and Myanmar, as we're supposed to call Burma, I suppose.[29]

But then newspapers can hardly be let off the hook, either. Arthur Brooks referred to the combined efforts of newspapers and social media as the 'outrage industrial complex', a system that stirs up anger at the opponents, 'affirming our worst assumptions about those who disagree with us'.[30] This polarisation also makes us unhappy, stimulating the stress hormones cortisol and adrenaline, which is why over 90 per cent of Americans are sick of polarisation.[31]

There is something early modern about this return to polarisation, even down to the phenomenon of social media rumours about the outgroup committing horrible acts.[32] In one of the most retweeted and shared of examples, a Texas waiter showed the racist note a customer had left, stating 'we don't tip terrorist' [sic], a horrible incident that received vast amounts of social media coverage. None of those people sharing it bothered to check if it was true – and it wasn't. Lots of other stories about ignorant racist conservatives, such as the case of a woman in a niqab responding to a bigot in Welsh, or of racists pretending to post a letter through the eye-slit of a similarly dressed Muslim woman, at least inspire some scepticism about whether the witness was entirely sure about the details. Others recall quaint little speeches by children making profound comments about how stupid the conservative outgroup are, to great applause from passers-by.

And even these have a historical parallel with the first great ideological schism. The anonymous 1659 tract, *Strange & Terrible Newes from Cambridge,* 'recounted how one Margaret Pryor had been victimized by a Quaker witch who temporarily turned her into a mare'.[33] And then the whole bus clapped, or maybe it should be 'and then ye whole stagecoach exalted'.

The popularity of these tales can be explained by 'narrative selection', the theory that the most popular and memorable stories are those that have an optimum amount of truth, enough to be believable but not too much, because reality rarely perfectly matches our prejudices. A successful narrative must establish 'the goodness of the ingroup and the badness of the outgroup . . . The category of legends known as "subversion myths" refers to stories that an outgroup is plotting against us, is responsible for our troubles, and possibly eats our babies in Satanic rituals. Today, the ingroups and outgroups evoked are primarily political.'[34] One study found that the most commonly shared stories on Facebook are ideological sectarian folk tales, the most successful being those that 'confirm and inflame the outgroup-hatred of any given ingroup'.

What these stories have in common is suspicion towards opponents' motives. A report from the National Academy of Sciences on 'motive attribution asymmetry', the belief that one's opponent is driven by hate and one's own group by love, found that Republicans and Democrats had the same level as that of Palestinians and Israelis, who after all don't enjoy a fantastic relationship.[35] This was in 2014, and it's fair to say that things have not improved since.

It's hard to imagine now but back in the 1940s American politics was so bland and boring that Congress authorised a committee to see how they could create some sort of gap between the two main parties, which had become 'razor-thin'. People feared that bipartisanship had gone too far and was a 'destructive force'.[36] To address this, in 1950 the American Political Science Association released a report calling 'on Republicans and Democrats to heighten their contradictions' and so provide 'the electorate with a proper range of choices between alternatives of action'. Safe to say it's 'mission accomplished' on that one – in the US House of Representatives polarisation is now higher than even in the era just after the Civil War.[37]

Many commentators have observed how US partisans have ceased viewing each other as mere opponents but as dangerous enemies. By 2014, 27 per cent of Democrats and 36 per cent of Republicans believed their rivals were 'so misguided that they threatened the wellbeing of the nation'.[38] Another poll found a third of Democrats and Republicans consider the other party 'a very serious threat to the country'.[39] The proportion of Republicans and Democrats who say they 'hate' the other party has also risen, from around 15 per cent in the 1980s, to the 20s and low 30s in 2008, to 50 and 48 per cent respectively in 2016.[40] Around 40 per cent think the other party has the country's best interests at heart 'none of the time'. In this sort of atmosphere it is not surprising that people don't wish to extend Lockean tolerance to their opponents.

There is also a measurement called 'the thermometer', whereby people are asked to rate their feelings towards the other party, 100 being the warmest and 1 being absolute hate. In 1980, voters gave the opposite party a 45 on the thermometer and their own 72, but by 1992 'the opposing party was down to 40; by 1998, it had fallen to 38; in 2012, it was down to 30'.[41] Partisans' views of their own parties had stayed the same, suggesting this was mainly the phenomenon of negative partisanship, identity based on what you hate rather than what you are. One academic warned 'that rising political polarization was showing something more fundamental than political disagreement – it was tracking the transformation of party affiliation into a form of personal identity that reached into almost every aspect of our lives.'[42] Party affiliation was no longer an expression of disagreement but something closer to a religious attachment.

American politics is so tedious, like a warring, divorcing couple who drag you into their endless conflict and force you to take sides. And indeed the two groups have come so far apart that they have taken on another aspect of sectarianism – hostility to exogamy, or marrying out.

My parents had what once would have been called a mixed marriage, something that two generations previously in England or southern Ireland would have been looked down upon, and more recently still a real problem in Ulster or the west of Scotland. As religious belief has declined so marrying across sectarian lines has become less of an issue and likewise racial barriers have come down too. Pollsters Gallup in 1958 found 'only 4 percent of Americans approved of an interracial marriage between blacks and whites,' a figure that is now '87 percent', although that may be inflated by social desirability bias – few people are going to answer 'Yes' to the de facto question 'Are you a big horrible racist?'[43]

Two years after the Gallup poll another study asked Americans if they would be 'upset' if a child married someone who supported the other party. The percentage of Republicans who answered yes was 5 per cent, for Democrats 4 per cent, a figure known as the 'Lizardman's Constant' because that number claim to believe the royal family are reptilians from outer space (in other words a number so low that people could be answering yes for a laugh, or because they are confused by the question). In 2008 Republicans were asked the same question, to which 27 per cent replied yes, they would be upset; in 2010 it was 49 per cent.[44] Among Democrats the figure had risen to 33 per cent. And they are getting their wish, with the proportion of Americans marrying people with the same political views increasing in recent decades, from 72 per cent to 82 per cent.[45]

Mixed marriages are bound to decline further, indeed a number of dating apps now match people based on political preferences.[46] It has accelerated since the 2016 election, with one expert claiming that 'millennials singles . . . are more interested in having similar politics and talking about good politics than actually having good sex'. Dating site OkCupid says that since 2016 the number of women who prioritised shared political views over enjoyable sex had doubled, a shift the company described as 'unprecedented'.[47] Dating sites now openly use this as a selling point, the *Guardian* 'Soul Mates' promising 'to play Cupid for the ideologically suited'.

Of course, the same pattern is developing in Britain, too, so from 2008 to 2016 the proportion who said they would be upset by a child marrying a member of the other main party doubled, although Labour supporters were more hostile (28 Labour v. 19 per cent Tory).[48] The gaps opened by the Brexit referendum are even worse, and rising; in 2016, some 18 per cent of Remainers said they would be unhappy with a Leave-voting in-law, compared to just 3 per cent of Leavers.[49] By 2019, this figure had risen to 37 per cent of Remainers, and 11 per cent of the other side.[50] This huge gap could partly reflect snobbery, although some form of asymmetrical tribalism is the most likely explanation.

The whole liberal ideal was that we could go on beyond the divisions in the past but political sectarianism has simply replaced the religious or racial variety. According to one study in the States, 'Prejudice based on political affiliation is stronger these days than prejudice based on race, ethnicity, language, or religion.' In the US, Britain, Spain and Belgium 'partisans discriminate against their opponents to a degree that exceeds discrimination against members of religious, linguistic, ethnic or regional out-groups'.[51]

But at least if everyone's educated then everything will get better, right? After all, late nineteenth-century Germany had the highest level of school-ing and university attendance and they turned out fine. Back in the 1890s Prussia had two and a half times as many students as England, relative to its population, and it also had enforced school attendance from the 1820s, half a century ahead of England, so German illiteracy levels were half those of Britain.[52] Unfortunately an educated population is just as prone to extrem-ism and violence: the Bolshevik Revolution would have been impossible without the growth of universities in tsarist Russia, 'the recruiting grounds for revolutionaries, ranging from nonviolent "propagandists" to the most extreme terrorists', in Richard Pipes's words.[53] Hitler was also consistently 'most successful on the campus, his electoral appeal to students regularly outstripping his performances among the population as a whole'.[54] The Nazis' most evil army corps, the Einsatzgruppen, was disproportionately comprised of graduates.

It's true that 'education reduces individuals' prejudices toward people who belong to different groups' – when it comes to race.[55] Analysis of American National Election Studies data from 1964 to 2012, however, also shows that education is related 'to *increases* in ideological (liberal vs. conservative) prejudice'.[56] Self-reported political anger among Americans is overall higher among Democrats but 'the angrier Democrats are those who have higher education' and the angrier Republicans are also the better schooled.[57] They're angry, but not necessarily because they're right – since the highly educated can be just as biased.

One meta-analysis suggested that while 'misinformation about politics is harder to correct than misinformation about health', it is 'particularly hard' among the better-educated political partisans.[58] In an experiment, academics from Yale Law School took a thousand subjects and tested them for numeracy and political leanings, after which they gave them basic puzzles and then politically charged ones. 'Those with stronger numeracy skills demonstrated more bias. They were more likely to err in the direction of their political predispositions, possibly because of their superior ability to manipulate data.' The smarter you are, the more likely you will simply twist the evidence to suit your beliefs and group identity, something replicated in numerous studies.[59] To think that John Stuart Mill suggested that we should have a plural voting system in which students had more than one vote, a nightmare idea.[60]

Today, partisan hostility in America is 'stronger among more highly educated supporters of both parties', but especially on moral issues, or those related to the environment.[61] The more that partisan Republicans know about global warming, the less likely they are to believe in it, the better they are at tracking down biased articles that would reinforce their own wrong opinions. (Some progressives have their own version of this with opposition to nuclear power and GM crops.) Likewise, while people tend to 'discredit issue polls that suggest their views are in the minority . . . those with greater political knowledge and methodological knowledge displayed this bias more strongly'.[62] At every education level the proportion of moderates in America has shrunk, but the least educated are now by far the most moderate demographic, with 48 per cent of high-school graduates having mixed views, compared to 22 per cent of postgrads.

Bigotry inevitably brings discrimination, another thing the post-war progressive era was supposed to eliminate. So while partisan hostility is now stronger than that of race, partisan discrimination is also more common, and for a similar reason – there are no social taboos against it. Psychologists at DePaul University 'found that both liberals and conservatives supported discrimination against groups that violated their respective values', even among liberals for whom 'non-discrimination' is one of their values.[63] The researchers 'measured the participants' willingness to deny basic rights and support vandalism against a variety of opponents. When outgroups were seen as violating core values, by opposing same-sex marriage, liberals were just as likely to support discrimination, just as conservatives were in favour of discriminating against feminists or atheists.[64]

Unsurprisingly, there is also strong evidence of ideological discrimination in the jobs market. Eighty per cent of Democrats and Republicans will award a scholarship to a co-partisan if some political identity cue is included in a CV, and 'When the Republican student was more qualified, Democrats only chose him 30 percent of the time, and when the Democrat was more qualified, Republicans only chose him 15 percent of the time.'[65] Both sides do it, because tolerance is not natural; the big problem for us, of course, is that these institutions have now become overwhelmingly progressive and they're holding all the cards.

Everyone loves being a part of the tribe. People who proclaim not to understand why someone would feel uncomfortable surrounded by foreign languages or niqabs often find the idea of living among UKIP voters horrific. Like the people who occasionally sell socialist newspapers outside my local Tesco while crying out, 'Refugees in, Tories out!' they would be deeply offended at the idea they are prejudiced. But tolerance is unnatural, and 'liberals and conservatives express similar levels of intolerance toward ideologically dissimilar and threatening groups'.[66]

Liberalism and pluralism developed as a sort of compromise between numerous different sects, whereas societies have historically struggled to reconcile such varying worldviews. 'This liberty, that men may openly profess diversity of religion, must needs be dangerous to the commonwealth,' wrote Edwin Sandys, the Bishop of London in 1571.[67] At the time, it was just obvious that a society could not accept rival belief systems without falling into conflict, and European history at the time seemed to confirm that pessimism. Before the American War of Independence eight of the thirteen colonies had established churches, but in order to create a Bill of Rights a compromise was reached where people could practise whatever they want.[68] Liberalism was a form of religious disarmament where ideologically divided people metaphorically left their guns at home. Pluralism meant no religion having dominance over others and a competing marketplace of ideas.

America's 'moral polarisation', and the similar trends happening across the West, puts a strain on that. As Will Wilkinson wrote of the ideological divide, it is 'basically a war of religions, of identity-constituting moral worldviews, in which neither side is very clear about what their religion is'.[69]

25

WEAPONISE THIS!

In the autumn of 2014 I was offered a job through fellow former *Telegraph* blogger James Delingpole. It paid double what I was on at the *Catholic Herald* and meant the chance to lead a politics website right in the heart of Westminster, in an office literally opposite Conservative HQ.

James had been by far the most popular of *Telegraph* bloggers, both in terms of absolute hits and the adoration of its readers. The commenters rather regarded him as their leader, or 'God-Emperor' as he referred to himself, and it seemed obviously insane that the *Telegraph* didn't give him a column in the newspaper; he was the funniest writer and had an instinctive bond with a good portion of their readers.

We had only ever met a handful of times, including one occasion when the *Telegraph* blogs editor Damian Thompson took James, Douglas Murray and me out to dinner at his club along with the eighty-something Norman Tebbit, who he had also managed to get as a blogger. I remember that we had foie gras as a starter, which was a sort of joke since James said this was the most 'sound' – i.e. Right-wing – dinner he'd had in ages.[1] There I was at an exclusive West End gentlemen's club with the Conservative Party legend, the very man who said 'get on your bike' to the unemployed, eating the cruellest form of food available on any modern menu. I felt like I was in the *Simpsons* scene where the Republican Party leadership meet and it's basically Mr Burns, Dracula and some oil barons. When the pudding wine came around I was tempted to toast

'Gentlemen, to evil' but wasn't sure Lord Tebbit would get the cultural reference.[2]

It was certainly the 'soundest' evening I'd had for a while, but then I didn't have that many, and just a few days later I would have the usual Crouch End dinner party with people from the third sector or publishing or whatever, discussing *The Bridge* or *Girls*. It was a weird double life between my Bobo world in north London and conservative political circles in west London. One day at Finsbury Park station I bumped into a liberal friend from New England who had previously worked at the *Guardian* and we had a lovely chat, not mentioning that I'd just been at the Tory party conference that very day and had literally shared a cab with the guy who came up with the poll tax.

The *Telegraph* blogs series was being dismantled; it was unprofitable and had become a bit of a swamp, the below-the line commenters an embarrassment to the brand. James was soon poached by Breitbart, a highly successful Right-wing American website, which was expanding into the European market, while I started blogging at the *Spectator*. I was allowed to write about whatever I liked, with less expectation to keep up with the daily outrage at what the Left were up to. I had also begun to read a lot more about the psychology of partisanship, and felt a bit less angry anyway. I suppose Breitbart meant going the other direction, deep and hard into the culture war.

The website's founder, Andrew Breitbart, had been raised in a liberal Jewish family in California, but had an 'epiphany' during the 1991 Thomas Clarence saga, when the conservative Supreme Court nominee was accused of sexual misconduct. The event pushed him to the other side, and many conservatives seem to have similar moments when Leftist overstretch converts them, making them feel their way of life is somehow threatened. Breitbart was also motivated by a belief that people on the Left were bullies, which seems an increasingly common experience among some men who grow up to be conservative partisans. But then, as more positions of power are held by the Left, that seems logical.

James had recommended me to run the Breitbart UK site after the regular guy Raheem Kassam had been seconded to work for Nigel Farage for the upcoming general election in 2015. He told me I'd be called at home one Sunday morning by the company's chief executive, some American I'd never heard of called Steve Bannon. I looked Bannon up and learned that he was a former US Navy Lieutenant and banker for Goldman Sachs, as well as an executive producer in Hollywood. The more I read the more terrifying he sounded, the epitome of American aggression and kick-ass determination, and I was nervous about the call, even though they were courting me. It didn't help my anxiety that on all the Google Images photos he seemed to look really angry, shouting and purple-faced with Irish rage.

On the phone Bannon talked *a lot*. He kept on using the word 'weaponise' in regard to every subject, even when I mentioned I was working on a book (not this one, incidentally, it wasn't even about politics): 'We can weaponise this, Ed!' He was super energetic, totally convinced of victory, confident that the tide was turning and the elites were going to be swept away; he sounded a bit like a revolutionary, in fact. At one point in the conversation Bannon told me they were going to overthrow the tired old Republican establishment and put their own nationalist candidate in the White House, after which they would focus on Europe. As he talked about this vision of the future I raised my eyes to the sky and, in that pasty effete English way, I thought to myself, 'What on earth is he on about? They'll never get some crazy outsider with no experience elected president on a populist ticket!' This was September 2014. I imagine if there was a film about this encounter I'd be played by Mark Gatiss, or a similarly supercilious British civil servant type who possesses the unjustified confidence of a nineteenth-century naval power and is always wrong.

America, because of its size, much larger religious population and greater diversity of opinion, has a much more active conservative movement than Britain, and so the ongoing Leftification of institutions, which over here is seamless and almost unopposed, has been countered by an active, and sometimes pretty eccentric, conservative counter-counter-culture, including an alternative media.

They often have a conspiratorial, anti-elitist nature, but then this was not entirely unwarranted, since surveys consistently show journalists to be much more liberal than Americans generally.[3] This has been the case for some time but has become more pronounced. Back in 1962 a study of 273 Washington correspondents found that '57 percent described themselves as "liberal," vs. 28 percent who called themselves "conservatives"', while a 1971 report suggested that 40 per cent identified as Left-wing compared to 20 per cent on the Right. By May 2004 a Pew survey of journalists found that just 7 per cent identified as conservative, compared to 33 per cent of the public, a figure repeated in a report a decade later.[4] At the very minimum, roughly three times as many American journos place themselves on the Left as Right.

Unsurprisingly, in 1997 Pew found that two-thirds of the American public felt that news organisations were biased, up from 53 per cent in 1985. And while about 30 per cent of Republicans trusted the mainstream media in 2004, that number was down to 14 per cent around the time of Trump's election.

Distrust in the American media really ramped up with the Barack Obama election campaign, again with good reason. In July 2008 a poll found Americans believed by 3 to 1 that journalists favoured Obama; by October that figure was 8 to 1. By September 2009 a large majority of Americans believed the media were 'promoting the Obama presidency' and Obamacare 'without objective criticism'.[5] Politico's John Harris, referring to his time at the *Washington Post*, wrote: 'A couple years ago, you would send a reporter out with Obama, and it was like they needed to go through detox when they came back — "Oh, he's so impressive, he's so charismatic," and we're kind of like, "Down, boy."'[6]

The Obama election to me was another one of those Diana moments when I thought everyone around me had lost their minds, except in this case it was upper-middle-class graduates and media folk rather than *Daily*

Express readers at it. He seemed articulate and a nice enough bloke, but also very inexperienced, and yet his supporters thought he would heal ancient racial divides in a society becoming more not less diverse, attaching to him an almost divine and royal power. Perhaps the lowest point of that election was the cringingly bad 'I Pledge' video put out by a bunch of actors led by Demi Moore and Ashton Kutcher, featuring stirring speeches by Obama, poignant music and celebs promising to be better people. I couldn't believe it wasn't a wind-up at first; it was like watching people caught up in a demented millenarian cult who poison themselves while dressed in identical trainers; no one has even talked about it since, perhaps because it was too traumatic.

So, if conservatives could not trust the media to give them the truth — as they saw it — perhaps they could start their own media organisations. I mean, what could go wrong?

Orchestra Pits

Jonathan Haidt identified fourteen causes of polarisation in the US, among which was the spread of media ghettos.[7] Although social media gets routinely blamed for almost everything these days, political polarisation is more acute among people who don't use Facebook or Twitter, because cable television is even worse.[8]

The old media, whatever its faults, had institutional checks, including editing, fact-checking and verifying pundits. If someone appeared as an expert, viewers could expect that he or she was in fact an expert, not just a random guy with an opinion. Even if channels were biased, they were obliged to have some semblance of balance. Today, however, people can spend their entire days in media ghettos where their views are not seriously challenged, and indeed become hardened. Analysis becomes propaganda and people are increasingly only exposed to the most crazed and extreme members of the opposing tribe. And because it's all an insane shouting match the only way to get noticed is to be more insane and shoutier than the next person.

The break-up first began in 1987 with the US Federal Communications Commission's abandonment of the 'Fairness Doctrine', which meant radio stations no longer had to maintain impartiality. This heralded the rise of shock-jocks, most of them Right-wing, of which Rush Limbaugh was the most high-profile. Limbaugh was an inspiration for 1995 culture war black comedy *The Last Supper*, in which a group of progressive housemates invite around conservatives and murder them. The Right-wingers they kill include an idiotically misogynistic rape apologist, a gay-bashing Protestant preacher, a guy who beats up tramps and, of course, an actual Nazi. The film was a satire on liberal intolerance, but of course the conservatives were mostly gargoyles and caricatures, except the final one, the Limbaugh-esque pundit 'Norman Arbuthnot', who makes such persuasive arguments that they don't know how to argue back and waver about killing him. Tellingly, he also says he exaggerates his views for effect, which is a common liberal idea about conservative commentators.

Right-wing radio stations in the US became the equivalent of tabloids in Britain, drawing on an all-encompassing pool of rage against the establishment and elite, mostly catering to middle-aged men in cars. David Foster Wallace wrote of these new radio shows that 'the ever-increasing number of ideological news outlets creates precisely the kind of relativism that cultural conservatives decry, a kind of epistemic free-for-all in which "the truth" is wholly a matter of perspective and agenda'.[9] There was a certain amount of truth in that, and as the twentieth century turned into the twenty-first the Right increasingly came to adopt the logic of cultural relativism. This was related to a worldview in which all politics was a zero-sum game. Limbaugh argued that the 'core institutions and norms of American democracy have been irredeemably corrupted by an alien enemy. Their claims to transpartisan authority – authority that applies equally to all political factions and parties – are fraudulent. There are no transpartisan authorities; there is only zero-sum competition between tribes, the Left and Right. Two universes.'[10]

Then things accelerated in the early 1990s. With conservatives losing the culture war a new television station appeared on the scene to challenge the three established networks. Fox News emerged out of the election victory of 'ex-hippie, pro-choice, and sexually liberated Bill Clinton (and his feminist, power-wielding wife)', an election which also saw Pat Buchanan's culture war convention, the rise of the televangelist religious Right and what some liberals saw as the radicalisation of the Republican Party.[11]

Fox News's founder Roger Ailes came up with the 'Orchestra Pit Theory' of news sensationalism, after his adage that 'If you have two guys on a stage and one guy says, "I have a solution to the Middle East problem," and the other guy falls in the orchestra pit, who do you think is going to be on the evening news?' Thoughtful conservatives had mixed feelings about this new force: 'On the one hand, Ailes reinvigorated American conservatism in a way matched or surpassed in modern times only by the likes of William F. Buckley, Ronald Reagan, and Rush Limbaugh . . . On the other, he did it in what was arguably the most demagogic, crude, fear-mongering fashion possible.'[12] He also somewhat blurred the line between political news and tabloid TV, which critical conservatives saw as further dumbing down, and yet without him neither George W. Bush nor Trump would have won.

Limbaugh and others had already set the tone on radio and in books, 'treating not just Democrats but country-club Gerald Ford Republicans . . . as though they were flag-burning hippies and dangerous radicals,' while on the Left Ralph Nader and Michael Moore were attacking 'Right-wing' Democrats like Gore or Clinton.[13] America's increasingly hyper-individual society was opening up a gap in politics.

Today just under half of 'Consistent conservatives' in the US cite Fox as their main source of information about politics.[14] Those with consistently liberal views rely on a far wider range of news outlets, including the *New York Times*, and most trust PBS, NPR and the BBC. But there is a difference between the makers of Fox's political programmes and the BBC, in that the former believe they are in a battle of ideas while the latter genuinely think they are reporting the truth. Conservative partisans accept the postmodern idea that there is no neutral truth, while the BBC is so keen to respond to criticism of bias, not just because of their public funding, but because they really do believe they are impartial and such a thing as impartiality is achievable. Some on the centre-Left still hold to the idea of objective truth in politics, while conservatives are more likely to agree with my social anthropology tutor that it's all subjective.

The proliferation of sites such as Breitbart feeds the belief that mainstream media is biased – something felt far more by conservatives than liberals – but then it is often true.[15] In one of the most notorious scenes, CNN filmed the sister of a black man killed by police in Milwaukee telling protesters: 'Don't bring the violence here and the ignorance here', but cut out her next breath where she says, 'take that shit to the suburbs,' i.e. white areas.[16] That's outright Soviet levels of propaganda, and there are plenty of similar examples, such as in 2019 when the same station was one of the worst offenders in broadcasting a highly distorted and edited version of a confrontation between a Native American 'Vietnam vet' and a group of white Catholic boys in Washington. It led to various high-profile journalists fantasising about beating up the teenagers, who had in fact just been subjected to racist and homophobic abuse from black extremists and were now getting shouted at by a former convict who hadn't in fact served in Vietnam.[17]

But while Fox might help win elections, in a wider cultural sense the rise of shouty Right-wing media coincided with conservatism rapidly losing ground in the culture sphere and among the young. And while Breitbart was a response to our growing defeat, perhaps it signalled a darker future, conservatism unrestrained by institutional checks. This was reflected in the coinage and spread of the abusive term 'cuck' to denounce high-ranking conservatives whom the foot soldiers felt had deserted them, and indeed conservatism had rather lost its elite, becoming a sort of 'left-behind community', to use that overused political cliché.

The expansion of higher education and the rise of the meritocracy have stripped many communities of local leaders, with the brightest sucked into the economically productive big cities. Shorn of its best, any community begins to wilt, or becomes prey to any unscrupulous person who wants to claim the leadership mantle. Likewise a political community, with declining numbers of conservative academics, doctors, teachers and other professionals, leaving the movement at the mercy of people who can get the most attention owning the libs. Among high-status individuals who still identify with the Republican Party and conservatism, many have also come to accept basic progressive premises, especially on multiculturalism, so much so that many conservatives no longer recognise them.

The void is therefore left to smaller organisations with lower editorial standards or concerns about balance. And Breitbart is like the *New York Review of Books* compared to InfoWars, or the various popular vloggers who inform large numbers of people and whose entire focus is on winning against the outgroup.

Years ago, when we first got Sky+, I had this brilliant idea that with interactive TV you should be able to press a button to shift the slant in news reporting to suit whatever prejudice you had. Press the Red Button for a *Guardian* view of the world, Blue for a *Telegraph*. Well, we're basically getting there.

This creates a positive feedback loop. Right-wing shock-jocks do well because they appeal to the mob, but the Leftist intelligentsia also get a kick out of them because they feed their worst prejudices about how heartless and stupid conservatives are, so guaranteeing coverage. As psychiatrist and blogger Scott Alexander wrote: 'The Republicans unilaterally seceded from those shared gatekeeper institutions, so that now we're in the weird position of having two sets of institutions: one labeling itself "neutral" and the other labeling itself "conservative".' New conservative institutions, 'by attracting only the refugees from a left-slanted system . . . ensured they would end up not just with conservatives, but with the worst and most extreme conservatives'.[18]

The process becomes self-propelling, creating a vicious cycle so that as conservatives move to their ghettos the mainstream media therefore moves to the Left, causing more conservatives to leave. And, as Alexander points out, these ghettos therefore get more grotesque and so liberals feel more justified in perceiving Right-wingers to be vile morons, further accelerating the exodus. This reaches an equilibrium, where 'The neutral gatekeeper institutions lean very liberal, though with a minority of conservative elites who are good at keeping their heads down and too mainstream/prestigious to settle for anything less.' Then there are ghettos which contain a 'few decent conservatives who are increasingly uncomfortable but know there's no place for them in the mainstream'.

The wider problem is the decline in institutions and public spaces that can legitimately be called neutral, when instead across various formerly politically diverse areas such as workplaces or universities overt liberalism is basically the norm. In some of these institutions, conservatives try starting their own spaces, 'which began as noble attempts to avoid bias, and ended as wretched hives of offensive troglodytes who couldn't get by anywhere else', as Alexander says, further justifying more purges in mainstream liberal spaces.

And so conservative media has become defined by its own outsider status, self-consciously brash and offensive because this is the only way to get noticed. The old ethos of the *Daily Telegraph* – a mixture of conservatism and classical liberalism with a heavy layer of irony and humour – has made way for something less endearing. Indeed, some Right-wingers revel in their role as bad guys, playing up to it so that, in Shylock's words in *The Merchant of Venice*, 'the villainy you teach me I will execute – and it shall go hard but I will better the instruction'.[19] They actually want to be the guys wearing the skull and crossbones because it gets them attention and from some quarters even admiration; while the ostracism and hostility towards conservative thinkers have selected the sort of person who can handle hostility, or even revels in it.

And declining trust in media must in part be caused by increasing numbers of journalists seeing the medium as a form of activism, and the boundaries between comment and reporting blurring (and I have been part of the problem). As one journalist complained after a colleague called for his fellow professionals to campaign for a cause: 'Journalism isn't activism; it's presenting the facts, honestly and objectively. It's this mentality that's killing trust in our profession.'[20] Yet many clearly don't see it that way. And if centre-Left mainstream news coverage is also often activism, why shouldn't the Right have its activists too? So along came Breitbart, which catered for the growing populist revolt that in Britain expressed itself through the rise of UKIP. The party were now polling around 14 per cent, although they had lost the support of Britain's twenty-three or so libertarians, and had just won their first seats in Parliament. It seemed like a rising force, and being part of Breitbart would make me part of the insurgency.

On the big issues I basically agreed, in particular that mass migration to the West was a bad idea that would, at best, turn us into a sort of America or Brazil. I'd written a book about it, copies of which I kept hidden in a drawer at home in case any of my SWPL neighbours saw it. But the issue always left me feeling troubled; what worried me about 'diversity' was that it would make us less civil, more bitterly divided, even bring about religious violence, a fear that I suppose was influenced by my Irish background. I worried about it because I don't like conflict and division, I'd rather live in a state of Japanese-style harmony. The inevitable political nastiness that would come about from such a diverse society was not something I wanted to be part of, and yet, by opposing it, inevitably I would be drawn into that poisonous atmosphere. Although diversity brings division, once it exists we should do our best to mitigate it and bring people together; and yet by doing so we encourage politicians to promote multiculturalism as a good in itself, so allowing interested parties both to lobby for more immigration and actively promote identity politics, so increasing the future likelihood of conflict.

In contrast, there just aren't many forums for making serious critiques of multiculturalism while avoiding sensationalism or stirring hatred, and I didn't want to end up as that guy from *Hotel Rwanda* who shouts 'cockroaches' on the radio; I hated myself enough already without this on top of it, whipping up anger about the latest outrages committed by young Muslim men. Maybe I was just being cowardly, and my British irony was masking a basic unwillingness to face a difficult fight for an unpopular cause. The temptation for conservative journalists to abandon their beliefs and seek the approval of the mostly Left-of-centre high-status figures in the media and their social circles is overpowering, and Breitbart would kill that off forever. It would mean being hated and shunned, while being praised and supported by some absolutely terrible people. That's the true definition of decadence, knowing we're all going to hell and yet feeling so fatalistic about it that you just want to enjoy the ride. As the Yiddish proverb goes: 'Money lost, nothing lost; courage lost, everything lost'.

But I could probably handle being a social leper; I couldn't the thought of hating myself. I personally feel some weary hostility towards the people who support and enable mass migration, because they are causing unnecessary problems out of motivated naivety or narcissism, or perhaps personal gain. But not towards the immigrants themselves. Many are indeed unwelcome, and I certainly shared the widespread dismay that so many unsavoury individuals are allowed to swan around because our rulers consider immigration controls a bit déclassé. But at the same time I feel shame and awe when I meet or read about immigrants working twelve-hour days, or doing life-saving work in the health sector, in order to support a family or just out of a sense of open-minded adventurousness. When I compare their lives with media gobshites such as myself, on Left and Right, who earn a living making the world an angrier place, and who almost all come from pretty comfortable backgrounds, it's hard not to feel like half a person. I turned down the job.

26

SAFE SPACES

It's not just the media: conservative mistrust of mainstream institutions in general is increasing, and with good reason. One paper, called 'Does Activism in Social Science Explain Conservatives' Distrust of Scientists?', suggested that this 'reflected the fact that scientists in certain fields, particularly social science, have increasingly adopted a liberal-activist stance, seeking to influence public policy in a liberal direction'.[1] This institutional slant has become most pronounced in universities, which have for several years gone through a 'purity spiral' as conservatives left the field, culminating in a sort of collective meltdown in the mid-2010s.

American academia has always leant Left to some extent, and for most of the twentieth century the ratio of liberals to conservative was about 3 to 1, but since the 1990s it has rapidly increased to 10 or 20 or even 50 to 1 in some areas. While 39 per cent of American academics defined themselves as being on the Left in 1984, by 1999 that figure was 72 per cent.[2] An average ratio of about 4.5 Democrat academics to 1 Republican in the 1980s has increased to between 10.4 and 12.7 today.[3] A study of social psychologists found that seventy-five times as many voted for Obama as Romney.[4] In contrast to the endangered conservatives, some 18 per cent of social science professors identify as Marxist.

The purity spiral accelerated when wartime-generation academics began to retire and were replaced by the far less diverse baby boomers, and it seems extremely unlikely that the next cohort coming in will lower the ratio.

Today 'Republicans make up 4% of historians, 3% of sociologists, and a mere 2% of literature professors', and these tend to be concentrated in religious colleges, while secular universities in New England and California are 'one-party campuses'. The faculty ratio at Williams College is 132 to 1; at Swarthmore it is 120 to 1; and at Bryn Mawr it is 72 to 0. US college administrators are, however, even more skewed to the Left than professors, if that is possible, with just 6 per cent identifying as conservative and 71 per cent as liberal.[5]

A 2018 study by the National Association of Scholars 'found that Democrats outnumber Republicans among professors of Religion by 70 to 1, English by 48 to 1 and Sociology 43 to 1. There were no Republican Anthropology or Communications professors at all. Only Engineering, with a ratio of 1.6 to 1, had a vaguely balanced total while even with Chemistry it was 5.2 per cent.' In history departments the ratio is 33.5 to 1.[6] While 18 per cent of academics describe themselves as conservative on economics, just 4 per cent do on social issues. Three-quarters of university departments in the US 'have either zero Republicans, or so few as to make no difference'.[7] Even military college West Point has a Democrat: Republican ratio of 1.3 to 1 and Annapolis a ratio of 2.3 to 1.[8]

Of course, universities lean Left because people high on openness are more creative and intellectually curious, and so have a natural predisposition towards both progressive politics and intellectually stimulating careers. But that cannot explain such a rapid shift, and neither can the claim that 'reality has a liberal bias', which even if true would show a much greater imbalance in areas where conservative politicians are more scientifically illiterate, such as chemistry. More likely is that universities have undergone a purity cycle, becoming so politically one-sided that non-progressive thinkers are leaving and new ones are not joining (or not being hired). Whatever one's views, that degree of ideological homogeneity is not healthy for an institution whose very reason for being is the debating and testing of ideas, which requires a certain level of ideological diversity and adversity.

George Yancey, professor of sociology at the University of North Texas, has researched bias in academic hiring practices, finding that a quarter of academic philosophers were unwilling to hire a Republican, more than three times as many who wouldn't want to employ a Muslim (and about the same as those who would bar a transgender person or communist working with them).[9] Yancey also found that 'some 30% of sociologists acknowledged that they would be less likely to hire a job applicant if they knew he was a Republican', as would 24 per cent of philosophy professors, and that female professors expressed more of an anti-conservative bias. Around 19 per cent of academics admitted they 'would have a bias against a conservative-leaning paper' and 'thirty-seven and a half per cent, against choosing a conservative as a future colleague'. The same study also found that most believed that no discrimination existed in hiring.[10] A 2016 study by another academic found that conservative and libertarian law professors produce more publications and are cited more often, 'which suggests that they are held to a higher standard by university gatekeepers'.[11]

One professor from Georgetown University described the various drives they had in order to look for more female and minority professors, and yet none enquired about political diversity: 'On the contrary, I have been involved in searches in which the chairman of the selection committee stated that no libertarian candidates would be considered. Or the description of the position was changed when the best résumés appeared to be coming from applicants with right-of-center viewpoints.'[12] While progressives see female or minority underrepresentation as *a priori* evidence of discrimination, the same conclusion does not leap to people's minds when conservative representation is far smaller. Paul Bloom, a psychologist at Yale, wrote that 'The same people who are exquisitely sensitive to discrimination in other areas are often violently antagonistic when it comes to political ideology, bringing up clichéd arguments that they wouldn't accept in other domains: "They aren't smart enough." "They don't want to be in the field."'[13] But then this parallel is not so odd, since liberals are in some ways the whitest of white people, the most into typically white interests, and holding the most characteristically Western social attitudes and opinions. This is why the most stereotypically liberal political movements and hobbies, whether the march against the Pope, the Liberal Democrats, climate activism, yoga, cycling or hipster beer-making, tend to be very white.

This bias inevitably affects the quality of work, because 'politically favored conclusions receive less-than-normal scrutiny while politically incorrect findings must scale mountains of motivated and hostile reasoning from reviewers and editors'.[14] One University of California psychologist studying institutional creativity looked at organisations that encouraged dissent, concluding that 'even when it's wrong, it actually improves the quality of thought in decision-making'.[15] Likewise a study of Wikipedia pages, 'The Wisdom of Polarized Crowds', found that 'polarized teams consisting of a balanced set of ideologically diverse editors produce articles of a higher quality than homogeneous teams. The effect is most clearly seen in Wikipedia's political articles, but also in social issues and even science articles.'[16] There are conservatives and liberals who think reality has a bias towards their side, but, almost by definition, quality of thought and analysis is improved by the tension between the two. As individuals we are all good at finding evidence to support our worldview, which is why it's important to have ideological diversity within any organisation.

The purity spiral is happening in Britain too, the proportion of Conservative-supporting academics falling from 35 per cent in 1964 to 11 per cent in 2015. A poll that year by *Times Higher Education* suggested that 46 per cent of university staff vote Labour, 22 per cent Green and just 11 per cent the Conservatives, in an election the Tories won. Only 0.4 per cent of academics said UKIP, compared to 12.6 per cent of the public.[17] This poll included all university staff, and Conservatives did worse with actual academics, at just 8 per cent.[18] The same publication a year later found that 89 per cent of academics planned to vote Remain and 10 per cent Leave, and I'm amazed the Brexiteer percentage was that high.[19]

Understandably, a third of conservative academics feel there is a hostile climate on campus, compared to just 7 per cent of the liberal respondents, although it should be caveated that the sample survey of the former was inevitably small.[20] (Strangely, however, conservative academics are just as happy as their liberal colleagues, perhaps even happier, and were 10 per cent more likely to say that, if they had to start their career again, they'd be academics.[21]) Perhaps more worrying, more than three-quarters of American students say they have self-censored their political views in class.[22]

This snowballing of campus radicalisation reached a tipping point in the 2010s with a series of protests at Yale, Missouri, Evergreen and elsewhere, which partly reflected the ideological conformity and intolerance of the institutions. People across the world saw students and in some cases professors screaming hysterically over the most petty of arguments; the Yale protest erupted because a dean had not taken sufficiently gravely a warning about culturally sensitive Halloween costumes. It all came with a new vocabulary, much of it possibly used more in newspaper columns than on actual campuses. 'Triggering' was first spoken of in late 2013 and the following year Oberlin College urged that texts have trigger warnings in case students were upset by subject matter, a trend that led to the tiresome pejorative 'snowflake'. 'Safe spaces' became popularised around the same time, and Brown University was the first to create such an area when it held a debate on whether America was a rape culture. A student said of that debate, 'Bringing in a speaker like that could serve to invalidate people's experience', invalidate being another term that rose in popularity, to denote challenging someone's subjective worldview or their feelings.[23] As college radicalism increased, so did the number of 'no-platforming' incidents, where colleges were forced into disinviting speakers because of protests or threats of violence. This increased heavily in the 2010s, and outside of private religious colleges, the vast bulk of disinvitations came from the Left, as did attempts to drown out a speaker.[24]

The student uprising was a strange sort of protest, demanding that society adopts more of its already existing norms, not fewer. At the time of the 1968 protests the military, business establishment and other institutions were still conservative, and even academia was quite mixed Their successors were protesting against a liberal establishment that already supported the students' progressive values; the protestors just wanted the establishment to be more like it already was. Most curiously of all, in 1964 students were campaigning for free speech. In 2017 they were rioting against it. Sixties student leader Mario Savio wrote that freedom of speech was 'something that represents the very dignity of what a human being is'.[25] Today, that would represent a minority view and, in 2017, 58 per cent of college students agreed it is 'important to be part of a campus community where I am not exposed to intolerant and offensive ideas', rising to 63 per cent for liberal students (45 per cent for conservatives).[26] Similarly, while one 68er recalled 'the noisy entrance of the first mass group of African-American students into the previously segregated American universities',[27] some of their successors in the 2010s were even arguing for segregated spaces based on race.

Today in America white liberals aged between eighteen and twenty-nine are the most in favour of free speech restrictions, against the historic trend of liberals being the most 'free speech absolutist', as older liberals still are.[28] (In Britain, students are about equally in favour of banning speech as the general public, although the two groups tend to differ on who should be banned.[29]) It's not that surprising, in one sense; self-identified liberals are probably opposed to free speech for the same reason that members of established religions tend to be more opposed to religious freedom. If you had the megaphone, would you want to hand it over?

According to a Cato Institute study, Democrats are much more supportive of blocking controversial ideas on campus than Republicans.[30] A clear majority of Democrats, by 2 to 1, would ban someone saying that men are on average better at maths than women. Many US colleges now have full speech codes stating with some detail what is permissible to say on campus, so that the University of California states that such statements as 'America is a land of opportunity' should be avoided because it would insult minorities or women. The idea of academia being a place of open exchange is clearly in decline, and this has implications for society in general, beyond Right-wing clickbait articles about snowflakes.

Arguing that colleges have never been bastions of free speech, and this was a moral panic, one *Vox* article quoted a college statement of student responsibilities from the 1960s, which warned that any behaviour that 'offends the sensibilities of others (whether students, faculty members or visitors) . . . will result in disciplinary action . . . vulgar behavior, obscene language or disorderly conduct are not tolerated'.[31] Yet institutions have always had rules about behaviour, and against bringing 'scandal' to the organisation; what is different now is the belief that ideas and speech are offensive, while in contrast people with protected ideas or identities are allowed to behave exactly as they like.

Some blame the rising intolerance of the twenty-first century on 1960s intellectuals such as Herbert Marcuse and his concept of repressive tolerance. John Stuart Mill had laid down the liberal principle that society should allow almost unrestricted speech and assembly, so long as it did not incite violence, so that the best arguments would win. Marcuse argued that this is what allowed the Nazis to win. His belief was that Left-wing arguments were about freeing people from oppression, while the Right wanted to keep them oppressed, and so the Right needed to be crushed. The Right are bad people and the Left good people, and everything came down to that basic dichotomy. To counter the threat posed by demagogues turning people against each other, he argued for the restriction of free speech and free assembly. By his logic violence might be needed to stop the Right, because they are all potential Nazis, although there is an obvious problem in deciding who is a Nazi, and in the twenty-first century the definition certainly seems to have broadened. (Marcuse's influence can also be seen in the idea that 'silence is violence', by which silence is not speaking up for Leftist causes.)

The groundwork for this Manichean view of the world as inhabited by good and bad people had been laid by decades of labelling and 'mind-reading' opponents. If you assume people are motivated by bigotry, then you are creating an atmosphere in which certain opinions become less acceptable to express, and potentially even a form of psychic violence. And if they are indeed motivated by hate, and their words a form of violence, then isn't the next logical step that the law should protect people from their bile, and perhaps they should even be physically stopped?

Among older people, for whom university attendance was limited, the political–cultural gap between graduates and non-graduates is small, which suggests that it is not just a function of being highly educated that moves people to the Left, but rather that in the past two or three decades merely attending university has become associated with becoming more Left-wing. And with universities becoming far more imbalanced, so inevitably conservatives are turning against them, with the number of Republicans seeing higher education having a negative effect on America going from 37 to 58 per cent from 2015 to 2017.[32] In contrast, a huge majority of Democrats are in favour, and so yet one more shared institution loses the confidence of one side of the political–religious divide.[33]

Universities have often been home to political activism, subversion and extremism. Thomas Hobbes wrote in his 1668 work *Behemoth* that Oxford and Cambridge had been 'The core of rebellion' in the civil war: 'The Universities have been to the nation, as the wooden horse was to the Trojans.' He was somewhat exaggerating but Oxford had been home to dangerous ideas since the Lollard heresy of the fourteenth century, founded by Oxford theologian John Wycliffe.[34] But the recent purity spiral means universities reverting to their original function, as centres of orthodoxy. In the Middle Ages philosophy had been the 'handmaiden of theology', as Thomas Aquinas put it, whereas the idea behind the seventeenth-century scientific revolution was about finding the truth, however disconcerting. In contrast, activism-based disciplines such as critical theory are more religious, in the sense that the purpose of inquiry is already decided before any conclusions are reached. And so the old intolerance for heretics seems to be returning.

April Kelly-Woessner of Elizabethtown College spelled out how a monopoly of ideas by the liberal-Left had forged a new generation. 'Young people are less politically tolerant than their parents' generation,' she observed from data analysis, 'and that this marks a clear reversal of the trends observed by social scientists for the past 60 years.' Tolerance, she defines, 'as the willingness to extend civil liberties and basic democratic rights to members of unpopular groups [and] recognize the rights of one's political enemies to fully participate in the democratic process, by giving talks, teaching at colleges or having their books used by libraries'. For people under forty, intolerance correlates with support for 'social justice', that is, 'people who believe that the government has a responsibility to help' marginalised groups, namely black and poor people. [35] Older supporters of social justice do not reject free speech and 'this tension between leftist social views and political tolerance is something new', and was linked to reduced exposure to opposing views in their everyday lives. And so, with the best will in the world, a generation has been bred with almost total confidence in the purity of their ideals and the malignance of their opponents.

27

THE GREAT AWOKENING

Progressivism is in many ways Christianity 2.0 and like the parent faith it's a proselytising religion. As the Spanish-American philosopher George Santayana observed: 'If you refuse to move in the prescribed direction, you are not simply different, you are arrested and perverse.' The existence of non-believers is almost a provocation, and so the faith must be spread, a development also pushed by activists who by their very existence encourage the creation of fresh causes, like landless knights whose restless energy drove medieval wars. Alice Dreger, author of *Galileo's Middle Finger*, explained much of the impetus behind this when she recalled her own activities: 'We weren't in this for lifelong identities as intersex activists, as leaders of the "intersex community." The goal really was our goal. This again distinguished us, in ways I only later understood, from many activists, who bank on always being able to keep fighting over an identity issue. We wanted to retire.'[1] But for many activists there is no point when, as with the Roman Cincinnatus, they return to their farm and they have no farm. Indeed, many have no hinterland beyond the political struggle.

So, once one cause is won against the forces of conservatism, the battle must immediately move to the next. Unsurprising, then, that things change in such a rapid time, and at quicker pace. Gay marriage came into the political debate at rapid speed, and after being decreed by court order across the United States, soon small businesses that refused to celebrate it were suffering vindictive legal campaigns. The trans-rights issue would have just seemed baffling even to a liberal at the start of the century; indeed even in 2003 Jon Stewart was making fun of 'chicks-with-dicks', a joke that would be genuinely career-ending by 2016. In the US at the turn of the century the Democrats had an immigration programme that in terms of policy if not language was very similar to Donald Trump's 2016 policy, widely compared to Nazi Germany by America's hysterical, gibbering columnists.

There is a line from *Ride with the Devil* where one Confederate rebel is explaining why they won't win the Civil War and the Yankees will, and which explains why their progressive descendants are also victorious: 'They rounded every pup up into that schoolhouse because they fancied that everyone should think and talk the same free-thinkin' way they do with no regard to station, custom, propriety. And that is why they will win. Because they believe everyone should live and think just like them. And we shall lose because we don't care one way or another how they live.'[2]

And so during the second Obama term, after decades of the culture shifting Left, things accelerated. Someone on Twitter christened this process 'The Great Awokening', a pun on the eighteenth-century Protestant religious revival the Great Awakening, and reflecting the semi-religious nature of the movement. Woke was originally an African-American term meaning someone literally 'awake' to social justice issues, and its use has been recorded since at least the 1970s, although it only became widespread from 2013. Wokeness is driven by the central dogma that 'All demographic groups are roughly biologically the same . . . Bigotry is pervasive. Almost all disparities among demographic groups are caused by bigotry. If we all work really hard, we can create a more just, multicultural society. Diversity is almost always a good thing.'[3] One academic paper stated that 'unlike scientific theories or other empirical claims, the basic tenets of Wokeness are held with sacred fervour. Those who challenge them are not debated; rather, their motives are denounced, and they are cast out of polite society like heretics.'[4]

This Great Awokening quite soon developed an overtly authoritarian edge. There was the 'call out culture', the tendency to 'call out' – or 'denounce' as it used to be called – people accused of being insufficiently Woke. On social media this leads to mobbing from hundreds or thousands of hostile accounts until the whole thing blows over, although not before the victim has deleted her account, publicly cried or even cancelled a publishing deal. A lot of this is just straight up girl-on-girl bullying, the type of thing women used to talk about when you mentioned the physically violent but psychologically quite basic abuse common in boys' schools. But it is also to do with the faith. Accusing others of offending the faith is a signal of faith, and the less plausible the accusation, the more trivial, so the stronger the signal. There's nothing to be gained by accusing an obvious racist of racism, but 'calling out' a progressive female professor immediately brings kudos and the support of disappointed academics whose entrance to the ivory tower has not led to the elite status for which they hoped.

This creates an air of anxiety, with people desperate to prove their Woke credentials by moving to the Left or perhaps accusing others of some unspecified ideological crime. These public displays of irrational anger and hatred, almost to the verge of meltdown, may be seen as professions of commitment by a member of the faith group.[5] Indeed, it's the very implausibility of Woke-era PC ideas that make them so attractive to true believers. Anyone can say something that is self-evidently true, but stating that someone with a beard and a penis is actually a woman, and organising a hate mob for anyone who disagrees suggests commitment and power, especially when the craven authorities – and even the police – take your side. After all, you're not scared about being laughed at for saying something outlandish and so the only possible explanation is that people fear you, an enticing prospect for many who find that their new religion gives them a strange new hold over others. As with any situation where institutional checks crumble, people with personality disorders can quickly rise to the top in the marketplace of ideas.

Many young people are attracted to causes that allow them to be the ideology police, to decide what others can say or think, and to lead mobs with the power to destroy. They can change the world – and destroy their enemies. Samuel Adams supposedly said: 'It does not require a majority to prevail, but rather an irate, tireless minority keen to set brush fires in people's minds' – although tiresome minority might be more accurate.

One of the curious symptoms of this culture change is the impact it has had on comedy, a medium tells underlying truths about society. Partly this is because British comedy reflected a liberal ideal about getting on with people we fundamentally can't stand, or disagree with, an idea that requires a certain tolerance and sympathy; think of Blackadder and his Puritan relatives or Basil Fawlty and just about everyone. That is something certainly in retreat. Worse still, the boundaries of what is permissible have become arbitrary. In the *Guardian* Zoe Williams wondered if the edgy mid-1990s satire *The Day Today* would be tolerated in 2016 and whether it belonged 'to another age'.[6] Citing one scene in which a presenter announces in a deadpan manner that the Bank of England had issued 'an emergency currency based on the Queen's eggs, several thousand of which were removed from her ovaries in 1953 and held in reserve', she suggested it would be stopped by both feminists and 'a pearl-clutching, royalist faction (let's term it, for brevity, the *Daily Mail*)'. Yet does anyone genuinely think that the threat of censorship still comes from the Right? There are no Mary Whitehouses any more, there are only two types of effective censors in action now: on the one hand, the Volunteer Woke Thought Police who will make your life a misery if you offend some perceived victim group, and, on the other, the rather more hands-on Islamists.

When Jennifer Saunders told the Cheltenham Literature Festival that 'There is always someone tutting in the back of your mind every time you write a joke that is on the edge: "Don't you think someone might be offended?"' she was not referring to pearl-clutching *Mail* readers. She added: 'I do look back at stuff we've done in the past and think: Oh God, the Twittersphere would go mad.'[7]

The Lord Chamberlain's Rule was abolished in 1968, yet the revolutionaries who tore down the Bastille built their own. We certainly have de facto censorship in the arts, although perhaps all societies must do because all societies must have sacred spaces. Certain sexual no-nos from the pre-1950s might have become edgy again because they also offend the new Woke authorities, taboos which conservatives are pretty fine about (an example was the space probe engineer who attracted feminist ire for wearing a shirt depicting breasts, which led to some conservatives defending him – which is rather odd, surely). But lots of issues are way more censored than ever, and the worst thing about it is that no one knows what is permissible. Comedy has been impoverished for a similar reason that many industries go downhill – uncertainty. You can't run any business if the law is unclear, if you don't know what will get you in trouble, or if El Presidente's psycho younger brother will just take your property on a whim. Likewise, you can't be free unless you know with great certainty what is legal and what isn't. With artists there can't be freedom if no one is sure what joke will pass approval and which will lead to thousands of hateful tweets and demands for their resignation; or while activists are trawling the internet for damaging material.[8]

Public morality has gone through a revolution in the past fifty years or so – a revolution that continues, and is arguably accelerating. Moral anarchy leads to moral tyranny as surely as political anarchy leads to dictatorship, and when there is no authority various individuals and factions will try to move in to claim society's sacred spaces. Just as in revolutions, they vie for power by outdoing each other with their ferocity, making demands that are deliberately unreasonable and focused on facetious or non-existent injustices. The more absurd, the better. Everyone knows their complaints are ridiculous, but no one has the authority to say so, and no institution or private company wants to suffer the effects of a boycott. People are also aware that appearing to be unduly uncaring about a perceived victim group is dangerous, and on top of this many of the activists are, to put it in the more archaic and unforgiving language of my adolescence, mental.

Rule-breaking artists of the past – take, for example, actors in edgy theatre during the 1950s – were able to transgress moral boundaries only because they knew what those boundaries were. A comedy writer can know pretty easily what will offend the *Daily Mail* and what won't, just as you know what might upset the Catholic Church. It hasn't changed in centuries. There are plenty of subjects that merit satire today, but these areas really are too edgy for satirists, most of whom hold quite conventional political views and fear the next wave of revolutionaries more than they do the *ancien régime*. That's why they make jokes about the *ancien régime*, just as French revolutionary theatre mocked the enfeebled Catholic Church.

Other comedians have moved away from trying to be funny completely, because it no longer serves political goals. The essentially religious nature of the Woke movement is reflected in the style of comedy nicknamed 'anti-comedy', the aim being to rebuke rather than amuse. This anti-comedy 'marks liberal culture's switch from post-Sixties libertinism to the progressive authoritarianism of today. Boundaries are enforced rather than pushed; where comedy helped us work through life's perversities and injustices, anti-comedy scolds our laughter as "problematic".'[9] One writer in *Slate*, on the subject of Sacha Baron-Cohen's character Borat, suggested that 'Twelve years later, we have higher standards for what counts as politically useful comedy.'[10] But what kind of person defines or measures comedy by whether it's 'useful'? This is your brain on politics.

The Great Awokening almost certainly represented an authoritarian turn by the Left, 'a spreading social, cultural, and ideological conformism . . . this relentless drive for conformism, which constantly works to extinguish the illiberal'.[11] Progressivism can never rest, there must always be a new battle to be fought, or to use that dreaded phrase, 'there is still much work to do'.

Yet just as this political activism was intensifying, new academic research began to overturn the long-held belief that conservatism correlated with authoritarianism. The dogmatism scale had been thought up in 1960 by psychologist Milton Rokeach, defining 'closed belief systems', which were shown to correlate with political conservatism. Likewise Bob Altemeyer's 2006 work *The Authoritarians* argued that authoritarianism was essentially a Right-wing thing.[12] It was almost established as fact that conservatives are more dogmatic – until researchers from Montana University in 2015 began looking at the questions asked in the surveys, and found that they only looked at issues of concern to Right-wingers; indeed, by switching the subjects, from religion to environmentalism for example, it was found that those on the Left could also be dogmatic, with questions about whether 'we must be careful not to compromise with those who believe differently from the way we do'.[13] Most studies had also found that conservatives are 'less willing to think about issues from different points of view', but again the Montana researchers found that previous studies had used topics of particular concern to Right-wingers. Overall, 'they report that liberals showed no greater complexity in thinking than conservatives did'.[14]

Left-wing authoritarianism had previously been found in eastern Europe, most obviously, as it had been ruled by communists for half a century, but it had not been found in the West before, except among Belgian communists.[15] They were just not looking in the right places, however, and a 2017 paper found that the Authoritarian Personality 'occurs equally frequently on the political left as on the right'.[16] Likewise a 2014 study found that 'Liberals are just as obedient as conservatives, but to different authorities', depending on whether the powers that be are conservative or liberal.[17] Past research had only looked at obedience to *conservative* authorities, such as the military, but when the powers that be were seen as Left-leaning, liberals were more likely to be obedient.

Authoritarianism is found both on the Left and Right; it just manifests itself in different forms.[18] Recent findings argue for the 'authoritarianism symmetry hypothesis', one example being the way that progressives tend to see deviant political views, the response often similar to how conservatives view crime, alternative lifestyles or other transgressive behaviour. Another popular idea that's broken down is that conservatism is more closed-minded and dogmatic, associated with 'intolerance of ambiguity' and valuing 'conformity and obedience'.[19] This 'rigidity of the right model', however, partly came about because mostly liberal social scientists were asking participants questions that conservatives were more dogmatic about. This was challenged in 2008 by New York University's John Jost, who found that 'Liberals scored as more dogmatic than conservatives' when it came to issues of concern to them; likewise the supposed 'prejudice gap' between conservatives and liberals, where research was biased because the subjects of prejudice were 'disproportionately left-wing groups' such as feminists and sexual minorities'.[20] Three research teams found that when Right-wing targets were used liberals expressed more prejudice.

The Great Awokening, which coincided with Obama's second term but was probably most connected to the growth of social media and the iPhone, saw a rapid radicalisation of progressives on social issues, by any measurement, with various polls showing a huge shift on social issues such as immigration.[21] With that there came a genuine – and to me, quite frightening – ramping up of hostility towards people who didn't agree with this worldview, driven by a new moral absolutism about progressive core values. It made me wonder about how my children's generation would interact, compared to that of my parents.

As a small boy, and here I go back to Grandpa Simpson mode, I remember Sunday lunches that culminated with my Provo-supporting godmother storming out after Dad had said something especially offensive about Ireland. Yet she'd be back a fortnight later and all was forgiven, until the next drink-fuelled argument. My dad's best man Bill Driscoll, an Irish journalist and fantasist I mainly remember smelling of whisky and offering us £50 if we learned Gaelic, had turned up to visit Mum in hospital after she'd given birth to me with his new girlfriend in tow, apparently a Red Army Faction terrorist on the run (this might have been untrue, like his earnest claim to have captured von Ribbentrop at the end of the war). Mum had more friends who were of the soft-Left variety, people who just couldn't understand how educated people could hold 'reactionary' views, but still loved her as a dear friend. In retrospect, I learned how important it is to have loved ones with whom you profoundly disagree, which like a lot of unsettling things is good for your soul. It's also fun, and Dad took a perverse pleasure in riling his friends, a smile on his face as he paraphrased John Knox's *The First Blast of the Trumpet against the Monstrous Regiment of Women* to an old feminist colleague.

This last paragraph is, of course, classic reactionary nostalgia for the Lost Golden Age but I think that sort of scenario is maybe less common now, as political sectarianism has overcome us; dinner parties are not so likely to be mixed, and we've lost our ability to argue with a spirit of charity.

After the 2015 election I found it hard not to feel great schadenfreude at the public grieving of people so utterly convinced of their righteousness, and baffled that the Tories could still win. It always springs to mind the famous quote of the New York socialite who said 'none of my friends voted Nixon', although that, curiously, is a good example of a Right-wing urban myth. The phrase 'I am mystified. I know only one person who voted for Nixon', was attributed to *New Yorker* film critic Pauline Kael, but what she said was, 'I live in a rather special world. I only know one person who voted for Nixon. Where they are I don't know. They're outside my ken. But sometimes when I'm in a theater I can feel them.'[22] The full quote showed she was aware how atypical her crowd was, if a little paranoid (although post-2016 that would sound positively restrained; now half those people in that theatre would be making secret 'Alt-Right' hand signals and the rest of them would be Russian spies).

My generation grew up with casual assumptions about the benefits of democracy, as if it's the default setting. Yet people forget just how unnatural it is, and that it's not normal for human beings to live with people with whom they profoundly disagree. We instinctively see people who have a very different vision of the tribe as potential enemies. A population certain of its own moral righteousness and used to getting its own way is not best suited to such a relaxed system of government, especially if it brings a mindset in which compromise is impossible because the other side is morally suspect. I wonder if the sort of life my parents lived, of long-held friendships across the political divide and politically diverse dinner parties, might soon look as anachronistic as the cigarettes they all smoked around the table.

28

REDPILLED

Tradition is not the cult of ashes, it is the transmission of fire

Attributed to Gustav Mahler

And so, eight years on from Obama came a figure who was almost the anti-Obama, and instead of hope and change there was fear and hate and anger, at least from the media.

Donald Trump seemed to be almost a caricature of Left-wing ideas about conservatives, brash, callous, casually racist, abusive towards women and absurdly rich thanks to his background. His son, posing with some poor dead animal he had killed, looked like one of the bad guys from *Animal House*. If someone this awful had turned up in a BBC satire I'd have been the first to write a piece complaining about the Left's ridiculously stereotyped view of us. He was also something from outside the normal political parameters, so that while most politicians lie to some extent, he would tell multiple lies within a sentence, his lies containing meta-lies within. It was almost done as a joke, like the wrestling he used to take part in, a little wink to the camera to suggest this is all a persona (or is it?); and yet he managed to get elected, and progressives seemed clueless about how their own behaviour was pushing people towards this awful man.

Political psychologist Karen Stenner argued that there are three types of conservatism, one of which is 'an enduring inclination to favour stability and preservation of the status quo over social change', what she called 'status quo conservatism'; another 'a persistent preference for a free market and limited government intervention in the economy', laissez-faire conservatism; and a third 'an enduring disposition, in all matters political and social, to favour obedience and conformity . . . over freedom and difference' – authoritarianism.[1]

Analysis of what was driving Trump's supporters showed they 'perceive that the moral order is falling apart' and 'the country is losing its coherence and cohesiveness'.[2] Indeed, Trump was less a conservative than an authoritarian who appealed to people who saw moral chaos, as well as an increasingly threatening world. Stenner, in her book *The Authoritarian Dynamic*, defined authoritarianism not as a personality type but something triggered by 'normative threats', things that threaten the moral order: 'authorities unworthy of respect, nonconformity to group norms or norms proving questionable, lack of consensus in group values and beliefs and, in general, diversity and freedom "run amok"'.[3] The behaviour of anti-Trump campaigners, whether it was Black Lives Matter, campus activists or actors getting naked to encourage people to vote against him, all seemed designed only to reinforce this not entirely irrational fear. There is also good evidence that the sort of radical activism seen on campus increased support for Trump, pushing away more people than it attracted.[4]

But then politics comes down to who's on your side, or as former political strategist Kevin Phillips said, 'knowing who hates who'.[5] Negative partisanship, defining oneself in opposition to another party or group, is very important to how we vote.[6] As America's upper-middle class became far more radical on issues of race and culture in the 2010s, and far more hostile to the lower class and rural whites, so more people have pushed towards the other side in response. During the election, commentators seemed to express surprise that Evangelical Christians would support a three-times married serial adulterer and sexual predator who had probably broken at least eight commandments regularly; yet Hillary Clinton's

Democrats were clearly against them, while Trump was not, so it was no kind of choice at all.

Richard Dawkins used to annoy me because he had a rather smug crowd following his pronouncements against 'the religiots'. Dawkins had once called Catholicism 'the world's second most evil religion', which made us at the *Herald* feel rather proud, but it was obvious what was number one in his book, and once he got fed up with the progressive *omertà* about Islam and started openly criticising the religion, he became hated by all right-thinking people; suddenly I remembered that I really liked him. In fact, as I got older I came to accept all my political stances are effectively based on irrational feelings of annoyance about smugness and sanctimony, or other forms of negative partisanship. Even my increasing scepticism of capitalism was probably partly driven by the fact that big business was getting irritatingly right-on about everything.

Rebels with a Cause

Soon before Trump was elected, I took my kids to the Efteling, which is a sort of Dutch Disneyland, and among many delights features a massive screen where the kids got to pretend to be a YouTube vlogger. Why not pretend to be an actual TV presenter, I asked, since after all *anyone* can be on YouTube? Am I really out of touch with the kids? Unpossible.

While I had been writing blogs about how the West was doomed – itself obviously paranoid nominative determinism – younger, fresher Right-wing types were instead going onto YouTube. These vloggers seemed to be obviously motivated by anger at the powers that be, the fashionable crowd among their peers, and the moral authorities telling them off. A *National Review* article about the phenomenon suggested that 'YouTubers are concerned less with progressivism per se than basically anyone wielding political or cultural power in the contemporary US: a list that runs the gamut from comic-book publishers to the Pentagon, from Google to the GOP itself.' These vloggers told 'sensational tales of sinister elites conspiring to censor and screw the little guy'.[7]

Around the same time, I heard a curious story about Gary, the old rogue who used to date my wife's friend Lottie, and who I hadn't seen since he'd spotted me campaigning with the Tories six years earlier. After they had broken up, he'd rather disappeared for several years until a mutual friend who works in the same industry went to look him up. He tracked Gary down to his dad's old council house where he found all the curtains drawn, his old friend sitting on his sofa with a huge ashtray in front of him, featuring a pile of roaches from smoking joint after joint, staring at his laptop. On the computer screen was a pale man with a northern accent speaking to the camera in very agitated tones. 'Watch this,' Gary said, furious and wide-eyed and pointing at the screen: 'Hillary Clinton and the globalists are trying to screw us, they're trying to screw the working class, this is exactly what's been happening for years, I've been fucking telling you.' He'd been like this for ages apparently, watching nothing but Paul Joseph Watson videos on InfoWars. Like many instinctively rebellious and angry working-class men, Gary had moved to the Right. But then, where else was he going to go?

Stephen Miller, Trump's much hated immigration guru, who does admittedly have a slight resemblance to a young Montgomery Burns, was described by the *Atlantic* as being 'a man of inherently "trollish" disposition, inclined to his ideas largely because they're disruptive and rebellious'. Miller told them, 'I've always been a nonconformist. In today's culture, the nonconformists are conservatives.'[8] There is a certain truth in this, but then nonconformists and rebels don't have to be James Dean or Marlon Brando in *The Wild One* – they can also be very uncool.

'If there is hope it lies in the proles' – George Orwell's quote from *Nineteen Eighty-Four* has often been cited by conservatives who argue that opposition to mass migration and other forms of social engineering will come from the working class. Perhaps that is true, but the system also seems to be breeding a hardcore of highly educated ultra-conservatives. So while the proportion of American students identifying as consistently liberal has rapidly increased, the percentage of postgrad and college graduates with 'consistently conservative' views also went up between 2004 to 2014, from 4 to 11 per cent.[9] Perhaps this is inevitable intra-elite conflict, or maybe also that Anglophone societies are becoming more isolated and atomised, and since liberalism is associated with higher sociability and social trust, it's now producing more conservatives, too.

It might also be the case that, since so many liberals have grown up in environments where their ideas are not challenged, so those ideas have become weaker, like immune systems raised in spotless homes. As Nassim Nicholas Taleb argued in the book of the same name, some things are 'antifragile' in that they need stress and challenges to grow and adapt. 'Just as spending a month in bed . . . leads to muscle atrophy, complex systems are weakened, even killed, when deprived of stressors.'[10] Perhaps political ideas are antifragile too.

The obvious example is the highly contentious issue of race and multiculturalism. Calling your opponents 'racist' is not an argument; if you believe that *a priori* any opponent is racist, using racist arguments or 'racist-adjacent' (which is equally invalid), you have no incentive to subject your argument to stress tests. Why, for instance, is 'diversity' a good thing? You might believe it, but it's handy to take your opponents seriously so you can understand the true strength of your own argument. In many areas of public life, and in many institutions, almost no conservative is taken seriously or read, because every conservative argument can be labelled as racist, sexist or at best misanthropic, because by definition conservatism *is* all those things – if you accept the parameters set out by progressives. Sure, some conservatives are praised in the media, but only for making completely un-conservative points and attacking other conservatives. This is not to score points; if we were able to dismiss rivals with the same rhetorical weapons, if labelling any enemy of the free markets 'communists' could put their arguments beyond the pale, we would most certainly use them. In a knife fight, who isn't going to use a gun if they can? But when people's ideas aren't challenged, they get sloppy and out of shape, and it's hard to counter arguments when you don't really understand them because you're comfortable that they're wrong. Moral certainty makes for laziness.

There are other problems that come with dominance. If political views denote status, then the masses will follow the elite and adopt those opinions, just as the masses will adopt prestige languages or religions, but this removes the very advantage those opinions have, of making you sound smart. Swedish academic Carl Ritter observed: 'If ideology x is the ruling ideology, aspiring elite persons will find that the easiest way to make the ruling elite is to opportunistically adhere to x. This will lead x to degenerate intellectually even if its premises are sound.' He called it 'hegemonic degeneration'.[11]

As Scott Alexander explained, counter-signalling hierarchies are what drives a lot of things. Looking at how fashions differ between class, and how upper-class people work to keep their style secret from those below them, he wrote:

> new trends carry social risk, and only people sufficiently clued-in and trendy can be sure the benefits outweigh the risks. But as the trend catches on, it becomes less risky, until eventually you see your Aunt Gladys wearing it because she saw something about it in a supermarket tabloid, and then all the hip people have to find a new trend. There's another solution to this problem too: the upper-class copies trends from the underclass . . . If the rich deliberately dress like the poor, then the middle-class have nowhere to go – if they try to ape the rich, they will probably just end up looking poor instead. It is only the rich, who are at no risk of ever being mistaken for the poor, who can pull this off.[12]

And so while liberal-progressive opinions were once reliable indicators of high status, now the least intelligent people instinctively follow Leftist fashions, where they would have been default conservative even twenty years before. Now, whenever a culture war issue blows up, Alexander observed that it is the least intelligent people from his high school who post on Facebook the most obviously progressive responses. He argued that, where every average and below-average person adopts progressive views, more intelligent people will try to differentiate themselves.

And the kind of 'stodgy conservatives' who disapproved of a hip young intellectual in the 1950s for having strange values are now exactly the kind of people who have adopted mainstream progressive views, thinking it scandalous that people read books of which she disapproves or believe in controversial ideas, trying to get them banned from speaking at universities or sacked from television shows. Naturally people who want to distinguish themselves from these holier-than-thou censorious types go to the Right.

The proliferation of clickbait media focusing on identity politics may also be aiding the appearance of hegemonic degeneration. With the digital media having emptied the journalistic profession of jobs and led to the rise of a semi-professional commentariat, provocative opinion writing has come to be used as r-selection strategy – the ecological reproduction strategy of multiple offspring applied, for example, by frogs. Websites churn out dozens of articles in the hope one strikes clickbait gold, and headlines have become increasing shrill and bizarre, a daily parade of articles tackling such issues as racism and sexism in the game *The Legend of Zelda*, or is *Game of Thrones* too white, or why *Seinfeld* episodes are racist and sexist and why that's not OK, and why *Friends* is 'problematic'. And of course, the favourite clickbait topic of all – white privilege, found absolutely everywhere, visible, invisible and all-consuming, and unfalsifiable. It's arguable that the dominance of Right-wing tabloids in the late twentieth century harmed conservatism as a movement in Britain, presenting it as essentially low-status and lacking reason or self-reflection. Perhaps clickbait media now damages the liberal-Left in a similar way.

In contrast, many bright young men who perhaps aren't hugely socially skilled increasingly find themselves drawn to the Right, isolated by those they call the normies, 'normal people' who just go along with the prevailing cultural winds. One of the most popular memes of the 2010s was that of the

'Non-Player Character' (NPC). The terms comes from *Dungeons and Dragons*, the online role-play game in which NPCs appear in the background and are designed to look like they have human agency behind them. A real-life NPC is 'a vessel for received opinion', trotting out all the conventional beliefs the prevailing liberal culture has told them to believe, 'echoes of the dumb slogans one incessantly hears on MSNBC or VICE or the latest Netflix special'.[13]

One version of this meme portrays a character called Wojack who is grey and robot-like and uses phrases like 'Did you catch the big game?', 'The future is female', 'Reality has a liberal bias' and 'I am excited for Disney-Marvel tentpole production #2881.' He looks void and empty, reflecting the empty slogans we're supposed to believe, but also perhaps the emptiness of life in an atomised society. Memes, most often created and spread by alienated young men, are perhaps the first art form in two hundred years in which the Right has excelled. They were the product of an online subculture in rebellion against the prevailing orthodoxy by rejecting the basic premises of liberal society, although everything is done with layers of irony masking the true intentions. But when public comedians act as cheerleaders for the dominant ideology, and even encourage the censorship of opposing views, the truly alienated will find humour elsewhere.

As the outer culture, the Right has naturally come to borrow arguments from the Left. Young online 'neoreactionaries' talk of the 'cathedral' in the same way feminists talk of the 'patriarchy', an all-encompassing network that has no formal existence and yet controls the system. They argue that we are living in a progressive society and so should be sceptical of everything the authorities tell us, because it will inevitably be used to justify and further that ideology, echoing critical theory. Conservatism is linked to institutions and in a world where shared institutions are crumbling, and the strength of gatekeepers is declining, the temptation for conservatism to turn to reaction is strong.

One of the most compelling attractions for the online Right is the claim to be empirical, whereas the liberal narrative is one of make-believe, the insistence on people using their preferred pronouns just the most obviously bizarre example. At some point they began to use the term 'redpilled', a phrase from the film *The Matrix*, a 'consensual hallucination' as William Gibson called it in his 1984 science-fiction novel *Neuromancer*, which coined the term. In *The Matrix* everyone goes about their life without realising it's all an illusion created by their real masters to keep them docile; take the red pill and you see what the world really looks like. Pretty awful, as it turns out.

The term 'redpilled' also crops up in reference to the 'Alt-Right', a phrase that's come to just mean 'neo-Nazi' and so effectively a meaningless term of abuse. 'Alternative Right' was originally coined by American historian Paul Gottfried and defined a branch of conservatism that didn't see race as irrelevant; people who believed that if America, and Britain for that matter, became majority-minority then it would no longer be the nation as they understood it. This was certainly a legitimate conservative tradition and not a 'fascist' or even authoritarian idea; indeed, nationalism and liberalism have often co-existed and in some senses the latter depends on the former. The American constitution refers to 'ourselves and our posterity', while Burke spoke of a nation being a pact between dead ancestors and descendants yet unborn. Many progressives believe nations to be essentially unrelated to concepts of race or ancestry, defined instead by overarching political philosophies or 'values' – usually their values, funnily enough – and mainstream conservatives have largely come to accept their terms, partly out of cowardice or because it's not the particular hill they want to die on, and surrounded by Orcs. Gottfried's idea of nationhood was not based on racial supremacy or purity – his Jewish parents had fled fascist Hungary – but as with many conservative concepts the brand became beshitten by its inability to police its borders. More broadly some young European Right-wingers refer to themselves as 'identarian' to suggest they don't believe their homeland belongs to everyone, but whatever neologism is coined to describe this worldview it inevitably becomes associated with its worst elements, some of whom are genuinely dangerous.

The actual Nazi component of the nationalist Right is a fringe of a fringe of a fringe, but as per Roger Ailes's logic, when some softly spoken American conservative intellectuals are making carefully phrased critiques of multiculturalism, and elsewhere Richard Spencer and some of his friends are making Nazi salutes, you're probably going to remember the latter. And yet the asymmetry of indulgence towards the Left and Right has obvious logic. Generally speaking, there are more nasties on the hard Left, many more street thugs willing to spit at their political opponents and intimidate them; but among the seriously violent and demented, the Right definitely has more bad guys. In Europe, Left-wing terrorism is far more common, for instance, but almost all the very deadly political terror attacks are by Right-wing extremists.

Political identity is formed by opposition, and so the future of the Right will be defined by the Left. In the US, if the Democrats continue to identify as the diversity party, and their politicians and cheerleaders continue to normalise rhetoric about 'muh white people', then I imagine the main thing holding the broad Republican coalition together will be whiteness. And inevitably something similarly depressing will follow in England. Politics comes down to who is on your side: if you read and see people repeatedly attacking your ethnic group for its privilege – especially people clearly more privileged than you – then you will side with whomever is against them, however terrible their economic policies, however venal, corrupt and just stupid their leaders. And if the opposition aren't smart enough to understand that aspect of human psychology, they don't deserve to win.

Among the countless examples, one blue-tick journalist and self-described 'public relations expert' tweeted that 'Brexit is dying right before everyone's eyes. Meanwhile, the gammon-faced white men who wanted it are dying too.'[14] Of course, individuals have far more incentive to increase their status within a political tribe than to advance a political tribe's broader interests, a variation of tragedy of the commons that pushes polarisation, but social media has ramped up the dangers in a way no one knows how to stop.

And there is some evidence young white men in America are moving towards the Right, the endless stream of crap opinion pieces in which 'white men' is used as a lazy term of abuse presumably having some effect.[15] Although millennials are most hostile to Trump and 'self-identify much less as conservative and much more as liberal than previous generations',[16] one Reuters poll found the Democrats losing some younger voters, their support dropping in just two years from 55 to 46 per cent, that decline being concentrated among white men.[17] Another found that among white millennials, Republicans were on level pegging, making up a 14 per cent gap in two years. Yet another found that among white male millennials, Republicans now hold an 11 per cent lead, where previously Democrats had a 12 per cent advantage.[18]

While the campus safe-space campaign is heavily female, the Alt-Right is overwhelming male, another facet of hyper-individualism; the more freedom we have, the more there will be very feminine and masculine subcultures, and this includes gendered political groups. In recent years there has been a steep rise in the proportion of female students, especially in the humanities, so it would seem logical, therefore, that already heavily Left-leaning institutions filled with single women would be the perfect breeding ground for a progressive movement, one in which members are in competition to display their political zeal.[19] In contrast, increasing numbers of men are moving into all-male worlds by dropping out of dating altogether, and the online Alt-Right grew out of a heavily male subculture, where angry single men made ideal recruits to a cause. This was something noticed long ago by Steve Bannon during his venture into *World of Warcraft*, when the future Breitbart boss said that 'These guys, these rootless, white males, had monster power.'[20] Men are less sociable on average than women, which explains why they are more willing to join political movements seen as beyond the pale. Across twenty-eight different countries, 'men's generally lower sensitivity to social cues makes them more likely to vote for stigmatized and small parties' than women.[21] Radical Right-wing groups do far better among men, the Sweden Democrats scoring 10 per cent more support among males, for instance.

Many young men are increasingly repulsed by the radical Leftism they find at college and online, which they find intolerant and suffocating. As one writer in the *Atlantic* observed: 'A lot of students, going off to the campuses in which political discourse was heavily discoursed, began listening and watching more and more blogs that offered them something else, something that wasn't conformist. Most of all they listened to one man, the Canadian psychologist Jordan Peterson.'[22] Peterson, a professor whose YouTube videos built up a huge following among young males, many fairly centrist, offered a more gentle and humane version of this reaction, not that this made any difference to the hostility facing him.[23] Peterson emerged from a cultural landscape that had forgotten conservative ideas, and which was shocked when someone in public life actually articulated them; naturally Cambridge University rescinded its offer of a visiting fellowship after protests.[24]

The popularity of the term 'redpilled' also came to reflect a growing belief that popular culture and political debate rest on imaginary ideas, a fantasy in which human nature doesn't exist. Even as the Great Awokening was pushing culture to the Left, scientific findings undermining their worldview have been stacking up. Pretty much every aspect of human culture and the variation between us has a large genetic factor that makes equality of outcome impossible, something of which almost no public debate takes account. Among the top-ten replicated findings from behavioural genetics are that 'all psychological traits show significant and substantial genetic influence' and 'the heritability of intelligence increases throughout development'.[25] One study of four thousand school pupils in England and Wales found that the type of school they attended had little impact on their relative performance, which was mainly determined by several hundred genes.[26] Twin studies show that 60 per cent 'of individual differences in school achievement' are down to genetics.[27] Countless studies have repeated this finding.

Meanwhile, the 'evidence for innate sex-linked personality differences in humans is overwhelmingly strong', something found in nearly every species studied, including all our closest relatives, 'especially in traits like aggression, female choosiness, territoriality, grooming behaviour, and parental care'.[28] Likewise our ability to exercise self-control is largely determined by genes and our parents have little influence on it, while even criminality has a genetic component.[29] Perhaps those two boys I saw attacking the old Polish lady might not have been victims of circumstances any more than the awful parents whose nature they inherited; maybe Augustine was more realistic than Pelagius.

Likewise with personality: a recent meta-analysis published in *Nature Genetics* looked at 2748 publications surveying 17,804 traits, and found that pretty much all the variation in personality traits is about 50 per cent genetic.[30] Indeed, it turns out there is an association between parents' child-raising behaviour and children's authoritarianism, but it is based on nature, not nurture.[31] So the Freudians were wrong, once again.

Even our political beliefs are to some extent hereditary.[32] A Danish twin study of twelve thousand participants showed that genetics account for about 60 per cent of the variation in political ideology.[33] Social attitudes generally have a genetic basis, which is further strengthened because of assortative mating, whereby people increasingly marry those with similar personalities and worldviews.[34] Perhaps most startling, and rather depressing, neurologists can predict your political beliefs with 83 per cent accuracy just by examining brain structure.[35]

According to a study by California, San Diego and Harvard universities, ideology is affected by a dopamine receptor gene called DRD4, but only if they had an active social life in adolescence.[36] Likewise where there is 'evidence of intergenerational transmission of party identification' it is down to genetic similarities in personality.[37] In other words, conscientious conservative parents will pass on those character traits that make their children conservative, too; open-minded liberal parents will pass on those same characteristics to their open-minded liberal children. That family members share similar values has always been put down to nurture but twin studies show even this is 'primarily due to shared genetic makeup'.[38]

No wonder, then, that as I enter my forties, I find myself turning into my dad. All those ideas fed from television and popular culture about how we are all free to decide our destiny and be what we want – all a fantasy. The older stories, going back as far as ancient Greece, that we are destined to be who we are meant to be, seem closer. Needless to say, Right-wing authoritarianism 'in particular shows high levels of heritability'.[39]

As this evidence – and even more controversial findings – has piled up, journals such as *Nature* have adopted an open agenda of social justice while science journalists increasingly double as political activists, further undermining the idea of scientific neutrality. Instead, these controversial-but-obvious ideas about human nature whizz around obscure websites full of men who come to think of the political world as a Matrix, a fantasy built to please progressive egos. They look at their political opponents, who in their heads think of themselves as being on the side of Galileo and Darwin against the bigoted establishment, as more resembling a modern-day Inquisition, ruthless in enforcing orthodoxy wherever they can.

Likewise many of the establishment beliefs trotted out in top-selling pop psychology books and repeated at TED Talks and then parroted in high-status postcodes turn out to be rubbish. Among the theories that have crumbled from psychology's 'replication crisis' of the 2010s is 'stereotype threat', the idea that preconceived beliefs about people become self-fulfilling prophecies and affect their outcomes. Stereotype threat explains that there are fewer women than men at the top of maths and science-based professions because they are put off by the perception that men are better, an idea so comforting that one 1995 paper has been cited over five thousand times. Yet it has completely failed to replicate. In contrast, the less hopeful idea of stereotype accuracy, once assumed by the psychology profession to be largely wrong, has in recent years been shown to be resilient and accurate.[40] Humans are very good at pattern recognition: we wouldn't have made it this far if we weren't.

The same goes for 'implicit bias', the idea that people's unconscious prejudices against minorities can actually have a negative effect on their outcomes. 'Early claims about their power and immutability have proven unjustified,' which is hardly surprising when it's basically hexing; today, vast amounts are spent by corporations and government agencies sniffing implicit bias out, despite there being no evidence it actually exists in a meaningful way.[41] If high-status progressives believe in such fairy tales, it is little surprise that some intelligent people begin to feel that public debate is a fantasy set in the Matrix.

Of course, conservatives accept that nurture and social norms play a huge role, too, usually around the 50 per cent mark. After all, you're going to find wildly different numbers of female science and maths graduates in egalitarian societies such as Sweden or Norway compared to conservative Muslim states such as Malaysia. The latter, of course, have far *more*, a curious pattern called 'the gender equality paradox'. Myanmar, Oman and Morocco have more female science majors than Scandinavian social democracies because the more gender freedom and equality we have, the more that women go for more stereotypically feminine careers. 'American women are 15 percent less likely to reach a managerial position in the workplace than are men – but in Sweden women are 48 percent less likely, in Norway 52 percent, in Finland 56 percent, and in Denmark 63 percent.'[42] Likewise Swedish men and women 'are worlds apart' in personality, while those in highly conservative Malaysia are far closer.[43] If culture were responsible for gender differences, then as culture becomes egalitarian so gender differences should narrow. Instead, when people are given more personal freedom, they express that freedom by becoming more diverse and dispersed.

Although social conservatives have often been alarmed by androgyny – I can still just about remember when men into heavy metal got called 'girl' because of their long hair – sexual freedom in many ways makes men more typically masculine and women more feminine. On top of gay or transgender people coming out, others will join weightlifting subcultures or spend fortunes on beauty products.

Perhaps this applies to wider society, too: that the freer a society, the more dispersion. Technology might cause huge alienation to some people, but to others it makes them hyper social, meeting more people through social media; likewise the number of very sexually active individuals has hugely increased in the twenty-first century, but so has the number of celibates.[44] Perhaps the hyper individualism of modern life pushes us to extremes, making us more exaggerated versions of ourselves, so that liberals and conservatives become more liberal and conservative in some ways; maybe the great divisions in American and British politics are a manifestation of this. Society in general is becoming more liberal, overall, but then by many measures it has also become more feminine, too, yet these gaps still get larger. And if this is the case, with so many people seeing politics as a form of self-actualisation, then modern, rich, free societies will find it increasingly hard to maintain legitimacy and democracy, and a shared faith in institutions.[45]

29

EVERYONE IS STUPID EXCEPT ME

I am a Christian, and indeed a Roman Catholic, so that I do
not expect 'history' to be anything but a 'long defeat'.

J. R. R. Tolkien, letter to Amy Ronald (15 December 1956)

Today the tide has turned. We are destroying them.

Mohammed Saeed al-Sahaf aka Comical Ali, Baghdad

(March 2003)

Children are the most conservative of people, in the very basic sense of
needing stability. Even the most twee of social media progressive trends,
the Woke eight-year-olds who repeat their parents' viewpoints in a naive
way, reflects an inherent conformity. And yet, after I'd written at least three
articles mocking kids who said pseudo-profound things about open borders
or gender or whatever, my actual eight-year-old said something quite
meaningful – to me – when on the morning of 23 June 2016, she told me:
'Daddy, I don't want to leave the EU.' This definitely happened, by the way.

I just smiled, but I also felt a bit sad. I smiled because it felt like a meme
come to life, as if I had actually entered Twitter, *TRON*-style, but I felt
saddened because I understood she just wanted stability, and continuity,
and parents have a responsibility to provide that. I'd been an opponent to
EU membership for years, and by this point had worked for a Eurosceptic

MP campaigning to leave, but had begun to lose faith in the idea. I smiled indulgently, thinking that I would explain the issue properly when she was grown up and understood it. Now I'm not sure when that conversation will be, to be honest, and whether I will just go down the 'ask your mother' route like I do when the kids ask zoological questions.

From the 1970s there had been a persistent decline in the number of people in Britain who identify with a party, and a very sharp drop in those who do so strongly.[1] And yet the Chinese curse 'may you live in interesting times' never seemed so apt. Today, as I write this, nine of out ten people identify as a Remainer or Leaver, and some 44 per cent identify as a 'very strong' partisan in that divide, whereas just 9 per cent now view themselves as 'a very strong supporter of a political party'. Remainer identity is in fact much stronger, suggesting their side is not lacking in tribal emotion, because supporting the EU means being part of the global community of liberals.[2]

I remember feeling great schadenfreude over Ed Miliband losing in 2015, laughing at all the people having meltdowns on social media: but that schadenfreude sure came back to bite me (and I have no idea if there is a German word for such a thing). Personally, I completely underestimated how intense passions would get over the vote; I wrote once, in an almost supernaturally un-prophetic blogpost, that the referendum would be 'boring'. Well, it was boring in one sense but not in the one that I meant, like a meeting of Swiss insurance analysts, but rather boring in the sense of your warring neighbours on the verge of divorce having yet another loud row at midnight is boring.

After the referendum result came through so many friends, from various different parts of my life, turned up on Facebook filled with rage and hatred. Many people said the country was overtaken by a wave of xenophobia, although most of the incidents seemed pretty minor, especially compared to the general level of violence in London. There were three murders or attempted murders in my postcode in the six months after the referendum, so stories about xenophobic language being used, while sad, didn't strike me as earth-shattering. It certainly encouraged the worst people to express their worst instincts, and that included ill-disguised snobbery, the lucky middle class's complete contempt for those lower down the social spectrum and those unfortunate enough to be closer to death.

Yet for all my horror at this snobbery, I felt I had allowed politics to blur my mind. I began the referendum as maybe 90 per cent pro-Leave, since it just seemed obviously a bad idea to try to turn Europe into a superstate. On top of this the euro had screwed southern Europe, a mistake that was backed at the time by most of the economic elite – the 'experts'. There were lots of other problems I had with the institution, including the absence of democracy. But if I was honest a lot of my opinion was based on pretty basic reasons, a visceral loathing for the kind of person who supported the European project, the smug types who appeared in the *Times*, *FT* or *Economist*, dismissing 'little Englanders' and 'loonies'. I also had an instinctive dislike of people who were contemptuous of patriotism because they looked like try-hards aping fashionable beliefs, when I felt patriotism was actually a good thing and a useful restraint on privilege.[3] The European project was supported by human rights lawyers, Liberal Democrats, *Guardian* columnists, wealthy politicians who went on about how wonderful vibrant, multicultural London was while living every angry Right-wing columnist's cliché of a secluded upper-middle-class existence. The sort of people who mention on Twitter that they went to Oxford and isn't it bad how un-diverse it is because . . . did I mention I went to Oxford?

Likewise, many on the other side had a similar instinctive loathing of Eurosceptics – the hanging and flogging Tory MPs, golf-club bores, Nigel Farage, men in stripy blazers, the gammons. I understand that, and if I'm honest a lot of the people in the Leave movement slightly repulsed me, too. Most voters didn't have intricate knowledge of a hugely complex issue, they just looked at the other side and knew whom they hated. But I also saw it in Hobbesian terms, that since progressivism could never settle and had to keep on reaching for new frontiers, a victory for Remain's cosmopolitan, global vision would just encourage them further. There would be speeches about how leavers were on the Wrong Side of History and there was 'still much work to do', and they took our concerns seriously but were still going to bury us.

Yet I was also by nature not a populist; I didn't like the anti-institutional rhetoric made by some Leavers, which smacked of revolution, and when some began going on about 'Goldman Sachs' it triggered alarm bells.

Four months before the referendum I had begun working at a think-tank founded by the former cabinet minister Owen Paterson. The original idea was for an organisation devoted to solving numerous different problems but this got swallowed up by Brexit – as did the entirety of British politics afterwards.

Paterson was lovely to work for, a very kind man, although as agriculture secretary he had become another hated Tory figure because he seemed quite keen on killing TB-infected badgers. On the other side of that battle was one of my childhood idols, Queen guitarist and badger-lover Brian May, who called him 'the nastiest kind of straightforward, old-fashioned, bloodthirsty bastard Tory'.[4]

Now here I was, in my suit working for the bloodthirsty bastard Tory as he went around student debates arguing why we should turn our backs on the EU. Owen was invariably the bad guy while the pro-Remain politicians told the kids they were in favour of diversity, openness, freedom to travel; pretty much all the students were hostile to us, although there would usually be one weird libertarian guy who stood up and argued against the EU on esoteric free-trade grounds that no one in the audience probably understood, including me. I would sit in the audience in my suit, standing out quite recognisably as one of the villains, while Caroline Lucas or whoever explained that the EU represented social justice, and fighting bigotry, and women and stuff.

I wrote speeches about how terrible the EU was, so in just a few months I read huge amounts about the working of it all, and talked to people who knew how it worked. I thought I knew a lot about the area, although in retrospect I was probably in that anti-Goldilocks zone of knowing enough about a subject to become prejudiced. And the more I read, the more I realised how unfathomably complex it would be to exit, and how many people on the Leave side didn't know what they were talking about when they claimed otherwise. Of course, that also undermined the Remainer argument that we weren't caught up in Brussels's web. We were, but leaving would be a mammoth task for Britain's politicians and civil service, and the economic risks were real.

I didn't like the EU, but I began to realise that however bad things were, they can always get worse. As the referendum went on, and some Leavers became more filled with revolutionary zeal and optimism, my instinctive pessimism took over. By 23 June 2016 I had wavered and eventually that day decided I wouldn't vote at all, and just felt miserable by how divisive the whole thing had become – but then, I thought in the late afternoon, what the hell? We wouldn't win and this would be my chance to register my protest. I felt it would be annoying that Remain won, and its supporters would be insufferable, but it might be the lesser of two evils. Then, when I sat at my computer later, I saw the Sunderland result come in. I went to bed, feeling anxious about the whole thing, and when I looked at my iPhone first thing in the morning the headlines said that Sinn Féin were calling for a united Ireland, the SNP wanted a new referendum, and the pound had crashed. That currency movement probably quite accurately mapped my endorphin levels. What had we done? I wondered. As Lord Salisbury is supposed to have said: 'Change? Aren't things bad enough as they are?'

It's hard to describe a feeling that you might be completely wrong, a strong hormonal reaction that is the opposite of a dopamine hit. It didn't help that my area on 24 June was like the day after England get knocked out of the World Cup. For the first time I heard middle-class English people arguing loudly in the street, expressing their shock and anger at what had happened. I was in a pub that evening and the atmosphere was one of astonishment and real rage; since then pretty much all politics has been like that. The Remainers have become more insufferable and partisan, while the Brexiteers have gone way beyond what they proposed in 2016, filled with revolutionary fervour and prepared to sacrifice everything in the revolution's name. When I read about their radical ambition for earth-shaking change, I sometimes wonder if Michael Oakeshott would agree: *To prefer the familiar to the unknown, to prefer the tried to the untried, fact to mystery, the actual to the possible, the limited to the unbounded, the near to the distant, the sufficient to the superabundant, the convenient to the perfect, present laughter to utopian bliss.*[5]

Those simmering divisions in Britain were in most ways more extreme in the US, which later that year ignored the teacher's adage that if your best friend sticks his hand into a fire you shouldn't do the same. After Trump's election, it was odd watching Hollywood stars conceiving themselves as a sort Confessional Church in their strange historical live action role-playing in which the new administration was the Third Reich. The same people who had rebelled against civility and boring middle-class norms for decades now expressed disgust when a politician came to power who broke all conventional rules of politeness and morality. Robert De Niro, star of *Casino* (422 fucks) and *Goodfellas* (300), warning the public that a presidential candidate was outside the normal moral boundaries of American life. Surely if any group stands for ethics, manners, politeness and respect for women, it's Hollywood!

A coarse and vulgar public culture, which encouraged shock value and rudeness, certainly helped lay the way for Trump. The media had relentlessly attacked his predecessor Mitt Romney, journalists mocking his old-fashioned deference to women, something they didn't have to worry about in the 2016 election. So many of Trump's loudest opponents had come from showbusiness, the same people who had made a career by casually insulting whole groups and pushing the boundaries of taste.[6] Even before the Weinstein scandal broke there was something quite sad about how the entertainment industry presented itself as the moral conscience of America, with Lady Gaga, Madonna and Miley Cyrus as modern-day Martin Niemöllers. Historically it has been the role of actors to upend and challenge the norms and roles of society, and in *ancien régime* France they were prohibited from taking part in politics. But the irony of this meta-ironic age was that the acting establishment now dreaded American political norms being upended by a latter-day Nero for whom politics is all one big show.

Much of the hysteria following the Brexit vote was surely explained by the fact that liberals hadn't really lost anything for decades. Their parties were defeated in elections, but those events only slowed their unstoppable progress and victory, and sometimes, as with Cameron's election, made no difference to the pace of change. Brexit and Trump seemed like something different, an actual reversal, and the result was genuine nastiness.

It doesn't help that the media makes everyone think they're losing; for progressives they fear they're living in an age of reactionary backlash with a white supremacist sympathiser in the White House. And yet both British and American public opinion continues to become more Left-wing, in particular on such issues as legalising cannabis, government intervention, gender issues, race and especially immigration.[7] Liberals are still very much winning, although they could be forgiven for opening Twitter and believing otherwise.

Likewise, after the referendum the media ran a narrative of the Tories launching a culture war, reversing the Cameron-era detoxification of the party and taking us back to the 1950s, or the Victorian era, or maybe 1065. During this time the government announced that prisoners could now get the vote, suggested that returning jihadis might get priority in social housing, brought out a report aimed at pursuing racial equality of outcome, and declared that the highly problematic, controversial term 'pregnant woman' should not be used in a United Nations treaty as it excluded transgender people.[8] They made no-fault divorce easier, recognised non-married relationships as having the same legal weight as marriage and introduced plans to make it easier for people to decide their own gender, which I'm sure won't have any unintended consequences whatsoever.[9] This was despite Brexit having killed off their hope of ever winning over urban liberals; the Tory modernisation project sails on like a ghost ship, although no one is on board, and no one cares.

A lot of people just feel fatigued by politics. Months after the 2016 election, most Americans found it 'stressful' arguing about Trump with someone of a different opinion, although this was considerably higher among Democrats.[10] Some 68 per cent of Americans feel 'worn out' by the news, and during the 2016 election a majority expressed feelings of exhaustion over the whole thing.[11]

I was so bored with it, too. During the school holidays it was actually a joy to go away to rural Herefordshire where you couldn't get any internet connection unless you stood on top of a nearby hill. Ironically Owen, who represented neighbouring Shropshire, had been trying for years to get the tight-fisted government to upgrade coverage in that part of England so that it was better connected than, say, Antarctica, but to me it was wonderful. I had spent too much time on the internet, so that on the motorway while tired I even misread the 'check your speed' signs as 'check your privilege'. Everything in life had become about how it affects the culture war. I remember reading some article about how AI would get out of control and we would end up with terrifying nanobots getting inside our bloodstream and then simultaneously killing us all or enslaving the population. And my first thought was, 'But how will this affect the Left's hegemony?'[12]

Now, for a week at least, I was freed from my iPhone. On Easter Sunday we went to the local church, a thirteenth-century jewel, which like everything in this part of the world was overwhelmingly filled with old people. We've not just become segregated along education or class lines but also age, and while most people in my area are between thirty and fifty, there are parts of England where there are defibrillators on street corners because so many of the locals are elderly.

The vicar, who looked relatively youthful – maybe in his sixties – gave a sermon about love, and I couldn't help looking over at one of the churchgoers, a man in late middle age, besides a woman in a wheelchair whom he had pushed in. She was overcome by a terrible-looking wasting illness, her body being destroyed by some malevolent force, and the strain was written all over his face. God knows what his daily life was like as her carer, but the power of love that led human beings to make such noble sacrifices never ceased to impress me. Now on the subject of universal love, the priest started suggesting that what the village (population: about 126. Median age ≈ 83) really needed was a load of (young, male) refugees from the Middle East, because Christianity is all about welcoming the stranger. As the vicar continued on this kind-hearted but naive theme my two-year-old began loudly singing the *Thomas the Tank Engine* tune, the description of the eight engines and their various qualities drowning out the priest's progressive Leftist-infused version of Pauline Christianity. Normally I get into an embarrassed rage when my children make a noise in church, hissing at them to be quiet, but this time I let it go.

Percy pulls the mail on time, Gordon thunders down the line . . .[13]

The demographic of that church was a foretaste of conservatism in the future, I thought. That will be us one day, just a shrinking number of elderly believers in the old faith, a curiosity to the young people outside as they go about their lives.

And yet, maybe not. Perhaps one of the most common stories in folklore is that of the 'good king, bad counsellor', of a kingdom that has fallen to corruption and evil in the hands of malevolent rulers. The land can only return to its rightful state when some brave men, often from a humble background, can restore the rightful ruler or his heirs. *The Lord of the Rings* is the most famous and beloved example, although *RoboCop* is a more recent interpretation. It is the most conservative, indeed reactionary, of myths, and it offers the most important of values: hope.

30

POLITICS POISONS EVERYTHING

A few men possess Ideas; most men are possessed by them.

Russell Kirk[1]

After the British conquered North America in 1763 it was the boast of the defeated French Canadians that they would still be victorious because they would win 'the battle of the cradle'. Indeed, Quebecers for many years had exceptionally high birth rates – Céline Dion, for instance, was the youngest of fourteen children. Across the world, differences in fertility levels have always been a feature of tribal conflicts, whether in Northern Ireland or the Holy Land, since when democracy becomes the established rule by which status is settled, then a group with consistently more children will inevitably win. And while in Israel/Palestine the most consistent factor determining birth rates for both Jews and Arabs is religion, in almost all societies 'religious attendance is the strongest predictor of higher fertility'.[2]

The contraceptive pill led to a huge drop in fertility rates across the West, and Europe's ethos was summed up by a *Time* magazine cover story with the strapline: 'The Childfree Life: When Having It All Means Not Having Children'.[3] Yet it has had a little-appreciated, unintended consequence, since this decline is much more pronounced among liberals than conservatives; so while modern breakthroughs in reproductive technology have made culture more liberal, in the long term they are making the electorate more conservative.[4] In the US conservative birth rates are still above replacement rate of 2.1 per woman, while for self-identified liberals the fertility rate is 1.48, and for 'very liberals' just 1.34; red states having much higher fertility, although part of this comes back to housing costs.[5] Even accounting for class and race, French women who oppose abortion have on average 0.5 more children than women who support it.[6] Men who voted for Trump fathered on average 0.6 more children than men who voted for Clinton (once age was taken into account). It is partly that liberals want to have fewer children than conservatives, and this is often down to a desire for economic stability beforehand.[7] Republicans are also much more likely to see parenting as essential to a fulfilling life than Democrats.[8]

Some conservative men actually like the idea of having lots of children, fitting into their *pater familias* ideal, standing by the fireplace like Captain von Trapp while all their smartly dressed kids sing a traditional folk song; even if the actual reality involves being on the point of tears most mornings trying to get them ready for school. This conservative–liberal baby gap has increased because, as with every other kind of freedom, sexual freedom makes us more different by allowing us to pursue a more individually tailored lifestyle. While once upon a time everyone was expected to have a family, now open-minded liberals can choose to go travelling and discover themselves in their late thirties, while their super-conservative peers go off on a wild one by attending traditional Latin Mass and having seven kids with names like Sixtus and Boniface. Desired family size among very conservative Americans has also increased, perhaps because it's sort of countercultural and appeals to slightly bohemian Catholics.

Fertility now correlates with the Big Five personality traits much more than it once did, with openness most negatively affected.[9] Since the evidence for the heritability of psychological traits is 'immense', this will probably favour a future population that is low in openness. The bad news is that America and Britain's artistic output in the late twenty-first century is going to be dreadful at this rate, but maybe that's the least of our troubles, what with the hellish Beijing-dominated dystopia the world is heading towards.

We're now two generations since birth control became available, which according to some is plenty of time to have a selection effect.[10] One study suggested those born after 2000 had very conservative views but it seems pretty dubious.[11] The liberal–conservative baby gap, however, has certainly grown in recent decades: for those born in the 1940s there was virtually no difference, but a generation later there is a one-child gap between the two ends of the political spectrum.[12] So long as marriage rates remain low the Left will have a huge advantage, but perhaps in the long-term conservatism always wins; socialist countries run out of money and liberal ones run out of people. Perhaps liberal societies, from a selection point of view, favour conservatives.

Fertility is also related to education, another issue that will trouble the Left's domination. Progressivism is boosted by the expansion of university places, especially in the humanities, because if you put loads of people together, allow them unlimited coffee and underwhelm them with a lack of productive work, they will become communists. But that can't last forever, since the costs involved are staggering, and hard to justify when so few jobs actually require a degree. There is also a fair bit of evidence suggesting that expanded higher education is leaving more people poorer, less happy, less open-minded and less likely to have children. By 2017 US student debts totalled $1.5 trillion, and some 40 per cent of debtors are expected to default.[13] Meanwhile only 19 per cent of executive secretaries and executive assistants currently have a degree, yet 65 per cent of jobs demand one.[14] Some have argued for making college degrees a protected characteristic under equality laws, so employers can't ask whether someone has one; others have made this argument on civil rights grounds, since focusing on degrees has a 'disparate impact' on minorities who are less likely to hold them.

If conservatism does return, however, the question is what kind of conservatism? Thatcher's hope that the free market would lead to Gladstonian Victorian morality was clearly wrong; instead, it led to obscenely wealthy banks distracting attention from their profits by cheering on progressive sexual causes while armies of homeless rot in city centres. Today, conservatism is increasingly moving in another direction, away from the legacy of Reagan and Thatcher, with less talk of freedom and more of solidarity. Its support base is far more working-class, a trend called the Great Realignment and speeded up by the Brexit and Trump votes.

During a recent debate between Ben Shapiro and Tucker Carlson, Shapiro made the Norman Tebbit argument that there are jobs out there and people will have to move to find them. But what if they don't want to uproot themselves, Carlson responded, leave their elderly parents and move their kids, just to become a cog for some billionaire, working in low-waged, non-unionised jobs with no security? I cheered for Carlson, whereas ten or fifteen years ago I would have thought him a socialist, but then I have roots now. And I suspect his vision is the future of conservatism, and rightly so, being one that is more genuinely in tune with its spirit. I like to think that, as Tucker spoke those words, the ghosts of Burke, Kirk and Oakeshott were looking down and smiling benevolently, like Obi-Wan and Anakin Skywalker at the end of *Return of the Jedi*. There are some things more important than the economy, but nothing is more serious to conservatives than 'home'.

The Right has long been an alliance between conservatives and liberals but that is fraying. That economically liberal vision of my childhood was a response to the times, but it can't alone deliver what we need. For conservatives, economic growth is less important than family, tradition and community, but we also believe the wealthy and powerful have a duty to take care of those less fortunate and less intelligent. Modern progressivism gives us some vague idea about looking after all unprivileged people, anywhere on earth, humanity in the abstract, but the real effect of that is not having to care about anyone. Conservatives argue that people have a responsibility to help the interests of their neighbours – and yes, their compatriots. Progressive denial of human nature also makes it easier for the new elites to confuse their own genetic good fortune with the idea that they deserve their success, while Right-wing economic liberals can use the same argument to claim that 'anyone' can make it with just enough hard work. That's simply not true.

The decline of Christianity will also have huge implications, especially as many of the Left's arguments rely on basic Christian underpinnings. The universalistic idea, emphasised in Tom Paine's maxim and seen in phrases such as 'no one is illegal', seems self-evident to its believers and may outlive the parent religion, but it might not. More darkly, who knows what path the Right will go without Christianity keeping the insanity in check? Already we see where declining religious observance in the US is leading, with conservatives more likely to embrace false messiahs. Alex Wagner observed in the *Atlantic* that while there is much emphasis on Donald Trump's 'brand of fear-driven, divisive politics . . . this would leave out an equally important part of the Trump phenomenon, and something critical to its success: the elation. Go to a Trump rally, speak to Trump supporters, and the devotion is nearly evangelical.'[15]

Indeed, American churchgoers, even controlling for social class and other characteristics, 'are considerably less racially prejudiced or hostile than other Republican voters'.[16] Even Trump voters who regularly attend church are more likely to have 'warm feelings toward racial and religious minorities, be more supportive of immigration and trade, and be more concerned about poverty'. Churchgoing Republicans are significantly more likely 'to have favorable attitudes toward black people, Hispanics, Asians, Jews, Muslims, and immigrants, even while holding other demographic factors, such as education, constant'. These religious voters have higher social capital, are more trusting, more likely to volunteer and more satisfied with their neighbourhood and with family relationships, all things that correlate with lower prejudice. Since 1992 the share of Americans with no religion has quadrupled, and trebled even among conservatives.

This has all been said before; some warned in the nineteenth century that declining faith in Europe would unleash the unrestrained 'blond beast' and it's hard to argue they were wrong. Indeed, there is also strong evidence from Germany of a link between declining religious attendance and rising populism.[17] The decline of churches 'and also other community institutions – leaves a gap which populist politics is well placed to fill'.[18] But I'm sure it will turn out fine this time.

The World Is All a Carcass and a Vanity

The Victorian novelist George Gissing, famous for writing about the London underclass in books such as *New Grub Street* and *Workers in the Dawn*, was known as a rage-filled radical until one day he concluded that all his anger at society was really about himself. 'I often amuse myself with taking to pieces my former self,' he later wrote:

> I was not a conscious hypocrite in those days of violent radicalism, working-man's-club lecturing, and the like; the fault was that I understood myself so imperfectly. That zeal on behalf of the suffering masses was nothing more nor less than disguised zeal on behalf of my own starved passions . . . I identified myself with the poor and ignorant; I did not make their cause my own, but my own cause theirs. I raved for freedom because I was myself in the bondage of unsatisfiable longing.[19]

I suppose I was coming to the same conclusion.

I deleted Twitter on my phone on 16 June 2016, at half-time while watching an England game being screened at our local town hall, after seeing the breaking news that a Labour MP had been shot by a Right-wing extremist. Jo Cox's killer opposed her work helping refugees and saw Labour's pro-immigration policy as 'treason', and so he murdered the young mother of two, the first MP assassinated since the IRA ceasefire.

Whenever an Islamist atrocity takes place it's become a sort of routine that we hear commentators say the killers were not 'really' Muslims because Islam teaches the sanctity of innocent life. Well, that's their interpretation of the faith, and yet the suicide bombers and enslavers of ISIS clearly fought in the name of their religion. That's an upsetting idea to most Muslims, the vast majority of whom find such violence appalling and senseless, indeed incomprehensible. Jo Cox's killer was a conservative and a nationalist, and I suppose we shared a certain worldview even if he did something most of us view with horror. It would be comforting to think otherwise, but untrue. Reading her obituaries in the days following the assassination felt humbling, her tireless efforts helping the most vulnerable putting most of us to shame. The refugee crisis is also a crisis of our future, and I am deeply uncomfortable with the scale of migration into Europe; as a group I fear the people crossing the sea in such large numbers, but as individuals I wish them well, and it is impossible not to admire those working to help them.

Our society is becoming more divided and Cox's death marked something new, and frightening, but then this division only really animates a minority of people, political junkies who are small in number but able to push politics to extremes. Most people just get on with their lives.

Just a couple of months earlier our two-year-old son had developed a chest infection, following what seemed like a pretty routine bug. All parents will experience these stressful moments but on this occasion the infection spread to his lungs and it soon became apparent by the hollowness of his cough that this was not normal. On the fourth day James deteriorated badly, and had become so hot and listless that I took him to the local A & E (the one the communist was petitioning to save, successfully as it turned out). I sat in the waiting room holding my son, watching my boy's laboured breaths, feeling so scared and hoping the doctors could work some magic – I don't know what – to make it OK. I felt powerless as my son struggled to take in air; pure fear overwhelmed my stomach.

They confirmed it was pneumonia, an illness still dangerous today to very young children but once a cruel throw of the dice; my grandmother, I remember, had an ancestral terror of the illness, passed down from generation to generation in the west of Ireland. In the ward, we waited with our son as he watched a cartoon, encouraging him to take in liquids and helping him to breathe with an oxygen mask. We were prescribed antibiotics, and told that we could take him home – but the next day he got worse, much worse. His temperature shot up to over 40 degrees, an ambulance was called and I followed in the car as my wife held his hand in the emergency vehicle. The illness was viral so he had not responded to the medicine, but for a few terrifying minutes they even thought it might be meningitis.

James was back on the oxygen mask that gave him breath, his mother holding it to his mouth so he could draw in the air, those tiny lungs now unable to do so unaided. All this time his chest was hooked up to a machine that monitored his oxygen levels, with an electronic reader flickering as he took in air, indicating how his breathing rate responded as he gulped in the precious oxygen. The scale went to 100 and whenever it fell below 90 a piercing, anxiety-inducing alarm would beep; Emma stayed overnight for three nights and if she drifted off the mask would fall off James's mouth and the shrill alarm would rouse her again. Just watching his tiny chest trying to take in the air was devastating; I had no idea how this would turn out, because even in this lucky age sometimes the worst still happens. And at that moment, as every parent knows, every previous anxiety before the illness cast its shadow becomes irrelevant, so meaningless.

In the hospital corridor and fiddling with my iPhone, as I do when I'm stressed or nervous, I opened Twitter; my eyes glazed over the feed about the now almost surreal outside world, and honed in on someone who was writing a serious of angry tweets because she had seen a film which she thought, in furious tones, had been insufficiently sensitive to her ancestral culture. I just thought, almost in tearful frustration: who gives a shit, you stupid fucking moron? If that's what's upsetting you, then you have literally no problems in your life.

That's what politics has become, just people making themselves upset about non-issues because they don't have enough actual problems to be worried about. Some people care about real things such as poverty, while others just waste their lives, sitting at the top of the hierarchy of needs feeding their own anxiety and others' too. Public discourse is now dictated by a small minority of angry, anxious and disappointed people who would once have faced strong disapproval for such outbursts or just been laughed at. Now, in the cause of group identity, such mania is affirmed, even encouraged, a sort of toxic validation where people are told their unreasonable and bizarre behaviour is praiseworthy or normal. We have political gatekeepers – and these are people with blue ticks and tens of thousands of followers – engaging in political rhetoric that even ten years ago would have been considered completely bizarre, the sort of stuff a psychotic vagrant at a bus shelter would think twice before shouting.

None of this really matters, these silly political arguments, and the poisonous and tedious online tribalism. While James was in hospital our daughters were looked after by good friends of ours, solid Labour members and activists who used to knock on doors for their party and have all the social values of the progressive Left. They are very good people. I'd trust them to raise my children if we ever died in a plane crash, perhaps with the proviso that they promised to make them watch Kenneth Clark's *Civilisation*. Yet the outrage machine is dividing thousands of similarly good people in a completely needless way, and as society has become more individual-orientated so more people have turned to the hit of political outrage to fill the void. Perhaps politics is just a drug for atomised people, the opioid crisis for elites; delivered straight to the brain via our iPhone, the most easily available addictive material around.[20] Political partisanship is addictive, and like most addictions not just personally destructive, but also socially corrosive, inflaming the same sense of moral outrage and righteousness that once inspired sectarian conflict in Europe.

At any rate politics is making lots of us deeply unhappy and unkind, warping our view of our fellow human beings, and poisoning public debate; there is also strong evidence that partisanship rots the brain, especially with the more intelligent, altering 'memory, implicit evaluation, and even perceptual judgments'.[21] I've developed the impression that, since Brexit, many people on both sides with strong feelings on the issue have noticeably got stupider, nuance and logic long given way. To paraphrase Christopher Hitchens, politics poisons everything.

Maybe normal people will lose interest in politics altogether, and it will just become an obsession of weirdos. There are already signs that this is happening in Britain, and it has long since begun in the States; while an overwhelming majority of Americans born in the 1930s and 1940s say they are interested in politics, less than half of young Americans do. The *Today* programme has been losing listeners throughout the decade, a sign that perhaps Britons are driven away by political debates.[22] Some attribute this to Brexit, but everywhere people are deserting mainstream media in droves, and not just newspapers. In the US television news suffered audience losses of around 10 per cent in 2017 alone, and while the internet is the main culprit, maybe polarisation itself is further driving viewers away.[23] A core of people are becoming more obsessed with politics, but more are put off altogether.

I was one of the latter. After a decade and a half of being a political news junkie I felt the whole thing just seemed pointless and idiotic, and there are more things to life. Brexit, however it turns out, has turned many people in public life into fanatics and fantasists, or at least revealed their true nature, which is almost as bad. So now I just turn on Radio 3 with its nice soothing classical music; occasionally they'll interrupt the tunes to have something about encouraging diversity in the arts but I imagine it's just one of those things they have to say, like in communist systems where, whatever your job, you had to repeat some token quote by Marx once in a while so they didn't hassle you.

One day, it finally dawned on me how obsessing about politics was actually making me unhappy. Dad had died the previous spring, having endured an agonising last few years after two strokes. The care workers who helped him through these miserable final stages of his life made me feel awe, and I suppose losing a father is a time to assess your life. Creative alcoholics often talk about how the drink, despite its association with Dionysus and art, had stunted their development, stopped them growing and maturing, and I wonder if there is a similar mechanism with politics. You end up cutting yourself off from more interesting things in life. When

I get to my dad's stage towards the end, when all there is left is the comfort of memories and whatever amazing painkillers they've developed by then, I don't want to think about the times I ignored my kids because I was looking at my iPhone arguing with a moron on Twitter. I'd also seen people whose whole identity had been swallowed by politics, on both sides; some sacrificed the chance to be a better writer because of politics; even worse, they had thrown away the chance to be a more interesting human being.

I think the nadir came for me with a news report about a two-year-old boy drowning in America, which a journalist I follow on Twitter took as an opportunity to tweet about 'white privilege' and how the media wouldn't have focused on a similarly aged black boy. That's an interesting hot take, I thought, a really normal thing to home in on with the painfully tragic death of a young child, who clearly enjoyed his two years of white privilege. But I was no better really; after years of writing about it, I concluded that politics was making me deeply miserable, and a bad person; well, an even worse one. In contrast, I look at my truly apolitical friends and they all seem so much more content but also much better human beings. People who are really into politics really do have emptier lives. In a 1979 German study it was found that two-fifths of students had a 'conscious commitment to politics' but the other three-fifths better 'valued their family life, their privacy, their detachment from the public virtues'.[24] I look at people who spend all their time tweeting about nothing but politics, and usually only about the same two or three issues, and wonder what inner lives they have. In contrast most political moderates don't awfully care that much about politics, and that seems healthier.[25]

As one writer put it: 'There is *so much more* by which to judge a person than his or her politics. Honesty, thoughtfulness, compassion, judgment, industriousness, prudence, self-control. Their interests, aptitudes, personality, piety, and sense of humor . . . Shared experience and common ground – outside of the politics – is key to reminding people of this truth.'[26] In my life I have met many people who have been friends, teacher and mentors, inspirational figures who have had very different political outlooks, sometimes wildly different to me. Without getting too saccharine and vom-it-inducing, they have hugely enhanced my life and made it richer. We all face difficulties and hardships, but I wonder if politics is making people forget this, so that others seem less than recognisably human.

As politics becomes more identity-focused and therefore awful, some look to the 'Political Benedict Option', Rod Dreher's premise that Christians should take themselves away from mainstream society, just as St Benedict did during the last days of the Roman Empire. His argument was that Christians can no longer take part in public life and so must rebuild from the ground, a retreat echoing what was called the 'inner migration' of life inside Hitler's Germany, or the 'dacha culture' of the DDR where people retreated into their private lives.

During the sixteenth-century Wars of Religion one Frenchman, the philosopher Michel de Montaigne, grew so tired of the conflict and depressed by the unending hatred that he simply retired to his chateau – although it helps to have a big country house in the Dordogne if you wish to pursue this strategy. Instead, he focused on the inner self because, as he cheerfully put it, 'the world is all a carcass and vanity. The shadow of a shadow, a play.'[27]

Some conservatives may want to escape progressive overreach, which in any case might be inescapable; others might want to avoid what the Right might become, inevitably populist and nationalistic, perhaps quite nasty. Then when the time comes, we will return to the mainstream, emerging out of our caves when conditions are more favourable. But for the meantime this digital reformation will continue apace, making many more people both miserable and insufferable, as the secular religions continue their fight for the West's soul. If that sounds all a bit downbeat, then so did Cassandra and she turned out to be right, too.

BIBLIOGRAPHY

Anthony, Andrew, *The Fallout: How a Guilty Liberal Lost His Innocence* (London: Jonathan Cape, 2007).

Berman, Paul, *A Tale of Two Utopias: The Political Journey of the Generation of 1968* (New York: W. W. Norton, 1996).

Bloom, Allan, *The Closing of the American Mind: How Higher Education Has Failed Democracy and Impoverished the Souls of Today's Students* (New York: Simon & Schuster, 1987).

Born, Georgina, *Uncertain Vision: Birt, Dyke and the Reinvention of the BBC* (London: Vintage, 2011).

Brooks, Arthur, *The Conservative Heart* (New York: HarperCollins, 2015).

Brown, Peter, *The Rise of Western Christendom: Triumph and Diversity 200–1000 AD* (London: Wiley, 1995).

Burke, Edmund, *Reflections on the Revolution in France* (London: James Dodsley, 1790).

Burleigh, Michael, *Moral Combat: A History of World War II* (London: HarperPress, 2011).

Butler, Eamonn, *Classical Liberalism: A Primer* (London: Institute of Economic Affairs, 2015).

——, *The Rotten State of Britain: How Gordon Brown Lost a Decade and Cost a Fortune* (London: Gibson Square, 2014).

Chua, Amy, *Political Tribes: Group Instinct and the Fate of Nations* (New York: Bloomsbury, 2018).

Cohen, Nick, *What's Left?: How Liberals Lost Their Way* (London: HarperPerennial, 2007).

Dawkins, Richard, *The Blind Watchmaker: Why the Evidence of Evolution Reveals a Universe without Design* (London: Norton & Co, 1986).

——, *The God Delusion* (London: Bantam Press, 2006).

——, *The Selfish Gene* (Oxford University Press, 1976).

Delingpole, James, *How to Be Right . . . In a PC World Gone Mad* (London: Headline, 2007).

Deneen, Patrick, *Why Liberalism Failed* (New Haven and London: Yale University Press, 2018).

Derbyshire, John, *We Are Doomed! Reclaiming Conservative Pessimism* (New York: Crown Forum, 2009).

di Lampedusa, Giuseppe Tomasi, *The Leopard* (English translation, New York: Vintage, 2007).

Dreger, Alice, *Galileo's Little Finger: Heretics, Activists and the Search for Justice in Science* (New York: Penguin, 2015).

Dreher, Rod, *Crunchy Cons* (New York: Crown Forum, 2006).

Durkheim, Émile, *Selected Writings*, selected by Anthony Giddens (Cambridge: Cambridge University Press, 1972).

Fest, Joachim, *Hitler* (English translation, New York: Harcourt Brace Jovanovich, 1974).

Fielding, Helen, *Bridget Jones: The Edge of Reason* (London: Picador, 1999).

Fischer, David Hackett, *Albion's Seed: Four British Folkways in America* (Oxford: Oxford University Press, 1989).

Frank, Thomas, *What's the Matter with Kansas? How Conservatives Won the Heart of America* (New York: Metropolitan, 2004).

Goldberg, Bernard, *Bias: A CBS Insider Exposes How the Media Distort the News* (New York: HarperCollins, 2003).

Goldberg, Jonah, *Liberal Fascism: The Secret History of the American Left, from Mussolini to the Politics of Meaning* (New York: Doubleday, 2008).

Gray, John, *Black Mass: Apocalyptic Religion and the Death of Utopia* (London, Macmillan, 2007).

Greene, Joshua, *Moral Tribes: Emotion, Reason and the Gap Between Us and Them* (London: Atlantic Books, 2014).

Haidt, Jonathan, *The Righteous Mind: Why Good People Are Divided by Religion and Politics* (New York: Penguin, 2012).

Hannan, Daniel, *How We Invented Freedom & Why It Matters* (London: Head of Zeus, 2013).

Hibbert, Christopher, *The French Revolution* (London: Viking, 1980).

Hibbing, John et al., *Predisposed: Liberals, Conservatives and the Biology of Political Differences* (New York: Routledge, 2013).

Hitchens, Christopher, *God Is Not Great: How Religion Poisons Everything* (New York: Hachette, 2007).

Hitchens, Peter, *The Abolition of Britain: From Lady Chatterley to Tony Blair* (London: Quartet, 1999).

——, *The Broken Compass* (London: Continuum, 2009).

Holland, Tom, *Dominion: The Making of the Western Mind* (London: Little, Brown, 2019).

——, *Dynasty: The Rise and Fall of the House of Caesar* (London: Little, Brown, 2015).

Horne, Alistair, *Seven Ages of Paris* (London: Pan Macmillan, 2003).

Johnson, Paul, *Intellectuals* (London: HarperCollins, 1988).

Johnston, Philip, *Bad Laws: An Explosive Analysis of Britain's Petty Rules, Health and Safety Lunacies and Madcap Laws* (London: Constable, 2010).

Kahneman, Daniel, *Thinking, Fast and Slow* (New York: Macmillan, 2011).

Kalder, Daniel, *Dictator Literature* (London: Oneworld, 2019).

Kaufmann, Eric, *Shall the Religious Inherit the Earth? Demography and Politics in the Twenty-First Century* (London: Profile, 2010).

Kirk, Russell, *The Conservative Mind: From Burke to Eliot* (Chicago: Henry Regnery, 1953).

Kling, Arnold, *The Three Languages of Politics* (Washington, DC: Cato Institute, 2019).

Lasch, Christopher, *The Revolt of the Elites and the Betrayal of Democracy* (New York: W. W. Norton, 1994).

Legutko, Ryszard, *The Demon in Democracy* (New York: Encounter Books, 2018).

Levin, Yuval, *The Great Debate: Edmund Burke, Thomas Paine, and the Birth of Right and Left* (New York: Basic Books, 2013).

Lilla, Mark, *The Once and Future Liberal: After Identity Politics* (New York: Hurst, 2018).

——, *The Shipwrecked Mind: On Political Reaction* (New York: New York Review of Books, 2016).

Lipset, Seymour Martin, *American Exceptionalism: A Double-Edged Sword* (New York: W. W. Norton, 1996).

Lukianoff, Greg and Haidt, Jonathan, *The Coddling of the American Mind: How Good Intentions and Bad Ideas Are Setting Up a Generation for Failure* (New York: Penguin, 2018).

Mason, Lilliana, *Uncivil Agreement: How Politics Became Our Identity* (Chicago: University of Chicago Press, 2018).

Moore, Charles, *Margaret Thatcher: The Authorized Biography* (London: Penguin, 2013).

Mortimer, Ian, *A Time Traveller's Guide to Elizabethan England* (London: Vintage, 2012).

Mounk, Yascha, *The People v. Democracy: Why Our Freedom is in Danger and How to Save It* (Cambridge, MA: Harvard University Press, 2018).

Mount, Ferdinand, *Mind the Gap: The New Class Divide in Britain* (London: Short Books, 2010).

Muller, Jerry, *Conservativism: An Anthology of Political Thought* (Princeton: Princeton University Press, 1997).

Murray, Charles, *Coming Apart: The State of White America, 1960–2010* (New York: Crown Forum, 2012).

Norenzayan, Ara, *Big Gods: How Religion Transformed Cooperation and Conflict* (Princeton: Princeton University Press, 2013).

Norman, Jesse, *Edmund Burke: Philosopher, Politician, Prophet* (London: William Collins, 2013).

Oakeshott, Michael, *Rationalism in Politics and Other Essays* (London: Basic Books, 1962).

Orwell, George, *The Lion and the Unicorn: Socialism and the English Genius* (London: Searchlight Books, 1941).

——, *Nineteen Eighty-Four* (London: Secker & Warburg, 1949).

Phillips, Kevin, *The Cousins' War* (New York: Basic Books, 1999).

Pinker, Steven, *The Better Angels of Our Nature: Why Violence Has Declined* (New York: Viking, 2011).

———, *The Blank Slate: The Modern Denial of Human Nature* (New York: Penguin, 2002).

———, *Enlightenment Now: The Case for Reason, Science, Humanism, and Progress* (New York: Viking, 2018).

Pipes, Richard, *Communism: A Brief History* (New York: Random House, 2001).

Pye, Michael, *The Edge of the World* (London: Pegasus, 2014).

Read, Piers Paul, *The Templars* (London: Phoenix, 1999).

Ryan, Alan, *On Politics* (London: Penguin, 2012).

Sacks, Jonathan, *Not in God's Name: Confronting Religious Violence* (London: Hodder & Stoughton, 2015).

Scruton, Roger, *Fools, Frauds and Firebrands: Thinkers of the New Left* (London: Bloomsbury, 2015).

———, *How to Be a Conservative.* (London: Bloomsbury Continuum, 2014).

———, *A Political Philosophy: Arguments for Conservatism* (London: Continuum, 2007).

———, *The Roger Scruton Reader* (London: Bloomsbury, 2009).

———, *The Uses of Pessimism* (London: Atlantic Books, 2010).

Sewell, Dennis, *The Political Gene* (London: Picador, 2009).

Siedentop, Larry, *Inventing the Individual: The Origins of Western Liberalism* (Cambridge, MA: Harvard University Press, 2014).

Stein, Harry, *I Can't Believe I'm Sitting Next to a Republican* (New York: Encounter Books, 2009).

Stenner, Karen, *The Authoritarian Dynamic* (Cambridge: Cambridge University Press, 2005).

Taleb, Nassim Nicholas, *Antifragile* (London: Penguin, 2012).

Tombs, Robert, *The English and Their History* (London: Allen Lane, 2014).

Tuchman, Barbara, *A Distant Mirror* (New York: Alfred A. Knopf, 1978).

Turchin, Peter, *Ages of Discord* (New York: Beresta Books, 2016).

Waite, Robert G. L., *Hitler: The Psychopathic God* (New York: Basic Books, 1977).

Waters, Natasha, *Living Dolls: The Return of Sexism* (London: Virago, 2010).

Watson, Peter, *The German Genius: Europe's Third Renaissance, The Second Scientific Revolution and the Twentieth Century* (London: Simon & Schuster, 2010).

West, Patrick, *Get Over Yourself: Nietzsche for Our Times* (London: Societas, 2017).

Worden, Blair, *The English Civil War* (London: Orion, 2009).

Ziegler, Philip, *The Black Death* (London: Collins, 1969).

ACKNOWLEDGEMENTS

Thanks most of all to my agent Matthew Hamilton, very much the midwife or perhaps surrogate mother to this whole idea, and to my publisher Andreas Campomar for having such faith in the book. I'm also very grateful for all the help from commissioning editor Claire Chesser and assistant editor Bernadette Marron, to Howard Watson for copy-editing, and to Jo Wickham on the publicity side of things.

I'd also like to thank Ben Sixsmith and Andrew M. Brown for reading the manuscript and giving valuable feedback.

The idea behind this book germinated during my time at the *Catholic Herald*, so I also thank my former colleagues Luke Coppen, Mark Greaves, Madeleine Teahan, Will Gore, Stav Sherez, Miguel Cullen, David V. Barrett, Anna Arco, Simon Caldwell and Andy Leisinger. Various of the ideas within were developed in *Spectator* articles, so I'd better thank Freddy Gray and Lara Prendergast there; likewise Melanie McDonagh at the *Standard*. There are many others who have provided intellectual inspiration or assistance in some way, but in particular I'm grateful to Jacob Hartog for all the ideas I've blatantly stolen. Also mainly Twitter-based people: Ben Southwood, Michael Brendan Dougherty, Michael Story, Peter Hurst and Dan Jackson, as well as Eric Kaufmann, Tom Holland, Douglas Murray and Jonathan Haidt. If I mention anyone else it'll start to sound like an Oscar speech but I'd also like to thank my brother Patrick, my mother Mary Kenny and my wife Emma, who has had to endure me shouting at the radio all these years. And, of course, to my father Richard West, no longer with us but I hope smiling down from Valhalla and feasting with our ancestors, and all that sort of thing.

ENDNOTES

Introduction

1   https://www.weeklystandard.com/shapiro-win-back-young-americans.

2   http://quillette.com/2018/02/01/
    lawsuit-exposes-internet-giants-internal-culture-intolerance/.

3   http://www.pewresearch.org/fact-tank/2016/09/15/educational-divide-in-vote-pref-
    erences-on-track-to-be-wider-than-in-recent-elections/.

4   https://twitter.com/JamesKanag/status/876789923738681344.

5   It was created out of two previous seats, though, and Kensington North was
    Labour voting, but overall the area has had a Tory majority since the year dot.

6   https://www.forbes.com/sites/andrewdepietro/2018/11/08/
    democrats-wealth-inequality-congressional-districts/#1042d7a06c9b.

7   https://theconversation.com/young-women-are-more-left-wing-than-men-study-
    reveals-95624?utm_source=twitter&utm_medium=twitterbutton.

8   https://www.ncpolitics.uk/2015/03/history-voting-patterns-gender.html/.

9   http://reutersinstitute.politics.ox.ac.uk/sites/default/files/research/files/
    Journalists%2520in%2520the%2520UK.pdf.

10 https://twitter.com/rcolvile/status/874927927590301696.

11 Jonathan Haidt, *The Righteous Mind: Why Good People are Divided by Religion and Politics*
    (New York: Penguin, 2012).

12 http://heterodoxacademy.org/2015/09/14/bbs-paper-on-lack-of-political-diversity/.

13 Harry Stein, *I Can't Believe I'm Sitting Next to a Republican* (New York: Encounter Books,
    2009).

14 https://www.nas.org/articles/homogenous_political_affiliations_of_elite_liberal.

15 https://nypost.com/2016/04/17/
    conservative-professors-must-fake-being-liberal-or-be-punished-on-campus/.

16 https://static1.squarespace.com/static/56eddde762cd9413e151ac92/t/58b5a7cd-
    03596ec6631d8b8a/1488299985267/Left+Wing+Bias+Paper.pdf.

17 https://spottedtoad.wordpress.com/2017/04/18/radical-privilege/.

18   Helen Fielding, *Bridget Jones: The Edge of Reason* (London: Picador, 1999).

19   https://www.nytimes.com/2016/05/08/opinion/sunday/a-confession-of-liberal-intol-erance.html.

20   *Conan the Barbarian*, written by John Milius and Oliver Stone, directed by John Milius (1982).

21   This was said to military cadets in 2010. https://www.cbsnews.com/news/obama-tells-cadets-us-will-win-afghan-fight/.

1. 1989

1   Roger Scruton, *The Roger Scruton Reader* (London: Bloomsbury, 2009).

2   https://www.theguardian.com/commentisfree/2018/may/02/democracy-crisis-plan-trump-brexit-system-politicans-voters.

3   *Falling Down*, written by Ebbe Roe Smith, directed by Joel Schumacher (1993).

2. Cassandra Was Right

1   Interviewed in the *Sunday Times* (11 December 2005), https://www.thetimes.co.uk/article/interview-tony-allen-mills-talks-to-george-clooney-72mnsbrkr6p.

2   Stein, *I Can't Believe I'm Sitting Next to a Republican*.

3   http://journals.plos.org/plosone/article?id=10.1371/journal.pone.0050092.

4   Daniel Kahneman, *Thinking, Fast and Slow* (New York: Macmillan, 2011)

5   https://www.sciencedaily.com/releases/2013/08/130822090326.htm.

6   Augustine, *The City of God Against the Pagans*, trans. R. W. Dyson (Cambridge: Cambridge University Press, 1998).

7   Alan Ryan, *On Politics* (London: Penguin, 2012).

8   Innocent III, *On the Contempt of the Worlds*, quoted in Charles Freeman, *A New History of Early Christianity* (New Haven and London: Yale University Press, 2009).

9   Barbara Tuchman, *A Distant Mirror* (New York: Alfred A. Knopf, 1978).

10   Michael Pye, *The Edge of the World* (London: Pegasus, 2014).

11   Robert Tombs, *The English and Their History* (London: Allen Lane, 2014).

12   Philip Ziegler, *The Black Death* (London: Collins, 1969).

3. Another Brick in the Wall

1   Roger Waters, 'Another Brick in the Wall' (© BMG Rights Management, 1979).

2   Thomas Hobbes, *Leviathan* (London: Andrew Crooke, 1651).

3   Ryan, *On Politics*.

4   Ibid.

5   Ibid.

6   Jean-Jacques Rousseau, *The Social Contract* (Amsterdam, 1762, English translation by G. D. H. Cole, 1782).

7   https://twitter.com/ZachG932/status/1039698612949839872.

8   Paul Johnson, *Intellectuals* (London: HarperCollins, 1988). When he drew up plans for a Corsican constitution, Rousseau suggested everyone swear the following oath: 'I join myself, body, goods, will and all my powers, to the Corsican nation, granting her ownership of me, of myself and all who depend on me.'

9   http://www.dailymail.co.uk/news/article-3094904/Five-pupils-west-London-comprehensive-dubbed-socialist-Eton-killed-waging-jihad-Syria-Iraq.html.

10 http://www.civitas.org.uk/pdf/cs26.pdf.

11 Written in an article for the *Financial Times*, https://www.ft.com/content/39a0867a-0974-11e7-ac5a-903b21361b43.

4. Revolution (Don't You Know that You Can Count Me Out)

1   Jerry Z. Muller, *Conservatism: An Anthology of Political Thought* (Princeton: Princeton University Press, 1997).

2   John Locke, 'Second Treatise', in *Two Treatises of Government* (London: Awnsham Churchill, 1690).

3   See Kevin Phillips, *The Cousins' War* (New York: Basic Books, 1999).

4   Jesse Norman, *Edmund Burke: Philosopher, Politician, Prophet* (London: William Collins, 2013)

5   Ibid.

6   Ibid.

7   Edmund Burke, *Reflections on the Revolution in France* (London: James Dodsley, 1790).

8   Quoted in Yuval Levin, *The Great Debate: Edmund Burke, Thomas Paine, and the Birth of Right and Left* (New York: Basic Books, 2013).

9   Ibid.

10 William Wordsworth, *The Prelude*, written originally in 1798–9.

11 Tombs, *The English and Their History*.

12 Ibid.

13 Friends are allowed to drink alcohol, but in moderation, and they were often involved in the temperance movement.

14 Thomas Paine, 'The Crisis', first published in the *Pennsylvania Journal*, 1776.

15 Ibid.

16 Thomas Paine, *Rights of Man* (London: J. S. Jordan, 1791).

17 Burke, *Reflections*.

18 Paine, *Rights of Man*.

19 Levin, *The Great Debate*.

20 Christopher Hibbert, *The French Revolution* (London: Viking, 1980).

21 Ibid.

22 Ibid.

23 Ibid.

24 William Wordsworth, 'England! the time is come', *Poems by William Wordsworth, Volume II* (London: Longman, Hurst, Reese, Orme and Brown, 1815).

25   Tombs, *The English and Their History*.

26   Quoted in Russell Kirk, *The Conservative Mind: From Burke to Eliot* (Chicago: Henry Regnery, 1953).

5. These Things I Believe

1   Tombs, *The English and Their History*.

2   Peter Mandler (ed.), *Liberty and Authority in Victorian Britain* (Oxford: Oxford University Press, 2006).

3   https://arcdigital.media/conservatism-an-intellectual-defense-db37af1879e7?sk= 321dca4075f874a07c3996fba1255821.

4   Muller, *Conservatism*.

5   Burke, *Reflections*.

6   Burke, *Reflections*.

7   Muller, *Conservatism*.

8   Ibid.

9   Roger Scruton, *A Political Philosophy: Arguments for Conservatism* (London: Continuum, 2007); William F. Buckley in the *National Review* (November 1955), https://www. nationalreview.com/1955/11/our-mission-statement-william-f-buckley-jr/.

10   Kirk, *The Conservative Mind*.

11   Muller, *Conservatism*.

12   Burke, *Reflections*.

13   Emmanuel Kant, 'Idea for a General History with a Cosmopolitan Purpose' (1784), in H. S. Reiss (ed.), *Kant* (Cambridge: Cambridge University Press, 1991).

14   Kirk, *The Conservative Mind*.

15   Edmund Burke, *A Vindication of Natural Society* (London, 1756).

16   https://arcdigital.media/conservatism-an-intellectual-defense-db37af1879e7.

17   Kirk, *The Conservative Mind*.

18   Edmund Burke, *Appeal from the New Whigs to the Old* (London: James Dodsley, 1791).

19   Levin, *The Great Debate*.

20   Michael Oakeshott, *Rationalism in Politics and Other Essays* (London: Basic Books, 1962).

21   Richard Dawkins, *The Blind Watchmaker: Why the Evidence of Evolution Reveals a Universe without Design* (London: Norton & Co, 1986). As Professor Dawkins wrote: 'Suppose that the lens is slightly lower than it ought to be for perfect focus, say a tenth of an inch too close to the slide. Now if we move it a small amount, say a hundredth of an inch, in a random direction, what are the odds that the focus will improve?'

22   From Arthur C. Brooks, *The Conservative Heart* (New York: HarperCollins, 2015). Americans measure poverty in absolute terms, whereas in Britain it is usually relative poverty. https://www.irp.wisc.edu/resources/ how-is-poverty-measured/.

23   Levin, *The Great Debate*.

6. Maggie and Madiba

1   In Tristram Hunt's words, in Anne McElvoy's documentary, *Conservatism: The Grand Tour* (BBC Radio 4, 2013).

2   Francis Gorman (ed.), *The Cambridge Companion to John Ruskin* (Cambridge: Cambridge University Press, 2015).

3   Benjamin Disraeli, *Sybil* (London: Henry Colburn, 1845).

4   Gorman, *The Cambridge Companion to John Ruskin*.

5   This is not my observation, but that of Kristian Niemietz of the Institute for Economic Affairs.

6   George Orwell, *The Lion and the Unicorn: Socialism and the English Genius* (London: Searchlight Books, 1941).

7   Brooks, *The Conservative Heart*.

8   A 2013 survey found Americans are five times as likely to say the Republican Party is uncompassionate as compassionate – but even a majority of conservatives agree with this idea. As Arthur Brooks put it in *The Conservative Heart*, 'Compassionate conservatism' is a terrible phrase because it grafts the word on 'like an unnatural appendage'.

9   Welsh Labour Party conference in 1983, https://www.newstatesman.com/uk-politics/2010/02/kinnock-major-jenkins-speech-warn.

10 Richard Littlejohn was the star of the Right-wing commentariat, with his catch-phrase 'You couldn't make it up', usually about crazy political correctness and with a swipe at the gay-obsessed diversity bureaucracy or the nanny-staters forcing him to slow down or pay more for petrol. I used to enjoy reading his column and he's a lovely man in real life, although I did laugh at the *Viz* cartoon 'Robin Hood and Richard Littlejohn', in which the outlaw's sidekick complains that Sherwood Forest is full of gay men cruising, encouraged by the progressive Sheriff of Nottingham.

7. Are We the Baddies?

1   'Jeremy Makes It', *Peep Show*, series 2, episode 2, written by Jesse Armstrong and Sam Bain, directed by Tristram Shapeero (Channel 4, 19 November 2004).

2   It was attributed to him although he denied it; http://news.bbc.co.uk/1/hi/uk_politics/8320241.stm.

3   'Are We the Baddies?', *That Mitchell and Webb Look*, series 1, episode 1, written by David Mitchell and Robert Webb, directed by David Kerr (Channel 4, 14 September 2006).

4   Michael Burleigh, *Moral Combat: A History of World War II* (London: HarperPress, 2011): 'No such shared cultural heritage exists for our perception of what was done to Chechens, Chinese, Kazakjs or Koreans, and our common humanity seems too weak to stimulate sustained attention beyond the "isn't it dreadful?" reaction to starving Africans shown on television.'

5   Ryan, *On Politics*.

6   Ibid.

7   Ibid.

8   Kirk, *The Conservative Mind*.

9   Ibid.

10   Ryan, *On Politics*. Many 'were skilled artisans such as clockmakers who were threated economically and psychologically by changes that made their skills obsolete and their old social ties harder to sustain'.

11   In 1813 Owen had outlined his philosophy in *A New View of Society, or Essays on the Principle of the Formation of the Human Character* (London: Cadell and Davies, 1813).

12   Dr Lyman Warren, recorded in the *Periodical Letters* (1856) from New Harmony, Indiana.

13   He misquoted William Gladstone deliberately to make him seem more evil, quoting 'this intoxicating augmentation of wealth and power is entirely confined to classes of poverty' without the context of the passage beforehand. He also falsified quotations by Adam Smith and even in the 1880s two Cambridge scholars found that the sources he cited were entirely out of date.

14   Steven Pinker, *Enlightenment Now: The Case for Reason, Science, Humanism, and Progress* (New York: Viking, 2018).

15   Zeev Sternhell, *The Birth of Fascist Ideology* (Princeton: Princeton, 1995).

16   Giovanni Gentile, 'The Doctrine of Fascism', *Enciclopedia Italiana* (Roma: Treccani, 1932).

17   https://www.theguardian.com/commentisfree/2016/jan/25/wristbands-red-doors-refugees-history-rhyming-holocaust-echoes-of-past.

18   https://twitter.com/adhofstra/status/691665680450637824.

8. This Country Is Going Straight to Hell

1   Walt Whitman, *Leaves of Grass* (New York: Walt Whitman, 1855).

2   Theodor W. Adorno, Else Frenkel-Brunswik, Daniel Levinson and Nevitt Sanford, *The Authoritarian Personality* (New York: Harper & Brothers, 1950).

3   With anti-Semitism 'the visible edge of a dysfunctional personality revealed in the many "ethnocentric" and "conventional" attitudes of the general American population'.

4   Peter Watson, *The German Genius: Europe's Third Renaissance, The Second Scientific Revolution and the Twentieth Century* (London: Simon & Schuster, 2010).

5   Else Frenkel-Brunswick, 'Intolerance of ambiguity as an emotional and perceptual personality variable', *Journal of Personality*, vol. 18, no. 1 (September 1949).

6   *American Beauty*, written by Alan Ball, directed by Sam Mendes (1999).

7   https://www.sciencedirect.com/science/article/abs/pii/S0092656605000632.

8   Stein, *I Can't Believe I'm Sitting Next to a Republican*.

9   http://www.sulloway.org/PoliticalConservatism(2003).pdf. He added that Stalin and Castro 'might be considered politically conservative in the context of the systems that they defended', which sounds like a bit of a cop-out.

10   https://www.psychologytoday.com/gb/blog/the-big-questions/201106/homophobic-men-are-aroused-gay-male-porn; https://slate.com/technology/2012/04/homophobic-maybe-you-re-gay-the-new-york-times-on-a-new-study-of-secret-sexuality.html.

11   https://link.springer.com/article/10.1007/s10508-018-1244-1; https://twitter.com/ DegenRolf/status/1017403089890902016.

12   Bob Altemeyer, *The Authoritarians* (Winnipeg: University of Manitoba, 1981), https://theauthoritarians.org/Downloads/TheAuthoritarians.pdf. There were three types of authoritarianism, according to the original theory: high degree of submission to authorities; 'a general aggressiveness, directed against various persons, that is perceived to be sanctioned by established authorities'; and conventionalism, 'a high degree of adherence to the social conventions' endorsed by the authorities.

13   http://www.econ.cam.ac.uk/research-files/repec/cam/pdf/cwpe1745.pdf.

14   Toke Aidt and Christopher Rauh, 'The Big Five Personality Traits and Partisanship', working paper (Cambridge: Cambridge University Faculty of Economics, 2015), http://www.econ.cam.ac.uk/research-files/repec/cam/pdf/cwpe1745.pdf. In fact, 'the only common denominator is that the supporters of both parties tend to be extraverted', since outgoing people get into party activism.

15   Ibid. 'In terms of magnitude, a one standard deviation increase in conscientiousness, for instance, is associated with a 1.77 percentage point increase in the stable preference for the Conservative Party.'

16   Greg Lukianoff and Jonathan Haidt, *The Coddling of the American Mind: How Good Intentions and Bad Ideas Are Setting Up a Generation for Failure* (New York: Penguin, 2018).

17   Aidt and Rauh, 'The Big Five Personality Traits'.

18   John Hibbing et al., *Predisposed: Liberals, Conservatives and the Biology of Political Differences* (New York: Routledge, 2013).

19   'Across three studies, words related to resistance to change, but not perceived threat, were related to political ideology such that conservatives were more likely to include resistance-to-change-related words in their responses compared with liberals'. https://twitter.com/DegenRolf/status/972007272850243585.

20   https://dspace.sunyconnect.suny.edu/bitstream/handle/1951/52392/000000880.sbu. pdf?sequence=1.

21   https://www.scribd.com/document/36153065/ Political-Conservatism-as-Motivated-Social-Cognition.

22   http://journals.sagepub.com/doi/full/10.1177/1474704918764170.

23   https://washingtonmonthly.com/magazine/marchaprilmay-2014/ the-origin-of-ideology/.

24   http://faculty.virginia.edu/haidtlab/jost.glaser.political-conservatism-as-motivated-social-cog.pdf.

25   George Lakoff, *Moral Politics: How Liberals and Conservatives Think* (Chicago: University of Chicago, 1996).

26   Arie W. Kruglanski, *The Motivated Mind: The Selected Works of Arie W. Kruglanski* (New York: Routledge, 2018).

27   https://www.vox.com/xpress/2014/10/8/6945871/ liberal-conservative-parenting-pew-chart.

28   http://www.demos.co.uk/blog/political-emotions-what-do-tories-feel.

29   https://www.cambridge.org/core/journals/
politics-and-the-life-sciences/article/effects-of-physical-attractiveness-on-po-
litical-beliefs/D5214D0CAE37EE5947B7BF29762547EE; https://
www.washingtonpost.com/news/wonk/wp/2017/01/10/
conservatives-really-are-better-looking-research-says/?utm_term=.4d2f7768baf9.

30   https://www.sciencedirect.com/science/article/pii/S0047272716302201.

31   https://www.cambridge.org/core/journals/british-journal-of-political-science/
article/height-income-and-voting/2B6875BFB8B956963D1DBBD510A581CF.

32   http://dailycaller.com/2014/02/14/rich-liberal-women-prefer-conservative-men/.

33   Tyler Okimoto and Dena Gromet, 'Differences in sensitivity to deviance partly
explain ideological divides in social policy support', *Journal of Personality and Social
Psychology*, vol. 111, no. 1 (2016), https://www.ncbi.nlm.nih.gov/pubmed/26571208.

34   https://ir.stonybrook.edu/xmlui/bitstream/handle/11401/71957/000000880.sbu.
pdf?sequence=1.

35   Philip E. Tetlock, 'Cognitive style and political belief systems in the British House of
Commons', *Journal of Personality and Social Psychology*, vol. 46, no. 2 (1984), http://faculty.
haas.berkeley.edu/tetlock/Vita/Philip%20Tetlock/Phil%20Tetlock/1984-1987/1984%20
Cognitive%20Style%20and%20Political%20Belief%20Systems.pdf.

36   https://www.newscientist.com/article/
mg23631560-800-effortless-thinking-why-were-all-born-to-be-status-quo-fans/.

9. Zombie Apocalypse

1   https://www.eurekalert.org/pub_releases/2015-11/au-rpp112415.php.

2   https://twitter.com/ZachG932/status/1088631735024267265.

3   https://onlinelibrary.wiley.com/doi/abs/10.1111/pops.12505.

4   http://uk.businessinsider.com/
how-to-turn-conservatives-liberal-john-bargh-psychology-2017-10.

5   Professor Bargh also tried some experiments, asking his subjects to imagine they
could fly like Spider-Man, after which they apparently responded with more liberal
views.

6   https://www.researchgate.net/
publication/10726978_Political_Conservatism_as_Motivated_Social_Cognition.

7   https://link.springer.com/chapter/10.1007%2F978-1-4613-9564-5_10.

8   Kruglanski, *The Motivated Mind*.

9   https://guilfordjournals.com/doi/abs/10.1521/soco.2017.35.4.450.

10   https://www.sciencedirect.com/science/article/pii/S0191886913002778. 'In the journal *Personality and Individual Differences*, the researchers describe a study where 237
participants provided a set of opinions to determine the extent to which they are
aligned with right-wing authoritarianism – that is, a tendency to submit to authority, condemn those who violate the rules, and uphold established traditions.'

11   https://psmag.com/social-justice/a-new-take-on-political-ideology-24683.

12   https://www.theatlantic.com/magazine/archive/2019/03/the-yuck-factor/580465/.

13   https://www.ncbi.nlm.nih.gov/pmc/articles/PMC3092984/.

14   Haidt, *The Righteous Mind*.

15   Other papers have found a few other differences between liberal and conservative brains, and nearly all are related to threat sensibility or openness to experience.

16   https://psmag.com/social-justice/bugs-like-made-germ-theory-democracy-beliefs-73958.

17   Ibid.

18   https://slatestarcodex.com/2013/03/04/a-thrivesurvive-theory-of-the-political-spectrum/.

19   https://www.city-journal.org/html/how-criminologists-foster-crime-12272.html.

20   https://www.researchgate.net/publication/238586358_Contemporary_penality_and_psychoanalysis.

21   http://journals.sagepub.com/doi/abs/10.1177/1462474508101490.

22   Johnson, *Intellectuals*.

23   In Theodore Dalrymple's words, https://www.city-journal.org/html/how-criminologists-foster-crime-12272.html.

24   Ibid.

10. The Sixties, Man

1   'Dance Class', *Peep Show*, series 2, episode 1, written by Jesse Armstrong and Sam Bain, directed by Tristram Shapeero (Channel 4, 12 November 2004).

2   Mark Lilla, *The Shipwrecked Mind* (New York: New York Review of Books, 2016).

3   https://twitter.com/SteveStuWill/status/831659342805889024/photo/1.

4   From this book, which I don't claim to have read seeing as it's in Danish: https://books.google.co.uk/books?id=xdtPDwAAQBAJ&pg=PT115&redir_esc=y.

5   https://freebeacon.com/columns/genuine-civil-war-potential/.

6   https://washingtonmonthly.com/magazine/marchaprilmay-2014/the-origin-of-ideology/.

7   Thomas Sewell, *A Conflict of Visions* (New York: William Morrow, 1987).

8   https://twitter.com/epkaufm/status/1064139824028950529.

9   William Buckner, writing in *Quillette*, https://quillette.com/2017/12/16/romanticizing-hunter-gatherer/: 'From 1920–1955 the !Kung had a homicide rate of 42/100,000 (about 8 times that of the US rate in 2016)', although that declined after an outside police force was imposed on them.

10   So that 'Two sentiments became increasingly powerful in the 1960s and early 1970s. The first was the sense that affluence had not given life the meaning that an increasingly well-educated and increasingly leisured society looked for. The other was a sense that society was, in some deep way that was hard to analyse but easy to feel, simply irrational.' Ryan, *On Politics*.

11   Johnson, *Intellectuals*.

12   http://www.freerepublic.com/focus/news/836210/posts.

11. Reality Is a Social Construct

1   http://monitor.icef.com/2014/04/
    english-universities-record-first-international-enrolment-drop-in-29-years/.

2   https://www.psychologytoday.com/us/blog/the-imprinted-brain/201702/
    margaret-mead-and-the-great-samoan-nurture-hoax.

3   In fairness, Alice Dreger wrote that Mead was a 'mensch for science – for free
    inquiry and free speech' and stood up for a key ideological rival being hounded in
    academia. Alice Dreger, *Galileo's Little Finger: Heretics, Activists and the Search for Justice in
    Science* (New York: Penguin, 2015).

4   https://twitter.com/CarlWRitter/status/1047724327234416641.

5   Stephen Hilgartner, 'The Sokal Affair in context', *Science, Technology,
    & Human Values*, vol. 22, no. 4 (Autumn 1997), https://www.jstor.org/
    stable/689833?seq=1#page_scan_tab_contents.

6   https://datausa.io/profile/cip/05/.

7   Richard Dawkins, 'Postmodernism disrobed', *Nature* (9 July 1998), https://physics.
    nyu.edu/sokal/dawkins.html.

8   https://www.city-journal.org/html/how-criminologists-foster-crime-12272.html.

9   https://static1.squarespace.com/static/56eddde762cd9413e151ac92/t/58b5a7cd-
    03596ec6631d8b8a/1488299985267/Left+Wing+Bias+Paper.pdf.

10 Noah Carl, 'Cognitive ability and socio-political beliefs and attitudes', https://ora.
    ox.ac.uk/objects/uuid:856fc58a-120f-4a51-a569-422e201e9f61/download_file?safe_file-
    name=Thesis%2BCarl.pdf&file_format=application%2Fpdf&type_of_work=Thesis.

11 https://www.theguardian.com/world/2018/feb/08/
    france-is-50-years-behind-the-state-scandal-of-french-autism-treatment.

12 https://www.latimes.com/archives/la-xpm-2004-feb-18-oe-dufresne18-story.html.

13 Mao Zedong, 'Introducing a Cooperative' (15 April 1958).

14 https://osf.io/ezg2j/.

15 Locke argued that we were born without any preconceived ideas and so could all
    acquire the necessary knowledge to make us rational.

16 Broadly speaking. As Steven Pinker wrote in *The Blank Slate: The Modern Denial of
    Human Nature* (New York: Penguin, 2002), there are two types of feminism: 'Equity
    feminism is a moral doctrine about equal treatment that makes no commitments
    regarding open empirical issues in psychology or biology. Gender feminism is an
    empirical doctrine committed to three claims about human nature. The first is
    that the differences between men and women have nothing to do with biology but
    are socially constructed in their entirety. The second is that humans possess a sin-
    gle social motive – power – and that social life can be understood only in terms of
    how it is exercised. The third is that human interactions arise not from the motives
    of people dealing with each other as individuals but from the motives of groups
    dealing with other groups – in this case, the male gender dominating the female
    gender . . . In embracing these doctrines, the genderists are handcuffing feminism
    to railroad tracks on which a train is bearing down.'

12. PC Gone Mad

1   Theodore Dalrymple in an interview with Jamie Glazov in *Front Page Magazine* (2005), http://www.orthodoxytoday.org/articles5/GlazovDalrymple.php.

2   Scruton, *A Political Philosophy*.

3   Seymour Martin Lipset, *American Exceptionalism: A Double-Edged Sword* (New York: W. W. Norton, 1996).

4   'How Tom Wolfe became Tom Wolfe', *Vanity Fair* (October 2015), https://www.vanity-fair.com/culture/2015/10/how-tom-wolfe-became-tom-wolfe.

5   Pinker, *The Blank Slate*.

6   https://www.nybooks.com/articles/1975/12/11/for-sociobiology/.

7   Pinker, *The Blank Slate*.

8   https://www.thecut.com/2015/12/when-liberals-attack-social-science.html?mid=twitter_nymag.

9   Someone has made a comprehensive list: https://handleshaus.wordpress.com/2013/12/26/bullied-and-badgered-pressured-and-purged/.

10 Debra Schultz, *To Reclaim a Legacy of Diversity: Analyzing The 'Political Correctness' Debates in Higher Education* (New York: National Council for Research on Women, 1993), https://files.eric.ed.gov/fulltext/ED364170.pdf.

11 https://blogs.scientificamerican.com/beautiful-minds/the-personality-of-political-correctness/.

12 Chris C. Martin, 'How Ideology Has Hindered Sociological Insight'. https://www.researchgate.net/publication/272790441_How_Ideology_Has_Hindered_Sociological_Insight.

13. 'I Want to See How a Culture War Is Fought, So Badly'

1   'I want to see how a war is fought, so badly', in 'Major Star', *Blackadder Goes Forth*, episode 3, written by Ben Elton and Richard Curtis, directed by Richard Boden (BBC One, 12 October 1989).

2   https://www.theamericanconservative.com/articles/social-justice-warriors-are-the-democrats-electoral-poison/.

3   It's arguable that Democrats had moved to the Right on welfare, with Clinton's Personal Responsibility and Work Opportunity Act of 1996. But welfare had also increased to such a degree that any cutting back on it was almost inevitable, and driven less by ideology.

4   Thomas Frank, *What's the Matter with Kansas? How Conservatives Won the Heart of America* (New York: Metropolitan, 2004).

5   https://www.independent.co.uk/voices/commentators/dominic-lawson/alan-clark-was-not-wonderful-he-was-sleazy-and-cruel-1787343.html.

6   Giuseppe Tomasi di Lampedusa, *The Leopard* (English translation, New York: Vintage, 2007).

7   The Who, 'Won't Get Fooled Again', written by Pete Townshend (1971).

8   Michael Oakeshott, 'The New Bentham', in *Rationalism in Politics*.

9   https://twitter.com/ZachG932/status/1044089863685967878. This is even when you take sexual differences into account.

10   In her introduction to her 1957 translation of *Chanson de Roland* for Penguin.

11   As Professor Basil Willey put it (quoted in Kirk, *The Conservative Mind*).

12   This reached over a thousand, although Harold Shipman slightly bumped up the figures.

13   https://djbooth.net/features/2015-10-20-platinum-hip-hop-albums-year-breakdown.

14   John Robinson, *Honest to God* (London: SCM Press, 1963).

15   Tombs, *The English and Their History*.

16   https://www.theatlantic.com/magazine/archive/1926/07/the-russian-effort-to-abolish-marriage/306295/.

17   https://publications.parliament.uk/pa/cm200809/cmselect/cmchilsch/111/11106.htm.

18   http://blogs.lse.ac.uk/politicsandpolicy/culture-wars-urban-left/.

19   https://www.bsa.natcen.ac.uk/media/38457/bsa30_gender_roles_final.pdf.

14. All the Good Songs

1   https://www.closer.ac.uk/data/infant-mortality/.

2   https://twitter.com/BobbyIpsosMORI/status/1036886639979765760.

3   Émile Durkheim, *Selected Writings*, selected by Anthony Giddens (Cambridge: Cambridge University Press, 1972).

4   Lilla, *The Shipwrecked Mind*.

5   Johnson, *Intellectuals*.

6   Tombs, *The English and Their History*.

7   https://www.aei.org/economics/extreme-poverty-declining-americans-have-no-idea/.

8   That's according to E. G. West's *Education and the State: A Study in Political Economy* (London: IEA, 1965).

9   http://www.kirkcenter.org/bookman/article/a-cause-lost-and-forgotten/.

10   https://twitter.com/AlexNowrasteh/status/925771803259260929.

11   http://www.unz.com/isteve/nyt-dallass-role-in-kennedys-murder/; https://www.nytimes.com/2013/11/17/opinion/sunday/dallass-role-in-kennedys-murder.html?pagewanted=1&hp&rref=opinion.

12   Tom Lehrer, 'The Folk Song Army' (1965), https://twitter.com/SilverVVulpes/status/925014104305274880.

15. Gryffindor v. Slytherin

1   Johnson, *Intellectuals*.

2   Ibid.

3   https://www.redstate.com/dan_mclaughlin/2016/05/04/politics-still-downstream-culture/.

4   Haidt, *The Righteous Mind*.

5   Lilla, *The Shipwrecked Mind*.

6   The narrative ends with Billy Zane's callous capitalist escaping but there is an explanation that he killed himself after the Wall Street Crash – so there's a happy ending then, awesome! http://www.icyousee.org/titanic.html.

7   https://www.nytimes.com/2014/01/23/us/politics/leaning-right-in-hollywood-under-a-lens.html?hpw&rref=arts.

8   https://twitter.com/Glinner/status/431751158756294656.

9   https://twitter.com/Glinner/status/431752242690277376.

10   https://twitter.com/MWStory/status/994933942699659264.

11   https://www.telegraph.co.uk/culture/theatre/3670229/Would-an-Enoch-Powell-play-be-staged.html.

12   Tom Holland, *Dynasty: The Rise and Fall of the House of Caesar* (London: Little, Brown, 2015).

13   Johnson, *Intellectuals*.

14   Ibid.

15   Watson, *The German Genius*.

16   https://www.spectator.co.uk/2008/01/unthinking-dogmatism/.

17   Burke, *Reflections*.

18   Brooks, *The Conservative Heart*.

19   https://www.newstatesman.com/politics/2013/04/where-are-all-right- wing-stand-ups.

20   *Knowing Me, Knowing You*, season 1, episode 4, written by Steve Coogan and Patrick Marber (Radio 4, 22 December 1992), http://www.bbc.co.uk/comedy/partridge/life/kmky_radio4.shtml.

21   https://www.firstthings.com/web-exclusives/2018/05/decline-and-fall-of-the-bbc.

22   The country was also becoming more ethnically diverse, which the corporation had to reflect, and so we had the paradox that the BBC proclaimed itself committed to 'diversity' to reflect the population, a large proportion of whom opposed the very idea of diversity.

16. Conquest's Law

1   The original Chown tweet is here: https://twitter.com/marcuschown/status/267564491011682304.

2   Roger Scruton, *How to Be a Conservative* (London: Bloomsbury Continuum, 2014).

3   The three laws are quoted in Scruton, *The Uses of Pessimism* (London: Atlantic Books, 2010). There is, however, some question about whether Conquest actually coined them. Others refer to 'every organisation becomes Left-wing unless explicitly Right-wing' as O'Sullivan's First Law, after John O'Sullivan, https://twitter.com/JohnOSullivanNR/status/1008655036048728064.

4   http://www.dailymail.co.uk/news/article-1344779/YWCA-drops-word-Christian-historic-Platform-51.html.

5   https://www.spectator.co.uk/2009/12/all-in-a-good-cause/.

6   National Audit Office, report into 'Public Funding of Large National Charities', https://www.nao.org.uk/wp-content/uploads/2007/08/charity_funding.pdf.

7   According to veteran Anglo-American commentator John Derbyshire, https://www.nationalreview.com/corner/conquests-laws-john-derbyshire/.

8   http://catholicherald.co.uk/issues/october-16th-2015-2/where-amnesty-went-wrong/.

9   In 2010 Amnesty employee Gita Sahgal was sacked after criticising the group's links with Cage, a group that campaigns on behalf of people captured in the 'War on Terror', https://en.wikipedia.org/wiki/Cage_(organisation).

10 Dennis Sewell, 'Where Amnesty went wrong', *Catholic Herald* (16 October 2015), https://catholicherald.co.uk/issues/october-16th-2015-2/where-amnesty-went-wrong/.

11 https://www.amnesty.org.uk/have-your-say-gender-recognition-act?utm_source=TWITTER&utm_medium=social&utm_content=20181001123500&utm_campaign=Amnesty&post_ID=1810746615.

12 https://twitter.com/ACLU/status/1063456843706585089.

13 https://www.spectator.co.uk/2014/03/im-scared-to-admit-to-being-a-tory-in-todays-c-of-e/.

14 Philip Johnston, *Bad Laws: An Explosive Analysis of Britain's Petty Rules, Health and Safety Lunacies and Madcap Laws* (London: Constable, 2010).

15 https://publications.parliament.uk/pa/ld200910/ldhansrd/text/100311-0010.htm.

16 Dan Lewis, *Essential Guide to British Quangos* (London: Centre for Policy Studies, 2005).

17 Eamonn Butler, *The Rotten State of Britain: How Gordon Brown Lost a Decade and Cost a Fortune* (London: Gibson Square, 2014).

18 In a 1973 interview with Playboy, quoted in Eamonn Butler, *Classical Liberalism: A Primer* (London: Institute of Economic Affairs, 2015).

19 'Waldorf Salad', *Fawlty Towers*, season 2, episode 3, written by John Cleese and Connie Booth, directed by Bob Spiers (BBC One, 5 March, 1979).

20 Butler, *Classical Liberalism*.

21 Isabel Paterson, *The God of the Machine* (New York: G. P. Putnam's Sons, 1943).

22 Thomas Jefferson, *Notes on the State of Virginia* (first written in note form 1781, published in Paris, 1785).

23 https://twitter.com/DegenRolf/status/976435602089529344; https://www.sciencedirect.com/science/article/pii/S0160289618300552.

24 http://www.ncbi.nlm.nih.gov/pubmed/22927928?dopt=Abstract.

25 http://blogs.independent.co.uk/2012/03/02/where-are-all-the-libertarians-coming-from/.

26 It's sad that the smoking ban almost certainly led to the closure of pubs, but if your business model depends on increasing people's risk of lung cancer twenty-four times then you can't really expect that much sympathy.

17. Religiots

1   *Illustrated London News* (3 January 1920).

2   https://www.theguardian.com/world/2017/sep/04/half-uk-population-has-no-religion-british-social-attitudes-survey; https://www.theguardian.com/world/2016/jan/12/church-of-england-attendance-falls-below-million-first-time.

3   A quote from me appeared on the paperback blurb even though I thought the central argument was pretty weak.

4   https://www.prri.org/research/prri-rns-poll-nones-atheist-leaving-religion/.

5   https://www.theamericanconservative.com/dreher/
     europe-is-dying-douglas-murray-italy-benedict-option/.

6   https://www.theguardian.com/commentisfree/2009/jan/13/
     polly-toynbee-harriet-harman-social-mobility.

7   https://www.bbc.co.uk/news/uk-scotland-glasgow-west-30514054.

8   Richard Dawkins, *The God Delusion* (London: Bantam Press, 2006)

9   Back in the early 1980s a Catholic campaigner called Victoria Gillick fought a legal case against the state giving out contraception to underage children without their parents' knowledge or consent. She lost the case and years later, when the full horror of the grooming scandal in towns such as Rotherham unfolded, it emerged that many of the victims had indeed been given contraception by local authorities without their parents knowing. More recently, government-funded trans charities have been sending out breast-binders to underage girls without their parents' knowledge. https://www.dailymail.co.uk/news/article-6450485/Trans-activists-send-free-breast-binders-13-year-olds.html?ito=amp_twitter_share-bottom.

10   https://www.dailymail.co.uk/news/article-2052319/Adrian-Smith-demoted-backing-gay-marriage-criticising-new-law-Facebook.html. Tatchell is one of those strange types who is instinctively and on principle liberal, and possibly would fight to the death for someone's right to say 'I hate Peter Tatchell'. http://www.petertatchell-foundation.org/adrian-smith-victory-for-free-speech-fair-play/.

11   https://www.bbc.co.uk/news/uk-england-manchester-26816850.

18. The Right Side of History

1   https://www.washingtonexaminer.com/weekly-standard/how-conservatives-can-win-back-young-americans; https://www.people-press.org/2018/03/01/the-generation-gap-in-american-politics/.

2   https://www.theamericanconservative.com/dreher/pew-politics-crisis-of-meaning/.

3   Tombs, *The English and Their History*.

4   https://wiserd.ac.uk/news/praying-brexit-christianity-and-euroscepticism-britain.

5   http://blogs.lse.ac.uk/brexit/2018/09/20/how-anglicans-tipped-the-brexit-vote/.

6   Larry Siedentop, *Inventing the Individual: The Origins of Western Liberalism* (Cambridge, MA: Harvard University Press, 2014). His scholarship was influenced by two nineteenth-century French historians: François Guizot and Numa Denis Fustel de Coulanges.

7   https://hansard.parliament.uk/commons/2018-11-21/debates/
     BE06C5D4-E549-4F94-87B1-9B77F32EA155/Self-IdentificationOfGender.

8   William Graham Sumner, *What the Social Classes Owe Each Other* (New York: Harper & Brothers, 1883).

9   Clarence Karier, *The Individual, Society, and Education* (Chicago: University of Illinois Press, 1986).

10   Jonathan Haidt wrote in *The Righteous Mind*: 'The worship of reason is itself an illus-
      tration of one of the most long-lived delusions in Western history . . . It's also a claim
      that the rational caste (philosophers or scientists) should have more power, and it
      usually comes along with a utopian program for raising more rational children.'

11   http://journals.sagepub.com/doi/abs/10.1177/1745691617746796?journalCode=ppsa.

12   https://papers.ssrn.com/sol3/papers.cfm?abstract_id=2952510.

13   https://twitter.com/derekmhopper/status/525953741824860164.

14   https://srconstantin.wordpress.com/2014/06/09/do-rationalists-exist/.

15   Durkheim, *Selected Writings*.

16   https://jacobitemag.com/2017/06/14/political-violence-is-a-game-the-right-cant-win/.

17   Ibid. 'Righties who like to build churches will build a church and worship in it.
      Lefties who like to build churches will build a church, write a book telling people
      how to build churches, go out and convince people church-building is the thing to
      do, run workshops on how to finance, build, and register churches, and then they'll
      offer to arrange church guest speakers who'll come preach the Lefty line.'

18   https://www.firstthings.com/article/2017/01/liturgy-of-liberalism.

19   Hibbert, *The French Revolution*.

20   https://unherd.com/2018/09/camus-rejection-tyranny-worth-remembering-today/.

21   Daniel Kalder, *Dictator Literature*. (London: Oneworld, 2019).

22   https://quoteinvestigator.com/2012/11/15/arc-of-universe/.

23   https://www.reuters.com/article/canada-us-canada-politics-idCAKCN0ST0EV20151104.

24   https://www.theglobeandmail.com/news/politics/trudeaus-because
      -its-2015-retort-draws- international-cheers/article27119856/.

25   https://www.firstthings.com/article/2017/01/liturgy-of-liberalism.

26   Ryszard Legutko, *The Demon in Democracy* (New York: Encounter Books, 2018).

27   Harvard law professor Adrian Vermeule wrote that Progressives believe in 'the irre-
      versibility of Progress and the victory over the Enemy, the forces of reaction. Taken
      in combination, these commitments give liberalism its restless and aggressive
      dynamism, and help to make sense of the anomalies.' https://www.firstthings.com/
      article/2017/01/liturgy-of-liberalism.

28   Eric Voegelin, *The Collected Works of Eric Voegelin Volume 5: Modernity without Restraint: The
      Political Religions; The New Science of Politics; and Science, Politics, and Gnosticism*, edited by
      Manfred Henningsen (Columbia: University of Missouri Press, 1999).

29   https://www.nytimes.com/2017/10/24/well/family/transgender-gender-nonbinary-
      students.html?smid=tw-nytimes&smtyp=cur.

30   Nigel Lawson, *The View from Number 11: Memoirs of a Tory Radical* (London: Bantam, 1992)

31   Christopher Lasch, *The Revolt of the Elites and the Betrayal of Democracy* (New York: W. W.
      Norton, 1995).

32   https://www.theguardian.com/commentisfree/belief/2013/mar/06/
      church-hypocritical-sex-guilty.

33   https://www.theguardian.com/commentisfree/2010/sep/18/
      pope-visit-turbulent-priest.

19. The Creed

1 https://amp.theguardian.com/commentisfree/2018/aug/04/
fiona-miller-labour-membership-corbyn-brexit?__twitter_impression=true.

2 In terms of proportion of tweets sent to them that are abusive. Six per cent of
tweets sent to male Tory MPs are abusive, compared to about 4 for female Tories,
3.5 for male Labour MPs and 2.3 for female; https://www.conservativehome.com/
thetorydiary/2018/09/which-mps-get-the-most-abuse-on-twitter-conservatives.
html. https://arxiv.org/pdf/1804.01498.pdf. https://www.buzzfeed.com/tomphillips/
twitter-abuse-of-mps-during-the-election-doubled-after-the?utm_term=.yiwek-
PVdBj#.loadwNrqm4.

3 http://hopisen.com/2013/on-being-on-the-far-right-of-the-centre-left/.

4 https://jacobitemag.com/2017/06/14/political-violence-is-a-game-the-right-cant-win/.

5 https://link.springer.com/article/10.1007/s11109-016-9382-4.

6 Brooks, *The Conservative Heart*.

7 Ibid. Liberals may be more likely to be from groups excluded from giving blood, but
the difference can't be that big. Only 2 per cent of the population are gay men, and a
sizeable minority of them are conservatives.

8 http://blog.practicalethics.ox.ac.uk/2015/05/if-youre-a-conservative-im-not-your-friend/.

9 https://medium.com/@NoahCarl/who-doesnt-want-to-hear-the-other-side-s-view-
9a7cdf3ad702.

10 http://www.journalism.org/2014/10/21/political-polarization-media-habits/; http://
fortune.com/2016/12/19/social-media-election/.

11 http://www.pewinternet.org/2012/03/12/social-networking-sites-and-politics/.

12 https://www.washingtonexaminer.com/conservatives-social-media-diet-more-bal-
anced-than-liberals; https://www.statsocial.com/social-journalists/.

13 https://www.prri.org/research/poll-post-election-holiday-war-christmas/.

14 https://www.sciencedirect.com/science/article/pii/S1364661318300172.

15 https://yougov.co.uk/news/2015/10/02/why-right-wing-so-righteous/.

16 https://yougov.co.uk/news/2016/02/10/left-wingers-keep-family/; https://twitter.com/
robfordmancs/status/995969314976141312.

17 www.people-press.org/2017/07/20/since-trumps-election-increased-atten-
tion-to-politics-especially-among-women/1_51-2/.

18 https://www.theguardian.com/theguardian/2010/jun/05/roger-scruton-interview.

19 http://malcolmpollack.com/2014/01/24/casting-out-the-devil-2/.

20 https://twitter.com/shadihamid/status/1025391824494649345.

21 http://journals.sagepub.com/doi/abs/10.1177/1948550617729410?journalCode=sppa.

20. Sex and the Suburbs

1 Kirk, *The Conservative Mind*.

2 https://en.wikipedia.org/wiki/Stuff_White_People_Like.

3 John Derbyshire, *We Are Doomed: Reclaiming Conservative Pessimism* (New York: Crown
Forum, 2009).

4   http://www.dailymail.co.uk/news/article-2751437/Why-leaning-Right-make-happy-opposition-power.html.

5   https://www.newstalk.com/Rural-pensioners-are-Irelands-happiest-people-says-survey.

6   https://twitter.com/TheEconomist/status/1063724705591541760.

7   https://twitter.com/page_eco/status/1001788008633319425; http://www.henrikkleven.com/uploads/3/7/3/1/37310663/kleven-landais-sogaard_gender_feb2017.pdf; https://www.ifau.se/globalassets/pdf/se/2018/wp2018-09-the-career-dynamics-of-high-skilled-women-and-men-evidence-from-sweden.pdf; https://theconversation.com/how-parenthood-continues-to-cost-women-more-than-men-97243.

8   http://takimag.com/article/the_secret_history_of_the_21st_century_steve_sailer/print#axzz4kASRWobo.

9   He found 'not only that Sailer was correct – lower median home values are closely linked to Republican voting – but that one of the key factors linking home values and Republican voting is marriage'. https://www.weeklystandard.com/jonathan-v-last/start-a-family.

10 https://papers.ssrn.com/sol3/papers.cfm?abstract_id=2820613.

11 http://anepigone.blogspot.co.uk/2017/03/marriage-and-gender-gaps-in.html.

12 https://isteve.blogspot.com/2012/11/marriage-gap-around-20-points-or.html.

13 http://www.unz.com/isteve/a-new-study-starts-to-look-into-my-dirt-gap-theory/.

14 https://www.washingtonpost.com/gdpr-consent/?destination=%2fnews%2ft-he-fix%2fwp%2f2018%2f03%2f19%2fclinton-said-she-meant-no-disrespect-by-com-ments-about-white-women-who-voted-for-trump%2f%3f.

15 https://twitter.com/rcolvile/status/874895457683636224.

16 https://twitter.com/lymanstoneky/status/1011247792411594752.

17 https://onlinelibrary.wiley.com/doi/full/10.1111/pops.12447.

18 http://www.sciencedirect.com/science/article/pii/S0191886917305111.

19 https://spottedtoad.wordpress.com/2016/02/01/why-have-marriage-rates-declined/.

20 The proportion of people married at each income and education level is steadily dropping, with lower education and lower income individuals dropping much faster. http://www.stat.columbia.edu/~gelman/research/published/rb_qjps.pdf.

21 Whereas 60 per cent of American women aged eighteen to twenty-nine were married in 1960, the figure today is 20 per cent. https://twitter.com/conradhackett/status/1014276459068841987.

22 https://www.thecut.com/2016/02/political-power-single-women-c-v-r.html.

23 https://www.heri.ucla.edu/monographs/TheAmericanFreshman2016.pdf.

24 https://twitter.com/salonium/status/933005022216097794, via https://quillette.com/2017/11/21/wilfrid-laurier-creep-critical-theory/.

25 https://twitter.com/epkaufm/status/1009516132607365120.

26 https://www.wsj.com/articles/the-yawning-divide-that-explains-american-poli-tics-1540910719.

27   https://twitter.com/ArtirKel/status/898949673011904512.

28   https://www.sciencedirect.com/science/article/pii/S0191886918301466.

29   http://news.gallup.com/poll/137357/four-moral-issues-sharply-divide-americans.aspx.

30   https://www.theguardian.com/uk/2006/jan/29/health.publicservices.

31   https://www.theamericanconservative.com/dreher/liberal-women-are-lustier-regnerus/.https://roosevelt.ucsd.edu/_files/mmw/mmw12/RodneyStarkReconstructingRiseofChristianityWomen.pdf.

32   Ibid.

33   Piers Paul Read, *The Templars* (London: Phoenix, 1999).

34   https://roosevelt.ucsd.edu/_files/mmw/mmw12/RodneyStarkReconstructing RiseofChristianityWomen.pdf.

21. Tinker Bell and the Globalist Plot to Impose Open Borders

1   Michael Morpurgo and Emma Chichester Clark (illustrator), *The Pied Piper of Hamelin* (London: Walker Books, 2013).

2   https://www.telegraph.co.uk/culture/books/6866648/Bestselling-authors-of-the-decade.html.

3   https://www.spectator.co.uk/2014/01/agitprop-for-toddlers-the-oddly-strident-politics-of-cbeebies/.

4   http://www.spectator.co.uk/features/9121001/agitprop-for-toddlers-the-oddly-strident-politics-of-cbeebies/.

5   http://people.stern.nyu.edu/jhaidt/articles/LoBue.nishida.2010.when-getting-something-good-is-bad.pub075.pdf.

6   https://www.theguardian.com/commentisfree/2018/dec/19/reverse-working-week-six-year-olds-vote-political-demands.

7   https://www.tes.com/news/school-news/breaking-news/exclusive-teachers-vote-shifting-dramatically-towards-labour.

8   https://www.telegraph.co.uk/education/secondaryeducation/10216388/Its-no-wonder-none-of-my-friends-are-teenage-Tories.html. As one analysis of marking schemes found, 'The "correct" answer as to why Conservatives might wish to alleviate poverty is out of "a pragmatic concern . . . in the interests of the rich and prosperous".' Meanwhile 'Authority is valued because it ensures individuals know "where they stand" and what is expected of them.' In a similar vein a marking scheme for the question 'The Coalition government's deficit-reduction programme goes too far, too fast. Discuss' provided nine bullet points in support of the idea and just one against.

9   https://www.news24.com/World/News/leftist-teddy-bears-corbyn-group-launches-kids-wing-20160920.

10   https://yougov.co.uk/news/2016/09/29/child-labour-what-age-it-acceptable-get-child-enga/.

22. The Blob

1   G. K. Chesterton, *The Collected Works of G. K. Chesterton*, volume 33 (London: Ignatius Press, 1986).

2   The *Sunday Telegraph* (17 March 2013) analysed jokes on the national broadcast-
    er's comedy programmes, and found that 'perhaps unsurprisingly, as the main
    party in power, the Conservatives were most ridiculed, on the end of 35 separate
    punchlines. Their Coalition partners, the Liberal Democrats, were the subject of
    10, while Labour was targeted by seven.' The paper reported: "The most common
    political subject in the surveyed comedy shows was the Government's austerity
    programme."' http://www.telegraph.co.uk/culture/tvandradio/bbc/9934902/Have-
    you-heard-the-one-about-BBC-Radio-4-and-the-Left-wing-bias.html.

3   Brooks, *The Conservative Heart*.

4   http://news.bbc.co.uk/1/hi/uk_politics/election_2010/8655846.stm.

5   http://www.guardian.co.uk/commentisfree/2013/feb/05/
    gay-marriage-debate-uncovered-nest-of-bigots.

6   https://twitter.com/KSoltisAnderson/status/1060246627573731329.

7   http://www.people-press. org/2016/04/26/a-wider-ideological-gap-between-more-
    and-less-educated-adults/.

8   http://www.people-press.org/2015/04/07/a-deep-dive-into-party-affiliation/ #party
    -id-by-race-education.

9   http://www.telegraph.co.uk/news/newstopics/howaboutthat/7887888/Champagne-
    socialists-not-as-left-wing-as-they-think-they-are.html.

10 https://twitter.com/whyvert/status/881572294430150656.

11 https://twitter.com/DegenRolf/status/953901373296398336.

12 http://journals.sagepub.com/doi/abs/10.1177/0093650215623837.

13 'And if ability to correctly explain a position leads almost automatically to agree-
    ment with it, that position is more likely to be correct . . . the ability to pass
    ideological Turing tests – to state opposing views as clearly and persuasively as their
    proponents – is a genuine symptom of objectivity and wisdom.' https://www.econ-
    lib.org/archives/2011/06/the_ideological.html.

14 For *The Righteous Mind* Jonathan Haidt, along with two other academics, conducted a test
    to identify how well people understood the beliefs of the other team. He writes: 'the
    results were clear and consistent. Moderates and conservatives were most accurate in
    their predictions, whether they were pretending to be liberals or conservatives. Liberals
    were the least accurate, especially those who described themselves as "very liberal".'

15 http://csi.nuff.ox.ac.uk/?p=1153.

23. Mechanical Jacobins

1   https://www.theguardian.com/commentisfree/2018/jul/25/
    conservatives-brexit-big-business.

2   Kirk, *The Conservative Mind*. Kirk adds that the National Coal Board basically did this
    with Hamilton Palace, the elegant country house demolished in 1927.

3   As I write this the Tories are trying to build a tunnel under Stonehenge because,
    although the site contains hugely important artefacts going back tens of thousands
    of years to the very birth of Britain, it would cut the journey time from London to
    Cornwall by a few minutes.

4   https://www.theguardian.com/uk-news/2016/aug/27/londoners-back-skyscraper-limit-skyline.

5   Kirk, *The Conservative Mind*.

6   Ibid.

7   https://edition.cnn.com/2014/01/06/opinion/frum-conservative-burke-today/index.html.

8   Kirk, *The Conservative Mind*.

9   Ibid. 'So it is, according to La Fontaine, in that of a wolf and I doubt whether it be much more rational, generous, or social, in one than in the other, until in man it is enlightened by experience, reflection, education, and civil and political institutions, which are at first produced, and constantly supported and improved by a few.'

10   Scruton, *A Political Philosophy*.

11   'Bart Gets an Elephant', *The Simpsons*, season 5, episode 17, written by John Swartzwelder, directed by Jim Reardon (Fox, 31 March 1994).

12   https://www.vox.com/policy-and-politics/2018/3/21/17139300/economic-mobility-study-race-black-white-women-men-incarceration-income-chetty-hendren-jones-porter.

13   http://faculty.chicagobooth.edu/emir.kamenica/documents/identity.pdf; https://spottedtoad.wordpress.com/2016/01/17/disaggregating-by-gender/.

14   Charles Moore, 'I'm starting to think that the Left might actually be right', *Daily Telegraph* (22 July 2011), https://www.telegraph.co.uk/news/politics/8655106/Im-starting-to-think-that-the-Left-might-actually-be-right.html.

15   Ibid.

16   https://quillette.com/2019/01/25/the-right-needs-to-grow-up-on-environmentalism/.

17   Peter Hitchens, *The Broken Compass* (London: Continuum, 2009).

18   http://www.spatialeconomics.ac.uk/textonly/SERC/publications/download/sercdp0221.pdf.

19   Kirk, *The Conservative Mind*. My own take is that cars are a liberating force that also have huge externalities, downsides shifted onto other people: if one person drives it has an impact on others, and if loads of people drive the consequences are terrible. We can only be happy if people agree to take up less road space and share public transport; there may be a metaphor there for economics and politics generally but I'm blocking it out of my mind.

20   https://www.theguardian.com/environment/2018/feb/11/how-build-healthy-city-copenhagen-reveals-its-secrets-happiness.

21   Kirk, *The Conservative Mind*.

24. Shown the Door

1   Of course, Americans use the word to mean 'left-liberal' or progressive, i.e. social liberals who argue for more redistribution and favour equality over liberty, and some British people still try to stave off the American definition of liberal becoming ubiquitous.

2   Ryan, *On Politics*: 'A society where individuals are uniformly subject to the "tyranny of opinion" – an idea that Montesquieu was the first to hit upon – could preserve an institutional separation of powers while losing its liberty, if the same convictions permeated all institutions.'

3   https://xkcd.com/1357/.

4   https://spectator.us/financial-blacklisting-sargon-akkad/.

5   https://www.nationalreview.com/corner/yes-universities-discriminate-against-conservative-scholars/.

6   Peter Brown, *The Rise of Western Christendom: Triumph and Diversity 200–1000 AD* (London: Wiley, 1995).

7   https://www.sciencedirect.com/science/article/pii/S0022103117307539.

8   https://papers.ssrn.com/sol3/papers.cfm?abstract_id=3162009.

9   https://onlinelibrary.wiley.com/doi/full/10.1002/jclp.22609; https://twitter.com/DegenRolf/status/976115912049938432.

10 https://ed.stanford.edu/sites/default/files/cohen_chap_hanson.pdf.

11 https://www.sciencedirect.com/science/article/pii/S0022103117304493.

12 https://twitter.com/DegenRolf/status/1019117630228221952.

13 https://www.economist.com/democracy-in-america/2012/05/21/the-big-sort.

14 https://www.theguardian.com/politics/2018/sep/22/cities-are-now-labour-heartland-as-traditional-working-class-desert.

15 https://www.theatlantic.com/amp/article/583072/.

16 http://graphics.wsj.com/blue-feed-red-feed/?utm_content=buffer1ab07&utm_medium=social&utm_source=twitter.com&utm_campaign=buffer.

17 http://thejsms.org/tsmri/index.php/TSMRI/article/view/359.

18 https://www.sciencenews.org/blog/scicurious/popularity-twitter-partisanship-pays.

19 https://www.aol.com/article/news/2017/02/07/poll-2016-election-breakups/21708912/; https://www.nytimes.com/2019/03/02/opinion/sunday/political-polarization.html.

20 https://www.washingtonpost.com/gdpr-consent/?destination=%2fnews%2ft-he-switch%2fwp%2f2014%2f10%2f21%2fliberals-are-more-likely-to-un-friend-you-over-politics-online-and-off%2f%3f&utm_term=.c1ae70fb459e.

21 https://twitter.com/ryanfazio/status/840268971362402304.

22 https://www.prri.org/research/poll-post-election-holiday-war-christmas/.

23 https://twitter.com/ZachG932/status/1042613089001238528.

24 https://www.washingtonpost.com/gdpr-consent/?destination=%2fnews%2ft-he-switch%2fwp%2f2014%2f10%2f21%2fliberals-are-more-likely-to-un-friend-you-over-politics-online-and-off%2f%3f&utm_term=.ebfa7072e6b1.

25 https://twitter.com/MattGrossmann/status/978367995817922560.

26 Yascha Mounk, *The People v. Democracy: Why Our Freedom is in Danger and How to Save It* (Cambridge, MA: Harvard University Press, 2018).

27 https://www.nytimes.com/2018/11/24/opinion/sunday/facebook-twitter-terror-ism-extremism.html?smtyp=cur&smid=tw-nytopinion.

28   https://www.nytimes.com/2018/08/21/world/europe/facebook-refugee-attacks-germany.html?module=inline.

29   https://www.nytimes.com/2018/04/21/world/asia/facebook-sri-lanka-riots.html?module=inline; https://www.nytimes.com/2018/10/15/technology/myanmar-facebook-genocide.html?module=inline.

30   https://www.nytimes.com/2019/03/02/opinion/sunday/political-polarization.html.

31   https://static1.squarespace.com/static/5a70a7c3010027736a22740f/t/5bbcea6b7817f-7bf7342b718/1539107467397/hidden_tribes_report-2.pdf.

32   https://twitter.com/lisatozzi/status/1021744997912248320.

33   https://twitter.com/holland_tom/status/1023501498133741568.

34   https://www.ribbonfarm.com/2016/06/02/the-theory-of-narrative-selection/.

35   https://www.pnas.org/content/111/44/15687.

36   http://nymag.com/intelligencer/2018/10/polarization-tribalism-the-conservative-movement-gop-threat-to-democracy.html.

37   https://www.washingtonpost.com/gdpr-consent/?destination=%2fpolitics%2fshutdowns-roots-lie-in-deeply-embedded-divisions-in-americas-politics%2f2013%2f10%2f05%2f28c0afe2-2cfa-11e3-b139-029811dbb57f_story.html%3f&utm_term=.2c80451b7069.

38   http://www.theguardian.com/politics/2016/feb/10/parents-disapprove-son-daughter-in-law-different-political-persuasion.

39   https://bakercenter.georgetown.edu/aicpoll/.

40   https://twitter.com/JonHaidt/status/1048543186896003072.

41   https://www.vox.com/2015/12/7/9790764/partisan-discrimination.

42   Ibid.

43   https://www.voanews.com/a/mixed-political-marriages-an-issue-on-rise/3705468.html.

44   http://pcl.stanford.edu/research/2012/iyengar-poq-affect-not-ideology.pdf.

45   https://niskanencenter.org/blog/how-marriage-and-inequality-reinforce-political-polarization/.

46   https://uk.askmen.com/news/dating/how-dating-apps-are-becoming-a-political-tool.html.

47   https://thehill.com/hilltv/rising/429593-politics-is-affecting-dating-intimacy-expert-says.

48   https://yougov.co.uk/topics/relationships/articles-reports/2019/08/27/labour-voters-more-wary-about-politics-childs-spou.

49   https://twitter.com/sexliesballots/status/780691814495969280.

50   Although the word this time was 'troubled by' rather than 'unhappy', which is arguably less strong. https://d25d2506sfb94s.cloudfront.net/cumulus_uploads/document/1muyphj16u/TheTimes_190114_BrexitFriendsandFamily_w.pdf.

51   https://onlinelibrary.wiley.com/doi/full/10.1111/1475-6765.12228; https://twitter.com/SteveStuWill/status/963731784180486144.

52   Watson, *The German Genius.* In Germany only 0.5 per cent of people were illiterate in 1900, compared to 1 per cent in Britain and 4 per cent in France.

53 Richard Pipes, *Communism: A Brief History* (New York: Random House, 2001).

54 Johnson, *Intellectuals*.

55 https://academic.oup.com/poq/article-abstract/81/4/930/4652248.

56 Ibid.

57 https://twitter.com/sundersays/status/1055443983659397120.

58 https://twitter.com/DegenRolf/status/996745636153319424.

59 Amy Chua, *Political Tribes: Group Instinct and the Fate of Nations* (New York: Bloomsbury, 2018).

60 Mill wrote in his 1861 *Considerations on Representative Government* that 'All graduates of universities, all persons who have passed creditably through the higher schools, all members of the liberal professions, and perhaps some others should be registered, and allowed to give their votes as such in any constituency in which they chose to register: retaining, in addition, their votes as simple citizens in the localities in which they reside.'

61 https://www.sciencedirect.com/science/article/pii/S0022103117304493#bb0215.

62 file:///C:/Users/Ed/AppData/Local/Packages/Microsoft.MicrosoftEdge_8wekyb3d8bbwe/TempState/Downloads/okuru_1%20(1).pdf; https://twitter.com/DegenRolf/status/1009696530859741189.

63 https://www.psypost.org/2013/11/its-not-just-conservatives-that-support-discrimination-against-their-ideological-foes-21225.

64 But within the liberal and conservative camps there was big variance, so conservatives who valued 'traditionalism' were in favour of discrimination while those in favour of 'self-reliance' were against. Likewise, liberals in favour of 'equality and tolerance' were in favour of discrimination and those who favoured 'egalitarianism and universalism' were against; what both groups of non-discriminators have in common is a close association with classical liberalism, the philosophy of John Locke.

65 https://www.washingtonpost.com/gdpr-consent/?destination=%2fnews%2fvolokh-conspiracy%2fwp%2f2015%2f12%2f17%2fanother-reason-viewpoint-diversity-matters-partisan-bias-can-exceed-racial-bias%2f%3f&utm_term=.0c39b7ceee31.

66 http://cdp.sagepub.com/content/23/1/27.abstract.

67 *The Sermons of Edwin Sandys* (Cambridge: Cambridge University Press, 1842).

68 https://www.facinghistory.org/nobigotry/religion-colonial-america-trends-regulations-and-beliefs.

69 https://www.niskanencenter.org/ tale-two-moralities-part-one-regional-inequality-moral-polarization/.

25. Weaponise This!

1 Which is strange – foie gras is something I definitely wouldn't eat now, as my kids would be furious with me. In fact, I'd quite happily see it banned although that's probably about 70 per cent genuine concern for animals and 30 per cent spite towards people who have more money than me.

2 Which is from another episode of *The Simpsons*, before any pedant thinks they can out-knowledge me on *Simpsons* trivia. 'Kamp Krusty', *The Simpsons*, season 4, episode 1, written by David M. Stern, directed by Mark Kirkland (Fox, 24 September 1992).

3 https://www.mrc.org/sites/default/files/uploads/documents/2014/MBB2014.pdf.

4 https://www.washingtonpost.com/news/the-fix/wp/2014/05/06/
just-7-percent-of-journalists-are-republicans-thats-far-less-than-even-a-decade-
ago/?utm_term=.8fb89e5d5ea1.

5 https://www.mrc.org/media-bias-101/exhibit-2-21-trust-and-satisfaction-national-
media-2009.

6 Bernard Goldberg, *A Slobbering Love Affair: The True (And Pathetic) Story of the Torrid
Romance Between Barack Obama and the Mainstream Media* (New York: Simon & Schuster,
2008).

7 https://twitter.com/JonHaidt/status/999971946317209600.

8 https://www.uscpublicdiplomacy.org/story/can-public-diplomacy-survive-internet.

9 *Atlantic* (April 2005), https://www.theatlantic.com/magazine/archive/2005/04/
host/303812/.

10 https://www.vox.com/policy-and-politics/2017/3/22/14762030/
donald-trump-tribal-epistemology.

11 http://www.theamericanconservative.com/articles/how-roger-ailes-remade-our-
reality/.

12 Ibid.

13 Ibid.

14 http://www.journalism.org/2014/10/21/political-polarization-media-habits/# media
-polarization.

15 https://www.tandfonline.com/doi/abs/10.1080/15456870.2017.1251434.

16 https://www.washingtontimes.com/news/2016/aug/16/
cnn-edits-out-milwaukee-victims-sister-sherelle-sm/.

17 https://twitter.com/CNN/status/1087083855826309121.

18 http://slatestarcodex.com/2017/05/01/neutral-vs-conservative-the-eternal-struggle/.

19 William Shakespeare, *The Merchant of Venice* (Act III, scene i).

20 https://twitter.com/HotlineJosh/status/978019910625452034.

26. Safe Spaces

1 https://link.springer.com/article/10.1007/s12108-017-9362-0.

2 Academic Stanley Rothman and colleagues found evidence that 'while 39 percent of the professoriate on average described itself as Left in 1984, 72 percent did
so in 1999'. https://www.conservativecriminology.com/uploads/5/6/1/7/56173731/
rothman_et_al.pdf.

3 https://www.nas.org/academic-questions/31/2/homogenous_the_political_
affiliations_of_elite_liberal_arts_college_faculty.

4 https://areomagazine.com/2018/03/17/the-reality-of-the-rise-of-an-intolerant-and
-radical-left-on-campus/.

5 https://www.nytimes.com/2018/10/16/opinion/liberal-college-administrators.html.

6 https://twitter.com/michaelshermer/status/1003741333377376257.

7 https://www.nas.org/articles/homogenous_political_affiliations_of_elite_liberal.

8   There are a few outliers, such as Thomas Aquinas College, which has thirty-three full-time faculty, all of whom are Republican, but then it is a Catholic institution.

9   http://dailynous.com/2018/04/10/philosophers-less-willing-hire/.

10 https://www.newyorker.com/science/maria-konnikova/social-psychology-biased-republicans.

11 https://static1.squarespace.com/static/56eddde762cd9413e151ac92/t/58b5a7cd-03596ec663d1d8b8a/1488299985267/Left+Wing+Bias+Paper.pdf.

12 https://www.nationalreview.com/corner/yes-universities-discriminate-against-conservative-scholars/.

13 https://www.newyorker.com/science/maria-konnikova/social-psychology-biased-republicans.

14 https://heterodoxacademy.org/new-study-finds-conservative-social-psychologists/.

15 http://freakonomics.com/podcast/creativity-3/.

16 https://www.nature.com/articles/s41562-019-0541-6.

17 The poll was done via email, for anyone with a university email address, so might not be completely reliable; 9 per cent said they would vote for the Lib Dems, 6 per cent for the SNP, 1 per cent for Plaid Cymru, and 5 per cent said other or that they did not intend to vote. https://www.timeshighereducation.com/news/general-election-2015-which-way-are-your-universitys-staff-likely-to-vote/2020070.article.

18 Conservative voters were most represented in business and law, still at less than 20 per cent, while humanities and arts were less than 5 per cent Tory. An age breakdown would be interesting, and I suspect the Tory academics are on average considerably older.

19 https://www.timeshighereducation.com/news/european-union-referendum-nine-out-of-ten-university-staff-back-remain.

20 https://journals.sagepub.com/doi/abs/10.1177/1948550616667617.

21 https://papers.ssrn.com/sol3/papers.cfm?abstract_id=2881527; https://www.insidehighered.com/views/2017/01/09/conservatives-are-actually-quite-happy-academe-essay#.WHPQcNoor5R.twitter.

22 http://blog.collegepulse.com/2018/11/pulse-plays-never-have-i-ever.html.

23 Lukianoff and Haidt, *The Coddling of the American Mind*.

24 https://heterodoxacademy.org/campus-speaker-disinvitations-recent-trends-part-2-of-2/.

25 https://www.ucpress.edu/blog/16940/free-speech-at-50-mario-savio-on-what-makes-us-human/.

26 https://quillette.com/2019/04/01/free-speech-for-me-but-not-for-thee/.

27 Paul Berman, *A Tale of Two Utopias: The Political Journey of the Generation of 1968* (New York: W. W. Norton, 1996).

28 https://twitter.com/ZachG932/status/1098413545182629888; https://anepigone.blogspot.com/2017/11/free-speech-absolutism.html.

29 Far more of the general public would ban a speaker who wanted to abolish the monarchy — 50 per cent of the public thought this should not be allowed,

compared to a third of students, both of which are surprisingly high in my view. In comparison students were keener on banning people who denied man-made climate change. https://yougov.co.uk/topics/politics/articles-reports/2018/06/27/are-students-really-more-hostile-free-speech.

30 They are even more in favour of banning speakers guilty of 'publicly disrespecting the police', something you would assume would be more of a conservative thing. https://twitter.com/PsychRabble/status/971492751002030080.

31 https://www.vox.com/policy-and-politics/2018/7/30/17505406/trump-obama-race-politics-immigration.

32 http://www.people-press.org/2017/07/10/sharp-partisan-divisions-in-views-of-national-institutions/.

33 http://www.pewresearch.org/fact-tank/2017/07/20/republicans-skeptical-of-colleges-impact-on-u-s-but-most-see-benefits-for-workforce-preparation/.

34 https://www.historytoday.com/miscellanies/medieval-university-monopoly.

35 'For people over 40, there is no relationship between social justice attitudes and tolerance. I argue that this difference reflects a shift from values of classical liberalism to the New Left.' https://heterodoxacademy.org/how-marcuse-made-todays-students-less-tolerant-than-their-parents/.

27. The Great Awokening

1 Dreger, *Galileo's Little Finger*.

2 *Ride with the Devil*, written by James Schamus, directed by Ang Lee (1999).

3 https://www.theaquilareport.com/the-preachers-of-the-great-awokening/.

4 https://www.researchgate.net/publication/282819379_A_social_science_without_sacred_values; https://quillette.com/2018/09/21/the-preachers-of-the-great-awokening/.

5 https://www.thetimes.co.uk/article/universities-are-reviving-the-notion-of-heresy-cmjvb87mz.

6 https://www.theguardian.com/culture/2016/oct/18/is-satire-dead-politicians-held-in-contempt-armando-iannucci-few-laughs.

7 https://www.thetimes.co.uk/edition/news/cheltenham-literature-festival-jennifer-saunders-says-trolls-are-killing-tv-comedy-0r0s6d5c2.

8 Poor Toby Young, who's constantly getting shit for reasons I'm not entirely clear about, christened this 'offence archaeology'. https://quillette.com/2018/07/23/the-public-humiliation-diet/.

9 https://blogs.spectator.co.uk/2018/10/identity-politics-and-the-rise-of-american-anti-comedy/amp/?__twitter_impression=true.

10 https://slate.com/culture/2018/07/rewatching-sacha-baron-cohens-borat-in-the-era-of-who-is-america-and-trump.html.

11 https://www.firstthings.com/article/2017/01/liturgy-of-liberalism.

12 https://home.cc.umanitoba.ca/~altemey/.

13 So when the question was changed to 'When it comes to differences of opinion in protecting the environment we must be careful not to compromise with those who believe differently from the way we do', liberals scored higher on dogmatism, just as

conservatives scored higher when protecting religion was the issue. Likewise with 'There are two kinds of people in this world: those who are for the truth that the planet is warming and those who are against that obvious truth.' Again the same thing, showing liberals to be more dogmatic on issues they're passionate about. https://onlinelibrary.wiley.com/doi/full/10.1111/pops.12304.

14   http://reason.com/archives/2016/01/15/liberals-are-simple-minded.

15   Alain Van Hiel et al., 'The presence of Left-wing authoritarianism in Western Europe and its relationship with conservative ideology', *Political Psychology*, vol. 27, no. 5 (2006), found authoritarian traits, 'measured by willingness to use violence (aggression) and needing to obey left-wing leaders (submission)', in Flanders, both in its Communist Party and its Stalinist Party. Anarchists, meanwhile, were found to be not authoritarian by nature – as you would expect. https://www.jstor.org/stable/3792538?seq=1#page_scan_tab_contents.

16   https://twitter.com/DegenRolf/status/944126788980170752.

17   https://twitter.com/SteveStuWill/status/884172411267985409.

18   https://onlinelibrary.wiley.com/doi/full/10.1111/pops.12470.

19   http://nymag.com/intelligencer/2018/07/how-social-science-might-be-misunder-standing-conservatives.html?gtm=bottom&gtm=bottom.

20   http://nymag.com/intelligencer/2018/07/how-social-science-might-be-misunder-standing-conservatives.html.

21   This is probably the best article about it: https://www.tabletmag.com/jewish-news-and-politics/284875/americas-white-saviors.

22   https://www.vanityfair.com/culture/2012/10/The-Fraudulent-Factoid-That-Refuses-to-Die.

28. Redpilled

1   https://www.jstor.org/stable/40646411?seq=1#page_scan_tab_contents.

2   https://www.nytimes.com/2016/01/06/opinion/campaign-stops/purity-disgust-and-donald-trump.html.

3   Karen Stenner, *The Authoritarian Dynamic* (Cambridge: Cambridge University Press, 2005).

4   https://twitter.com/epkaufm/status/957908283943260160.

5   https://www.newyorker.com/news/news-desk/nixon-memorial.

6   https://onlinelibrary.wiley.com/doi/full/10.1111/pops.12479.

7   https://www.nationalreview.com/2018/06/youtube-conservatives-changing-right-wing-disposition/.

8   Ibid.

9   http://www.people-press. org/2016/04/26/a-wider-ideological-gap-between-more-and-less-educated-adults/.

10   Nassim Nicholas Taleb, *Antifragile* (London: Penguin, 2012).

11   https://twitter.com/CarlWRitter/status/953570199164342273.

12   http://slatestarcodex.com/2014/04/22/right-is-the-new-left/.

ENDNOTES

13   https://jacobitemag.com/2018/10/02/empty-realm/.

14   https://twitter.com/mikeh_pr/status/918966398826762240?lang=en.

15   https://anepigone.blogspot.com/2017/08/gen-z-is-wests-last-great-hope.html.

16   https://www.theguardian.com/commentisfree/2018/jun/24/
      democrats-losing-millennial-vote-change-message.

17   https://www.theguardian.com/commentisfree/2018/jun/24/
      democrats-losing-millennial-vote-change-message.

18   https://twitter.com/wesyang/status/1012418245826109440. As *Tablet* columnist Wesley
      Yang suggested, 'viral hate-read clickbait' may have played a part.

19   http://www.bbc.co.uk/news/uk-40504076.

20   http://nymag.com/selectall/2017/07/steve-bannon-world-of-warcraft-gold-farming.
      html.

21   https://www.cambridge.org/core/journals/british-journal-of-political-science/
      article/gender-differences-in-vote-choice-social-cues-and-social-harmony-as-
      heuristics/DB58CD40104BABA70AF2917DD5C89AF4.

22   https://www.theatlantic.com/ideas/archive/2018/08/why-the-left-is-so-afraid-of-
      jordan-peterson/567110/.

23   https://www.wsj.com/articles/jordan-peterson-and-conservatisms-rebirth-1529101961.

24   http://quillette.com/2017/11/12/non-believers-turning-bibles/.

25   https://pdfs.semanticscholar.org/7a6b/ad93d88b0158d449881e56749d5443b3ff80.pdf.

26   https://www.theguardian.com/science/2018/nov/11/nature-or-nurture-debate-three
      -identical-strangers-film?CMP=share_btn_tw.

27   https://www.nature.com/articles/s41539-018-0030-0.

28   https://twitter.com/SteveStuWill/status/1048403867031887873.

29   https://twitter.com/DegenRolf/status/960541924250783744; https://www.ncbi.nlm.
      nih.gov/pmc/articles/PMC3404054/.

30   https://www.ncbi.nlm.nih.gov/pubmed/25985137.

31   https://twitter.com/DegenRolf/status/989072773560655872; https://onlinelibrary.
      wiley.com/doi/abs/10.1002/per.2144?campaign=woleearlyview.

32   https://www.ncbi.nlm.nih.gov/pmc/articles/PMC3809096/.

33   http://sciencenordic.com/political-colour-half-genetic.

34   https://www.pnas.org/content/83/12/4364.

35   https://www.smithsonianmag.com/science-nature/ study-predicts-political-
      beliefs-with-83-percent-accuracy-17536124/.

36   http://journals.cambridge.org/action/displayAbstract?aid=7909320; https://twitter.
      com/DegenRolf/status/973513569353551872.

37   https://link.springer.com/article/10.1007/s11109-017-9429-1.

38   https://onlinelibrary.wiley.com/doi/abs/10.1111/cdev.12452.

39   https://onlinelibrary.wiley.com/doi/full/10.1111/jopy.12055.

40   http://www.spsp.org/news-center/blog/stereotype-accuracy-response; https://twit-
      ter.com/SteveStuWill/status/980230845851090944.

41   https://www.psychologytoday.com/gb/blog/rabble-rouser/201712/mandatory-implicit-bias-training-is-bad-idea.

42   http://www.epicenternetwork.eu/blog/the-swedish-gender-equality-paradox/.

43   https://arstechnica.com/science/2018/10/gender-differences-in-personality-are-bigger-in-egalitarian-countries/.

44   https://www.ipsos.com/ipsos-mori/en-uk/millennial-myths-and-realities.

45   This is on top of the obvious problems of ethnic diversity, which I've already covered in one book and would rather spend a week in the Louisiana State Penitentiary than go over again.

29. Everyone Is Stupid Except Me

1   http://ukandeu.ac.uk/a-nation-of-remainers-and-leavers-how-brexit-has-forged-a-new-sense-of-identity/; www.econ.cam.ac.uk/research-files/repec/cam/pdf/cwpe1745.pdf.

2   https://ukandeu.ac.uk/a-nation-of-remainers-and-leavers-how-brexit-has-forged-a-new-sense-of-identity/. And so as one academic concluded, although Leave voters' views are seen as being 'rooted above all in emotion and identity . . . the large proportion of very strong identifiers on the Remain side suggests that in practice emotion and identity underpin the views of many a Remainer too'.

3   A friend of mine, Niall Gooch, wrote a blogpost explaining these confused feelings better than I could: http://niallthinksandwrites.blogspot.com/2019/01/some-where-anywhere-leave-remain.html.

4   https://www.facebook.com/notes/save-me/owen-paterson-the-embarrassing-kind-of-tory-by-brian-may/583957688281355/. I used to love Queen when I was a kid; I gave my daughter the middle name Mercury in tribute and would have named my son after Freddie if it wasn't for the fact this would make him Fred West.

5   Oakeshott, *Rationalism in Politics*.

6   As Stephen Daisley wrote in a *Spectator* blog (October 2018, https://blogs.spectator.co.uk/2018/10/identity-politics-and-the-rise-of-american-anti-comedy/), 'only a few years ago, Stephen Colbert was still yukking it up with the word "retard" and Bill Maher was cracking down syndrome jokes. Before Trump launched his White House bid with a peroration about Mexican rapists, Amy Schumer was dropping this gag into her stand-up routine: "I used to date Hispanic guys, but now I prefer consensual."'

7   https://twitter.com/robertwiblin/status/1099557871828709376.

8   https://www.telegraph.co.uk/news/2017/10/29/prisoners-day-release-will-allowed-return-home-vote-reports/; https://www.standard.co.uk/news/uk/jihadis-suspected-of-fighting-in-syria-could-jump-queue-for-council-houses-and-get-help-finding-jobs-a3670946.html; https://www.thetimes.co.uk/article/its-not-women-who-get-pregnant-its-people-w3mmzbgwh.

9   https://www.bbc.co.uk/news/uk-politics-45714032; https://www.independent.co.uk/news/uk/politics/transgender-rules-reform-gender-dysphoria-changes-2004-gender-recognition-self-identify-a7855381.html.

10   http://www.people-press.org/2017/07/20/since-trumps-election-increased-attention-to-politics-especially-among-women/?utm_content=buffer868a0&utm_medium=social&utm_source=twitter.com&utm_campaign=buffer.

11   http://www.pewresearch.org/fact-tank/2018/06/05/
      almost-seven-in-ten-americans-have-news-fatigue-more-among-republicans/.

12   That was actually the following year. I'm obviously not cured. https://www.vanity-
      fair.com/news/2017/03/elon-musk-billion-dollar-crusade-to-stop-ai-space-x.

13   'Engine Roll Call' by Thomas and Friends, from *Thomas the Tank Engine*.

30. Politics Poisons Everything

1   Kirk, *The Conservative Mind*.

2   https://link.springer.com/article/10.1007/s10680-018-9487-z.

3   *Time* (12 August 2013).

4   https://twitter.com/toad_spotted/status/1002637331692703744.

5   https://jaymans.wordpress.com/2012/08/19/just-a-reminder/; https://jaymans.word-
      press.com/2012/08/23/another-tale-of-two-maps/; http://www.jcrt.org/archives/12.3/
      ramos.pdf.

6   Eric Kaufmann, *Shall the Religious Inherit the Earth? Demography and Politics in the Twenty-First
      Century* (London: Profile, 2010)

7   https://jaymans.wordpress.com/2012/11/30/expectations-and-reality-a-window-into-
      the-liberal-conservative-baby-gap/.

8   https://twitter.com/WilcoxNMP/status/1068541891279503360.

9   http://journals.sagepub.com/doi/abs/10.1177/0956797612439067.

10   https://twitter.com/toad_spotted/status/1002638763883945985.

11   http://www.dailymail.co.uk/news/article-3790614/They-don-t-like-drugs-gay-
      marriage-HATE-tattoos-Generation-Z-conservative-WW2.html.

12   https://twitter.com/toad_spotted/status/1003716412362444805.

13   In 2006 to 2011 median inflation-adjusted household income in the US fell
      by 7 per cent while average real tuition at public four-year colleges increased
      by 18 per cent. In 2007 total student debt in the US was $545 billion; in 2017
      it was $1.5 trillion. Some 40 per cent will default. https://www.american-
      progress.org/issues/education-postsecondary/reports/2019/06/12/470893/
      addressing-1-5-trillion-federal-student-loan-debt/.

14   http://www.hbs.edu/managing-the-future-of-work/Documents/dismissed-by-de-
      grees.pdf.

15   https://www.theatlantic.com/ideas/archive/2018/08/the-church-of-trump/567425/.

16   https://www.voterstudygroup.org/publications/2018-voter-survey/
      religious-trump-voters.

17   https://unherd.com/2018/09/catholics-bring-merkel/.

18   https://unherd.com/2018/09/worships-church-trump/.

19   Kirk, *The Conservative Mind*.

20   The blogger Spotted Toad came up with this theory, https://twitter.com/
      toad_spotted/status/1055864889019895808.

21   https://psyarxiv.com/ak642/.

22 https://www.thetimes.co.uk/edition/news/today-programme-loses-65-000-listeners-as-audience-tunes-out-lc67xxsw7?CMP=Sprkr-_-Editorial-_-thetimes-_-Unspecified-_-TWITTER.

23 https://twitter.com/pewjournalism/status/1047286758034100225.

24 Ralf Dahrendorf, *Society and Democracy in Germany* (New York: W. W. Norton, 1979).

25 http://anepigone.blogspot.com/2018/06/centrists-find-politics-boring-wish-it.html.

26 https://medium.com/@ryanfazio/politics-are-not-the-sum-of-a-person-378102f25334.

27 Burton Egbert Stevenson, *The Macmillan Book of Proverbs, Maxims, and Famous Phrases* (London: Macmillan, 1948)

INDEX

INDEX

Brooker, Charlie 249
Brooks, Arthur 82, 191, 299
  Who Really Cares 237
Brooks, David 244
'brotherhood of man' 71, 100
Brown, Dan 213
Brown, Gordon 203, 265, 281
Brown era 203–4
Bruinvels, Peter 194
B'Stard, Alan 89
Buchanan, Pat 154–9, 313
Buckley, William F. 68, 295–6, 313
Bullingdon Club 267
Burke, Edmund 47, 53–5, 57–9, 61–3, 65, 66, 68,
  70–2, 82, 89–90, 159, 163, 181, 190, 191, 198,
  230, 274, 279, 280, 345, 365
Burleigh, Michael 88
Bush, George, Sr 86, 156
Bush, George W. 27, 201, 236, 248, 313
buttons 34–5
Byrne, Liam 266

C2DE social class 5
cable TV 311
Cafod 233
California 4, 320
Calvin, John (Jean) 48, 49, 293
Calvinism 45, 49, 64
Cambridge 49
Cambridge University 52, 55, 145, 151, 326, 348
Camden Labour Party 18
Cameron, David 237, 265, 266, 267, 270, 272, 359
Cameron faction 266, 270, 359
Campaign for Nuclear Disarmament (CND) 81
Campbell, Alistair 159–60
Camus, Albert 226
Canada 178, 201
capitalism 15, 64, 78, 93, 97, 280, 339
Caplan, Bryan 275
Capra, Frank 123
Captain America comics 237
Carlson, Tucker 365
Carlyle, Thomas 41, 75, 76
cars 285–6
Cash, Johnny 24
Cassandra 28–9, 62, 373
Catharism 254–5
Cathedral, the 202–3, 271
Catholic Church 48, 116, 212, 212–14, 217–18, 232,
  233, 269, 333
Catechism 137
Catholic Emancipation Act 289

Catholic Herald (newspaper) 212, 213, 216, 219, 233,
  241, 272, 307, 339
Catholicism 11–13, 33, 37, 41–3, 45, 49, 51–2, 54,
  57, 62, 64, 75, 134–5, 142, 155, 158, 176, 199,
  202, 211–13, 217–18, 222, 230–1, 241, 243,
  272–3, 291–2, 294, 296, 339, 363
  see also anti-Catholicism
Cato Institute 324
Cavaliers 53, 57
Ceauşecu 46
censorship 148, 166, 188–9, 290, 331
Central Intelligence Agency (CIA) 61
'centrist dad' 8
Chagnon, Napoleon 147
Change 3
Change UK 3
Channel 4 168, 232
charities 57, 199–202, 233, 237
Charles I 49, 55
Charles II 36, 37, 52
Charles-Roux, Fr Jean-Marie 210–11
Chartists 175
Chelsea FC 47
Chesterton, G. K. 69, 210, 265
Chick-fil-A 228–9
child abuse scandals 218, 232
child-rearing 242–7, 250–1
children, indoctrination 256–64
children's stories 261
China 97, 139, 226–7, 230
Chindamo, Learco 122
Chinese Revolution 256
chlamydia 168
Chown, Marcus 197
Christian Judeophobia 88
Christian saints 105–6
Christian socialists 240
Christian-run colleges 145–6, 152
Christianity 2, 4, 12, 54, 95, 100, 173, 208, 211,
  215–23, 225, 227–9, 229, 264, 275–7, 280, 289,
  291–3, 361, 366, 373
  and charities 199–200, 202
  evangelical 86, 219–20, 243, 338–9
  and gender bias 254–5
  and human nature 261
  'Judaising' 64
  and the Left 19
  and Marx 93
  national 97
  norms 79
  and original sin 28
  Roman 254, 275–6

413

INDEX

natural selection 147
Nature Genetics (journal) 349
Nature (journal) 350
nature-nurture debate 138–40
Nazis 20, 24, 87–9, 96–100, 105, 126, 139, 155, 157, 161, 172, 179, 196, 197–8, 205, 210–11, 237, 303, 312, 325, 329, 346
   see also national socialism
NCT *see* National Childbirth Trust
neoconservatives 240
nepotism 70–1
Netflix 137
Netherlands 49, 52
neuroticism 108
New Atheism 215–16, 218, 224
New Atheism Internet Wars 214–15
New Deal 96
New England 49, 55, 57, 320
New Labour 153, 156–60, 163, 200, 265
New Left 146
New Model Army 49
'New Moral World' 93
New Statesman, The (TV show) 89, 272
New Tories 267
New York 153–4
New York Times (newspaper) 99, 177, 178, 229, 236, 298–9, 313
News of the World (newspaper) 283
NHS *see* National Health Service
Nicaraguan civil war 14–15
Niemietz, Kristian 197
Niemöllers, Martin 358
Nietzsche, Friedrich 229
Night to Remember, A (1958) 162
Nike 4–5
Niskanen Centre (think-tank) 295
Nixon, Richard 24, 148, 153, 154, 336
noble savage 130–1
non rapid eye movement (NREM) sleep 180
Non-Player Characters (NPCs) 344
non-whites 127
Nonconformism 65, 92
Norman, Jesse 54
norms
   Christian 79
   cultural/moral 70
   shifting 2–3
   traditional gender 246
Norodom Sihanouk 17
Norris, Chuck 24
North America 362
North Korea 97, 226

Northern Ireland 5, 158, 214, 362
Norway 351
Norwich, John Julius 259
Notting Hill 42, 81, 266, 269–70
novelty seeking 137
Nowrasteh, Alex 177
NPR 313
nuclear families 246
Nugent, Ted 24
Nuts (magazine) 169, 212, 238–9
NWA 122

Oakeshott, Michael 72, 159, 358, 365
Oath of Supremacy 291
Obama, Barack 13, 24, 27, 30, 227, 249, 256, 265, 310–11, 319, 329, 335, 337
Obama, Michelle 11
Oberlin College 323
Obi-Wan Kenobi 365
O'Brien, James 186
Observer (newspaper) 245
OkCupid 302
Old Sarum 17
Oman 351
openness 108–9, 137
optimism 37–8
'Orchestra Pit Theory' 313
Original Sin, doctrine of 28, 33, 129, 229
O'Rourke, P.J. 22
orthodoxy 65–6, 128, 240
Orwell, George 80, 179, 341
   Animal Farm 143–4
   Nineteen Eighty-Four 144
Osborne, George 250, 270
Oscars 4
Oswald, Lee Harvey 178
Owen, Robert 92–3, 97
Owenites 93
Oxfam 233
Oxford University 36, 37, 52, 80, 145, 151, 166, 326

paedophiles 18
paganism 6, 12, 173, 254, 255, 276, 291
Page Eight (play) 189
Paine, Thomas 56–9, 61, 63, 71–2, 366
Paisley, Revd Ian 296
Pakistan 292
Palestine 300, 362
Pandora's box 29
Pantisocracy 91
Papua New Guinea 18
Paris 36, 38, 55–6, 90, 131–2, 190